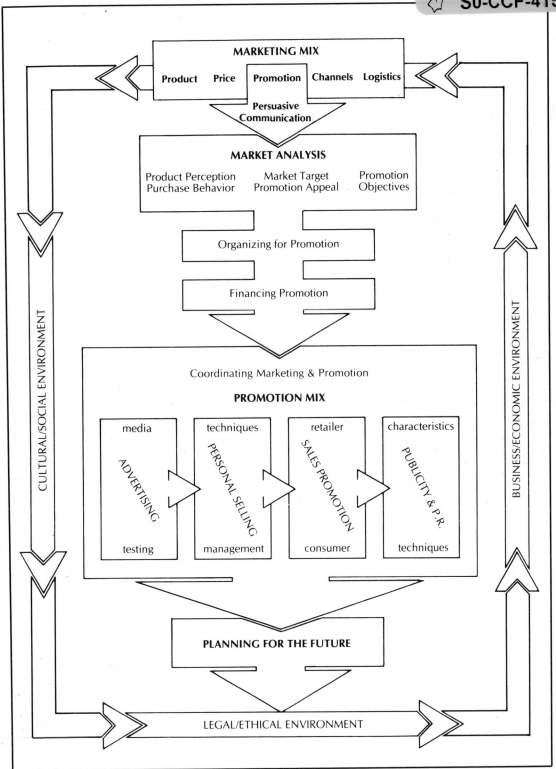

PROMOTION
PRODUCTS, SERVICES, AND IDEAS
SECOND EDITION

WILLIAM M. KINCAID, JR.
Oklahoma State University

Charles E. Merrill Publishing Company
A Bell & Howell Company
Columbus   Toronto   London   Sydney

Published by Charles E. Merrill Publishing Co.
A Bell & Howell Company
Columbus, Ohio 43216

This book was set in Optima and Bookman.
Cover photo: Larry Collins
Cover Design Coordination: Cathy Watterson
Production Coordination: JoEllen Gohr

Library of Congress Catalog Card Number: 84-61299
International Standard Book Number: 0–675–20346-5
Printed in the United States of America
1 2 3 4 5 6 8 9 10—89 88 87 86 85

To Rosann

PREFACE

Promotion encompasses the diverse fields of advertising, personal selling, sales promotion, and publicity. These areas must be considered individually and collectively to understand the promotion function.

The primary audience for this book is junior and senior students in colleges and universities. Although it emphasizes product promotion, this text can be used by people outside the business community because it deals with the promotion of ideas as well as products and services.

This book stresses the *conceptual* and *managerial* aspects of promotion, although certain of promotion's creative aspects are introduced to help the reader understand problems encountered in the creative process. More detailed discussions can be found in textbooks specifically written for students in advertising, selling, and public relations. In addition to learning basic promotion concepts, the reader will be challenged by the pros and cons of controversial issues presented throughout. Thus the book is as much thought provoking as it is encyclopedic.

To enhance understanding and perspective, a schematic of the promotion function is presented at the beginning of the book, and again at the beginning of each part with the topic of the part highlighted on the schematic. The flow of ideas throughout the book, then, logically develops the function. Part One provides background and perspective. Part Two presents a discussion of the environment in which promotion takes place and its effects on promotional strategy. Part Three moves the discussion from the general environment to the specific market, and Part Four deals with the problems of organization and finance with respect to promotion. Part Five concerns the specific elements of the promotion mix, and Part Six looks at promotion in the future.

Much of the material in the first edition has been rewritten and reorganized for purposes of clarity. New sections have been added, and the material in each chapter has been expanded considerably.

It is rarely possible for any textbook author to identify all the people who helped in the effort since they include family, friends, students, colleagues, and others. However, I do want to mention William Lochner of Charles E. Merrill Publishing, as well as Boris W. Becker of Oregon State University, Walter Gross of the University of Georgia, Leonard J. Konopa of Kent State University, William Pride of Texas A&M University, George Prough of the University of Akron, Bennett L. Rudolph of Grand Valley State Colleges, and David Seigel of Los Angeles Pierce College. Each of these reviewers read the manuscript for the first edition in its entirety, or in part, and offered many useful suggestions. I also want to acknowledge the help of George Prough of the University of Akron, Larry Knight of Indiana State University, Denise Smart of Texas A&M University, and William L. James of the University of Alabama, who provided critiques of the first edition for use in this revision.

William M. Kincaid, Jr.

CONTENTS

PROMOTION

PART ONE

BACKGROUND AND PERSPECTIVE

Part I establishes the background and perspective necessary for a clear understanding of the promotion function. There are no isolated decisions in business; nor does any single facet of business operate by itself. In order to perceive promotion in its proper light, we must first see how it fits into the total operation of business. Significant in this regard is the relationship of promotion to marketing. Chapter 1 develops this relationship.

Chapter 2 discusses the role of communication in promotion. Promotion *is* communication, and communication theory should be understood to fully understand the promotion function and how it is implemented.

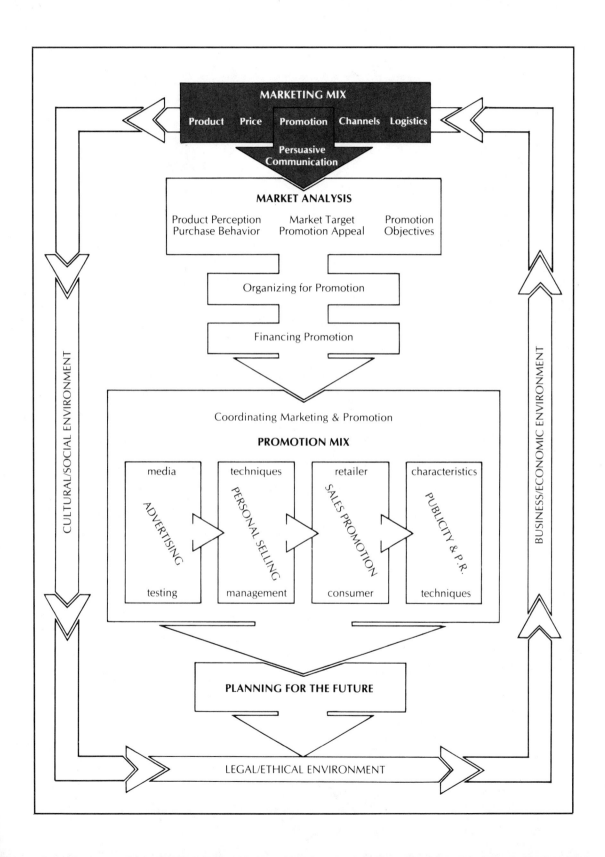

PROMOTION AND MARKETING

This book is about promotion. The purpose of promotion is to persuade, and for persuasion to take place, there must be communication. Therefore, this book deals with the communication of messages about products, services, and ideas.

The book focuses on the *conceptual and managerial* aspects of promotion. While such creative aspects of the function as advertising layout and copywriting and the development of sales presentations in personal selling are extremely important, they are highly specialized areas and require special treatment. We shall examine such topics only enough to indicate their significance to the promotion function.

PERSUASION

Promotion persuades. It also provides information, but its emphasis must be on persuasion. As we shall see later, the kind of information presented is determined by its persuasive potential in a given situation.

Persuasion is the ultimate objective of promotion whether we are dealing with products, services, or ideas. In each case we are attempting to persuade people to accept our intended message and to respond or react accordingly. We want to convince them that our product or service can do a better job of satisfying their wants than the alternatives. We want them to believe the ideas we are presenting are worthy and desirable.

But to say the purpose of promotion is to persuade does not endorse unethical practices. Not only are such practices morally wrong, they are not good strategy!

PROMOTION AND THE CONSUMER

Exposure to promotional messages is inescapable in today's society. We are the targets of messages from dawn to dusk. We turn on the radio in the morning to get the news and hear several commercials. Scanning the newspaper before going to work or class, we see advertisements. On the way we pass by billboards and shop signs. Throughout the day we use ball-point pens, calendars, or magazines — all of which may have advertising messages. In the evening, we put up with countless commercials in order to watch our favorite television programs. In addition to this bombardment, it is quite likely that we will enter a store, see innumerable sales messages on signs and packages, and be approached by a salesperson who will attempt to persuade us to buy.

We seem to know what promotion is. But we see only the end product of a complicated activity. It is somewhat like a spectator sport; as we watch the game, we really have no appreciation for each team's hard work and preparation. We take it for granted that the players are ready, and we subconsciously assume that their playing skills just happen.

THE MARKETING FUNCTION

Promotion is rooted in the marketing function. To understand promotion, we must have a basic understanding of marketing. Only then is it possible to see how promotion fits into the total picture.

Marketing is initially a matching process — matching products or services or ideas with consumer needs. The astute marketing manager is quick to capitalize on newly identified needs. For example, the health craze of the early 1980s generated many new needs associated with health care. Marketers responded with products to match them. Calorie-counting consumers created a wide-open market for low-fat food and beverage items such as Lean Cuisine, Diet Coke, and Diet Pepsi. Miller introduced the concept of light beer, and other breweries followed.

The caffeine concern in the early 1980s prompted a marketing response from a number of companies. A decaffeinated variety can be found among the traditional brands of coffee along with the original brand, Sanka. Royal Crown Cola Company offers RC 100 and Diet Rite, 7-Up Company offers regular and Diet 7-Up, and Coca-Cola's no-caffeine version of Coca-Cola, Tab, and Diet Coke are other examples of a marketing response to the needs of caffeine-conscious consumers.[1] Lipton has introduced a decaffeinated tea, and Bayer came out with caffeine-free super-strength aspirin.[2]

Of course, the marketing process does not end with the initial matching of products with consumer needs. Somehow consumers must be made aware of the match and be persuaded it is a good match. And somehow the products must be made available to consumers and appear more desirable than competing alternatives or substitutes. This is what the marketing function is all about. The magnitude of the effort requires a structure that can only be called a *system*.

A Systems Perspective

The essence of the systems concept is that the whole is composed of a number of parts and that each part must work with the others. Maximum effectiveness requires perfect coordination of all the parts — an impossible achievement in the behavioral sciences, of course, but something to be strived for nevertheless.

We could consider the whole of society as a system whose component parts include government, education, religion, and business. Each of these parts would be composed of separate parts and would constitute a subsystem of the system of society. The concept could be continued through each successive layer of activity. Marketing would be included in the parts that make up the subsystem of business, and it must be harmonized with business's other components (such as production) so that business can operate effectively.

Marketing is *the system in which products, services, or ideas are conceived,*

---

[1]See "Seven-Up Uncaps a Cola — and an Industry Feud," *Business Week* (March 22, 1982): 98, 99; "Coke to Debut Caffeine-Free," *Advertising Age* (April 25, 1983): 1, 70; and "Coke Plunges into No-Caffeine Coke," *Business Week* (May 9, 1983): 35.

[2]"Lipton Jumps into Fray with De-caffeinated Tea," *Advertising Age* (May 2, 1983): 1, 70.

publicized, moved, distributed, and transmitted to appropriate market segments. Thus marketing is a system composed of a number of subsystems, each of which must harmonize with the others for maximum effectiveness.[3]

A MODEL OF THE MARKETING SYSTEM

Marketing both acts and is acted upon, since the very notion of a *system* implies a creative force and an arena in which it operates. To get the total picture of the marketing system, it is not only necessary to identify the components of the system but also to delineate the arena. The operation of the marketing system in its environment is illustrated in figure 1-1. The figure portrays, among other things, the need for all components of the system to work together.

As you examine the figure, visualize a wheel moving between two grooved tracks toward a receptacle designed to receive it at the end of the tracks. If the wheel is properly designed, it will roll into the receptacle. On the other hand, if one of the spokes is out of line, or if the condition of the tracks changes, the wheel will become lodged in the tracks and its movement toward the receptacle will cease.

The wheel represents the marketing system; the tracks symbolize the environment in which the system operates; and the receptacle denotes the marketing objectives. If the marketing system is properly conceived, with due consideration given to its environment, the marketing objectives will be accomplished. But if one

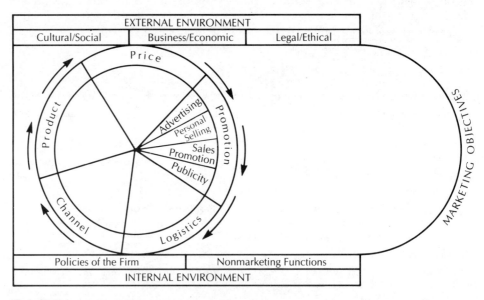

FIGURE 1-1 An analogy of the marketing system.

---

[3]See Lee Adler, "Systems Approach to Marketing," *Harvard Business Review* 45, no. 3 (May-June 1967): 105-18.

of the components of the system is out of proportion to the others, or if some element of the environment changes or has been misjudged, the system will fall short of reaching its objectives.

In the analogy we see that marketing is a system. For the system to work effectively each component must work together with all the others, and the total system must be designed to fit the environment. *Promotion, in the figure and in reality, is just one element in the marketing system.* Promotional strategy, therefore, must be planned and implemented within that constraint.

However, there is nothing static about the system. Rapid changes in the environment necessitate responsive changes in the system and require constant monitoring. The task of marketing management is to plan and effect the appropriate changes.

MARKETING IN ACTION

A brief overview of the marketing process provides additional perspectives. The marketing manager's task is to maintain consistency between the marketing activities of the company and its environment. A perpetual problem is that the environment is constantly changing, requiring constant adjustment in the marketing program. Thus planning and adjustment are continuous processes involving several activities and considerations.

Analyze the Situation

Alertness to the "situation" is mandatory for maximum effectiveness in marketing. It enables the marketing manager to locate problem areas in connection with the existing program; it makes the manager aware of any constraints on the program; and it furnishes clues to new marketing opportunities. Coca-Cola, after seeing an opportunity to create a mass market for wine, proceeded with mass-marketing techniques for its Taylor wines, although it has since abandoned the wine business.[4] Thus the focus of the situation analysis is on the environment.

Environmental factors exert enormous influence on the marketing system, yet they cannot be manipulated. They are the forces that act *upon* the system. Those individuals responsible for managing the marketing function must have a thorough knowledge of the environment's actual and potential impact and make decisions accordingly. These managers cannot change the environment, but must know it *will* change. The two groups of environmental factors are those that exist outside the organization and those that operate within it.

External Environmental Factors

External factors can be classified very broadly into three categories: cultural/social, business/economic, and legal/ethical.

---

[4]See "Creating a Mass Market for Wine," *Business Week* (March 15, 1982): 108–118; "Why Coca-Cola and Wine Didn't Mix," *Business Week* (October 10, 1983): 30.

Cultural/social. Culture refers to the composite ways of living as determined by a group of human beings over the years and transmitted from one generation to another. Attributes of culture are not innate, but are learned from parents and others and are passed on to children.

Because of interrelationships existing among people, culture is highly social. The people in any group associated with a particular "culture" have adopted, deliberately or without design, the attributes of that culture. Such adoption of cultural dictates stems from many causes, one of which is the desire for peer group acceptance or other group relationships.

Cultural/social forces have an enormous influence on the perceived needs of consumers and how they may be satisfied. The increasing emphasis on health and its influence on exercise and diet, the prevailing passion for computers and video games, and other aspects of the "ideal" life-style are obvious manifestations of the effect of cultural factors. Everything we do is a reflection of cultural influences. Marketers cannot afford to ignore such a force.

Business/economic. The activities of other businesses, both individually and collectively, are beyond the control of marketing management. They are a part of the environment and are reflected in the many facets of competition the firm must deal with. The number and kinds of retailers, wholesalers, and other business institutions may be virtually fixed, and the firm attempting to perform in that arena must accept it as it is and plan a marketing strategy accordingly.

Economic aspects must be considered in connection with marketing decision making. It is the willingness of people to buy that makes a marketing effort successful, and willingness to buy is affected by economic factors. General conditions such as prosperity, recession, and depression are extremely significant in this regard. Tax and spending policies of the federal government, inflation, the availability of money, agricultural crop conditions, recurring shortages of essential materials, and many other economic forces affect demand. All are beyond the control of marketing management; yet they must be considered when marketing decisions are made.

Legal/ethical. The third broad category of factors characterizing the external environment is identified as *legal/ethical.* These two terms are not synonymous. Some actions that are legal are not ethical, and vice versa. However, many actions viewed as unethical have been made illegal.

Promotion and other marketing decisions must not only be made with strict compliance to the law but also be consistent with good business ethics. Failure in this regard encourages severe antibusiness criticism and, of course, possible court action. In recent years, the legal/ethical environment of marketing has been increasingly significant. Consumer groups have influenced the passage of much legislation designed to regulate marketing activity, and industry itself has encouraged greater use of self-regulation to reduce the adverse criticism directed at marketing.

Internal Environmental Factors

In addition to these external forces, conditions within the firm itself must be considered part of the environment in which the marketing system operates. These conditions relate to those internal factors not directly related to the performance of the marketing function and over which the marketing manager has no control. Such factors may be controllable, of course, and may be changed as the need arises — but not by authority of the marketing manager. They include the general company policies and those nonmarketing activities that affect and are affected by marketing decisions.

Company policies.   Each company establishes policies to guide action in all the functional areas of the business. Marketing decisions must be consistent with these policies. General policies that place constraints on marketing decisions include growth, market share, extension of credit and credit terms, product, price, and relations with the various publics (consumers, government officials, stockholders, and so on).

Nonmarketing functions.   Further restrictions are placed on the freedom of the marketing manager by the operation of other functional areas of the firm. In some instances these nonmarketing functional areas directly constrain marketing action; in others, marketing action is restricted because of its effect on the other functions.

Financial managers, for example, may severely limit the promotional budget, limiting marketing action. On the other hand, although it does not directly constrain marketing action, a given production capacity should be considered in developing marketing strategy.

Establish Objectives

Objectives provide guides for action, and in most firms there is a hierarchy of objectives. The first tier of overall corporate objectives deals with such things as the niche desired in the market and the business community, rate of growth, merger and diversification goals, and return on investment. The second tier of objectives is established in the functional areas of the firm such as marketing. Successive layers of objectives, then, are established for the subdivisions in each area, and in *their* subdivisions. Promotion is a subdivision of marketing (third tier); and promotion is subdivided into advertising, personal selling, sales promotion, and publicity (fourth tier). Objectives at each level should support the objectives at the next higher level, and accomplishment of the lower level objectives should result in the accomplishment of the overall objectives. This relationship is illustrated in figure 1-2.

The results of the situation analysis provide clues for appropriate marketing objectives. Analyzing the situation not only identifies opportunities but also points up problem areas associated with the current marketing program. Thus directions for effort are indicated within the constraints of the corporate objectives.

FIGURE 1–2   Levels of objectives.

Marketing objectives are usually related to the market in some way, and can be either general or specific. General objectives suggest direction while specific objectives quantify the effort. Examples of general objectives are to increase and maintain market share, increase total sales volume, increase sales of a specific product, expand a particular territory, develop a new territory, and introduce a new product. Specific objectives apply numbers to the general objectives. The general objective to increase market share, for example, might be stated specifically as "to increase market share by 20 percent in Territory A in fiscal year 198–." Specific objectives are *measurable,* and the marketing manager can determine at the end of the year whether or not the objective was accomplished. All the "tools" available, promotion as well as others, will be used to accomplish the objective.

Define the Market

A major tenet of modern marketing is consumer orientation. Marketing begins and ends with the consumer. It begins before the product is developed, the service designed, or the idea formulated. It continues until consumer satisfaction is assured. Since all consumers do not want all products, nor do all consumers want any product for the same reasons, a marketing plan must be designed with certain consumers in mind. The market for the product, service, or idea must be defined.

Situation analysis provides much information for delineating the market. The only reason people buy products or services or accept ideas is to satisfy unfulfilled needs. The alert marketer, in analyzing the situation, will perceive certain consumer needs as not being satisfied or as being inadequately satisfied. Thus an opportunity is born and a market suggests itself. The need for ball-point pens with ink that could be erased led to the development of erasable ink. Because of the poor writing quality of the initial product, however, the market was limited. Later, the major firms in the industry — Paper Mate, Scripto, and Bic — made product improvements and saw opportunities to expand the market.[5] Seven-Up recognized a consumer need for products with no artificial flavors and colorings and created a stir in the

---

[5]See Gay Jervey, "New Scripto Erasable May Boost Market," *Advertising Age* (May 9, 1983): 30, 31.

industry by promoting their product as being free from such ingredients.[6] Shopping services evolved in the early 1980s, and exemplified a keen marketing reaction to an unfulfilled and unrecognized need. These complete shopping services are designed for people who do not have time to shop, such as professional women and families in which both husband and wife work outside the home, for example.

Once the market is defined, it must be reached by the proper approach. Basically the approach can take one of two forms, depending upon how the market is defined: market segmentation or product differentiation. If there is a relatively small group of consumers, or if there are different groups of consumers to whom the product might appeal for different reasons, the marketer might *segment* the market — that is, divide the total market into smaller groups and develop a product and a marketing strategy tailored specifically for each one or more of the segments.

On the other hand, if the marketer feels that the best approach is to consider the total market as one market — that is, if there appear to be enough people across the total range of the market to whom the product might appeal for the same reasons — the strategy calls for a mass-marketing approach. Consumers are not differentiated; the product is. It is differentiated from competing products sufficiently, it is hoped, to attract some people across the total market.

Determine the Marketing Mix

The major cogs in the marketing system (the wheel in figure 1-1) are referred to as the *marketing mix.*[7] Unlike the environmental factors beyond the marketing manager's control, the elements of the marketing mix are the tools of marketing. It is through their manipulation that the system is kept on track. The task of marketing management is to maintain these elements in the proportion necessary for maximum effectiveness of the system. The problem is compounded by the constant changes taking place in the environment. As a change in the environment is perceived, the marketing manager redesigns or rearranges the elements in the marketing system to counteract the change. The elements consist of product, price, channel, logistics, and promotion.

Product

The product (or service or idea) is the marketer's response to an unfulfilled or inadequately fulfilled need. The only reason for buying any product or service or accepting any idea is need satisfaction. There are no exceptions. The need may be real in that it must be fulfilled for purposes of survival (we must eat to stay alive), or it may be learned, such as the "needs" for tasty food, gratification, and ego

---

[6]See Robert Reed and Nancy Giges, "7-Up Ads to Hit Artificial Ingredients," *Advertising Age* (May 23, 1983): 2, 97; and Robert Reed, "7-Up Drive Tops $40 Million," *Advertising Age* (May 30, 1983): 3, 60.

[7]See Neil H. Borden, "The Concept of the Marketing Mix," *Journal of Advertising Research* 4, no. 2 (June 1964): 2-7.

fulfillment. We seek to satisfy these needs by purchasing products we perceive as capable of doing so. The same is true with ideas. We vote for a political candidate because we believe that person's ideas and conduct in office will better satisfy our needs than those of any other candidate.

Thus marketers develop products to satisfy specific needs — real, learned, or both. But even if there is initial success, the situation may change. A competitor may enter the market with a product perceived as better than the one being offered. Some change may have to be made in the product, package, or size to revive its acceptance in the market. Manufacturers of laundry detergents periodically introduce "new and improved" products. Candy companies increased the size of candy bars in recent years. And changes in the packages of items on supermarket shelves are so common it is sometimes difficult to find a specific, familiar "friend." In each case the marketer is reacting to changes in the environment by redesigning or adjusting the product.

Price

Price is an expression of value, usually but not always in monetary terms. Price equates consumer cost with consumer satisfaction. In shopping for a sweater, for example, you may see one that you like but you do not buy it because you think it is too expensive. What you are really thinking is that it would not provide you with satisfaction equal to the price (cost to you). You could be persuaded to buy the sweater only if the price were *reduced* to a figure matching your perceived satisfaction — or if your perceived satisfaction could be *increased* to a degree that matches the price. Thus the marketing response to your resistance could be either to lower price or to be more persuasive in the promotional effort (advertising and personal selling).

Yet a marketer could increase the marketability of a product by raising its price. Prestige may be a reason for purchasing the product (prestige is often associated with price) or a price/quality association may be connected with the product.

Price is often a very effective marketing tool, but its use can sometimes result in fierce "price wars." Most people are aware of the price battles between Coca-Cola and Pepsi, although of course these companies also use promotion in their competitive conflict.[8]

Channel

The channel of distribution is the combination of institutions directing the flow of goods from manufacturer or producer to the consumer. It begins with the manufacturer and ends with the consumer. The institutions between the two are intermediaries or middlemen. Intermediaries can be merchants or agents. Merchants take title to the goods they handle and consist of wholesalers and retailers, while agents do not take title to the goods. Examples of agent middlemen are manufacturers' agents, selling agents, or brokers.

---

[8]See "Coke's Big Marketing Blitz," *Business Week* (May 30, 1983): 58–64.

Figure 1-3 indicates several distinguishable channels. The actual channels may not be as clearly defined as the figure suggests, however.

The manufacturer often can choose the channel or channels that will be most appropriate for maximum effectiveness. Many considerations go into making the choice, but essentially they are cost, coverage of the market, promotion of the product, and control. Cost is obviously a factor, because the manufacturer certainly wants to minimize cost as much as possible without losing effectiveness. The market as the company has defined it must be adequately covered. Because manufacturers of convenience goods (products purchased by most consumers at the most convenient locations) must have their products in every retail outlet possible, they usually choose a relatively longer channel, enlisting the help of wholesalers and/or agents to reach the retailers.

Manufacturers of shopping or specialty goods (goods the consumer compares on some basis, or makes a special effort to find) do not attempt to appeal to "everybody," and can thus limit the number of retailers who handle the product. They can reach the selected stores with their own sales force without the help of wholesalers or agents. Sometimes, when a manufacturer decides to change a channel of distribution, it helps a competitor, such as, for example, when Levi Strauss & Co. started selling jeans through mass merchandisers. Some department stores that had formerly carried Levi's on an exclusive basis were not pleased, and looked for a replacement brand—and VF Corporation was ready to oblige with Lee brand.[9]

Manufacturers would like to use channels that assist in promoting the product. They like to have wholesalers and retailers supplement their national advertising with support in the local media, and push the manufacturer's brand in their personal selling efforts; and they like to have retailers display their brands prominently in the stores. It is becoming increasingly difficult to find such a channel, however, because more and more retailers and wholesalers are developing their own "private" brands and understandably promote them at the expense of the national brands.

Control is always an objective in choosing a channel. The manufacturer would like to dictate what goes on in the channel such as pricing, maintenance of

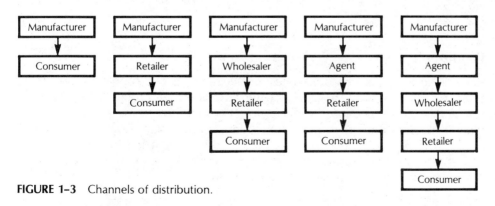

FIGURE 1-3 Channels of distribution.

[9]See "How Levi's Is Helping Lee Sell More Jeans," *Business Week* (May 23, 1983): 46.

prescribed inventory levels, promotion, etc. But this is totally possible only in the shortest channel—manufacturer to consumer. The longer the channel is, the less control the manufacturer has. Thus in reaching a mass market, the manufacturer must sacrifice some degree of control because of the need to use a relatively long channel to obtain adequate market coverage.

Channel decisions are not only concerned with the determination of the number of different levels of institutions (retailers versus retailers and wholesalers, for example) but also with the *types* of institutions at each level. What kind of retailer should be used—specialty shop, department store, supermarket? A classic example of a decision in this area that seemed to defy tradition at the time was Hanes' decision to sell L'eggs pantyhose through supermarkets instead of specialty shops or department stores. The product was successful so the decision was right.

There has been an enormous increase in direct marketing in recent years. Direct marketing is reaching consumers and making sales by means of direct mail advertising, catalogs, the telephone, and the use of such electronic marvels as computers, telecommunication systems, and interactive TV systems. While Sears, Montgomery Ward, and Spiegel were early pioneers in direct marketing, there are probably hundreds of firms today using this "channel."[10] And the pioneers have continued to be strong by adjusting to the times.

Logistics

The term logistics is used in marketing to refer to activities such as transportation and warehousing associated with the physical movement of goods. Good logistics management requires that the *total* costs of physical distribution be minimized without endangering the effectiveness of the marketing effort. This means that the focus should not be on, say, transportation with the commitment to use the cheapest method of transporting the goods. The objective should be to manage the activities in such a way as to keep *total* costs down. It may be better strategy, for example, to use air freight (an expensive mode) frequently rather than railroads (lower-cost transportation) less frequently. This procedure would result in higher transportation costs but lower warehousing costs because the need for maintaining large inventories at distribution points would be eliminated. Total costs might thus be minimized.

Promotion

Knowledge about products, services, and ideas does not spontaneously reach those for whom it is intended. No matter how good the product, how valuable the service, or how sensible the idea, its creation or existence will remain unknown without deliberate effort to make the information available. Contrary to the old adage, the world no longer beats a path to the door of the better mousetrap builder unless the builder persuades the world that the mousetrap is better. It is the job of promotion to persuade the world.

---

[10]See "Direct Marketing," *Advertising Age* (January 18, 1982): Section 2; and "Direct Marketing," *Advertising Age* (January 17, 1983): M-9–52.

Promotion is the deliberate attempt on the part of an individual, business, or other institution to communicate appropriate information in a manner persuasive enough to induce the kind of acceptance, reaction, or response desired. Thus promotion is communication — *persuasive* communication — and its effectiveness depends upon the talent and skill of those who design it.

Promotion is a system whose components consist of advertising, personal selling, sales promotion, and publicity. These are the tools of the promotion manager. Used in combination, they are referred to as the *promotion mix.* Like the marketing mix, the promotion mix must reflect a proper ratio of the components.

There is no best component; nor is there any generally accepted best combination of components. Rarely is one tool used without the others. The timing of a consumer's decision to accept, react to, or respond to the information is unpredictable — by the consumer or by the expert who designs the promotion strategy. In addition, the degree of persuasiveness of the message varies with different tools used among different people at different times. Effective promotional strategy, therefore, generally requires the use of all the components. Each is described briefly in the following sections (and is discussed at length in later chapters):

Advertising. Perhaps the most conspicuous of the components is advertising, which involves the use of mass media. The advertiser is always identified and pays for the opportunity of communicating a message.

Many firms rely heavily on advertising in their promotional strategy, devoting a major portion of their promotion budget to its use. Such media as television, radio, newspapers, and magazines, for example, are used extensively by manufacturers of consumer goods. Numerous other media play significant roles in effective advertising programs.

Personal selling. Unlike advertising, which is nonpersonal in nature, personal selling involves voice-to-voice contact. It may be a one-to-one situation, or it may be one individual attempting to persuade a group. It may be a face-to-face contact or it may be done over the telephone.

Manufacturers of industrial goods are among those companies that use personal selling more than advertising in their promotional strategies.

Sales promotion. *Sales promotion* consists of those promotional activities not considered advertising or personal selling. Such activities as games, contests, demonstrations, trade shows, trading stamps, and similar efforts are designed to help in promotional strategy.

Sales promotion is not to be confused with *promotion* — a broader term — of which sales promotion is a part.

Publicity. Publicity resembles advertising in that it generally uses mass media and it is nonpersonal. It differs from advertising, however, in that it is not paid for by its sponsor. Publicity involves the favorable presentation in a print or broadcast medium of some newsworthy event associated with the business or institution.

Publicity is an effective tool because the favorable light is not seemingly created by the firm itself. However, it is difficult to use because it always involves a decision by one or more outside parties such as an editor.

Consider the Marketing Mix a System

Although each component in the marketing mix is a subsystem with its own objectives and commensurate strategy, its actions must complement the other subsystems. If any of the actions conflicts with any of the other subsystems, the effectiveness of the total marketing system is reduced. A decision should not be made in one subsystem without first considering its effect on the operation of the others.

It would be counterproductive, for example, for a firm to generate a strong demand for its product through aggressive promotion, and fail to consider the logistics of making the product available to consumers. The product must be available at the place consumers expect it to be (the channel must be correctly chosen). If consumers are persuaded to buy the product, it must be obtainable; otherwise, the promotion would likely have a negative effect.

Or suppose that after a thorough market analysis a superior-quality product was determined to be necessary to obtain a share of a particular market segment, and thus *product* and all of its ramifications as an element of the marketing mix had been designed to create a certain image. Suppose that the *promotion* emphasized low discount prices. Clearly, the two subsystems would work against each other, and the result would be a less effective or ineffective marketing system.

Good marketing managers can increase the marketing system's effectiveness by using each of the subsystems (the elements of the marketing mix) in the way that can best accomplish the marketing objectives. This means making each of the subsystems responsible for a specific part of the overall task. If each of the subsystems performs effectively, then the total task will be accomplished. Promotion's part in the overall task is *communication*.

Figure 1-4 summarizes the mix concept in marketing, particularly as it relates to promotion.

Each element in the marketing mix has its own mix. The various products in a company's offerings, their price variations, the different channels through which they are sent, the variations in logistics, and the different methods of promotion constitute the respective mixes in each element of the marketing mix. Likewise, each element of the promotion mix has its own mix.

Evaluate Results

The dynamic nature of marketing demands careful monitoring of activity and evaluation of results. Changes are constantly occurring in the environment, and in the process of adjusting to these changes, marketers can never be sure the actions they take are the best. Despite the sometimes disputed justification for profit, businesses must make a profit to survive; and survival must be the underlying objective of any business. Thus unprofitable marketing actions must be eliminated or changed to make them profitable.

Most marketers find, for example, that the "80-20 principle" describes their

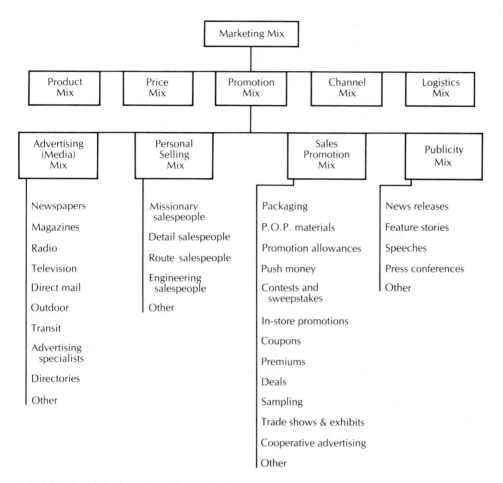

FIGURE 1–4   The mix concept in marketing.

situations. The principle means that 80 percent of the customers contribute 20 percent of the profit or that 20 percent of the customers contribute 80 percent of the profit. The percentage figures may vary, but a small part of the market is responsible for most of the firm's profit. Thus a portion of the unprofitable 80-percent segment could be eliminated altogether. This would change the ratio, but the marketer could then concentrate on the profit-producing segment.

Compounding the problem is the "iceberg principle." The principle takes its name from icebergs in the North Atlantic Ocean. Only the tip of an iceberg can be seen above the water while the enormous bulk of ice is submerged. Although an observer knows the iceberg is there, its size can only be surmised. Thus a marketer may know sales are down or profits are declining, but may not know why.

Effective evaluation of marketing performance requires a minimum of two kinds of analyses: sales analysis and marketing-cost analysis. A complete evaluation requires a marketing audit.

Sales Analysis

A sales analysis is a detailed study of sales data. These data include total sales figures — current figures, historical trends, and projected figures — and total sales broken down into various categories.

Sales can be itemized by territories or regions. For example, although *total* sales may have increased for the last five years, the increase could be the result of extraordinary success in one territory while sales in another territory have actually been decreasing. Total sales figures alone would not show this. But with specific sales-breakdown information the marketer might be able to adjust the marketing mix (perhaps redesign the promotional effort) to improve performance in the losing territory.

Total sales figures can similarly be classified by products, customer groups, or any other relevant category. Losers, winners, and problem areas can thus be identified and isolated, and the proper marketing focus indicated.

Marketing-Cost Analysis

Sales analysis may be misleading when used alone. The sales figures by themselves may look great until the cost of getting the sales is known. A marketer could probably always increase sales by lowering price and increasing promotion. But there is obviously a limit to which price could be lowered or expenditures on promotion made and still produce profitable sales.

A marketing-cost analysis is a detailed study of the costs associated with sales. Used in conjunction with a sales analysis it can expose the problem areas — such as sales whose costs of generation consume all the profit. The marketer can then determine the proper course of action.

The approach in preparing a marketing-cost analysis is to begin with the "natural," or ledger, expense accounts (salaries, rent, advertising, supplies, etc.), and reclassify them into "functional" accounts based on the purpose or activity for which the expenditures were made. Examples of such accounts include marketing administration, personal selling, advertising, transportation, and warehousing. The salary figure in the ledger account, for instance, would be broken down into these accounts, reflecting the activities for which salaries were paid. The functional costs are then further classified on the basis of products, regions, customer groups, and other appropriate bases. The result is an accurate picture of the profit or loss associated with sales, to whatever degree of division or classification the marketing manager desires.

Marketing Audit

The marketing audit is the ultimate evaluation procedure. It is a *total* evaluation approach in which the entire marketing program of the company is examined, from the conclusions drawn in the analysis of the situation to the sales that are eventually made. It is something like a CPA audit in accounting but is expensive because it should be performed by specialists from outside the company.

Whether a company uses a marketing audit or simply relies on a sales analysis and marketing-cost analysis, the marketing program should be evaluated at fairly frequent intervals. Only then can a company be sure that its marketing effort gets and stays on target.

EXPANDED CONCEPT OF MARKETING

Most of us tend to associate marketing and all of its components with businesses. But the concept of marketing can be applied appropriately to nonbusiness institutions and activities as well.[11]

Perhaps the most vigorous and pervasive nonbusiness marketing activity in the United States is that of political parties and candidates. Such activity is often planned for two distinct but related programs: marketing a philosophy to solicit funds and marketing a candidate to solicit votes. The entire effort should be planned and conducted according to sound marketing principles. Analyzing the situation is a necessary first step. Not only does this suggest the areas from which funds can be expected but it also provides the party leaders and campaign managers with clues to possible needs for government action. Objectives can then be established for both the solicitation of funds and voter response.

Effective political strategy also calls for defining and segmenting the market. Candidates use different marketing approaches in reaching several different groups, or segments, whom they identify as their markets, such as farmers, business people, labor unions, veterans, women, and minority groups. In reaching these various markets candidates must use different marketing mixes. The product (themselves or their ideas), for example, will be characterized differently to match each market because the people in each may have different reasons for "buying the product." Price reflects the value of what the voters give up if their candidate is elected and his or her ideas implemented — higher taxes or foregone benefits that might have been available if the other candidate had been elected. Channel and logistics are significant to the availability of the candidate to the voters.

The component of the marketing mix that reflects the most obvious use of marketing, however, is promotion; all elements of the promotion mix are used, although sometimes not wisely. Advertising often becomes so blatant during presidential election years that it becomes counterproductive for some candidates.[12] The national telethons sponsored by political parties sometimes create resentment by the viewing public. Personal selling is exemplified in the speeches made by and on behalf of candidates; sales promotion is used through bumper stickers, free refreshments, and other devices; and publicity for the party's cause is sought from all the media.

---

[11]See Philip Kotler, "A Generic Concept of Marketing," *Journal of Marketing* 36, no. 2 (April 1972): 46–54.

[12]Political advertising is not restricted to the United States. See Sean Milmo, "Hard-Hitting Ads Inflame U. K. Election," *Advertising Age* (May 30, 1983): 6.

Readin'. 'Ritin'. 'Rithmetic.

There's a fourth 'R' that's just as important to your child's future.

Regular physical activity.

If your children don't get at least one school period a day of vigorous exercise, then their future is being short changed.

60% of our children are overweight. 25% are obese.

Diseases of heart and blood vessels start with inactivity in the early years. Yet the number of schools requiring regular physical education has actually decreased.

Find out what's happening in your schools. And do something about it. That fourth 'R' is just as important as the other three.

Your child has a right to good health... exercise it.

FIGURE 1–5   Use of an advertisement by a nonprofit organization.

Finally, evaluation of results is essential both during and after the campaign. As the campaign progresses, the planners want to be sure their objectives are being met. If not, they will make some adjustments. When the campaign is over they want to know what went wrong and why, particularly if they lost.

Many other institutions and activities reflect similar application of marketing principles. Fraternities and sororities market their causes with "rush" activities; successful United Way drives are based on sound marketing concepts; states market their tourist attractions; and religious groups use marketing to increase their attendance and membership, through signs posted in front of the church announcing the day's sermon or religious discussions in both print and broadcast media. Success in connection with most social and civic causes requires the use of marketing techniques. (See figure 1-5.)

Although this book focuses on promotional strategy in business, the approaches, considerations, and techniques used in developing promotional strategy for firms can be adapted and applied to the promotion of nonbusiness causes and ideas.

We shall now "pull" promotion out of the marketing mix (see the schematic at the beginning of this section) and devote the remainder of the book to a discussion of that function.

SUMMARY

Promotion is a part of marketing and its strategy must be consistent with and complementary to marketing strategy. The purpose of this chapter has been to present an overview of marketing to see where promotion fits into the total picture.

The marketing function is a system operating in an environment beyond the control of marketing. External factors in the environment are cultural/social, business/economic, and legal/ethical. Environmental factors within the firm itself that bear on marketing strategy include the general policies of the firm and certain nonmarketing functions.

The components of the marketing system include product, price, channel, logistics, and promotion. These elements, referred to as *the marketing mix,* are the tools of marketing management. Promotion is one of the tools and must be used in conjunction with all the others.

Promotion is a system in itself. Its role in the overall marketing strategy is to communicate information in a persuasive manner. The components of the system include advertising, personal selling, sales promotion, and publicity. These elements, when combined into a promotional strategy, are referred to as *the promotion mix* and are the tools of promotion.

Finally, the concept of marketing may be expanded to include certain nonbusiness activities so the techniques of promotional strategy may be applied to nonbusiness ventures that require persuading the public.

QUESTIONS FOR THOUGHT AND REVIEW

1. If the purpose of promotion is to persuade, what part does providing information play in the process?
2. Could you argue that the purpose of promotion is to provide information? Why or why not?
3. Explain the statement that marketing is initially a matching process. Give some examples of this process.
4. What is *systems analysis?* Illustrate with an example of your own.
5. Define *marketing* in your own words.
6. What does it mean to say marketing "both acts and is acted upon"?
7. Explain the principle illustrated in figure 1-1.
8. Since environmental factors are beyond the control of the marketing manager, can such factors be ignored in developing marketing strategy? Explain.
9. Distinguish between external and internal factors in the marketing environment.
10. What are the three broad groups of external factors? Briefly describe each group.
11. Distinguish between *legal* and *ethical.*
12. How are the policies of the company considered a part of the environment for marketing?
13. Give an example of how the action of a nonmarketing function might constrain marketing action.
14. Explain how marketing action is restricted because of its effect on other functions.
15. What is the purpose of establishing objectives? Explain a hierarchy of objectives in marketing, using an example.
16. Distinguish between *product differentiation* and *market segmentation.*
17. What is the *marketing mix?*
18. Based on the text, how would you define *product* and *price?* Explain how they can be adjusted to a changing environment.
19. Describe the several channels of distribution and how a manufacturer chooses a channel.
20. What is *logistics?* How is it important in the marketing process?
21. Define *promotion* in your own words.
22. What is the *80-20 principle?* The *iceberg principle?* Explain how they relate to the evaluation of results in a marketing program.
23. What is a *sales analysis?* Explain why using a sales analysis alone may be misleading.
24. What is a *marketing cost analysis?* A *marketing audit?*
25. Discuss how promotional strategy can be applied to nonbusiness activities.

PROMOTION AND THE COMMUNICATION PROCESS

We communicate in many ways. We speak, write, whistle, raise our eyebrows, lift our arms, shake our heads, grunt, groan, cry, yawn, clear our throats, or leave the room. It is impossible to conceive of any social environment existing without communication in many forms.

There are many times when we try to communicate but are unable to do so. How many times have you talked with someone who obviously did not hear what you were saying? You could tell that your conversational partner was not listening because you could almost see his or her mind working on what to say when you stopped talking. The listener's response confirmed your observation.

There are also times when we think we have communicated only to find that the idea we *thought* we were conveying was not perceived by our listener. We were misunderstood and communication did not take place.

Because promotion is communication, we must understand the communication process to understand effective promotion.

THE CONCEPT OF COMMUNICATION

The term *communication* stems from the Latin, *communis,* meaning common. Our purpose in communicating is to establish something in common with another person or persons. We do this by imparting information, knowledge, thoughts, and opinions to those with whom we wish to establish the relationship.

It is often argued that in some instances we are simply attempting to *inform,* while in other cases we are trying to *persuade.* Others suggest that all communication is an attempt to persuade in some way — if only to accept the statements we make.[1] In any event, effective promotion requires persuasive communication.

Communication takes place when those with whom we are attempting to communicate attach a meaning to the message similar to the meaning we are trying to convey. This similarity of interpretation is necessary in all communication situations, but it is particularly significant in promotion because mass communication is often required.

A Communication Model

Communication literature is replete with models of the communication process.[2] The models are similar with respect to the elements they contain; however, they may differ in terminology, in the exact number of items included, and in the precise interpretation of relationships and effects.

The following elements are common in all communication situations and in most models: source, message, encoding, channels, decoding, receiver, noise, and

---

[1]See David K. Berlo, *The Process of Communication* (New York: Holt, Rinehart & Winston, 1960), p. 9.

[2]See, for example, S. Bernard Rosenblatt, T. Richard Cheatham, and James T. Watt, *Communication in Business* (Englewood Cliffs, N.J.: Prentice-Hall, 1977), p. 9; Wilbur Schramm, "How Communication Works," in Wilbur Schramm, ed., *The Process and Effects of Mass Communication* (Urbana: University of Illinois Press, 1954), pp. 3–26.

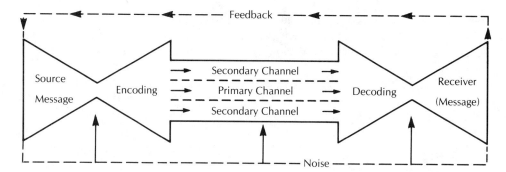

FIGURE 2-1   A diagram of the communication process.

feedback. For purposes of this discussion, encoding and decoding will be expressed as activities, rather than as people or things. The elements are depicted in the diagram in figure 2-1.

Basic Elements in the Communication Process

All communication contains the basic elements shown in figure 2-1. It is necessary to understand each element and its relationship to the others to develop an effective promotional effort.

Source

The source is the originator of the message. The source may be an individual, such as a salesperson talking to a customer, a minister preaching to a congregation, or a candidate for political office expounding to an audience. The source may also be an organization such as a business, a charitable institution, or a government agency. Each of these institutions originates countless messages to appropriate targets about products, services, and ideas it is trying to promote.

The receiver may or may not be aware of the source's identity. In a conversation between two people, of course, each knows the other as the source of the message. In an advertisement the source is identified in the message.

The source, however, is not always recognized. Sometimes receivers confuse the source with the vehicle of transmission — the newspaper or the radio, for example. You have no doubt heard such expressions as, "The paper says it's going to rain today"; or "According to the radio, the stock market was down yesterday." In these cases, the source is not the newspaper or the radio; it is some other institution or individual using the newspaper or the radio as the channel of transmission.

Confusion also arises when the person presenting the message is mistaken for the source. This frequently happens when well-known personalities such as athletes or entertainers present the commercials. When Billy Martin, Dorothy Hamill, or Jack Nicklaus, and Loretta Lynn, Ricardo Montalban, or Martha Raye, for example, star in television commercials, there is a tendency to perceive them as the sources of the messages. But the source is really the company whose product is being advertised. Sometimes such mistaken identity provides pseudocredibility to the real source and thereby aids in the reception and acceptance of the message.

This latter notion suggests that the source's credibility in the eyes of the receiver is a significant factor in communication. Clearly, one is more likely to believe what is said if the source is considered reliable than if it is suspect.

Message

The message might be thought of as *an idea in transmittable form.* The message originates in the source, and its *content* is suggested by circumstances that gave rise to the idea in the first place. However, its *form* is determined by conditions and forces affecting perception and receptivity of the message once it has been transmitted. Designing the form is the task of encoding.

A significant step in promotion is determining the appropriate idea to communicate. The relevancy of the intended message determines whether or not communication takes place. Often, people are not aware of messages unrelated to their interests. They "tune out" such messages, and communication does not occur.

Therefore, the promotional strategist must be as certain as possible that the message is right for the purpose and audience. A careful and thorough analysis of the individuals or groups who make up the target audience puts the strategist in a better position to understand what the communication objectives must be and what ideas should be communicated to produce the desired effect. After *content* is determined, it is put into communicable form — encoded into a message.

Encoding

The purpose in communication is to transmit an idea. The originator of the idea hopes to recreate in the receiver's mind precisely the same thing he or she has in mind. "When we communicate, we are trying to establish a 'commonness' with someone."[3] Because we experience so much misunderstanding in communication situations, we know that commonness is often difficult to establish.

Encoding is the process of putting the message into a form that can be transmitted, received, and understood by the receiver. This form is usually a written or spoken language, although it does not have to be. For example, the symbols used on street and highway signs and the shapes of the signs indicate very clearly the intended message without the use of language. The devices used in the encoding process must mean the same thing to both source and receiver; otherwise communication will not take place.

We assign meaning to signs and symbols, whether language or other devices, on the basis of our past experiences.[4] We interpret whatever we see or hear on

---

[3]Schramm, *Process and Effects,* p. 3.

[4]See Wilbur Schramm, ed., *The Science of Human Communication* (New York: Basic Books, 1963) pp. 7–8.

that basis. Our experiences with certain makes of automobiles, for example, influence the meanings we assign to advertising messages about those cars. Although no two people ever have precisely the same experiences and therefore can never assign precisely the same meaning to signs and symbols, the past experiences of source and receiver must be sufficiently similar to result in some degree of "commonness." There must be some congruence of frames of references — the collective experiences and previously assigned meanings — of each. When the signs and symbols used in encoding the message reflect this common ground, the decoding process will reflect it, and the meanings assigned in the two processes will be similar. This is illustrated in figure 2–2.

Encoding is complicated by the fact that a word often has different meanings and shades of meanings. English people, for example, define *lift* as an elevator and *flat* as an apartment; Americans do not. Groups of people assign different meanings to these words appearing in a message as a result of their different frames of references. To some Texans the word *tank* means a farm pond, but Colorado natives think of a *tank* as some sort of metal container used to store liquids. Words must be very carefully chosen in the encoding process so they have the same general meaning for source and receiver. Even so, since no two people ever have the same experiences, perfect communication between sender and receiver will probably never be achieved.[5]

One way to minimize communication error, assuming that the message's content has been properly determined, is to exercise some degree of empathy while encoding the message. An encoder who sees the communication situation through the receiver's eyes is more likely to use the language, signs, and symbols meaningful to the receiver to convey the idea. The same message, for example, might be encoded one way if it were being transmitted to a professional engineer and an entirely different way if the target were a high school student.

Market segmentation, breaking the market into smaller homogeneous groups, serves a number of purposes in marketing. Its primary significance in pro-

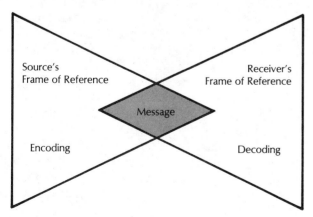

FIGURE 2–2   Congruence of frames of references.

---

[5]See Otto Lerbinger, *Designs for Persuasive Communication* (Englewood Cliffs, N.J.: Prentice-Hall, 1972), p. 117.

motion is related to the encoding process in mass communication. The receivers in a mass audience must be considered as a collective. The only way to do this is to segment the audience (market) into homogeneous groups and then communicate with each group as if the people in the group were one receiver.

External encoder.   The source is always the originator of the message but not always the encoder. In some situations the source may not be qualified to encode the message in transmittable form or in a form that would be accepted and understood by the receiver. The receiver may have insufficient knowledge or the source may lack the ability to encode the message. Such organizations as advertising agencies, media personnel, and public relations agencies often act as encoders of messages aimed at mass audiences. Senior salespeople and sales organizations also encode messages conceived by sales managers to be delivered by new salespeople.

Channels

The channel is the link between the source and the receiver — the means by which the message is transmitted. The channel may be the human voice in personal selling situations; it may be the printed word in magazine and newspaper advertising; it may be the spoken word on radio or television; or it may be something else or a combination of many things. There are both primary and secondary channels.

Primary channel.   The primary channel is the vehicle chosen to carry the message. Choosing the channel for promotional messages, however, involves much more than simply electing to use, for example, the human voice. Some messages are transmitted more persuasively by a female voice than a male voice. Credibility would be suspect, for example, if one heard a masculine voice extolling the benefits of women's lingerie. Or it would seem incongruous to hear the desirable features of a bulldozer described in a feminine voice. (This is no reflection on the capabilities of women who handle earth-moving equipment. It has to do with the images of ruggedness and daintiness, and ruggedness is associated more with masculine voices than feminine).

If the promotional strategist chooses to use the printed word as the primary channel, there are many options. Examples include newspapers, magazines, direct mail, billboards, transit (using public transportation systems), directory advertising (telephone and other), the product package signs in retail stores, and all kinds of advertising specialties such as calendars, ball-point pens, and match books. Different newspapers reach different audiences and specific magazines reach every special interest group imaginable as well as the general public. Radio and television can be characterized similarly, with respect to the stations themselves and their programs.

Thus the promotional strategist must choose the channel or combination of channels most appropriate for transmitting the message to the defined audience (market). Success in the promotional effort depends upon effective communication. Unless the intended audience receives the message, communication cannot take place.

Secondary channels.   As shown in figure 2–1, most communication situations involve one or more secondary channels along with the primary channel. These ''message carriers'' are deliberately used in connection with the primary channel or inadvertently accompany it. The secondary channel often has a greater impact on the receiver than the primary channel. If such impact reinforces the message being transmitted, the effect is good. When a father speaks (primary channel) to his son and says, ''I want you to tell me where you were last night,'' and punctuates his words with a shaking of his fist and a threatening look (secondary channels), the intended message comes through loud and clear.

On the other hand, the secondary channels may distort the intended message so much it is ineffective or even negated. For example, a meek salesperson may be selling a good product and have a good message; but making the sales presentation in an apologetic manner showing a complete lack of confidence negates the intended message. The secondary channels (mannerism and behavior) prevail over the primary channel (words spoken). The intended message in the primary channel, which points out the favorable aspects of the product, will be completely overshadowed by the message in the secondary channel, which says that the salesperson does not really believe in the product.

Secondary channels are not restricted to face-to-face situations, but are also significant in mass communication. Certain magazines are considered more prestigious than others. Their prestige will act as a secondary channel by adding impact to the message in them — impact that would not be present if the message were in other magazines. In a single magazine the size and style of type used in an advertisement will act as a secondary channel. The positioning of messages, both in print media and in broadcast media, creates secondary channels. Advertisers should very carefully consider the television programs with which they may be identified; the association itself could be a secondary channel.

Noise

In addition to the difficulties posed by multiple channels of transmission, the communicator is always faced with the problem of noise. Noise in this sense refers to *any* distraction from the reception and understanding of the message. The distraction may be some activity or condition in the environment of the source or receiver or it may be some condition internal to either that affects the encoding or the reception and understanding of the message.

Music blaring, children playing, the telephone ringing, interruptions by other people, conversations between nearby people, and other promotional messages are examples of outside noise. These kinds of annoyances can affect the person encoding the message and will result in a less than effective message. Such noise can also interfere with reception and understanding of a properly encoded message. Noise can also result from some condition within the source or receiver. Illness, anger, worry, preoccupation, discomfort, or uneasiness will tend to affect the way the message is encoded or received. Any distracting influence when a message is being encoded or transmitted may distort the meaning of the message, lessen its impact, or actually prevent its reception.

Feedback

Feedback refers to the clues that indicate whether or not the message is being received and the degree to which it is understood. Such clues may suggest changes in the presentation that will make the message more meaningful to the receiver and more consistent with the source's intent.

In face-to-face situations the sequential steps in the process are simply repeated *with the original source and receiver exchanging roles.* The clue may be nothing more than a frown, a raised eyebrow, or a nod of the head; it is a message in every sense of the word. Or feedback may be orally expressed by the original receiver through questions or statements. The good salesperson takes full advantage of the feedback and adjusts the presentation accordingly.

Such immediate feedback is most obvious in face-to-face situations involving the source and one receiver, but it also exists with more than one receiver, perhaps an audience of hundreds of people in direct contact with the source. Alert political speakers, ministers, college professors, and soapbox orators can pick up clues from the audience that indicate whether the message is being received and how. Furthermore, the shrewd speaker can adjust the presentation (revise the content or recode the message) accordingly.

When mass media are used, however, acquiring feedback is a problem. Yet the source must have some idea whether the target audience is getting the correct message. Since there is no direct contact between source and receiver, feedback must be obtained through indirect methods such as marketing research, opinion surveys, attitude studies, and perhaps sales of the product. Clearly, feedback obtained in this manner is much less reliable and timely than that received through direct contact.

Decoding

Decoding, the reverse of encoding, takes place at the receiver's end of the channel. The source, who wants to implant an idea in the receiver's mind, puts the idea into message form, encodes the message, and transmits it. If all goes well, the source's idea will be reproduced in the receiver's mind and communication will have occurred.

If perfect communication is to take place, the message must be decoded in precisely the same way it was encoded. Because no two people perceive things exactly the same way, the best thing that can be hoped for is for some degree of congruency.

The decoding process begins as soon as the receiver becomes aware of the message. He or she "translates" the message into an idea and if the idea matches what the source had in mind, communication has taken place.

The terms *denotative* and *connotative* are significant in both encoding and decoding. The denotative meaning of a word is universally accepted; it is the meaning that identifies the object to which the word refers. The connotative meaning is its unique meaning to an individual, stemming from emotions or feelings rather than thought. For example, the denotative meaning of *snow* (not the technical scientific definition, but the meaning to nonscientists) is "precipitation in the form of white flakes which can accumulate on the ground to several inches or feet." The connotative meaning of snow, on the other hand, is not the same to all individuals. To homeowners it may suggest the unpleasant task of shoveling the sidewalks and driveway. But to the children it may mean snowballs and sledding.

If the encoder uses the word *snow* in the message, there is no assurance that the decoder will translate it in the manner intended. Communication may not take place because the idea might not be recreated by the receiver. The encoder must make every effort to use language, signs, and symbols that will not only have the correct denotative meaning but also will have connotative meanings to the receiver consistent with the idea the source is attempting to transmit.

Receiver

It is impossible to divorce the decoder from the receiver as people because the receiver is the decoder. However, it is possible to discuss them separately, if we consider decoding as an *activity* and the receiver as a *person*.

The message must be encoded in terms of the receiver. If this is done well, the receiver is in a likely position to decode the message as the source intended. *Encoding the message in terms of the receiver* means using language, signs, and symbols whose denotative and connotative meanings are shared by both source and receiver — not meanings that are simply those of the source. The only way communication will take place is for both source and receiver to use the same referents in the encoding and decoding processes. A *referent* is the particular object, event, or concept that signs and symbols identify or describe and stems from one's frame of reference. Some degree of congruence of the frames of references of both source and receiver must exist for effective communication to occur.

Suppose that a restaurant operator has decided to add a line of Mexican dishes to the menu. One of the advertisements promoting the new line states, "Our chili is always hot." Such a statement seems simple enough. However, unless the audience has been identified very carefully, communication would not take place with all the receivers because the referents for the words *chili* and *hot* might not be the same for both source and receiver.

Chili is thought of by some people as a soup; to others it describes a special kind of meat sauce to be put on tamales and other kinds of Mexican food. The word *hot* might refer to the temperature of the chili, or it might refer to the strength of the ingredients used in the product. There are at least four different messages that could be decoded from the one simple statement, depending on the referents used in the process.

The foregoing illustration suggests a receiver may receive a message but not *the* message. If such is the case, of course, communication has not taken place because the idea in the source's mind has not been recreated in the mind of the receiver. Referents derive from the influence of one's culture and are tempered by a unique background and experience. This is why it is so difficult to communicate with people whose culture is different from ours. Language is an obvious difference, but the differences need not be that extreme. The many subcultures in any society present problems of communication because of the different referents associated with the same signs and symbols. In mass communication the logical approach to the problem is market segmentation—identifying groups of people with common referents.

PERCEPTION

Communication cannot take place unless the message is perceived; it is not completely effective unless it is perceived as the source intended. Thus perception is an important factor in the success of any promotional effort.

Berelson and Steiner define perception as "the more complex process by which people select, organize, and interpret sensory stimulations into a meaningful and coherent picture of the world."[6] A sensory stimulation results from the perception of a stimulus, which is an input to any of the senses. Examples of stimuli related to promotion include sales presentations, advertisements, commercials, signs in retail stores, products, packages, brands, labels, and any other device whose purpose is to convey a promotional message.

But a person cannot possibly detect all the stimuli to which he or she is exposed. Why, then, are people oblivious to some stimuli and susceptible to others? Why do people listen to some promotional messages and ignore others? The answer lies in the concept *selective perception.*

Selective Perception

The observer, in the face of the countless stimuli to which exposure is possible, sorts out particular aspects of the environment to be perceived. The shopper in the supermarket, potentially exposed to perhaps 15,000 different items, notices only a few. The individual watching television or thumbing through a magazine "sees" only a very few commercials or advertisements. The voter hears only certain political messages and the church-goer only listens to parts of the sermon. Perceived stimuli are organized and interpreted in different ways, resulting in different meanings for different people.

What is perceived and how is determined by the nature of the stimulus, the "set" or expectations of the individual, and the individual's current motives (based on needs, wants, interests, etc.).[7] The promotional strategist attempts to create a stimulus that will be included among those sorted out by the intended receiver.

---

[6]Bernard Berelson and Gary A. Steiner, *Human Behavior: An Inventory of Scientific Findings* (New York: Harcourt, Brace, and World, 1964), p. 88.
[7]Berelson and Steiner, *Human Behavior*, p. 100.

This is done by not only correlating the stimulus with the interests of the intended receiver but also by using more obvious attention-getting devices such as contrast. Advertisements are produced in color instead of black and white, or in contrasting colors. Sound, or the absence of it, is used to attract attention, as are large-size and "fold-out" ads in a magazine. The use of an attractive female in an advertisement, although now considered sexist when used in irrelevant situations and not necessarily effective with respect to communicating the message, attracts attention. Packages are designed to attract attention in retail stores; salespeople, political candidates, and other oral communicators use various techniques to insure their messages (stimuli) will be perceived.

People tend to perceive things according to their expectations. If they expect to perceive something, or perceive it in a certain way, they probably will. They bring a certain "set" to the perceptual situation. You expect to see more advertisements for radiator coolant (generally referred to as antifreeze by many people) in the fall and winter than in the summer. So you are likely to see such ads while looking through a mazagine in the fall but not even notice them in the summer. Or if someone tells you a certain TV commercial is terrible, you will likely perceive it that way because that is what you expect it to be. A stimulus that contrasts *sharply* with expectations may be perceived because of its novelty or shock value. Merrill Lynch's "bull" commercials in recent years, for example, are incongruous enough to be perceived because of this.

Finally, perception is influenced by one's unfulfilled needs or wants. How many advertisements for refrigerators did you see in last night's newspaper? Probably none if you are not in the market for a refrigerator. But if you intend to replace yours, it is likely that you saw all such ads. A hungry person will perceive more advertisements for food than one who has just finished eating dinner. Marketers and promotion strategists try to anticipate the needs of consumers in their markets and develop products and strategies accordingly.

The selective process in perception can be summarized as consisting of four stages: exposure, attention, interpretation, and retention. Each is a significant factor in the success of any promotional effort because they are all related to effective communication.

Exposure

Because we cannot perceive all the stimuli in our perceptual fields (our fields of awareness), we must pick and choose among them. We engage in *preattentive processing*.[8] The purpose of this activity is to identify those stimuli (messages) to which we will allow ourselves to be exposed. The process is virtually automatic, and stems from our desire to maintain consistency in the things we know. We try to avoid or reduce frustration by seeking out communications that support the things we believe in and avoiding those that challenge our beliefs.[9] The confirmed

---

[8]Neisser, Ulric, *Cognitive Psychology* (New York: Appleton-Century-Crofts, 1967), ch. 4.

[9]See Elihu Katz, "On Reopening the Question of Selectivity in Exposure to Mass Communications" in R. P. Abelson et al., eds., *Theories of Cognitive Consistency: A Sourcebook* (Chicago: Rand McNally, 1968), p. 789.

cigarette smoker is aware that he or she is more likely to contract lung cancer than the nonsmoker but does not want to quit smoking and experiences frustration. To reduce the discomfort, the smoker seeks out stimuli perceived as supporting the habit and ignores the conflicting stimuli. Republicans are attracted to political speeches of Republican candidates and avoid those of Democratic candidates. The same is true of Democrats and their party candidates.

Persuasion, the ultimate objective of any promotional effort, cannot be accomplished unless the intended audience receives the message. Exposure to the message (stimulus) is a necessary first step. The promotion strategist must think in terms of the intended receiver in designing an appropriate strategy. This means carefully defining the audience (market), identifying its characteristics, and designing the message consistent with the needs, wants, interests, attitudes, and values of the members of the audience.

Attention

Once a stimulus has been selected for exposure, it is examined further to determine if it is worth "attending." In this stage the individual attempts to confirm or refute the wisdom of the decision to allow exposure in the first place. Thus, he or she performs an *analysis for pertinence*.[10] Somewhat the same criteria are used in making this analysis as for the preattentive processing stage, except criteria are considered more carefully and the resulting decision is more studied. But the purpose is essentially the same. The individual is evaluating the message to see if it is pertinent to his or her personal needs and interests. If the message is pertinent, the individual will perceive it; selective attention has resulted.

Interpretation

Perception includes organizing and interpreting sensory stimulations into something meaningful. But it is a uniquely individual process and the same stimulus can be interpreted in different ways by different people. The same pervasive force present in all communication prevails here — the individual's own frame of reference, needs, wants, attitudes, interests, and expectations. How many times, for example, have you listened to a political speech on TV, made your own interpretations of what was said, and then at the end of the speech hear the "professional" analysts present an entirely opposite view? Or have you ever been to a football game with a companion who was a fan of the other team, and the referee made a close call? If the call was an advantage for your team you probably thought it was correct; your friend may have felt it was a bad call. Yet both of you were sincere in your interpretations.

This phenomenon poses a real problem for the promotion manager because the objective in the communication process is to transmit the intended message intact. There is no assurance this will happen. The only approach to solving the problem is to think in terms of the receiver.

---

[10]See Norman, Donald A., *Memory and Attention* (New York: John Wiley & Sons, 1969), pp. 33–36; 102–4.

Retention

Not only do we fail to perceive many of the promotion messages intended for us but we forget many we do perceive. We tend to remember only that which is relevant to our needs and interests. Since much advertising is intended for use by the consumer at some future time, this presents a problem. The promotion manager would like for the consumer to retain the message long enough to use it in the decision-making process — whenever that occurs.

The promotion strategist must associate the product, service, or idea with the needs, interests, attitudes, and predispositions of the people who are the target of the effort. Otherwise, the message will very likely be forgotten.

Subliminal Perception

Quite a stir was created in the late 1950s when it was alleged that advertisers were presenting some messages at rapid speeds or camouflaging them so the consumer was not aware of them but perceived them nevertheless. The process is referred to as subliminal perception and simply means that the stimulus is beneath the threshold of awareness but that it can still be perceived by the people at whom it is directed.

The impetus in the furor was the now classic study done by James Vicary in which the words "Drink Coke" and "Eat Popcorn" were flashed on a movie screen at speeds below the threshold of awareness. The sale of Coke and popcorn allegedly increased as a result.[11] Although the findings in the study have been discounted as lacking appropriate methodology and replications have not been successful, they have had a lingering effect in the minds of many people. The phenomenon of subliminal perception was further publicized by Vance Packard in *The Hidden Persuaders.*[12]

The issue was revived in the 1970s with the publication of several books by Wilson Bryan Key.[13] Key contends that subliminal "embeds" are placed in advertisements to manipulate purchase behavior through appeals to sexual motivations.

Although there appears to be little or no evidence that subliminal advertising is persuasive and therefore manipulative (primarily because consumers perceive selectively even at subliminal levels), it remains an issue.[14] Many people believe subliminal advertising is used frequently, widely, and successfully.[15] With so little evidence of its effectiveness however, and with the existing climate of ethical concern, it seems doubtful it would be extensively used.

---

[11]R. Wilhelm, "Are Subliminal Commercials Bad?" *Michigan Business Review* 8 (January 1956): 26.

[12]Vance Packard, *The Hidden Persuaders* (New York: McKay, 1957).

[13]Wilson Bryan Key, *Subliminal Seduction* (New York: Prentice-Hall, 1974) and *Media Sexploitation* (New York: Prentice-Hall, 1976); and *The Clam-Plate Orgy and other Subliminal Techniques for Manipulating Your Behavior* (New York: Prentice-Hall, 1980).

[14]See for example, M. L. DeFleur and R. M. Petranoff, "A Television Test of Subliminal Persuasion," *Public Opinion Quarterly* 23 (Summer 1959): 170–80.

[15]Eric J. Zanot, J. David Pincus, and E. Joseph Lange, "Public Perceptions of Subliminal Advertising," *Journal of Advertising* 12, no. 1 (1983): 39–45.

SUMMARY

Promotion is communication. If communication does not take place, the promotional effort will fail. This is true whether the object is a product, a service, or an idea — whether it is a can of green beans, a guided tour of the Orient, or a plea to support the United Fund. The promotional strategist must have some knowledge of the communication process.

The basic elements in all communication situations are source, message, encoding, channels, decoding, receiver, noise, and feedback. The *source* is the originator of the message, which was defined as an idea in transmittable form. *Encoding* is the process of putting the message into a form that can be received and understood. The *channel* is the means by which the message is transmitted. Usually in addition to the primary channel there are several secondary channels. *Noise* is any distraction that interferes with the reception and understanding of the message; it may be in the external environment of the source or receiver or may result from some internal condition of either. *Feedback* refers to the clues the source gets that indicate whether or not the message is being received. *Decoding* is the reverse of encoding and takes place at the receiver's end of the channel.

Perception is significant in communication for many reasons, but it is particularly significant in explaining why an individual is aware of some messages and ignores others. The term *selective perception* describes this phenomenon.

QUESTIONS FOR THOUGHT AND REVIEW

1. Can you conceive of any social environment in which communication does not occur? Explain.
2. Cite some examples of personal experiences where communication did not take place although it might have been expected to occur. Explain why it failed to occur.
3. Do you agree with the notion that the purpose in all communication is to persuade? Why?
4. Explain the relationship between the source and the encoder in the communication process. Under what conditions is the source different from the encoder?
5. What is *feedback?* Compare and discuss the problems associated with feedback with respect to personal selling and mass communication.
6. Explain why the source is not always recognized. Is it important that the source be recognized? Why?
7. How significant is the *credibility of the source* in communication? What are some of the factors that increase the credibility of the source in the eyes of the receiver?
8. Define *message* in the communication process and discuss the importance of the message *content* to effective communication.
9. What is meant by *establishing a commonness with someone?* Relate this notion to the encoding process.

10. Define *signs and symbols* as they are used in encoding and explain why they must mean the same thing to both source and receiver.
11. Define *empathy* and *market segmentation* and relate both concepts to the communication process.
12. What is the *channel* in the communication process? If leaving the room under certain circumstances is communication, what channel is involved?
13. Give some examples of how a secondary channel can negate the message being transmitted through the primary channel.
14. What is noise in the channel? Is there any way this can be eliminated? How?
15. List the denotative meaning and some possible connotative meanings for each of the following: coffee, car, tree, flower shop, picnic.
16. What is a *referent?* Describe a situation illustrating its significance in communication.
17. Explain how a receiver may receive a message but not *the* message. When this happens, has communication occurred? Why or why not?
18. Explain the notion of a *congruence of the frames of references* of source and receiver. Why is this necessary for effective communication?
19. Suppose you were told that a particular new brand of instant coffee tasted bitter. How would this influence your perception of it?
20. Discuss each of the following in relation to selective perception: *exposure, attention, interpretation,* and *retention.* Use examples in your discussion.
21. What is *subliminal perception?* Do you think it is used? Do you think it is effective?

PART TWO

THE EXTERNAL ENVIRONMENT

There are environmental factors over which the marketing manager and the promotion manager have no control but with which they must work. Some of these factors are directly related to the appropriateness and effectiveness of promotion decisions; others are indirectly related because they influence general attitudes toward the concept of promotion.

This section is divided into three chapters. Chapter 3 deals with cultural and social factors; chapter 4 examines business and economic aspects; and chapter 5 is concerned with legal and ethical considerations. The three areas make up the environment in which promotional activity is conceived and implemented.

MARKETING MIX

Product | Price | **Promotion** | Channels | Logistics

Persuasive
Communication

MARKET ANALYSIS

Product Perception   Market Target   Promotion
Purchase Behavior   Promotion Appeal   Objectives

Organizing for Promotion

Financing Promotion

Coordinating Marketing & Promotion

PROMOTION MIX

| media | techniques | retailer | characteristics |

ADVERTISING | PERSONAL SELLING | SALES PROMOTION | PUBLICITY & P.R.

testing | management | consumer | techniques

PLANNING FOR THE FUTURE

CULTURAL/SOCIAL ENVIRONMENT

BUSINESS/ECONOMIC ENVIRONMENT

LEGAL/ETHICAL ENVIRONMENT

THE CULTURAL/SOCIAL ENVIRONMENT

Generally, people do not seek out promotional messages but are inclined to avoid them, for the ever-present implication is that promotion's purpose is to elicit responses that would not otherwise occur. Therefore the promotion manager must make every effort to ensure the message will be noticed; this effort must include the development of a considerable amount of cultural empathy with respect to the targets of the promotional messages. Empathy is developed by understanding the forces and conditions that give rise to the behavior patterns of the potential message receivers. Predominant among such forces and conditions are the cultural and social aspects associated with the identified environment.

THE CONCEPT OF CULTURE

A person's way of life is necessarily conditioned by the social influences of time and culture. It is not possible for a person to behave in a manner that does not reflect such influences.

What is *culture?* Of course, it is *not* merely an appreciation of grand opera and Shakespearean drama. To refer to those who exhibit a fondness for such art forms as "cultured" is to misuse the term. Everyone has a culture — the Papuans of New Guinea as well as English nobility. Culture has been conceptualized many times in many ways, but its definition always refers to the learned behavioral traits that are shared by members of a society.

Thus every society has its own culture; a society's culture is reflected in the behavior of its members. Furthermore, the culture of one society is never quite the same as that of another; nor does the culture remain static. It changes as it ceases to gratify the members of the society with which it is associated.

Attempting to compile a list of all the components of a culture would be futile. By definition, such a list would include all the behavioral traits of society. Yet throughout the voluminous literature dealing with culture there are numerous classifications of culture components. Kuhn suggests that the content of culture consists of "a set of concepts and a set of motives or values . . . intertwined in the culture."[1] Herskovits divides culture into material culture and its sanctions, social institutions, belief systems, aesthetics, and language.[2] White uses four categories: "ideological, sociological, sentimental or attitudinal, and technological."[3] There are many other classifications, of course.

Thus, a society's culture is defined by its own peculiar manifestations of language, religion, social institutions, beliefs, values, customs, laws, attitudes, motives, skills, art, music, drama, folklore, mores, social norms, and all other aspects of its collective behavior.

Marketers in the United States are primarily concerned with the American culture. But recently the managers of many American and foreign firms have been

---

[1]Alfred Kuhn, *The Study of Society: A Unified Approach* (Homewood, Ill.: Richard D. Irwin and Dorsey Press, 1963), pp. 214-15.
[2]Melville J. Herskovits, *Man and His Works* (New York: Alfred A. Knopf, 1948), p. 634.
[3]Leslie A. White, *The Evolution of Culture* (New York: McGraw-Hill, 1959), p. 6.

devoting increasing attention to the international market. Success is highly dependent upon an understanding of the different cultures of the target countries. Mistakes can be costly and there have been many, particularly in promotion.

Pepsodent failed in Southeast Asia because in promising white teeth it violated a cultural tenet that black or yellow teeth are symbolic of prestige.[4] Maxwell House was not aware of the fact that Germans have little respect for American coffee and its appeal as the "great American coffee" did not go over.[5] In advertising its "rendezvous" lounges on flights to Brazil, a U.S. airline lost customers because "rendezvous" means *a place to have sex* in Portuguese.[6] Chevy Nova did not do well in Latin American countries because *no va* means *no go* in Spanish; in some countries General Motors' "Body by Fisher" translates into *corpse by Fisher;* and in Taiwan, Pepsi's slogan "Come Alive with Pepsi" means *Pepsi brings your ancestors back from the grave.*[7]

Promotion strategists must not only be careful with language in their efforts but also with their use of color on their products and packages. Different colors mean different things. Green is the national color of Egypt; its use on product packages is taboo. In some other countries, green is associated with death. In Latin America, purple is likewise so associated, and is to be avoided. Black and white are the colors of mourning in Japan.[8] White is the color of death in West Africa. Blue is a feminine color in Holland but masculine in Sweden. The international marketer must be fully aware of the cultural differences in the target countries.

SUBCULTURES

A society can be identified by the common behavior exhibited by its members in the components of its culture. But distinguishing characteristics in behavior modes serve to further delineate certain groups within the society. Such groups are called *subcultures.*

Subcultures evolve from numerous bases, some of which are natural and others contrived. Certain behaviors are sufficiently different in one group to set it apart from other groups in the culture while there is enough common behavior in all the subcultures to identify them as parts of the culture from which they originate.

Subcultures can be isolated by region. Within the United States, for example, distinctly different cultural traits can be observed between the South, the Southwest, and the Northeast. Such differences are evident in the pronunciation of words, tastes in food and clothing, mannerisms, and other displays of behavior.

---

[4]David Ricks, Marilyn Y. C. Fu, and Jeffrey Arpan, *International Business Blunders* (Columbus, Ohio: Grid Publishing, 1974), p. 15.

[5]S. Watson Dunn, "Effects of National Identity on Multi-national Promotional Strategy in Europe," *Journal of Marketing,* 40 (October 1976): 56.

[6]Ann Helming, "Culture Shocks," *Advertising Age* (May 17, 1982): M–8.

[7]Charles D. Schewe and Reuben M. Smith, *Marketing: Concepts and Principles* (New York: McGraw-Hill, 1983) p. 628.

[8]David Carson, *International Marketing: A Comparative Systems Approach* (New York: Wiley, 1967), p. 70.

Ethnic origin serves as another basis for the development of subcultures. Blacks, Spanish-Americans, Puerto Ricans, and American Indians have their own separate subcultures; and to a lesser extent, subcultures can be identified among people with strong ethnic ties such as the Irish, German, or Slavic. Age provides another natural basis; teenagers and senior citizens represent the two extremes.

Social classes, organizations, and religion also define subcultures. People in one social class share life-styles with each other but have different life-styles than people in other classes. Organizations such as fraternities and sororities, Freemasonry, The Order of the Eastern Star, and Rotary create subcultures of their own. Under the general concept "religion" can be found innumerable subcultures.

The concept of subcultures is particularly significant to marketers and promotion managers. It is important to understand the culture that comprises all of the people in the United States, but it is the subcultures that are the targets of much marketing and promotional effort. Designer jeans (Calvin Klein, Gloria Vanderbilt, and others) during their peak of popularity appealed to a definite subculture composed of fashion-conscious young women. Mexican foods were initially sold in the Southwest, and although they are gaining national acceptance, the Southwest is still the strongest market. Kosher meats are sold in the Jewish market, and uniquely spiced sausage is sold to Polish people. In some sections of the country brown eggs are preferred over white.

SUBCULTURES AND MARKET SEGMENTS

The two pairs of concepts — culture/subcultures and market/market segments — are not only analogous in their respective relationships but often the groups delineated in a particular culture/subculture relationship are the same groups identified for particular market/market segments. Recognizing this relationship emphasizes the need for marketers and promotion managers to understand the cultural environment.

A market develops where consumers respond favorably to the product, service, or idea offered to them and designed for their acceptance. Market segmentation is the policy of dividing the total market into smaller groups each of which is composed of people with a degree of homogeneous behavior.

This relationship of market to market segment is precisely the relationship that culture has to subcultures. Since culture is reflected in behavior and since the activity of individuals as consumers is part of behavior, cultural factors such as income, education, and religion that separate members of a culture into subcultures might also divide the members of a market into market segments.

Cultural Homogenization

Of particular significance to marketing and promotion is the sometimes disputed notion that the lines of demarcation between cultures and subcultures are breaking down. If there is homogenization of culture taking place, it must ultimately be reflected in marketing strategy and promotional methods. We shall use the international marketing arena as the focus for the discussion, although the principles can be applied equally well to subculture relationships within the United States.

It is customary in the marketing strategy of an American firm selling in Europe to consider each country a separate market and to consider both *cultures* and *markets* to coincide with established countries. This is not entirely logical because European countries have subcultures that are perhaps more distinct than those in the United States. Northern Italians, for example, have different food preferences than people in the southern part of the country. Nevertheless, it is presumed that people in a particular country share a common culture (because of national origin and other bonds of union) and therefore behave as consumers in ways unique to that country.

Yet both the market and the culture may transcend the boundaries of the country or fail to fill the area delineated. With the increasingly dominant role of television, for example, together with growing mobility, there must be an inevitable transfer and exchange of cultural characteristics among peoples with traditionally different cultures. To the extent that this happens, the cultures become less definitive. There are certain subcultures whose limits obviously have no national boundaries. The members of these groups have similar characteristics regardless of their national origin. One example of such groups is teenagers whose tastes in hair styles, music, and clothing seem to be universal. This mutual identification rises above national affiliation.

But there will always be national and regional cultural differences among societies and cultural changes will occur with changing environmental conditions. If marketing can be considered a social institution — a force that molds, directs, or responds to human behavior — it could very well be the impetus for some changes in culture.

In any event, marketing has its roots in the culture of a society.[9] The homogeneous nature of people in a "market" implies there are shared ways of behaving with regard to the purchase of a particular product or service or the acceptance of an idea. Therefore, marketers and promotion managers must be fully aware of cultural changes as they take place, whether in the direction of homogenization or not. More importantly, they must react to the changes.

GROUPS AND OTHER INTERPERSONAL INFLUENCES

It is generally accepted by contemporary marketers that the Marshallian concept of "economic man" does not completely explain purchase behavior.[10] Modern marketers have rejected the idea that consumers make their purchase decisions on the basis of economic factors alone. Decisions result from the interplay of forces and influences emanating from many sources, many of which are not economic.

---

[9]See Ronald D. Michman, "Culture as a Marketing Tool," *Marquette Business Review* (Winter 1975): 179–83; and Walter A. Henry, "Culture Values Do Correlate with Consumer Behavior," *Journal of Marketing Research* 13, no. 2 (May 1976): 121–27.

[10]Philip Kotler, "Behavior Models for Analyzing Buyers," *Journal of Marketing* 29 (Oct. 1965): 37–45. (Discusses application to marketing of several human-behavior theories.)

Primary Groups

By whatever collective name one chooses for them, the family, the church (or religion), and the school are the traditional primary institutions through which values are transmitted. The structure, objectives, and perspectives of these institutions change; and as they do so, the values transmitted through them change.

The mass media (television in particular) are becoming increasingly significant as agents of cultural transmission. The children in many homes today spend more time in front of a television set than they do in school or with their parents. A medium that pervasive surely must influence and transmit values. Since the mass media will be the focus of much of our attention throughout this book, we shall restrict our current discussion to the traditional triad of family, church, and school.

The Family

An individual's first contact with cultural values comes in relationships and associations with family members. All through childhood to the inevitable time the child leaves home, the opinions, attitudes, beliefs, and values of the adults and older siblings in the family influence character development.

Analyzing the family and its influence on promotional strategy would be much simpler if evolutionary changes were not taking place in the family as a social institution. In most Western cultures the very *structure* of the family is different from what it was a few years ago. The extended family is rare today; very few families in the United States include grandparents and other older relatives living under the same roof with parents and their children. Thus grandparental influence is less direct than it has been historically. In addition, there is a trend toward fewer children in the family.

Working wives and mothers are becoming the rule rather than the exception. The result is less time spent with the children who spend more time with baby-sitters or in day-care centers. Such changes in family relationships generate changes in values and the ways in which those values are transmitted.

Role assignment.   The traditional roles of husband and wife within the family unit are undergoing change and this change can have a profound effect on the design of promotional strategy.

For example, there is a greater degree of cooperation between American husbands and wives with regard to housework. There is a noticeable trend toward total egalitarianism. For example, one study showed that ``married women with children are spending four hours less on homemaking, and men about one hour more'' than in the 1960s.[11] It is not uncommon to see a husband with a basket full of clothes at the self-service laundry or a wife behind a power lawnmower. The

---

[11]Marianne A. Ferber and Bonnie Birnbaum, ``One Job or Two Jobs: The Implications,'' *Journal of Consumer Research* 7 (December, 1980): 263–71.

traditional distinction between man's and woman's work is blurring and the authoritarian role of the husband and the subservient role of the wife are disappearing. Decisions regarding the purchase of certain products, formerly made by one or the other, may now be made jointly or by either.

To be sure, there are still distinctions in their respective roles. There are still areas in which the husband is the decision maker and the principal role player, as there are areas in which the wife acts in similar fashion. But the promotion manager needs to know whether the decision to purchase a particular product or accept a specific idea is made by the husband alone, the wife alone, or by both acting together. Failure to get this information relative to the product or idea being promoted would mean that the appeal might be directed at the wrong person and communication would not take place.[12]

Family life cycle.   The concept of family life cycle refers to the phases through which a family progresses throughout its existence as an identifiable unit. The family begins as a husband and wife. The traditional concept is that there is a fairly typical pattern of successive distinguishable phases in family life as each new child arrives, enters school at each of the established levels, and finally leaves the family to begin another sequence. The time comes when all the children have left the home and the husband and wife are "back where they started." Eventually a single spouse is left until he or she, too, is gone. The cycle is then complete.

Because of the increasing prevalence of divorce in contemporary society, however, the traditional pattern is no longer necessarily typical.[13] Young married couples with no children divorce, each becoming a part of another cycle. If children are involved, one and sometimes two separate families are started. It is not uncommon to see divorces in couples with grown children, thus disrupting the "normal" cycle. Occasionally there are "singles" who have acquired children in one way or another and who thus may be considered families. Nevertheless, each of these departures from tradition can be identified with specific stages in the family life-cycle concept and can be dealt with accordingly in promotion planning.

The significance of the family life-cycle concept to promotion is that the purchase behavior of the family changes at each stage in the cycle. Such changes are reflected in the products and/or brands demanded, buying motives, decision-making procedures, buying power, and attitudes toward consumption in general. The astute promotion manager will be aware of these conditions as they relate to the product and how it can best be promoted.

---

[12]See E. H. Wolgast, "Do Husbands or Wives Make the Purchasing Decisions?" *Journal of Marketing* 23, no. 2 (Oct. 1958): 151–58; Robert Ferber and Lucy Chao Lee, "Husband-Wife Influence in Family Purchasing Behavior," *Consumer Research* 1, no. 1 (June 1974): 49–50; Harry L. Davis and Benny P. Rigaux, "Perception of Marital Roles in Decision Processes," *Journal of Consumer Research* 1, no. 1 (June 1974): 53.

[13]Patrick E. Murphy and William A. Staples, "A Modernized Family Life Cycle," *Journal of Consumer Research* 6 (June 1979): 12–22.

The Church

The influence of the church (church in the generic sense and not as applied to any specific denomination, sect, or religion) has fluctuated over the years, both in nature and degree. Sanctions today seem more loosely conceived and less severely imposed than they have been historically. Perhaps this change reflects the efforts of the church to overcome the current indifference of young people, or the changes taking place in the mores of society. Until recent times, the church has established a great many of the mores of society.

If the church has become a follower and not a leader in determining the values associated with our culture, its effectiveness in transmitting values has been lessened. Nevertheless, it must still be considered a source of influence on behavior. One measure of this influence is the effect of stands taken by various religious organizations on such controversial issues as the ordination of women, the status of homosexuals, and abortion.

The School

The importance of the school as a transmitter of values has increased in recent years. This is due, in part, to the relatively smaller roles now being played by the family and the church in this regard.

Western cultures are committed to educating the entire population. Virtually everyone is exposed to the educational process and the length of exposure is increasing. The school has become a kind of surrogate parent for many children whose values are largely developed through their associations in school. Their classmates, teachers, and administrators now have such diverse backgrounds that the values transmitted may not be considered traditional by many groups of parents.

Reference Groups

Reference groups have a significant effect on behavior, which includes consumer behavior and therefore promotion. A reference group is a set of people whose attitudes and standards of behavior are used by an individual in evaluating certain proposed actions. The person "refers" to the group when contemplating some specific action such as the purchase of a product or the acceptance of an idea.

Reference groups take many forms. Some are large; others are small. Some exert a positive influence, others, a negative. Some are groups of which the individual is a member; others are not. All that is necessary is that the group have some influence on a person's attitudes, values, and associated behavior. The three primary groups (family, church, and school) are special kinds of reference groups. With the possible exception of the church, they are not optional with the individual, as are others.

Influence

Reference groups serve as comparison points. They may be groups to which the individual belongs or would like to belong; or they may be groups whose perspectives the person adopts.[14] The latter notion is especially significant because a person often perceives the world from the standpoint of a group in which only vicarious participation is possible.

In some cases, the reference group is one to which the individual wants *not* to belong. Strongly negative feelings about a group may be reflected in behavior designed to prevent any possible identification with the group.

A particular reference group may have a positive influence on one individual and a negative influence on another. Country club sets, theater-goers, swingers, campus fraternities, motorcycle clubs, athletic groups, musical groups, liberals, conservatives, social classes, and occupational groups are examples of reference groups. In each case, the group may be one whose behavior in all its ramifications would be emulated by one individual and eschewed by another. For example, one person might want to be identified with the country club set and would adopt its behavior patterns; another might consider such a group to be snobs and would behave so as to preclude any possible membership inferences.

We are a society of conformists and much of our conforming behavior stems from reference group influence. Even those who proclaim their individuality and their opposition to traditional group behavior are conforming to the norms associated with any such deviate behavior. Thus these individuals have a reference group.

A person's total life-style is determined to a large extent by the influence of reference groups.[15] Not only is there a certain amount of psychological risk associated with independent behavior but it is difficult to isolate oneself from influential groups in society.

Promotional Strategy

Since a large part of one's behavior is a result of reference group influence, one's purchase behavior and other responses to promotional messages is affected likewise. Acceptance or rejection of a promoted idea is in many instances determined by the influence of one's reference groups. The persuasive effect of promotion for a product or brand is often influenced by one's reference groups.

Not all products or brands are subject to reference group influence and there are varying degrees of influence associated with different products or brands. Not

---

[14]See Tamotsu Shibutani, ''Reference Groups as Perspectives,'' *American Journal of Sociology* 60, no. 6 (May 1955): 562–69.

[15]See Joseph T. Plummer, ''The Concept and Application of Life-Style Segmentation,'' *Journal of Marketing* 38 (Jan. 1974): 33–37; William Lazer, ''Life Style Concepts and Marketing,'' in Stephen Greyser, ed., *Toward Scientific Marketing* (Chicago: American Marketing Association, 1964), pp. 130–39; 140–50.

all people are affected to the same degree by reference group influence for any one product or brand. For the highest degree of influence to exist there must be some association of its use with a particular group of people. Moreover, its ownership and use must be visible and conspicuous.

For example, there will not be much reference group influence in the purchase of a fingernail clipper that one keeps in a pocket or purse. But purchase and consumption of a bottle of beer might be the result of a good deal of reference group influence both with the generic product and the preferred brand. If beer has not been part of an eighteen-year-old college student's life-style at home, the student might perceive it as being associated with a particular reference group now. If the members of that group used one specific brand, the student would not only order beer but would also ask for that specific brand. Such behavior exists among people of all ages for many different products and brands.

In using the reference group concept in promotional strategy, it is necessary to determine first whether the purchase of the product or brand in question is influenced by reference groups. If the influence is established, the promotional effort should emphasize the people who use the product or brand. If there is no reference group influence on purchase of the product, the promotion should focus on the characteristics and attributes of the product.[16]

Social Class

That there is no such thing as a classless society is proven by extensive literature on the subject.[17] In some societies class distinction is more pronounced than in others. In the United States, for example, class lines are rather vaguely defined; there is a kind of blending of each class into the next. Nevertheless, each class is relatively identifiable by its tastes in food, clothing, literature, entertainment, and symbols designating class membership.

One of the landmark works on the subject of social class is the often quoted six-class concept developed by W. Lloyd Warner in the late 1940s.[18] Whether the promotion manager uses the Warner classification or some other index, he or she must recognize the fact that social classes exist and that they may have a bearing on the promotion of the product, service, or idea.

Members of identifiable social classes are distinguished more by their tastes and preferences than by their income (see figure 3-1, p. 54). It is not unusual to

---

[16]See Francis S. Bourne, ''Group Influence in Marketing and Public Relations,'' in Rensis Likert and Samuel P. Hayes, Jr., eds., *Some Applications of Behavioral Sciences Research* (Paris: UNESCO, 1957), pp. 217-24.

[17]See Dennis Wrong, ''How Important is Social Class?: The Debate Among American Sociologists,'' *Dissent* 00 (Winter 1972): 278-85; K. B. Mayer and Walter Buckley, *Class and Society* (New York: Random House, 1970); Pierre Martineau, ''Social Classes and Spending Behavior,'' *Journal of Marketing* 23 (Oct. 1958): 121-30; Sidney J. Levy, ''Symbols by Which We Buy,'' in Lynn H. Stockman, ed., *Advancing Marketing Efficiency* (Chicago: American Marketing Association, 1959), pp. 409-16.

[18]W. Lloyd Warner, Marcia Meeker, and Kenneth Eels, *Social Class in America: A Manual of Procedure for the Measurement of Social Class* (Chicago: Science Research Associates, 1949).

find a highly successful contractor with a six-figure annual income whose tastes have changed little since the contractor was a bricklayer earning $2.50 per hour. Conversely, people born into a socially elite class are not likely to change their tastes even if their wealth dissipates.

Differences in income *within* a social class, however, may be significant. Coleman has suggested the notion of *overprivileged* and *underprivileged* individuals in each social class.[19] Within each social class some individuals have an income above the average for the class (overprivileged) and some have incomes below the average (underprivileged). All the people in each social class share the same values, tastes, and so on, but the overprivileged can maintain the standards of living associated with their respective classes more easily than the underprivileged, and therefore have more discretionary purchasing power. In some cases the same products and brands are purchased by the overprivileged in each social class; similar behavior is exhibited by the underprivileged.

It was discovered, for example, that low-priced cars (Chevrolets, Fords, and Plymouths) were purchased by individuals with average income in each class, while the overprivileged members of each class bought Pontiacs, Buicks, Oldsmobiles, and Mercurys. Similarly, early color television sets were purchased by the overprivileged members of each class.

Some product brands are identified with certain social classes. For example, Michelob beer is associated with one class, Old Milwaukee with another. Chanel No. 5 cologne is associated with a particular social class. Price does not necessarily account for the differences. People in one social class are not only adamant in their use of a particular brand but also in their refusal to use brands associated with other social classes. Such differences in tastes and preferences extend also to services, magazines, books, entertainment, and ideas.

Thus the promotion manager must keep informed of any possible significance social class may have on the promotion of the product, service, or idea. Failure in this regard may result in failure to reach the people for whom the promotion was intended. Even worse, the promotion could alienate those people who had previously responded favorably.

ATTITUDES AND CHANGING VALUES

The promotion manager must not only understand the current impact of such social forces but must also be aware of the changes taking place in the influence these forces exert. Before we examine values in American society and their possible impact on promotional strategy, we must consider attitudes and their relationship to values.

---

[19]R. P. Coleman, "The Significance of Social Stratification in Selling," in Martin Bell, ed., *Proceedings of the 43rd Conference of the American Marketing Association* (December 1960), pp. 171–84.

Attitudes

Attitudes are those "enduring systems of positive or negative evaluations, emotional feelings, and pro or con action tendencies with respect to social objects."[20] Having an attitude means the individual is no longer neutral toward the object of the attitude but is either for it or against it. If the attitude is a strong one, the individual resists any attempt to change it; this influences what is perceived and how.

Any consideration of values requires some attention to attitudes since they are formed in relation to social values or norms. Attitudes can be general or specific. One can have an attitude toward socialism in general, for example, or toward nationalizing the oil industry in particular. An attitude can be so strongly entrenched that it is central to one's behavior or it can be somewhat superficial. In any event, attitudes are related to one's value system.

Since an attitude is a tendency to behave in a certain way under a given set of circumstances, the promotional strategist must correctly determine consumer attitudes to design appropriate communication strategy. As Rom Markin says, "A large amount of communication must function either to reinforce existing attitudes and behavior or to accelerate or stimulate the behavior sequences of consumers who are already predisposed to act in a given manner."[21]

Formation

The forces and conditions involved in attitude formation are numerous and variously interpreted. Some attitudes are in a sense inherited from one's parents. They become a part of an individual's attitude structure as a result of the transmission of values that takes place in the family. Attitudes toward religion and politics, for example, are often formed in very early years and persist into adulthood. However, not all attitudes are formed in this manner, and the strength of attitudes that are thus formed is not the same for every person. As a child matures he or she begins to question the parents' attitudes toward certain objects and to develop others. Peer groups also assume a more significant role in their formation.

Thus attitudes and group affiliations are largely determined by environmental forces — social, political, and economic. Because each person is a member of more than one group, attitude formation can become quite complex. Interests in and loyalties to the various groups differ in importance and are often conflicting. It then becomes necessary to reconcile, compromise, or choose between the differences. Sometimes one must associate with still other people to find support for the choice. The individual then becomes a member of a group whose only claim for homogeneity is the one particular common end of its constituents.[22]

---

[20]David Krech, Richard S. Crutchfield, and E. L. Ballachey, *Individual in Society* (New York: McGraw-Hill, 1962), p. 139.

[21]Rom J. Markin, *The Psychology of Consumer Behavior* (Englewood Cliffs, N.J.: Prentice-Hall, 1969), p. 197.

[22]See Reavis Cox and Wroe Alderson, eds., *Theory in Marketing* (Chicago: Irwin, 1950), pp. 89-109.

FIGURE 3-1   An advertisement appealing to particular tastes. *Source:* Saks Fifth Avenue.

The sophistication, the elegance—the splendour!—is pure Bill Blass. His
inspiration...the very drama of the seas! For there, he has stolen the design-intricacy
of coral for sequined black and white beading swirling from shoulder to waist.
And too, captured its graceful curves and arcs for the sweep of a great
fishtail hem. As photographed amidst the brilliant luxuries of
New York's Parker Meridien, truly this is a gown born of
nature and the natural genius of Blass. In black silk
crepe. In American Designers Collections.

Attitudes, Values, and Promotional Strategy

Current social values or norms provide the framework within which promotional strategy must be developed; if something about a strategy is not acceptable to contemporary society, the strategy is doomed to failure from the outset.

Much promotional effort is designed to take advantage of existing favorable attitudes that need stimulation. Since attitudes reflect values, the promotion manager must understand attitudes and their relationship to values and must keep abreast of the changes in the values of society.

Changing Values

Predominant among the criticisms leveled at advertising and promotion is that they promote causes contrary to our traditional American value system. It is argued that the emphasis is always on materialism, whereas our real values are primarily spiritual and aesthetic. It is further argued that because of their tremendous influence the institutions of advertising and promotion are eroding our value system.

Two arguments have been advanced in response to those criticisms. First, the formation and transmission of values takes place primarily in the *external* environment of promotion over which the promotion manager has little or no control. If advertising and promotion are not developed with due consideration for the consumer's interests and values, communication will not take place and the effort will fail. Thus values are *reflected,* not created, by advertising and promotion.

Second, values *are* changing but not as a result of advertising and promotion.[23] As values change, advertising and promotion change. The principle still holds: the nature of advertising and promotion must always be compatible with the behavior of the targets of the efforts. The promotion manager must be aware of the changes in the value system of American society and *respond* accordingly.

The Work Ethic, Leisure, and Security

Attitudes toward work and security have undergone change since the end of World War II. Before that time the so-called "Protestant work ethic" prevailed in America. Work was considered almost sublime; it was a reflection of one's character to "put in a full day's work for a day's pay." An individual felt responsible for personal and family safety and security. Leisure was associated primarily with either the independently wealthy or retired.

Today the situation has changed. There seems to be a trend toward minimizing the number of hours devoted to earning a living and increasing the number of hours for leisure activities regardless of the occupation. Loyalty to the firm has diminished, and some people even work for an employer for whom they have extremely antagonistic feelings. Where there is little loyalty, employees are less

---

[23]See B. G. Yovovich, "It's 1982 – Do You Know What Your Values Are?" *Advertising Age* (October 18, 1982): M–28–31.

FIGURE 3–2 An advertisement portraying a professional woman. *Source:* COMPUPRO.

likely to perform their jobs at maximum efficiency; there is no stigma attached to such behavior. Such individuals do not consider it necessary to assume responsibility for their own safety and future security; somebody will take care of them — perhaps the government. There is a tendency to shift many responsibilities traditionally accepted by the individual and the family to the government.

The foregoing characterization represents the extreme; perhaps very few people can be so categorized. But the trend toward these values must be reflected in promotional strategy. For example, promotion appeals related to leisure activities formerly restricted to high-income groups can now be used to reach people with moderate or low incomes. With a higher perceived discretionary income (less concern for saving for the future), people are more inclined to spend now and are thus more responsive to promotion efforts.

Ecology

Among the most significant changes in values occurring today, and accelerating every year, are those having to do with ecology. Until recently the majority of people have not greatly concerned themselves with ecological considerations, perhaps with the exception of Thomas Malthus and his dire predictions in 1798 about population and the food supply. Today more people are becoming concerned about the essentials for the survival of the human race.

Population.   Increasing numbers of people feel that unless we achieve a zero growth rate in population (not only in the United States but in the world) the prediction of Malthus will be fulfilled: population will outgrow the available food supply. As a consequence of this notion and other factors, the historical merit associated with large families is disappearing — a definite change in values. This has not only had an effect on family purchase behavior (fewer items purchased, more eating out, smaller cars, etc.) but the potential food supply problem has generated a demand for storable foods such as dehydrated fruits and vegetables.

Natural resources.   Many of our nonrenewable resources are becoming depleted; our oil and gas reserves may soon be exhausted. That portion of our value system that relates to the use of energy is being revised toward using less energy or using alternative energy sources. Oil companies no longer promote the sale of gasoline, and STP oil treatment is promoted as a gas-saver by making engines run more efficiently. Natural gas and electric companies have stopped urging people to go ``all electric'' or ``all natural gas'' in their homes. The federal government and other nonprofit institutions promote conservation of energy through the mass media.

Pollution.   Pollution of land, water, and air is the target of much concern. Many people are recognizing that our planet could become one large garbage heap unless we clean it up. Our values are shifting from a concern with the present to a concern for the future.

Legislators have attempted to solve many of the problems stemming from pollution and the depletion of natural resources. Some laws were passed in haste and are creating problems more severe than those they were designed to remedy. There are conflicting opinions about how to solve the problems. For example, coal could be used more as an energy source, but many environmentalists oppose its use because of its possible effect on the environment. One day we may be forced to choose between energy and clean air. Many ecological problems must be solved in the near future, requiring the cooperative efforts of government, business, and individuals.

The growing concern with pollution has affected marketing and promotion in many ways. Many manufacturers of products formerly sold in aerosol containers are now using nonaerosol dispensers and promoting them as nonpolluting. Soap companies exhibit concern over phosphates. Manufacturers charged with polluting lakes and streams are taking corrective measures and publicizing their actions. Nonprofit organizations as well as some businesses are using the mass media to promote litter consciousness on streets and highways.

The Role of Women

Women's roles in our society are changing (see figure 3-2, p. 55). Although this has been developing for many years, its impact has recently been more noticeable. Career opportunities formerly identified only with men are now available to women. Society is demanding that women be treated equally with men in employment and all other areas. Although in the early 1980s the Equal Rights Amendment to the Constitution failed because it was not ratified by the requisite number of states, it has been reintroduced; efforts to achieve ratification will be repeated if it is passed by Congress.

Advertisers must portray more women in professional roles to reflect these changes. Many family purchase decisions are now made jointly by husband and wife because of her increasing acceptance in the business and professional world. This means there is a changing target for promotion appeals.

Racial and Other Discrimination

Racial discrimination in our society has not disappeared, but much progress has been made in the last few years. Most people today are opposed to discrimination against blacks and other minorities and legislation has been passed to protect the rights of all races in America.

The gay liberation movement has been identified with the concept of discrimination. The issue is very controversial and there is no clear picture of the outcome. The very fact that the issue has been brought out into the open indicates there has been sufficient change in our society to permit that to happen.

Promotion's role in reflecting these changing values is difficult to implement. Minorities should be represented in mass media advertising as an equal part of society without calling undue attention to the fact that they are minorities (see figure 3-3, p. 86). But it must be recognized that they often comprise separate identifiable markets. In the latter case, media, designed to appeal to specific minorities (*Ebony,* for example), should be used to carry the advertiser's message.

Recognizing and reaching the gay community is touchy. Because it is a sensitive issue, advertisers must be careful not to offend consumers in existing markets; yet they must be aware of the fact that there may be a "new" market emerging. It would seem that advertisers should not recognize gays specifically in their general advertising, but they might use gay magazines to reach that community if they are certain the advertising would not be considered offensive to anyone else.

Morality

Perhaps because of the declining influence of the church or other reasons, society's view of "right" or "wrong" is changing. Behavior considered taboo twenty-five years ago is now generally accepted.

As with all social values, of course, acceptance is not universal. But there is an increasing prevalence of such things as cohabitation without marriage, divorce, and magazines, books, and movies that once would have been considered pornographic.[24] Our society is becoming more permissive in all respects; advertising and promotion have reflected the change. The sex appeal is used much more blatantly than in earlier years, and products are advertised now that would not have been a few years ago.

The Responsibility of Business to Society

In recent years attempts have been made to crystallize society's views on the social obligations of business. Consumerist groups, with the help of some elements of the press and some legislators, have succeeded in indicting business for failure to assume its social responsibilities. Some of their charges are justified; some are not. The effort has affected society's perception of the role of business in our system of social values. (We shall examine this issue further in chapter 5.)

SUMMARY

Cultural and social factors are parts of the external environment that influences promotional strategy. The *culture* of a society is its way of life and it distinguishes one society from another. Yet culture is not static but changes in an evolutionary way. *Subcultures* are smaller groups within a culture; while their homogeneous characteristics set them apart from similar groups, they can still be identified with the culture of the society. Although there is a certain amount of culture homogenization taking place, different cultures and subcultures still provide clues for strategies in marketing and promotion.

Purchase decisions result from the interaction of many kinds of influences, including cultural, social and economic factors. Because family, church, and school,

---

[24]See John Wilke, "Number of Unmarried Couples Living Together Triples Since '70," *Tulsa World* (July 2, 1983): C-3.

the primary social groups, have a great influence on values, the promotion manager must be alert to changes in these institutions.

Reference groups and social class also influence behavior. People often use certain social groups as standards or norms to guide their purchase decisions. The promotion manager must know whether the product, service, or idea is subject to reference-group influence and develop strategies accordingly.

Social values in the United States are changing and attitudes reflect a society's values. Since attitudes are often the target for stimulation by promotion, the promotion manager must be aware of the values held by the desired audience.

Among the values changing in American society (none of which is the direct effect of promotion) are those concerned with the work ethic, leisure and security; ecology; the role of women; racial and other discrimination; morality; and the responsibility of business to society. The promotion manager must be alert to the nature and magnitude of these changes and adjust promotion strategy accordingly.

QUESTIONS FOR THOUGHT AND REVIEW

1. Under what conditions might an individual seek out promotional messages? Do these conditions suggest anything about *cultural empathy?* Explain.
2. Define *culture.* How would you describe the culture of the American people to an outsider who was totally unfamiliar with life in the United States?
3. Name some subcultures in the United States. In what ways might the unique characteristics of each affect the promotional strategy of products? Of ideas?
4. Attack or defend the analogy made between culture/subcultures and market/market segments.
5. What is *culture homogenization?* Do you believe it is occurring? Why or why not? What is its effect on promotional strategy?
6. What are primary groups? Discuss the changes in each relative to its function of transmitting values.
7. What is the *family life-cycle concept?* Discuss its effect on promotional strategy. Use a specific firm and product line as an example.
8. What are *reference groups?* Give some examples. What is their significance to promotional strategy?
9. Name two products or brands whose purchase is influenced by reference groups and two not affected by reference groups. What differences in promotional strategy would you recommend for the two pairs?
10. What determines social class? Explain why income is not necessarily a determining factor. Are there implications to promotion?
11. Explain how attitudes can be *specific* or *general.* Give some examples of each and indicate the difference in their effect on promotion.
12. What are some of the ways in which attitudes are formed?
13. Do advertising and promotion create values? Discuss.
14. What causes the social values of a society to change?
15. Discuss some values in our society that are changing. Why do you think they are changing? Do you think promotion is responding effectively? Discuss.

THE BUSINESS/ECONOMIC ENVIRONMENT

Business has an impact on government, education, religion, welfare activities, youth programs, health care, retirement plans, and a host of other social institutions and issues. But the magnitude of the impact, whether favorable or unfavorable, is related to the success of business, and business success is determined in the *market*.

Stanton defines a *market* as ''people with needs to satisfy, the money to spend, and the willingness to spend it.''[1] Clearly, whatever serves to delineate a market is significant to business managers and to the development of promotional strategy. Many of the factors that determine a market are parts of the external environment which is beyond the control of business management.

ECONOMIC DEMOGRAPHICS

Since the external environment in which business operates is dynamic, its characteristics must be constantly monitored. It is essential not only to observe environmental changes as they occur but to search historical data to find possible patterns in the changes that take place. Such information can be valuable in defining trends and predicting future conditions.

Pertinent economic factors include population, income, and gross national product.

Population

In general, an expanding population creates an expanding market, for the more people there are the more total needs there are to satisfy.

As significant as the total figure is, however, it is perhaps less meaningful to the promotion manager of a specific firm than are the figures reflecting population composition, mobility, and regional distribution in some of the subdivisions. But the population data for a country are points of orientation for the promotion manager.

Total Population

To get a perspective of the total-population factor relative to the promotion environment, consider the population figures for the years 1950–1982 presented in table 4–1.

In the thirty-two-year period between 1950–1982 the total population of the United States increased by over 70 million. This average annual rate of approximately 2¼ million suggests a yearly increase in the size of the potential market for many firms. To maintain even a *constant* share of such a steadily growing market a firm must promote its product aggressively; if an *increase* in the share of the market is desired, promotional effort is even more essential.

The total population figure by itself can do little more than indicate the pos-

---

[1]William J. Stanton, *Fundamentals of Marketing,* 5th ed. (New York: McGraw-Hill, 1978), p. 72.

TABLE 4-1
Population of the United States, 1950-1982 (in millions)

Year	Population	Year	Population	Year	Population	Year	Population	Year	Population
1950	152.3	1957	172.0	1964	191.9	1971	207.7	1978	222.6
1951	154.9	1958	174.9	1965	194.3	1972	209.9	1979	225.1
1952	157.6	1959	177.8	1966	196.6	1973	211.9	1980	227.7
1953	160.2	1960	180.7	1967	198.7	1974	213.9	1981	229.8
1954	163.0	1961	183.7	1968	200.7	1975	216.0	1982	232.0
1955	165.9	1962	186.6	1969	202.7	1976	218.0		
1956	168.9	1963	189.2	1970	205.1	1977	220.2		

Source: Adapted from U.S. Bureau of the Census, *Statistical Abstract of the United States*, 1982-83 (103rd ed.), Washington, D.C., 1982, p. 6.

sible size of the national market to the promotion manager. The existence, size, and strength of a market must be determined for each individual industry or firm from an analysis of many other factors.

Projected Growth

Predicting the population of the United States for future years is perhaps more difficult now than in the past. Historically, trends in population growth seemed fairly obvious. However, in a climate of concern over the future availability of food and the accelerating depletion of traditional sources of energy, one cannot be so sure at what rate population will grow in the future. For the years reported in table 4-1, the annual growth rate dropped below 1 percent for the first time in 1981 (.9 percent) and remained at that figure in 1982.

Nevertheless, it is helpful in planning for promotional strategy and other business activities to have some idea of probable future population figures. Table 4-2 shows projected figures by sex, race, and age.

Table 4-2 suggests some interesting projected changes in population. The most likely projection of total population, for example, shows a growth of 70 million for the 43 year period; and as shown in table 4-1, total population increased by 70 million in only 32 years between 1950 and 1982. Thus the growth rate is declining. The disparity between males and females jumps from 6 million more females in 1982 to 9 million more in 2025. The black population shows an increase of 70 percent between 1982 and 2025 compared with an increase of 27 percent for the white population. The percentage of the population under 5 years of age drops from 7 percent in 1982 to 6 percent in 2025, while the population over 65 years of age increases from 12 percent in 1982 to 19 percent in 2025.

Any projected population figure is conjectural, of course, and is directly affected by the assumptions made in its determination. As well founded as the assumptions may be, they are really nothing more than educated guesses. There are simply too many variables that affect the fertility rate. For example, Dr. Richard A. Easterlin, Professor of Economics at the University of Pennsylvania, is quoted as saying, " . . . the fertility of young adults depends on their relative well-being —

TABLE 4–2
Projections of the total population by sex, race, and age: 1982 to 2025 (in thousands, as of July 1; includes Armed Forces overseas)

Sex, race, and age	1982	1983	1984	1985	1990	1995	2000	2025
TOTAL POPULATION:								
Lowest projection	231,769	233,675	235,544	237,366	245,507	251,550	255,638	259,673
Most likely projection	231,997	234,193	236,413	238,648	249,731	259,631	267,990	301,022
Highest projection	232,333	234,940	237,620	240,364	254,686	268,834	282,339	356,601
MOST LIKELY PROJECTION:								
Male	112,924	113,977	115,045	116,124	121,498	126,314	130,379	146,105
Female	119,073	120,216	121,368	122,525	128,234	133,317	137,611	154,917
White	198,538	200,092	201,661	203,237	210,964	217,587	222,801	240,663
Male	96,951	97,702	98,463	99,229	103,010	106,263	108,825	117,297
Female	101,587	102,390	103,198	104,008	107,955	111,324	113,976	123,366
Black	27,737	28,187	28,645	29,107	31,452	33,693	35,795	45,951
Male	13,166	13,382	13,601	13,824	14,957	16,046	17,072	22,029
Female	14,570	14,805	15,043	15,283	16,495	17,647	18,724	23,923
Under 5 years old	17,370	17,846	18,234	18,462	19,200	18,616	17,624	17,949
5–17 years old	45,363	44,668	44,350	44,352	45,123	48,514	49,762	48,403
18–24 years old	30,344	30,055	29,476	28,715	25,777	23,684	24,590	25,447
25–44 years old	67,614	68,677	71,745	73,779	81,351	82,483	80,105	78,253
45–64 years old	44,473	44,521	44,575	44,668	46,481	52,329	60,873	72,334
65 years old and over	26,833	27,427	28,035	28,673	31,799	34,006	35,036	58,636
16 years old and over	177,031	179,090	181,039	183,054	191,901	199,257	208,222	242,080
18 years old and over	169,264	171,680	173,829	175,834	185,409	192,501	200,604	234,671

Source: U.S. Bureau of the Census, *Current Population Reports*, P-25, No. 922.

how well-off they are compared to how well-off they would like to be."[2] Mortality and immigration are also affected by many variables. But businesses must anticipate and use population in long-range planning.

Composition

While the total population and its projected growth are important in the analysis of the promotional environment, its composition is perhaps more important. Among other things, the promotion manager is concerned with the number of people in various age and ethnic groups and the number of households.

Age. Manufacturers of certain kinds of products must often define their markets in terms of age groups. For example, the demand for products such as baby food, toys, children's clothing, and denture aids is obviously identified with age. Manufacturers of these products must know the current number of people in the relevant groups and anticipate any changes. Table 4-2 shows the population by age groups and indicates projected figures.

There will be a gradual reduction in the percentage of the population under five years of age. The percentage of people who are 65 and over in 2025 will more than double the percentage in 1950. These conditions are significant in the long-range planning of businesses, especially those firms whose markets primarily consist of people in either of the two age groups.

The post-World War II baby boomers born between 1946 and the early 1960s will be middle-aged in the 1990s. Thus there will be a greater demand for nondurable goods during those years. As this group enters the ranks of senior citizens shortly after the turn of the century, there will be an increase in the demand for products and services associated with health care.[3]

The over-65 group may pose more problems than are readily apparent. Not only is this group a market that has been largely neglected historically but its accelerated growth relative to the growth of the younger groups may generate resentment because of the increasing burden it places on the latter. The growing retirement benefits under the Social Security System will be financed by a decreasing number of young people in the work force.

Ethnic background. The markets of some firms are composed of people of a particular ethnic background. The market composed of black people, for example, has long been a subject of study for marketers.[4] As indicated in table 4-2, the percentage of blacks relative to whites in the population is increasing.

Other ethnic groups too are important markets for the manufacturers of

---

[2]Associated Press, "Fertility Rate in U.S. on Upswing, Economist Says," *Tulsa World* (16 November 1977): 2.

[3]See "You've Come a Long Way, Baby Boom," *Nation's Business* 71 (January 1983): 52–55.

[4]See Arnold M. Barban and Edward W. Cundiff, "Negro and White Response to Advertising Stimulus," *Journal of Marketing Research* 1 (Nov. 1964): 53–56; Pravat K. Choudhury and Lawrence S. Schmid, "Black Models in Advertising to Blacks," *Journal of Advertising Research* 14 (June 1974): 19–22.

some products. Jews and Spanish-Americans, for example, are the market targets of some firms. The 1980 census shows nearly 15 million people of Spanish origin.[5]

Any group of people with strong ethnic ties that relate to purchase behavior can compose a market. Examples of such groups are people whose ancestry is Irish, German, Italian, Greek, or Slavic. Firms appealing to such markets need to be aware of their size, yet census data may be incomplete or misleading for certain groups that could represent viable market segments. Certain groups tend to be underreported: Mexican citizens who have entered the country illegally, foreign students no longer attending American schools, Orientals crossing the Canadian border, or people who do not register in this country to avoid income taxes or possible military service.

Households.   The number of households is often more significant to the marketer or promotion strategist than the number of people; and the concept of household is not restricted to the notion of a married couple with two children. Many households do not reflect the traditional. Table 4–3 shows some of the changes taking place in households.

Between 1970 and 1981 the number of family households increased by 17.2 percent, but the number of nonfamily households rose by 84.7 percent. The latter group includes single adult households – divorced or widowed peole and young adults who live alone. These people comprise markets for household furnishings, cars, convenience foods, and housing units. Many of them have above-average incomes and can afford such "luxury" items as expensive stereos, sports cars, and prestige-label clothing. Included also in the nontraditional households is an increasing number of unmarried people living together.

Mobility

In the past, Americans generally remained in the localities of their birth; many never ventured beyond a few miles from home throughout their entire lives.

TABLE 4–3
Households, married couples, and unrelated individuals (in thousands except percent)

Type of unit	1970	1980	1981	Percent change 1970–1981
Households	63,401	80,776	82,368	29.9
Family households	51,456	59,550	60,309	17.2
Nonfamily households	11,945	21,226	22,059	84.7
Married couples	45,373	49,714	49,896	10.0
Unrelated individuals	14,988	26,426	27,348	82.5

Source: Adapted from U.S. Bureau of the Census, *Statistical Abstract of the United States,* 1982–83 (103rd ed.), Washington, D.C., 1982, p. 43.

---

[5]U.S. Bureau of the Census, *Statistical Abstract of the United States,* 1982–83 (103rd edition), Washington, D.C., 1982, p. 35.

But technological improvements in communication and transportation, particularly since World War II, have led to an increasing awareness of distant places and the means to see such places. The evolving shorter work week, increased leisure time and a rising level of income have given people the impetus to travel. Many return home, others find greener pastures, and still others continue to look. Many moves are job-related. Over 45 percent of the population changed residences in the five-year period between 1975 and 1980.[6]

A population on the move has obvious implications to marketing and promotion. It can drastically change the business/economic environment in which an industry or particular firm operates. Some areas grow at the expense of others; and the increase or decrease in population in the respective areas affects the value of the area as a present or potential geographic market. When people move their needs change, and the promotion manager must be alert to such changes.

Distribution

Table 4-4 shows the regional distribution of the population in the United States by divisions of states for the three decennial census years of 1960, 1970, and 1980.

In the twenty-year span between 1960 and 1980, the population of the states in the first four divisions indicated in the table declined in percent of the total U.S. population. Included in this group are the New England states and the more heavily populated Eastern and Midwestern states. Gaining as a result of this exodus are the Southern, Mountain, and Pacific states.

Figure 4-1 graphically illustrates the regional shifts in the distribution of the population between the years 1970 and 1979.

There are numerous reasons for these population shifts. The Southern states have attracted industrial moves from the North because of the relatively lower costs of operation in the South, and industrial activity generates population growth. People of retirement age have migrated to states with temperate climates — Florida, Arizona, and California. The recreational possibilities associated with the Mountain states are appealing to winter sports enthusiasts. Many moves may have been induced by the accelerated worsening of environmental conditions such as air and water pollution and more pronounced energy problems in the traditionally heavily populated areas.

Population shifts and trends in area population growth are factors in the external environment for promotion and must be considered in the development of marketing and promotional strategies. The two largest full-line department stores in Chicago, for example, have reacted to the population shift in different ways. Carson Pirie Scott & Co. has expanded into the food service business by acquiring an airline caterer, Dobbs House, Inc. Marshall Field & Co. is developing new stores in the South and West.[7]

---

[6]U.S. Bureau of the Census, *Current Population Reports,* P-20, No. 368, Washington, D.C., Dec. 1981, pp. 1-3.

[7]See Carson Pirie Scott, ''Hoping to Get Fat on Food Services,'' *Business Week* (March 23, 1981): 124-29.

TABLE 4-4

Distribution of population by divisions of states, 1960, 1970, 1980 (in thousands except percent)

Divisions of states	1960		1970		1980	
	Population	Percent of U.S. pop.	Population	Percent of U.S. pop.	Population	Percent of U.S. pop.
United States	179,323	100.0	203,302	100.0	226,546	100.0
New England	10,509	5.8	11,848	5.8	12,348	5.4
Middle Atlantic	34,168	19.1	37,213	18.3	36,787	16.2
East North Central	36,225	20.2	40,262	19.8	41,682	18.4
West North Central	15,394	8.9	16,327	8.0	17,183	7.6
South Atlantic	25,972	14.5	30,678	15.1	36,959	16.3
East South Central	12,050	6.7	12,808	6.3	14,666	6.5
West South Central	16,951	9.5	19,326	9.5	23,747	10.5
Mountain	6,855	3.8	8,289	4.1	11,373	5.0
Pacific	21,198	11.8	26,549	13.1	31,800	14.0

Sources: Adapted from U.S. Bureau of the Census, *Statistical Abstract of the United States, 1982–83* (103rd ed.), Washington, D.C., 1982, p. 10, 11.

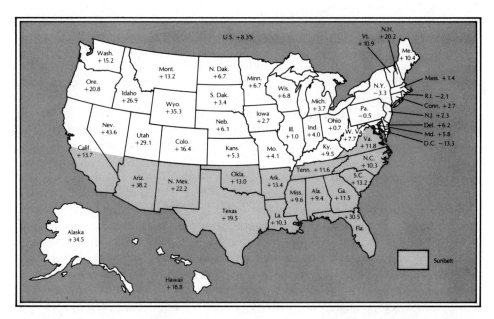

FIGURE 4–1 Geographical changes in population, 1970–1979. Source: U.S. Department of Commerce, Bureau of the Census, *Current Population Reports, Population Estimates and Projections,* P-25. No. 875 (January 1980), p. 12.

Urban, rural, and suburban shifts.   There has been a continuing decline in the rural population for many years. Fewer than 4 percent of the population lived on farms in 1980, as compared to about 25 percent in 1940. This has had an effect on marketing and promotion because the shift has been to urban areas, and urban people have different wants and needs than rural people.

Inner city dwellers have shifted to the suburbs. The older parts of many cities are becoming virtually abandoned. This shift has had a tremendous impact on the marketing of such products as patio furniture, lawn and yard equipment and supplies, and all kinds of do-it-yourself products. But there seems to be a developing trend among families with grown children to move back into the city. They are tired of the hassle of keeping up a suburban home and yard and are moving into apartments and condominiums closer to downtown.

Standard Metropolitan Statistical Area.   Despite the foregoing shifts, the people involved are still urban. Because of the population shifts, it is difficult to delineate markets in the traditional way of political boundaries of cities and counties. As a result, the U.S. Census Bureau has created a population classification called a Standard Metropolitan Statistical Area (SMSA). An SMSA consists of a county or a group of contiguous counties with a central city, or two closely located cities, having a population of at least 50,000. The population of the total area must be at least 100,000. Such areas can be used by a business in identifying target markets.

Income

Population alone does not make a market. If it did, the best markets for firms would be found in such countries as India and China. The more people in an area, the more needs there are to satisfy, but in order for a market to exist, people must have money to spend and be willing to spend it. They must have an income.

There are several ways of describing income for national income accounting purposes.[8] *Personal income* is the total income received by persons from all sources, excluding income that has been earned but not received (such as undistributed corporate profits). *Disposable income* is the income persons have left after they pay personal income taxes. Table 4–5 shows personal income and disposable income for selected years between 1960 and 1981. Disposable income is shown in both current and constant dollars.

Table 4–5 shows that, although personal income for 1981 was more than 4½ times what it was in 1960 and disposable income in current dollars increased more than 4½ times, disposable income in constant dollars was only slightly more than 1½ times greater. The constant dollar is of most concern to the promotion manager for it is more closely related to purchasing power.

The average annual total compensation for full-time employees was $17,218 in 1981—more than 2½ times the average income in 1965.[9] Such rising incomes indicate to promotion managers that people in their target markets are likely to have increasing amounts of money to respond to promotional efforts.

Another concept of income not included in national income accounting is *discretionary income*. Discretionary income is that portion of income left after the payment of personal income taxes and the purchase of necessities. It is the amount completely available to spend for whatever is desired.

TABLE 4–5
Per capita income for selected years between 1960 and 1981

Year	Personal income (current dollars)	Disposable income	
		Current dollars	Constant (1972) dollars
1960	2,226	1,947	2,709
1970	3,955	3,390	3,665
1975	5,857	5,075	4,051
1978	7,783	6,621	4,441
1979	8,668	7,331	4,512
1980	9,490	8,012	4,472
1981	10,510	8,827	4,538

Source: Adapted from U.S. Bureau of the Census, *Statistical Abstract of the United States,* 1982–83 (103rd ed.), Washington, D.C., 1982, p. 421.

---

[8]See Edwin G. Dolan, *Basic Economics* (Hinsdale, Ill.: The Dryden Press, 1977), ch. 6.

[9]U.S. Bureau of the Census, *Statistical Abstract of the United States,* 1982–83 (103rd ed.), Washington, D.C., 1982, p. 400.

It is not possible to derive precise figures for this amount because people disagree on what necessities are. What might be considered a necessity for one person would be thought of as a luxury by another. Nevertheless it would seem that discretionary income would rise along with personal income — albeit not to the same degree (an increase in personal income generally results in a more expensive life-style which redefines necessities for the individual concerned).

If a rise in personal income results in an increase in discretionary income, the size of the "nonnecessity" market is increasing. Not only does such a condition provide greater opportunities for the promotion of such items but it also broadens the appeals used in promotion. People are often more responsive to emotional appeals than to rational ones. Emotion can play a stronger role in making decisions concerning luxury items than it is allowed to play in connection with necessities. People with money to spare are also less constrained in their purchase of necessities and may respond more quickly to promotional efforts.

ECONOMIC CONDITIONS

In addition to delineating the business/economic environment by statistical data, it is also useful to describe it in terms of certain *economic conditions*. Each of these conditions is related to the health of the economy and is therefore significant in the development of long-range promotional strategy. We shall consider selected general conditions that are obviously significant to marketing and promotional strategy.

The Business Cycle

Economic activity in the United States is historically characterized as a series of ups and downs. Periods of full employment with a high level of spending have tended to be followed by periods of widespread unemployment and restricted spending. The concept *business cycle* refers to such recurring phases of business activity of several years' duration.

Phases

The four identifiable phases in the business cycle are prosperity, recession, depression, and recovery. Prosperity and depression describe the extremes in the cycle; recession and recovery are the transition periods between the extremes. Business cycles can vary in both severity and duration. The Great Depression of the 1930s lasted for ten years, and its effect was devastating. But the 1960s were years of expansion and prosperity. There have been numerous ups and downs over the years that were shorter-lived and less severe.

Until the 1940s, business-cycle theory was accepted as an explanation of the way things are in a free enterprise system. It was presumed that alternating periods of boom and depression were inherent in the system so no one could do anything about it. However, shortly after World War II the influence of the rapidly spreading

Keynesian economics led to the development of the *demand management* concept.[10]

It appeared to a number of economists that the various phases of the business cycle simply reflect the waning and gaining of consumer demand. If consumer demand could be "managed" in some way, economic activity could be stabilized thus eliminating depressions and the inevitable inflation always associated with prolonged periods of prosperity. Fiscal and monetary policies of the federal government have been used ever since, with considerably less than complete success. Economic activity still reflects various phases of the business cycle.

Significance to Promotional Strategy

Obviously prosperity provides the ideal climate for effective promotional strategy. Depression discourages promotional activities for people do not have money; if they did, they would not be willing to spend it. The severely contracted market reduces promotional activities.

The transition periods of recovery and recession are less definitive economic environments. In the recovery phase there is a developing market. People are beginning to think more positively, yet they are a bit skeptical having so recently experienced a depression. Businesses are optimistic, however, and are willing to use promotional efforts to accelerate the development of their markets.

Recession is another thing. Instead of the growing optimism that prevails in the recovery phase, there is a growing pessimism. People are apprehensive about the future and are inclined to curtail demand. It is in this stage of the business cycle that marketing managers and promotion managers are most undecided. They are aware of the possibility that the declining demand traditionally associated with a recession is the harbinger of a diminishing market, yet they cannot help but believe that with a little more promotional effort they can reverse the downward trend. Of course, the recession in the mid-1970s was even more complex. Not only was demand affected but supply was also affected by shortages of materials and energy. (We shall discuss this problem in more detail later in this chapter.)

A firm should maintain a substantial promotion program during periods of recession to hold its position in the market.[11] A vigorous effort could increase a company's share of the market during such times, although the greatest payoff usually comes with heavy promotion in prosperous times.

Inflation

Inflation has been with us since the 1940s, sometimes reaching double-digit magnitude. There is every likelihood it will continue indefinitely. Inflation is characterized by a rising price level. The consumer's money is devalued, and it takes pro-

---

[10]See Dolan, *Basic Economics,* ch. 17, for a detailed discussion of demand management.
[11]See Edward W. Cundiff, "What is the Role of Marketing in a Recession?" *Journal of Marketing* 39, no. 2 (Apr. 1975): 1, and "Marketing in a Recession: Comments from Our Readers," *Journal of Marketing* 39, no. 3 (July 1975): 78–79.

TABLE 4-6
Purchasing power of the dollar, 1940-1978, as measured by consumer prices (base year, 1967)

Year	Consumer prices	Year	Consumer prices	Year	Consumer prices
1940	$2.381	1956	$1.229	1968	$.960
1945	1.855	1957	1.186	1969	.911
1946	1.709	1958	1.155	1970	.860
1947	1.495	1959	1.145	1971	.824
1948	1.387	1960	1.127	1972	.799
1949	1.401	1961	1.116	1973	.752
1950	1.387	1962	1.104	1974	.678
1951	1.285	1963	1.091	1975	.621
1952	1.258	1964	1.076	1976	.587
1953	1.248	1965	1.058	1977	.551
1954	1.242	1966	1.029	1978	.518
1955	1.247	1967	1.000	1979	.461
				1980	.406
				1981	.367

Source: Adapted from U.S. Bureau of Labor Statistics, *Statistical Abstract of the United States,* 1982-83 (103rd ed.), Washington, D.C., 1982, p. 452.

gressively more money to buy things. The decline in the purchasing power of the dollar is shown in table 4-6.

Using 1967 as the base year, a dollar was worth $2.38 in 1940 and 37 cents in 1981. The decline in the purchasing power of money is frightening. Fortunately incomes in general have risen commensurately, and consumer demand has generally been sustained. Nevertheless, a rising price level makes consumers price conscious, and promotional strategists must be aware of the impact of inflation on consumer thinking.

Energy and Product Shortages

Economists have taken the position for years that our concern as a people should be with the proper allocation of scarce resources (all the natural, human, and manufactured ingredients used in the production of goods and services). There have always been differences of opinion as to how the allocation should be made, but never any disagreement with the idea that resources are limited.

Yet business, as a kind of a subset of economics, has rarely concerned itself with the possibility of shortages. Perhaps this is rightly so. After all, the underlying objective of business is survival, and survival depends upon profitable sales volume. Perhaps it is business's only responsibility to provide consumers with the things they want. If there are impending shortages, some other institution, such as government, should take restrictive action. Or perhaps consumers themselves should tailor their demands consistent with available supply. In any event, and whether it is right or wrong, it is extremely difficult for an individual company to take any action that is not aimed at stimulating sales.

But times change. Impending shortages in some cases become real. The depletion of oil and gas reserves, for example, may not be too far off. International economic and political actions such as the Arab oil embargo of 1973-74 and the Iranian situation in 1979 have brought home what we have long known to be true but have been reluctant to accept. Shortages in energy and in other resources are inevitable. Something will have to be done, and whatever is done will affect promotional strategy.

Kotler and Levy suggest that '' . . . excess demand is as much a marketing problem as excess supply.'' It is their contention that marketing must find ways of reducing demand to the level of supply, and their name for this activity is ''creative demarketing.'' They suggest that methods of reducing demand could include curtailing advertising expenditures, changing the content of advertising messages, reducing sales promotion expenditures, increasing price, and generally discouraging consumer demand. They point out that this effort could be general or aimed at selected market targets, and would be carried on to retain customer goodwill. The key to success seems to lie in the word *creative.*[12]

The promotion environment will change as shortages materialize. Consumers may be tempted to hoard, or they may be persuaded to prefer energy-saving products. Planned obsolescence may become a thing of the past. Government certainly will become more involved, possibly to the extent of rationing. This is bound to have an impact on the marketing strategies of businesses.[13]

BUSINESS INSTITUTIONS AND COMPETITION

So far our discussion of the business/economic environment has dealt with economic statistics and conditions in the aggregate that have an impact on promotional strategy. Any promotion manager must be aware of the current overall economic situation on the existence and health of current and potential markets.

However, the promotion manager of a specific firm must also be aware of characteristics of the business/economic environment more directly related to the firm's markets. Among such factors are the number, size, and kinds of business institutions and the intensity of competition.

If a company were the only manufacturer serving a particular market, its promotional strategy would be different than if there were several manufacturers — especially if the other firms were highly competitive. Strategy would also be influenced by the number and kinds of wholesalers and retailers serving the market. The use of manufacturers' agents or selling agents in the promotion of the product

---

[12]Reprinted by permission of the *Harvard Business Review.* Excerpt from ''Demarketing, yes, demarketing,'' by Phillip Kotler and Sidney J. Levy (Nov.-Dec. 1971). Copyright © 1971 by the President and Fellows of Harvard College. All rights reserved.

[13]See Nessim Hanna, A. H. Kizilbash, and Albert Smart, ''Marketing Strategy Under Conditions of Economic Scarcity,'' *Journal of Marketing* 39, no. 1 (Jan. 1975): 63-67; David W. Cravens, ''Marketing Management in an Era of Shortages,'' *Business Horizons* 17, no. 1 (Feb. 1974): 79-85.

might be contingent upon their availability in the area. The presence of strong retail department stores and/or discount houses might dictate different kinds of promotional efforts in a particular market than would be used in their absence.

Thus, the business/economic environment in which a company operates is characterized both by factors in the aggregate and by factors identified with specific markets. Both must be thoroughly analyzed and properly considered as a promotional strategy is planned.

SUMMARY

This chapter has been concerned with the business/economic dimension of the environment in which promotion takes place. The business/economic dimension is beyond the direct control of the promotion manager but must be considered in the development of promotional strategy.

Economic factors can be divided into two broad categories: economic demographics and economic conditions. Significant economic demographics include population, income, and gross national product. Several important aspects of population include composition, mobility, distribution, and total population figure. Total income, disposable income, discretionary income, and trends in the gross national product provide clues to the economic health of the nation.

The phases of the business cycle are prosperity, recession, depression, and recovery. They must be considered in the development of promotional strategy, as well as such current economic conditions as inflation and the possible shortage of energy and other materials. Conditions in the business/economic environment relating directly to the development of a promotional program for a specific company include the number, size, and kinds of business institutions operating in the firm's market, and the intensity of competition.

QUESTIONS FOR THOUGHT AND REVIEW

1. What is a *market?* Can marketers ''make a market?'' Discuss.
2. Do you believe that an expanding population creates an expanding market? What conditions might suggest that this is not true? Explain.
3. What is the concept of a *household?* What changes have taken place in households that affect promotion? Why is the number of households sometimes more important to promotion strategists than total population?
4. What is a *Standard Metropolitan Statistical Area* (SMSA)? Explain how it can be useful to promotion strategists.
5. Discuss the impact on promotion of rural-urban-suburban population shifts.
6. Discuss the impact on promotional strategy of changes in population composition. In addition to those mentioned in the text, what other identifiable groups within the total population would be significant to promotional strategy?
7. What causes people to move? How does mobility affect promotional strategy? Do you think mobility will increase or decrease in the next few years? Why?

8. Describe the population distribution in the United States as you envision it ten years from now. How does this differ from what it is now? Explain.
9. Distinguish between *personal income* and *disposable income*. Which is most significant to promotion? Has income in constant dollars been increasing or decreasing? Discuss.
10. What is *discretionary income?* Discuss its significance to promotional strategy.
11. Explain why the expenditures for food, beverages, and tobacco have declined as a percent of the total expenditures since 1950.
12. What does the gross national product show? What is its significance to marketing and promotion?
13. Briefly explain *business-cycle theory*. Why is it believed now that severe depressions can be prevented?
14. Discuss the influence on promotional strategy of prosperity and depression.
15. What should be the role of marketing and promotion in a period of recession? Why?
16. Discuss the possible effects of inflation on promotional strategy.
17. Whose responsibility is it to deal with the problem of product shortages — the government, business, or who? Speculate and discuss.
18. Explain how the number, size, and kinds of business institutions in a particular market area can affect the promotional strategy of a firm serving that market.

5

THE LEGAL/ETHICAL ENVIRONMENT

> Law is a circle with the same center as moral philosophy (ethics) but with a smaller circumference.[1]
>
> Jeremy Bentham (1748–1832)

Laws and sanctions governing the conduct of business have been societal issues from time immemorial. Three thousand years before Christ, Mesopotamian merchants were criticized for unethical operations just like the huge conglomerates of today. Generally, the criticism has been directed at marketing activities (called *trade* and *commerce* in earlier times) rather than production. Critics have typically taken the position that production is justified because it results in the creation of *form utility,* but marketing activities create nothing of value and are therefore parasitic.[2]

The charge that marketing activities create nothing of value is not true. Even if there were no marketing institutions, the activities associated with them would have to be performed for consumers to realize the benefits intended when the goods and services were produced.

It is advantageous to all business that its unethical practices be exposed. Such revelation keeps management alert to the reasonable demands of society and forces business to maintain a constant vigil over its own behavior.

Most of the practices society considers unethical are eventually made illegal. Laws passed to prevent truly unethical behavior are perhaps justified, but it is impossible to legislate ethical behavior completely. Business can engage in certain behavior that is unethical but not illegal. However, the failure of business to establish its own codes of ethics is today an invitation to pass more legislation.

Included in the criticism of business today is discontent with many legal and ethical aspects of the business environment that affect *promotion.* In the single area of "misleading advertisements," for example, a Harris poll of 2,000 persons showed that 46 percent of the people thought that TV ads are misleading and 28 percent held the same opinion about advertising in other media.[3]

CONSUMERISM

The catalyst in the accelerated expressions of discontent seems to be the movement referred to as *consumerism*. This movement is not really new.[4] For example, the writing of Upton Sinclair in the early 1900s was a major force resulting in the passage of the Pure Food and Drug Act in 1906, the Meat Inspection Act in the same year, and the creation of the Federal Trade Commission in 1914. In the depression years of the 1930s some kind of consumer pressure was undoubtedly

---

[1]Quoted in Henry Hazlitt, *The Foundations of Morality* (Princeton, N.J.: D. Van Nostrand, 1964), p. 69.

[2]For a brief sketch of this viewpoint's historical origin, see Robert L. Steiner, "The Prejudice against Marketing," *Journal of Marketing* 40, no. 3 (July 1976): 2–9.

[3]"Business Out of Sync with Public, Pollster Says," *Advertising Age* (23 May 1977): 4, 102.

[4]Max E. Brunk, "The Anatomy of Consumerism," *Journal of Advertising* 2, no. 1 (1973):9–11, 46; and Philip Kotler, "What Consumerism Means to Marketers," *Harvard Business Review* 50, no. 3 (May–June 1972): 48–57.

responsible in part for the strengthening of the Pure Food and Drug Act and increasing the legal clout of the Federal Trade Commission.

It is difficult to determine precisely when the current movement started. But the seeds were probably planted in the late 1950s with the writings of such diverse authors as Vance Packard and John Kenneth Galbraith.[5] Packard expressed the notion that consumers are being unwittingly manipulated by advertisers. Galbraith's thesis was that advertising creates artificial wants that would not exist in its absence.

Whether one agrees with these views or not, it is quite likely that their diffusion throughout their respective audiences started some people thinking. The movement gathered momentum with President John F. Kennedy's directive to the Consumer Advisory Council in 1962 in which he proclaimed certain rights of consumers: the right to safety, the right to be informed, the right to choose, and the right to be heard.[6] Although all of these rights have become cornerstones of the consumerist movement and have had an impact on the business environment, the right to be informed is the most relevant to promotional strategy. This right, concerned with false and misleading advertising and labeling, states that consumers be given the facts necessary to make an informed choice.

The real impetus came in 1966 with the well-publicized success of Ralph Nader's battle with General Motors over the dangers of the Corvair. Since that time the consumerist movement has ballooned, largely due to the increasing intensity of the efforts of Nader, his followers, and other sympathetic individuals and groups. The movement has received the support of the government and the press.

Contrasting Perspectives

Two of the many interpretations of consumerism are presented to stimulate constructive thinking about an important facet of today's business environment.

Philip Kotler defines *consumerism* as ''a social movement seeking to augment the rights and power of buyers in relation to sellers.''[7] Viewed in this light it may be considered simply as a phase in the development of our economic system that makes the system more responsive to social needs. Furthermore, it is not antithetical to marketing; it simply emphasizes the concern for societal needs embodied in the ''marketing concept'' — a tenet of modern marketing.

On the other hand, there are those who take the position that consumerism is not the hallowed movement it is purported to be.[8] It is argued that the movement is simply a vehicle by which certain activists attempt to further their personal causes and that consumer welfare is not the motivating force.

Obviously, supporters can be found for both points of view. Any movement

[5]Vance Packard, *The Hidden Persuaders* (New York: David McKay, 1957); John Kenneth Galbraith, *The Affluent Society* (Boston: Houghton Mifflin, 1958).

[6]Consumer Advisory Council, *First Report,* Executive Office of the President (Washington, D.C.: U.S. Government Printing Office, 1963), pp. 5–8.

[7]Kotler, ''What Consumerism Means,'' p. 49.

[8]See Brunk, ''Anatomy of Consumerism,'' pp. 9–11, 46.

with the impact that consumerism has had is bound to generate controversy. It is clear that consumerism will not go away, and it probably should not. Our political and economic philosophy invites the free expression of opinion; indeed, it is guaranteed by the First Amendment to the Constitution. Business must be alert to the charges made in the name of consumerism, ignore those that are simply outbursts of emotion, and respond to those that are justifiably made.[9]

The Response of Business

Whether or not certain questionable practices are prohibited by law is irrelevant. We are dealing with *ethics* as well as laws, and the justifiable demands of consumers for ethical behavior on the part of business must be met. Failure can only lead to more government regulation, which not only makes it more costly for business to operate but also increases the taxes consumers pay and adds to the prices of goods and services.

But business is responding. Perhaps its response is not recognized by some groups or is deemed insufficient, and perhaps those who do see some positive action feel it is only because of the threat of legal action. The reason does not matter as long as something is done.

More than 300 manufacturers and retailers now have consumer affairs departments.[10] Their effectiveness varies from a cosmetic alteration of the firm's public image to a sincere attention to the problem. But creation of such departments suggests a recognition of the complaints consumers have.

Each business must make certain that its own standards are high so it cannot be accused of unethical behavior. Further, it must express its disapproval of unethical behavior of *any* firm. Because there will always be some offenders, a business might even support *reasonable* regulation.[11]

One of the problems seems to be that business has remained silent for too long regarding the relevant issues. Many consumers are uninformed or misinformed of business' viewpoint. It is becoming more essential, despite the lack of credibility undoubtedly associated with such action, for business to present the public with its side of the story.[12] It has been suggested that to bridge the credibility gap business firms could sponsor ads that extol other firms — the gas company could inform the public of the praiseworthy characteristics of the telephone company, for example.[13] But above all, business must be certain that its house is in order.

---

[9]No attempt has been made to document here the voluminous literature on consumerism; libraries are replete with both scholarly and popular books and articles on the subject.

[10]"Disgruntled Customers Finally Get a Hearing," *Business Week* (21 Apr. 1975): 138.

[11]Fred T. Allen, "Should Corporate Ethics be Regulated?" *Management Review* 66, no. 5 (May 1977): 16-17.

[12]See "What Business Leaders are Doing to Polish a Tarnished Image," *U.S. News and World Report* 81 (13 Sept. 1976): 42-44.

[13]"High Ethical Standards Needed to Brighten Business' Murky Image," *Marketing News* (16 Dec. 1977): 8.

CRITICAL AREAS OF CONCERN

No business areas are out of bounds for critics. The major targets, however, are marketing activities; of these promotion seems to be the most significant, particularly advertising. It is logical that advertising would rank high among the targets because it is so visible. No one can escape exposure to advertising, and everyone has an opinion about it. Paradoxically, critics of advertising seem to believe that the persuasive powers of advertising are greater than do the companies who use it. But regardless of who is right about advertising's degree of persuasiveness, ethical considerations should be observed.

Content of the Advertisement

Content of the advertisement includes both explicit and implicit factors. Prominent issues include usefulness of the information, deception, obscenity and bad taste, and discrimination.

Usefulness of the Information

Society can justify advertising only to the extent that it provides consumers with the kind of information that helps them make purchase decisions. But there are two problems: opinions differ as to what constitutes *information,* and there are those who believe that although informational advertising is acceptable, ''persuasive'' advertising is not.

Advertising is criticized for not providing the consumer with factual information about the product, and facts about the product are important. The product's intrinsic characteristics (strength, durability, mechanical features, ingredients, and so forth) are often used by the consumer in making decisions. Such information is the only relevant kind for some products. In the purchase of other products, however, consumers look for information that is not necessarily factual. They may want to know if a product will increase their sex appeal, or enhance their status with their peer groups, or enable them to impress their friends. If this is the kind of information the consumer is seeking, advertising could be expected to supply it and should not be discouraged from doing so.

The results of one study showed that most television advertising is of the latter kind and therefore noninformative as far as presenting ''facts'' is concerned.[14] But the issue exists: What kind of information is important to the consumer? On what bases do consumers make their purchase decisions? Advertisers would be remiss if they ignored the reasons for buying that are beyond obvious facts. Nevertheless, promotional strategists must be aware of the pressure from both outspoken critics and government watchdogs to provide only the ''factual'' kind of information.

---

[14]Alan Resnik and Bruce L. Stern, ''An Analysis of Information Content in Television Advertising,'' *Journal of Marketing* 41, no. 1 (Jan. 1977): 50–53.

Moreover, advertisers must be able to prove the claims they make. Since 1971, the Federal Trade Commission has followed a policy of requiring advertisers to "submit on demand by the Commission data supporting advertised claims relative to product safety, performance, efficacy, quality, or comparative price."[15] Such substantiation of claims is not so difficult if the claims are objective enough to be proven through tests — although there is sometimes a question as to what tests are acceptable.[16] For subjective claims, substantiation is tough.

The substantiation requirement employed by the FTC is probably supported by most consumer advocates. However, the requirement can work to the consumer's disadvantage. For example, the replication of tests often required by the FTC can result in higher costs and discourage the entry of potential competitors, which cause higher prices for the consumer.[17]

At the time of this writing the substantiation requirement is being reexamined by the Federal Trade Commission. It is suggested that ad substantiation serves as a deterrent to advertisers in providing consumers with useful information. This is particularly true, it is argued, if the Commission demands excessive amounts of support for ad claims. While much of the advertising industry agrees with this point, it does not agree with attacking the *prior* substantiation rule — that advertisers have a reasonable basis *before* making a claim. Most of the industry supports the *concept* of ad substantiation — the unethical practices of one advertiser reflect on the entire industry — but would like to see the policy clarified and simplified.[18]

In any event, the advertiser must be alert to the possibility that the information provided is always subject to review by the Federal Trade Commission. For many years it had been presumed that the First Amendment's protection of freedom of speech and press did not apply to advertising. The courts had distinguished between "commercial speech" and other forms of speech and had drastically reduced the protection to commercial speech that the Amendment provides for other forms.[19] But some recent court actions have extended the Amendment's protection to advertising.[20]

---

[15]Robert E. Wilkes and James B. Wilcox, "Recent FTC Actions: Implications for the Advertising Strategist," *Journal of Marketing* 38 (Jan. 1974): 55–61.

[16]See for example, *Firestone Tire and Rubber Co.* versus *Federal Trade Commission* CCH #74,588 CA-6, June 1973 (D.C.) and *Crown Central Petroleum Corp.* CCH #20,348, FTC DKT 8851 (May 1973); BNA ATRR No. 618 (19 June 1973) A-23 (D.C.) in Legal Developments in Marketing section, *Journal of Marketing* 38 (Jan. 1974): 77, 78.

[17]Yale Brozen, "Are New FTC Advertising Policies Inhibiting Competition?" *Journal of Advertising* 2, no. 2 (1973): 28–31.

[18]See Richard L. Gordon, "Miller Questions Ad Proof Policy," *Advertising Age* (November 2, 1981): 3, 102; "FTC Aide Won't Dump Ad Substantiation," *Advertising Age* (November 16, 1981):66; "FTC Memo Leery of Support for Substantiation," *Advertising Age* (September 6, 1982): 2, 64; "Miller Asks for Ad Rule Review," *Advertising Age* (October 25, 1982): 1, 85–6; "Ad Groups Gird for FTC Review," *Advertising Age* (March 7, 1983): 58; Dorothy Cohen, "The FTC's Advertising Substantiation Program," *Journal of Marketing* 44 (Winter 1980): 26–35; and Debra L. Scammon and Richard J. Semenik, "The FTC's 'Reasonable Basis' for Substantiation of Advertising: Expanded Standards and Implications," *Journal of Advertising* 12, no. 1 (1983): 4–11.

[19]See Senator Sam J. Erwin, Jr., "Advertising: Stepchild of the First Amendment," speech before the Proprietary Assocation at White Sulphur Springs, West Virginia, on 16 May 1972, in John S. Wright and John E. Mertes, *Advertising's Role in Society* (New York: West, 1974), pp. 326–31.

[20]See Dorothy Cohen, "Advertising & The First Amendment," *Journal of Marketing* 42, no. 3 (July 1978): 59–68.

Critics of advertising have argued that informative advertising is justified but persuasive advertising is not. Actually, this issue is related to the problem of defining *information*. If an advertiser were to avoid appealing to the emotions of consumers and only emphasize the intrinsic characteristics of the product, the advertising would be acceptable to the critics — would not be persuasive. Advertising aimed at stimulating emotional motives is deemed persuasive and somehow not ethical.[21]

We shall not debate the issue except to suggest that *all* advertising is designed to be persuasive. If it were not so, it would hardly seem worthwhile to advertise anything — products, services, or ideas.

Deception

One of the major charges leveled against advertising is that much of it is false or misleading. There is no question that some advertising can be so characterized. There *is* a question, however, as to its amount and as to which specific ads are misleading.

No one but the most irresponsible individual or business would condone deliberately *false* advertising. To state in an advertisement that a product will do something it can't is unethical, illegal, and poor business judgment. Yet false advertising does exist.

Advertisements alleged to be *misleading* present the problem. It is one thing to say that misleading advertisements shoud not be allowed; it is quite another to positively identify such ads. Moreover, an ad that would be perceived as perfectly all right by one person might appear misleading to another. David M. Gardner says, "Deception in advertising is always going to take place, whether it is planned or not, for the simple fact that deception is in the 'eye of the beholder.' Therefore, some advertisements will always be deceptive to some."[22] Nevertheless, firms must make every effort to refrain from using advertising that might be construed as misleading. The task is not easy, however, because an advertisement does not have to be explicitly misleading to invite censure. It is only necessary that the ad has the capacity to mislead.[23]

Several examples of advertising deemed deceptive are particularly noteworthy because of the precedents they set for regulation. In the early days of television, certain commercials used actors wearing white jackets to demonstrate medical and dental products. The advertisements were judged to be misleading because viewers might believe the actors were really physicians and dentists recommending the products. To demonstrate the moisturizing qualities of Rapid Shave shaving cream, the product was applied to what appeared to be a piece of sandpaper, after which the sand was removed with a razor. In actuality, however, it was not sandpaper but Plexiglas. Although it was argued that use of the glass

---

[21]See Shelby D. Hunt, "Information vs. Persuasive Advertising: An Appraisal," *Journal of Advertising* 5, no. 3 (Summer 1976): 5–8.

[22]David M. Gardner, "Deception in Advertising: A Receiver Oriented to Approach to Understanding," *Journal of Advertising* 5, no. 4 (1976): 5–11.

[23]See "Ad Men Cautioned that It's More Than a Sin to Tell a Lie," *Broadcasting* (28 Mar. 1977): 78–79.

instead of paper was necessary for the demonstration, and that the intent was simply to illustrate a feature of the product, the commercial was ruled deceptive. Simulations should be identified as such.

The Campbell Soup Company was forced to discontinue a commercial in which some marbles were placed in the bottom of a bowl of soup to raise the meat and vegetables to the top. The company argued that in order to show the ingredients it was necessary to use such a device because otherwise the ingredients would settle to the bottom and could not be seen. But the commercial was judged misleading because it suggested that the soup contained more solid ingredients than it actually had.

In a lengthy case involving the ITT Continental Baking Company, it was alleged that the company used misleading advertising by showing Wonder Bread as unusually nutritious when it was really no more so than competing brands. A major outcome of this case was that advertising agencies are considered just as responsible for deceptive advertising as the advertisers themselves.

Obscenity and Bad Taste

Most companies try to keep their advertising within the bounds of propriety. Society provides sanctions for this. After all, cultural factors determine what is considered ethical behavior. But because culture is ever-changing, the limits of ethical behavior are not rigid. Therein lies the difficulty.

Advertising that would have been considered obscene or in bad taste twenty years ago is perfectly acceptable today. If advertising today were as staid as the social constraints of twenty years ago would have it, it would be considered unsophisticated. Yet the advertiser must not go too far. People still draw the line between what is acceptable and what is in bad taste. The advertiser must find where that line is.

The frankness and frequency of sex appeal in advertising is an important concern. How permissive *is* our increasingly permissive society? How does society determine when the expression of an idea with sexual overtones is not simply candid but is actually in bad taste or even obscene? The answers to these questions would keep the advertiser current and not offensive. But the answers are not easily found.

The questions of obscenity and bad taste are of concern to advertisers also regarding the television programs they sponsor.[24] Numerous organized groups, such as the Coalition for Better Television, the Knights of Columbus, the Joelton Church of Christ in Tennessee, Action for Children's Television, the Moral Majority, and Morality in Media have boycotted or threatened to boycott the sponsors of shows they consider objectionable.[25] Despite the countermeasures of such

---

[24]Janet Neiman, "Advertisers Want 'Major Change' in TV," *Advertising Age* (March 8, 1982): 1, 67.

[25]See Reverend Timothy S. Healy, "The Coalition: Advertising's Big Tug of War," *Advertising Age* (August 3, 1981): 3, 4; Colby Coates, "'Boycott' Reborn by Two Church Groups," *Advertising Age* (August 24, 1981): 1, 81; and Craig Endicott, "Television's Watchdog," *Advertising Age* (August 31, 1981): 29–31.

groups as Norman Lear's People for the American Way and The Screen Actors Guild, some advertisers believe "permissiveness" has indeed exceeded the bounds of propriety.[26] Complicating the issue is the increasing prevalence and popularity of cable TV which admittedly and overtly airs programs beyond the bounds of conventional TV. Morality in Media has also attempted to "clean up" cable programming.[27]

Discrimination

Discrimination is an emotional term. The response to the word is immediate. Discrimination in advertising content is sometimes alleged in the portrayal of women and minorities.

The representation of women in ads.   Advertising is accused of failing to reflect the changing role of women in our society. It is criticized for consistently portraying women in the stereotyped roles of homemaker, secretary, or sex object. Critics would like to see more ads showing women in professional and executive positions. Advertisers are charged with discrimination against women relative to the illustrations used in advertisements.[28]

There is justification for these charges. Career-oriented women fighting the battle for equality rightfully resent anything that seems to perpetuate limited roles. If advertising does reflect the changing behavior of society, it certainly should recognize the changes taking place in the professional world for those who occupy positions of influence.

Advertisers should not act blindly but should maintain a proper balance. Many women *choose* to be homemakers. These women resent being put down and are proud of their way of life. Advertisers must be careful not to degrade such women. A similar stance is taken by many secretaries. While some women in secretarial positions aspire to managerial roles, others enjoy working where they are and recognize the contributions they are making.

Both women and men are sexual beings. The facts of life cannot be ignored, and advertising should reflect reality. Thus the concern should not be with whether women are sometimes portrayed as sensuous; rather, it should be with the taste in which it is done.[29]

The portrayal of minority races in ads.   Because minority races are important segments of our society, advertisers should not ignore them in designing ads. But advertisers have been criticized with good reason for not using minority actors.

[26]"Actors Guild Joins Lear's TV Fight," *Advertising Age* (September 7, 1981): 61.

[27]Maurine Christopher, "Morality in Media Tackles Cable," *Advertising Age* (August 24, 1981): 12.

[28]See Joseph P. Dominick and Gail E. Rauch, "The Image of Women in Network TV Commercials," *Journal of Broadcasting* (Summer 1974): 259–65; and Roger A. Kerin, William J. Lundstrom, and Donald Sciglimpaglia, "Women in Advertisements: Retrospect and Prospect," *Journal of Advertising* 8, no. 3 (Summer 1979): 37–42.

[29]See *Advertising Age,* July 26, 1982, Section 2. The entire section is devoted to a discussion of women in ads.

This does not mean that advertisers should include members of minority races in all their advertising; nor does it mean that token representation is sufficient. Advertisers should carefully plan their advertising so minority races are represented fairly and wisely.[30] In addition, advertisers should be careful not to denigrate any race by using such devices as comical illustrations or exaggerated dialects.

Product Advertised

Another target of criticism is the product advertised. The ethical debate focuses on two opposite fronts: the elimination of advertisements for some products that have been advertised for years, and the advertising of some products for which advertisements have been considered taboo for years. Of course there are questions relative to the degree of regulation and control appropriate in the advertising of most products.

Included among the products for which efforts are made to eliminate advertising are cigarettes, "junk foods" and candy, and energy products. Examples of other products receiving a good deal of criticism on ethical grounds are liquor and over-the-counter drugs. Products for which advertisements are becoming increasingly acceptable include such heretofore nonsanctioned items as feminine hygiene products, lingerie, contraceptives, and prescription drugs.

Cigarettes

Traditionally any product that could be legally sold could be advertised since advertising is a part of the selling process. But that has changed. Cigarettes can no longer be advertised on radio and television as a result of an edict issued by the Federal Trade Commission on January 1, 1971. They can be advertised in other media, however, and they can be legally sold; but the manufacturers' promotion options were severely limited by the regulation. Furthermore, the following notice must be stated on the package: "Warning: The Surgeon-General Has Determined That Cigarette Smoking Is Dangerous To Your Health." A stronger warning is now being considered by a Senate Committee: "Warning! Cigarette smoking causes CANCER, EMPHYSEMA, HEART DISEASE; and may complicate PREGNANCY and is ADDICTIVE."[31]

Junk Foods and Candy

The term *junk foods* is used to refer to food items high in caloric content, low in nutritional value, and generally quite tasty. Potato chips, corn chips, salted nuts, popcorn, pretzels, cheese crackers, and other snack items are examples of such

---

[30]See Ronald F. Bush, Paul J. Solomon and Joseph F. Hair, Jr., "There Are More Blacks in TV Commercials," *Journal of Advertising Research* 17 (Feb. 1977): 21–25; C. Orpen, "Reactions to Black and White Models," *Journal of Advertising Research,* 15 (Oct. 1975): 75–79.

[31]"Cigarette Warnings Get Tough," *Advertising Age* (June 27, 1983): 83.

FIGURE 3-3   An example of a nondiscriminatory advertisement. *Source:* Courtesy of The Procter & Gamble Company.

WHAT HAPPENS WHEN 32 TEETH TRY TO FIT INTO A SIZE 28 MOUTH?

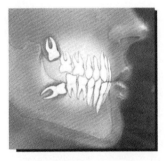

Well, frankly, it depends.

Four new wisdom teeth don't necessarily have to be a problem. If the individual is young enough so her jaw is still growing, it will hopefully become large enough to accommodate the teeth trying to come through. However, if the growth has stopped, it's a different story.

In that case, the wisdom teeth may become impacted, trapped beneath the gum line, with nowhere to go but sideways. This unfortunately can result in a variety of ailments, from serious infection and damage to adjacent molars, to serious jaw problems. So the sooner you take care of them, the better.

Don't ask for trouble. Ask your dentist.

The best way to find out if you have wisdom tooth problems isn't to wait for a wisdom tooth to tell you. It's to ask your dentist to check things out. If anything's wrong, chances are he'll refer you to an Oral and Maxillofacial Surgeon. A specialist with the kind of experience and advanced training in anesthesia that enables him to remove wisdom teeth skillfully and usually with a minimum of discomfort.

Concern for your total health.

The scope of an oral and maxillofacial surgeon's specialty is far wider than wisdom teeth.

He's concerned about helping people with poorly shaped jaws. About patients whose gums and jaws prevent their use of dentures. He cares for accident victims with serious facial injury.

Just as meaningful, the oral and maxillofacial surgeon is also actively involved in alerting us to hidden everyday hazards. A prime example is the safety bar on the back of most school bus seats, a frequent cause of childhood facial injury. Moreover, he's a major advocate of the mandatory and proper use of sports safety equipment; goalie masks, mouthpieces, and helmets. He also advocates the routine use

of automobile seat belts. Because prevention is always the best policy.

Write to us.

For more information about this dental surgical specialty, please send for our free brochure. Write:
The American Association of Oral and Maxillofacial Surgeons, P.O. Box 1024, Tinley Park, Illinois 60477.

Oh, and don't forget to ask your dentist about your wisdom teeth. If there's a problem, finding out from him is a lot better than finding out from them.

AMERICAN ASSOCIATION OF ORAL AND MAXILLOFACIAL SURGEONS
DENTAL SPECIALISTS WORKING TO INSURE YOUR TOTAL HEALTH

products. Similarly identified are the sugar-coated ready-to-eat cereals and, perhaps to a lesser extent, candy. It is argued that advertisements for these products minimize the importance of a balanced diet with the result that people rely too much on such foods and develop improper dietary habits.

Energy Products

Although the concern a few years ago with the immediate depletion of energy sources has subsided somewhat, there is still pressure for the curtailment of any advertising that stimulates the wasteful use of resources.[32] This notion is particularly obvious in connection with public utility advertising (gas and electric companies) and with oil companies in advertising gasoline. Gas and electric companies traditionally vied to persuade homeowners to use more of their respective products, and each oil company tried to persuade consumers to use more of its gasoline. These companies have responded to the pressure by either restricting their advertising or by changing their appeals. Oil companies rarely advertise gasoline; instead their approach is to inform the public about the "societal" activities in which they are engaged—such things as the search for new energy sources, and the development of products related to health care.

Feminine Hygiene Products

Certain products formerly considered too intimate to be advertised in the mass media (particularly television) now seem to be gaining acceptability.

One of the product categories traditionally considered too intimate for broadcast advertising is feminine hygiene products. Until 1972, advertisements for these items were prohibited by the National Association of Broadcasters (NAB). In that year, however, the NAB relaxed its ban and allowed the advertising of such products, although various restrictions were imposed by the networks.[33] In earlier years, such products were advertised very discreetly if at all and were sold with equal discretion. Kotex, for example, was sold in a plain-wrapped package which the customer could pick up herself. The intent was to prevent embarrassment, but in retrospect one wonders whether it actually did that since the contents of the package were known to any who saw it.

The frequency of television commercials for such products has steadily increased. But universal acceptance is far from complete. In a poll conducted by *People* magazine, for example, it was found that the most irritating commercials on television were for sanitary products—Brenda Vaccaro extolling the merits of Playtex tampons and Cathy Rigby advertising Stayfree Maxi-Pads.[34] Many people

---

[32]See Richard L. Gordon, "Pertschuk Hits Ads that 'Encourage' Energy Waste," *Advertising Age* (June 6, 1977): 10.

[33]See Maurine Christopher, "NAB Board to Study Rise in Feminine Hygiene Ads," *Advertising Age* (June 30, 1975): 1.

[34]Jennifer Alter, "A Delicate Balance," *Advertising Age* (July 12, 1982): M-2-8.

FIGURE 5–1 An advertisement for a professional group. *Source:* American Association of Oral and Maxillofacial Surgeons.

still think that because of the personal nature of the needs giving rise to the use of the products, public discussion of the products' attributes is in bad taste. Some people are quite uncomfortable when exposed to such commercials in mixed company. Nevertheless, advertising for such products will probably increase, particularly with the suspension in 1982 of the code of the NAB, which had formerly exerted some influence over such things.

Lingerie

The advertising of women's underwear has been accepted by most people for many years. So the issue here is not *whether* commercials for lingerie are in good taste; it is rather *how* they are presented.

Consistent with the general trend in society to relax traditional sanctions on human behavior, there is an increasing liberalizing of the methods by which lingerie is advertised. Illustrations in print advertisements considered in bad taste a few years ago are now quite common. But more significant is the impact of the trend on television advertising. A few years ago the NAB approved on-air tests of live models in bra commercials.[35] But the experiment did not spread, perhaps because of reluctance on the part of the networks, or perhaps because of reservations of the NAB and the fact that its code still really prohibited the use of live models in lingerie advertising. Even with the suspension of the code, however, the networks in conventional TV have not yet broken with tradition.

Cable TV does not seem to be subject to the same sanctions as conventional TV in the commercials it airs as well as in its programming. In the early 1980s, for example, Flexnit's Ce Soir intimate apparel pioneered the use of live models in TV commercials.[36] And a year or so later, Berlei USA showed the back of a model putting on her underwear.[37] What this means for lingerie commercials in the future remains to be seen. Given the climate of the times, however, we can expect to see more use of live models in television commercials for women's underwear.

Contraceptives

Perhaps most controversial of advertised products is the male contraceptive. Originally sold "under-the-counter" in gas stations and pool halls, the condom is now sold primarily through drug stores. But advertising the product has been an even more sensitive, ethical issue. It was not until 1969 that the first advertisement for condoms appeared in a consumer magazine, *Sport.* Such ads ran for a few issues and then were dropped. Later other magazines, primarily men's, ran the ads, and in the 1970s the ads appeared in women's magazines such as *Redbook.*[38]

Advertising in the broadcast media, however, is another thing. The product classification was banned under the NAB Code, and despite a short-run experiment with such ads on a noncode station in California in the mid-1970s, condoms are

---

[35]"NAB Widens Bra Spot Test; Contraceptive Ads Weighed," *Advertising Age* (April 25, 1977): 1.

[36]Pat Sloan, "NAB Ghost Keeps Lingerie Spots Well Clad," *Advertising Age* (June 14, 1982): 69.

[37]Pat Sloan, "Cable Outstrips Networks in Undie Ads," *Advertising Age* (June 13, 1983): 14.

[38]See Alter, "A Delicate Balance."

not advertised on TV.[39] With the suspension of the NAB Code, however, it is possible that the situation will change.

Prescription Drugs

Prescription drugs were advertised to the consumer on TV for the first time in 1983 when Boots Pharmaceutical Company launched a campaign for its Rufen prescription anti-arthritis drug.[40] Prior to that, prescription drugs were advertised only to medical doctors.

In allowing such advertising, the Food and Drug Administration has stipulated that the copy must focus on the company, health problems, or price comparisons with other products. It must avoid product-specific claims until the legal and ethical issues are resolved. Presently prescription drug advertising to consumers is very new and experimental. No doubt it will be closely watched and severely regulated for several years.

Liquor

The elimination of the advertising of certain products historically considered acceptable and the sanctioning of the advertising of certain products historically forbidden are extreme positions. Between the extremes is a host of products whose advertising has invited criticism, comment, and often legislation. Two such products are liquor and over-the-counter drugs.

Liquor advertising and the product itself have long been targets of criticism. Business institutions connected with the industry have been very careful to avoid any activity that might violate social sanctions. Hard liquor is not advertised on television, although commercials for beer and wine are plentiful. Print advertisements have always reflected the current conventions of society; they excluded women in earlier ads and gradually incorporated them into advertisements as the social tolerance for women's use of alcoholic beverages increased.

One would think the liberal trend will continue, even though some people feel that the use of alcohol should not be made so attractive by depicting glamorous people in the ads. The FTC has taken the position, however, that it should not take action against liquor ads that show glamorous people because any such action would affect other ads.[41]

Over-the-Counter Drugs

Advertisements for over-the-counter drugs have been controversial since the early days of advertising. The old patent medicines were advertised as having the capa-

---

[39]Maurine Christopher, "Freer Use of TV Sought for Male Contraceptives; Trojan on Two Stations," *Advertising Age* (Aug. 4, 1975): 1.

[40]See Susan Spillman, "Prescription Drugs Hit the Air," *Advertising Age* (May 23, 1983): 3, 94; and Susan Spillman and Stanley E. Cohen, "Boots Gets FDA Okay on New Drug Spots," *Advertising Age* (May 30, 1983): 10.

[41]Richard L. Gordon, "FTC Won't Try to Tackle 'Glamour' in Alcohol Ads," *Advertising Age* (Mar. 22, 1976): 55.

bilities of curing everything from bunions to scarlet fever. Such obviously false claims have not been made for years. But there is still concern that some advertisements for these products may have adverse effects. It is not so much the claims made in individual ads that are suspect as it is the cumulative effect of frequent exposure to them. There is the concern that people may be lulled into a false sense of health security by using them and neglect regular visits to their physicians.[42]

Even if control were desirable, implementation would be difficult, and as yet the courts have not supported extensive control. For example, the Federal Communication Commission once ruled that there was no evidence supporting a petition filed by 14 state attorneys general that TV spots for OTC drugs encourage "pill-popping."[43] But the concern still exists, and such advertising will continue to be controversial.[44]

Advertising Directed at Children

In recent years a major area of concern has been advertising directed at children. It is argued that advertisers take advantage of children's immaturity, causing detrimental effects to their health and well-being. It is said that very young children cannot distinguish between the commercial and the program and therefore are excessively influenced. It is also contended that because of their lack of sophistication older children are more susceptible than adults to the ideas presented in commercials. Represented by such vocal groups as Action for Children's Television (ACT), critics concentrated on candy and sugar-coated cereals.[45]

As in the case of the over-the-counter drugs, critics attack not so much the individual ad but the cumulative effect of watching the commercials over a period of time.[46] The result is a gradual build-up of undesirable attitudes and ideas about nutrition and health care. Critics argue that despite the efforts of well-intentioned parents who are sincerely trying to guide their children's growth and development, such subtle coercion is a difficult thing to cope with. And, of course, when the television set is used as a baby-sitter the problem is even greater.

No doubt there is some justification for concern. When our children are involved, we become "fighting mad." Ethical advertisers should be alert to any harmful effects their advertising might have on children. However, some people question the constitutionality or desirability of any law or bureaucratic edict aimed at banning such advertising. It has been suggested that advertising is not necessarily the culprit in the issue and that parents can be blamed because of their permissive attitudes. Parents can say "no" to the requests of their children to buy undesirable products; if they choose to give in to the demands of the children, the fault is theirs. Children have always tried to persuade their parents to buy the things they

---

[42]Gordon, "Pertschuk Hits Ads," p. 10.
[43]"FCC Refuses Bid to Restrict Drug Ads on TV to Late Hours," *Advertising Age* (Dec. 13, 1976): 2.
[44]"FDA Alarmed at Growth of Drug Promo Materials," *Advertising Age* (May 3, 1976): 31.
[45]See, for example, "Push on for TV Ban of Kids' Candy Ads," *Advertising Age* (13 June 1977): 35.
[46]Gordon, "Pertschuk Hits Ads," p. 10.

wanted, and it is up to the parents to use their own good judgment in purchasing the products.[47]

Furthermore, children may not be as gullible as we sometimes think. For example, the FTC claimed that when premium offers are advertised with products the child's attention is focused on something other than the product; therefore the child does not get the product information. An experimental test proved this not to be true.[48]

A report of Child's Research Service, Inc., suggested that a single false element in an ad causes children to tune the ad out. It was found that a commercial for a candy bar showing a Little League team boarding a bus after a game was not considered believable by the children tested because none of the players were dirty.[49]

The Federal Trade Commission wrestled with the problem for several years. Early in 1978, the Commission approved a rule-making process designed to curb such advertising. The proposal called for several things, including severe regulation of advertising on children's programs and advertising for highly sugared foods that will likely be seen by children. After lengthy hearings on the issue, the Commission staff recommended in 1981 that the FTC abandon the effort to write a children's TV advertising rule. It suggested that there is no effective rule it can develop now, but it still sees the issue as a cause for concern.[50] Thus it seems unlikely that any such rules will be written by the FTC in the foreseeable future. No doubt the activist organizations, however, will continue their efforts to curb advertising they view as detrimental to children.

Excessive Amount of Advertising

Some people believe that any amount of advertising is too much. These are the people who have never been convinced that advertising has any social or economic value. That viewpoint is not representative of the majority of people who believe that advertising generally provides benefits to the consumer.[51]

Other people are not opposed to advertising as an institution but do object to what they view as an excessive amount in some instances. Most television viewers probably think there are too many commercials; it is quite likely that advertisers feel the same way about the increasing number of spot commercials during station

---

[47]See Herbert Kay, "Children's Responses to Advertising: Who's Really to Blame?" *Journal of Advertising* 3, no. 1 (1974): 26–30.

[48]Terrence A. Shimp, Robert F. Dyer, and Salvatore F. Divita, "An Experimental Test of the Harmful Effects of Premium-Oriented Commercials on Children," *Journal of Consumer Research* 3 (June 1976): 1–11.

[49]Leah Rozen, "Kids Aren't Easily Fooled by Ads, Researchers Find," *Advertising Age* (12 July 1976): 6; Alan Resnik and Bruce L. Stern, "Children's Television Advertising and Brand Choice: A Laboratory Experiment," *Journal of Advertising* 6, no. 3 (Summer 1977): 11–17; and Pat L. Burr and Richard M. Burr, "Television Advertising to Children: What Parents are Saying About Government Control," *Journal of Advertising* 5, no. 4 (1967): 37–41.

[50]Richard L. Gordon, "Children's TV Ad Rule Dying," *Advertising Age* (April 6, 1981): 1, 82.

[51]See "What Does Advertising Do For The Consumer," *Journal of Advertising* 2, no. 2 (1973): 22–27.

breaks. The ratio of advertisements to reading matter in newspapers and magazines is considered disproportionate in the opinion of some people. But the two areas accused most for excesses are outdoor (billboard) advertising and direct-mail.

Outdoor Advertising

The familiar billboards along the streets and highways throughout the United States have been the subject of controversy for many years. It is argued that they violate the rights of travelers to enjoy the beauty of the countryside by blocking the traveler's line of vision and destroying the tranquillity of the scene. Furthermore, it is charged that they are distractions to drivers and are therefore conducive to accidents.

The defense says travelers *look* for signs, particularly those advertising motels and eating places. Moreover, instead of being dangerous distractions, the posters serve to minimize the hypnotic effect of otherwise monotonous highway driving. It is argued, too, that prohibiting property owners from leasing space for posters violates their rights.

It is the *excesses* in the use of the medium and not necessarily the medium itself that is of concern. The Highway Beautification Act of 1965 includes the restriction of poster placement to within 660 feet of the right-of-way on interstate highways under certain conditions. Enforcement is the responsibility of the individual states, but the incentive for enforcement comes from the authority given the federal government to withhold highway subsidy funds from those states that fail to comply with the provisions of the Act.

Direct Mail

The fact that many people object to receiving unsolicited advertising through the mail is reflected in the term used to refer to it — junk mail. Yet a Postal Service survey showed that 63 percent of direct-mail pieces received are opened.[52] Despite their objections more than half the people who receive such mail probably read it.

Here again, it is the perceived abuse of the medium that seems to rankle people more than the fact that the medium exists and is used. People resent the unrestricted inclusion of their names on mailing lists, which results in the receipt of an avalanche of mail promoting products in which they have absolutely no interest. Their feeling is that such lists are unethical and should be regulated by law.

The issue is sensitive, but control is difficult. There are laws prohibiting the use of the mails for fraudulent purposes, and there are laws against sending obscene material through the mail. Furthermore, people have means for having their names removed from mailing lists. The Direct Marketing Association (for-

---

[52]"Direct Mail — 'Quiet Medium,'" *Advertising Age* (Nov. 21, 1973): 116–17.

merly, the Direct Mail/Marketing Association), for example, initiated a service for this purpose in the early 1970s. But in the final analysis, the emotional resentment to direct-mail advertising must be an ethical consideration by advertisers in their evaluation of the legal/ethical environment.

Advertising by the Professions

Historically it has been contrary to the codes of ethics of such professionals as medical doctors, dentists, lawyers, and certain other groups to advertise their services. Their position has always been that their services are so highly personalized that they cannot be compared and therefore do not lend themselves to advertising. They say that if they were to advertise their services, people would tend to be persuaded by the power of the advertising and not by the qualifications of the professionals themselves; the result could be detrimental because their services are so crucial to the health and well-being of people.

A 1977 Supreme Court decision in *Bates vs. State Bar of Arizona,* however, opened the door to professional advertising. The decision was that bar association codes that prohibit advertising by lawyers are unconstitutional. Subsequent to that decision, the Federal Trade Commission ruled that the American Medical Association and the American Dental Association could no longer prohibit their members from advertising their fees and services.[53] Grounds for these actions include First Amendment considerations as well as charges that there is no competition among professionals and that advertising will tend to result in lower costs to consumers. Very soon after the rulings, some professionals did start to advertise.[54] A more recent consequence of these actions, however, is a growing number of shopping mall dental centers and dental departments in established retail stores.[55] It seems that more than 15,000 dentists are advertising; contrary to what was feared, according to a 1982 Gallup poll, the public's respect for dentists has not declined as a result.[56] (For an excellent example of such advertising, see figure 5–1, p. 87)

But the fight has been bitter. Both the American Medical Association and the American Bar Association have lobbied vigorously to get the rulings overturned.[57] As things stand at the time of this writing, however, the trade practices of all licensed professions remain under the jurisdiction of the Federal Trade Commission.[58]

---

[53]Dennis J. Moran, ``Moving Out of Infancy,'' *Advertising Age* (December 24, 1979): S-1.

[54]See ``Ads Start to Take Hold in the Professions,'' *Business Week* (24 July 1978): 122–23. See also *Advertising Age,* 24 Dec. 1979. Section 2 of this issue is devoted to professional advertising.

[55]Carol Galginaitis, ``Dental Services Cast in New Mold,'' *Advertising Age* (September 27, 1982): M-9, M-18.

[56]``Ads Don't Bite into Dentists' Ethics,'' *Advertising Age* (May 23, 1983): 88.

[57]See ``MDs, Lawyers Rap FTC,'' *Advertising Age* (July 20, 1981): 73; and ``The Medical Lobby Operates on Antitrust,'' *Business Week* (December 6, 1982): 42.

[58]``FTC Gets Full Budget; Senate Kills AMA Rider,'' *Advertising Age* (December 27, 1982): 2, 18.

Comparative Advertising

Comparative advertising is advertising in which the sponsor's brand is compared with one or more competing brands, usually by name but at least in such a way that the comparison is understood by the audience.[59]

Although it has never been prohibited by governmental restriction, with few exceptions the practice has been avoided by advertisers. Typically, the closest they came was to compare their brands with "Brand X" or with "other brands." It had always been a tenet of advertising that to mention a competitor's name in an advertisement was not good business. There was always the chance of inviting a libel suit; a further deterrent was the fear of retaliation by a competitor.

But in 1972 things changed. The Federal Trade Commission endorsed comparative advertising, believing that the consumer would be better informed through its use than with the more common practice of using vague comparisons to Brand X. A forerunner, perhaps, to the current viewpoint was the campaign that Avis ran in the 1960s suggesting that since it was number two in the rent-a-car business, it "tried harder."

Among the first examples of comparative advertising to appear after its encouragement by the FTC was the campaign of the over-the-counter headache relief medicine, Datril, compared with Tylenol. Since then, there have been many others. Examples include such comparisons as Behold furniture polish with Pledge; Mighty Dog with Kal Kan dog food; Tempo and Alka-Seltzer with Rolaids and Tums; Suave antiperspirant with Ban Ultra Dry; Gillette with Bic (shavers); and Chrysler with other makes of automobiles.[60] Such well-known battles as Pepsi/Coca-Cola and the now famous (or infamous) Burger King/McDonald's and Wendy's comparisons have sparked considerable rivalry and ill feelings. The Burger King/McDonald's/Wendy's comparative campaigns have generated some law suits.[61]

There is a good deal of uncertainty in the industry with respect to both the ethics of the practice and its effectiveness as an advertising technique.[62] No company likes to have its name or its brand publicly denigrated; when this is done viciously in a comparative ad, there is certainly a question of ethics involved. But there are many firms that use comparative advertising in a perfectly ethical way.

---

[59]See Thomas E. Barry and Roger L. Tremblay, "Comparative Advertising: Perspectives and Issues," *Journal of Advertising* 4, no. 4 (1975): 15–20.

[60]John J. O'Connor, "Gillette Slashes at Bic," *Advertising Age* (April 5, 1982): 2, 70.

[61]See Christy Marshall and Richard Kreisman, "Competitors to Fight Burger King Drive," *Advertising Age* (September 20, 1982): 2; "McDonald's Sues to Halt BK Effort," *Advertising Age* (September 27, 1982): 1, 80; Christy Marshall, "Burger King Thinks It's Found the Sizzle," *Advertising Age* (September 27, 1982): 4, 81; "Wendy's Asks Damages," *Advertising Age* (October 4, 1982): 3; "Burger King's Ads Cook Up a Storm," *Business Week* (October 11, 1982): 39; and Richard Kreisman, "Big Mac Ads Hit Back at BK," *Advertising Age* (November 1, 1982): 1, 78.

[62]For representative articles dealing with the effectiveness of comparative advertising see V. Kanti Prasad, "Communication-Effectiveness of Comparative Advertising: A Laboratory Analysis," *Journal of Marketing Research* 13 (May 1976): 128–37; Philip Levine, "Commercials That Name Competing Brands," *Journal of Advertising Research* 16, no. 6 (Dec. 1976): 7–14; Anthony C. Chevins, "A Case For Comparative Advertising," *Journal of Advertising* 4, no. 2 (Spring 1975): 31–36.

(See figure 5-2, p. 118, for an example of a comparative ad.) All advertising is designed to enhance the sponsor's cause, and when comparative advertising is not unduly caustic, it should be considered within the bounds of ethical procedure. It is further justified if it assists the consumer in making wise purchase decisions.

Although many firms are not convinced of its effectiveness as an advertising technique, there is a large number who are. Chrysler, for example, attributes much of its increase in market share in the early 1980s to the use of comparative advertising.[63] And certainly all the companies that use it consistently believe in its effectiveness. It has been argued that the technique is particularly good for introducing new brands.[64] However, the results of one study indicate that a noncomparative approach is more effective.[65] Perhaps the jury is still out.

If comparative advertising is to be used, it may be wise to follow the guidelines suggested several years ago by the American Association of Advertising Agencies:

1. The intent and connotation of the ad should be to inform and never to discredit or unfairly attack competitors, competing products or services.
2. When a competitive product is named, it should be one that exists in the market as significant competition.
3. The competition should be fairly and properly identified but never in a manner or tone that degrades the competitive product or service.
4. The advertising should compare related or similar properties or ingredients of the product, dimension to dimension, feature to feature.
5. The identification should be for honest comparison purposes and not simply to upgrade by association.
6. If a competitive test is conducted, it should be done by an objective testing source, preferably an independent one, so that there will be no doubt as to its validity.
7. In all cases the test should be supportive of all claims made in the advertising based on the test.
8. The advertising should never use partial results or stress insignificant differences to cause the consumer to draw an improper conclusion.
9. The property being compared should be significant in terms of value or usefulness to the consumer.
10. Comparatives delivered through the use of testimonials should not imply that the testimonial is more than one individual's thought unless that individual represents a sample of the majority viewpoint.[66]

---

[63]"Chrysler Ties Recent Success to Comparatives," *Advertising Age* (January 15, 1981): 82.

[64]Terrence Shimp and David C. Dyer, "The Effects of Comparative Advertising Mediated by Market Position of Sponsoring Brand," *Journal of Advertising* (Summer 1978): 13-19; and Linda L. Golden, "Consumer Reactions to Explicit Brand Comparisons in Advertisements," *Journal of Marketing Research* 16 (November 1979): 517-32.

[65]John H. Murphy II and Mary S. Amundsen, "The Communications—Effectiveness of Comparative Advertising for a New Brand on Users of the Dominant Brand," *Journal of Advertising,* 10, no. 1 (1981): 14-19.

[66]Leonard S. Matthews, "Slugging it Out Fairly in Comparative Advertising," *Advertising Age* (July 11, 1983): M-36. Reprinted with permission from the 11 July 1983 issue of *Advertising Age.* Copyright 1983 by Crain Communications, Inc.

REGULATION OF PROMOTION

Given the magnitude of ethical concern about advertising and other forms of promotion, it is no wonder that regulation and control are serious problems to both promotional strategists and government watchdogs. Strangely enough, the motivating forces for actions taken by both groups are the same — sincerity and reality. Many people in promotion strive to be ethical in their activities simply because they feel morally bound to do so. Others may attempt to be ethical only because of the reality of the continuing threat of increased government regulation.

The same can be said about government officials. There are some people in government who sincerely believe that the regulatory actions they take in making unlawful the things they perceive to be unethical are truly in the consumers' interests. Other government officials simply observe political reality as they see it in the decisions they make.

But for whatever reason, the regulation and control of promotional activities is increasingly a factor to be reckoned with in the development of promotional strategy. The sanctions and restraints take two forms: self-regulation and government regulation.

Self-Regulation

There is a good deal more self-regulation of advertising and other promotional activities than the average consumer realizes. Advertisers have not always been concerned about their actions but they are today. Although self-regulation is far from being completely effective, its influence is felt at the national, state, and local levels.[67]

At the National Level

The National Better Business Bureau was for years the primary vehicle of national self-regulation. In addition to the efforts of that organization, the National Association of Broadcasters (NAB) established a code for radio in 1937 and for television in 1952. These codes which the networks and most stations adopted were enforced through sanctions imposed by the NAB, and covered the regulation of time allotments for commercials; products advertised; and sex, nudity, and violence in commercials and programming. It was primarily because of the code, for example, that hard liquor was not advertised, that beer commercials did not show the product actually being consumed, and that lingerie commercials observed propriety with respect to nudity.

In the early 1980s, however, the Justice Department charged that the codes or portions of them were unconstitutional because they result in a restraint of

---

[67]See Priscilla LaBarbera, ''Advertising Self-Regulation: An Evaluation,'' *MSU Topics* 28 (Summer 1980): 53–63; Priscilla LaBarbera, ''Analyzing and Advancing the State of the Art of Advertising Self-Regulation,'' *Journal of Advertising* 9, no. 4 (1980): 27–38; and Stanley E. Cohen, ''Should Ad Policing Go Private?'' *Advertising Age* (March 21, 1983): 24, 28.

trade. The Department was specifically concerned with rules enforcing time standards and prohibiting the practice of piggybacking (sales pitches for two unrelated products in the same 30-second spot). The charges were upheld with a Federal District Court ruling. Since then, virtually the entire code has been suspended.[68]

Many people are concerned about the demise of the NAB code because they feel it was an effective method of self-regulation. It appears that if the code is not revived, the burden of regulation will fall on station managers with the result that decisions will vary from market to market. Furthermore, there seems to be the opinion that beer drinking may be allowed in commercials and that hard liquor will be advertised.[69]

A new code may be developed by the NAB. At the time of this writing, there are definite indications that a code will be established and that it will be done ''from scratch'' and will not be built on the skeleton of the old one.[70] The outcome of all this remains to be seen.

The strongest move toward effective self-regulation came in the early 1970s. The Council of Better Business Bureaus (CBBB) was established, and this organization became active in the regulation of national advertising through its National Advertising Division (NAD). By 1980, for example, it had handled over 1,000 cases, and had requested discontinuance of roughly half of the advertising involved on the grounds that it was deceptive.[71] Also established was the National Advertising Review Board (NARB), which consists of a chairman and 50 members who represent advertisers, advertising agencies, and the public. By means of a carefully worked out system involving these organizations and others wherein complaints and appeals are heard and judgments rendered, the workload of the government regulatory bodies has been enormously reduced.[72]

At the State and Local Level

It was in 1911, perhaps, that the advertising industry first reflected its acceptance of ethical responsibility. In that year the editors of the trade publication, *Printers' Ink,* sponsored the now classic ''Printers' Ink Model Statute,'' which became the basis for legislation enacted in a number of states.[73] The statute dealt with dishonest advertising and put the responsibility for ethical conduct on the advertiser. It not only showed concern on the part of one segment of the industry for ethical

---

[68]See Richard L. Gordon, ''Bell Raps U.S. in NAB Attack,'' *Advertising Age* (June 14, 1982): 3, 58; and Stanley E. Cohen, ''NAB Studies Future of Code,'' *Advertising Age* (November 29, 1982): 1, 68.

[69]''Now that the TV Code Is Dead,'' *Marketing & Media Decisions* 18 (May 1983): 72–74.

[70]See ''NAB Eyes New Direction for Code,'' *Advertising Age* (July 5, 1982): 3; ''NAB Ending Code; New Program Studied,'' *Advertising Age* (January 10, 1983): 64; and Maurine Christopher, ''Departing NBC Exec Urges NAB Changes,'' *Advertising Age* (June 27, 1983): 56, 57.

[71]National Advertising Division, Council of Better Business Bureau, *News from NAD* (January 14, 1980); and ''NAD — A Real Bargain,'' *Advertising Age* (January 24, 1983): 16.

[72]See Eric J. Zanot, ''A Review of Eight Years of NARB Casework: Guidelines and Parameters of Deceptive Advertising,'' *Journal of Advertising,* 9, no. 4 (1980): 20–26; and John S. Wright, Daniel S. Warner, Willis Winter, Jr., and Sherilyn K. Zeigler, *Advertising,* 4th ed. (New York: McGraw-Hill, 1977), pp. 680–82.

[73]The Statute is copyrighted by Printers' Ink Corporation.

behavior, but very likely it was also a strong impetus to the passage of the state legislation.

Another example of self-regulation at the state and local levels can be found in the activities of the Better Business Bureaus (BBB) in many cities and towns throughout the country. Although there are no legal teeth in the actions they take, the constraints are there because no firm wants to incur the ire of the local BBB. The bureaus are particularly effective in suppressing ''bait and switch'' advertising (baiting the consumer with a low-priced model and switching the pitch to something else once the consumer is in the store).

Local media, such as newspapers, radio, and TV stations, generally have guidelines relative to the kinds of advertising they will accept. Advertisers in adhering to these guidelines are thus encouraged to consider the ethics of their proposed promotional efforts.

In addition, local advertising review units are appearing in some cities.[74] The growth of such units had stopped in the 1970s when a local advertiser brought suit against a Denver ad self-regulation panel. The lawsuit ultimately went all the way to the U.S. Supreme Court.[75] Although no monetary damages were assessed against the review panel, potential boards were not inclined to want to take the risk. The revival of local review units could be an effective addition to the self-regulatory system, however.

Although business favors self-regulation over government regulation, it recognizes the need for some of the latter. The threat of government regulation is probably necessary to make self-regulation work. Nevertheless, to the extent that self-regulation can be made effective, government regulation can be minimized.

Federal Government Regulation

Despite the favorable results of efforts by various segments of business to regulate promotional activities, there will always be people who believe that government regulation is the only answer, and the trend is for ever-increasing amounts of it. The following discussion presents certain aspects of only some of the major acts. Promotional strategists should be aware of the kinds of constraints within which they must operate. Federal laws are only applicable in interstate commerce.

Federal Trade Commission Act

The superstar in government regulation is the Federal Trade Commission, established by the Federal Trade Commission Act in 1914 and since amended and strengthened. The Commission consists of a chairman and four other commissioners, all appointed by the President for seven-year terms subject to Senate confir-

---

[74]See ''17 Cities Operating Ad Self-Regulation Programs,'' *Editor & Publisher: The Fourth Estate* 115 (September 11, 1982): 18.

[75]''Local Ad Review Units Try Again,'' *Advertising Age* (April 27, 1981): 1, 90.

mation. There are four divisions in the Commission: Bureau of Economics, Bureau of Competition, Bureau of Consumer Protection, and twelve regional offices.[76]

The FTC not only investigates and prosecutes in its own right but is also the enforcing agency for numerous other laws. Under the original act, the FTC was to be primarily concerned with unfair methods of competition. However, the Wheeler-Lea Act, passed in 1938, amended the Federal Trade Commission Act so that deceptive practices that might be harmful to consumers could be attacked even though competition was not injured. It is only necessary to show that the overall impression is deceptive whether or not the specific claims are literally true.[77] Furthermore, until recently the FTC has policed ads for "unfairness" and used the results as a basis for industrywide trade rules against advertising. This latter power was temporarily removed, however, with the passage of the FTC Improvement Act of 1980, because of the difficulty in defining unfairness. Presently a bitter debate is raging over whether the removal should be permanent or not.[78]

Historically, the FTC has had three categories of "weapons" to use in carrying out its regulatory powers: conferences with the alleged violators that can result in a letter of compliance or a stipulation; consent orders that reflect the agreement of the company or industry to cease the alleged unfair practice; and formal legal action (which can be appealed through the courts) that could result in a cease and desist order.[79]

But in the early 1970s, the FTC began to get tougher. It took the position that it should concentrate more than it had on false advertising. Accordingly, it initiated a program under which advertisers could be required to substantiate their claims. If the FTC finds that an advertiser has made claims it cannot substantiate, the FTC can require *corrective advertising*. The advertiser then may not only be required to cease making the false claims but may also be required to devote a specified amount of advertising effort aimed at dispelling previous claims.

The rationale for requiring corrective advertising is that deceptive ads may continue to influence consumers even after the ads are discontinued. It is therefore necessary that the advertiser run corrective advertising to eliminate the "residual effects" of the deceptive ads. Furthermore, the FTC does not have to show proof that consumers have been deceived; it only has to show that the ad in question has a "fair probability" of deceiving.[80]

Corrective advertising first appeared in 1972 when the FTC required the ITT

---

[76]See Thomas G. Krattenmaker, "The Federal Trade Commission and Consumer Protection," *California Management Review* 18, no. 4 (Summer 1976): 89–104.

[77]See Loevinger, "The Attack on Advertising and the Goals of Regulation," *The Conference Board Record* 10, no. 1 (January 1973): 25.

[78]See for example, Richard L. Gordon, "Industry Off Target on 'Fairness'—FTC," *Advertising Age* (March 1, 1982): 1, 76; Richard L. Gordon, "FTC Seeks Narrower 'Unfair' Rules," *Advertising Age* (March 15, 1982): 3, 83; and "Senate FTC Bill Would Eliminate Unfairness Rules," *Advertising Age* (May 10, 1982): 2, 80.

[79]See Vernon A. Mund, *Government and Business* (New York: Harper & Row, 1960), pp. 294–99.

[80]See Robert F. Dyer and Philip G. Kuehl, "The 'Corrective Advertising' Remedy of the FTC; An Experimental Evaluation," *Journal of Marketing* 38 (Jan. 1974): 48–54.

Continental Baking Company, Inc., to run corrective ads in connection with its Profile bread. The bread had been advertised as being lower in calories than competing brands. The corrective advertising (25 percent of each advertisement run during the year) admitted that the only reason slices of Profile were lower in calories than competing brands was that they were thinner.[81]

The case that clinched the practice involved Warner-Lambert and Listerine mouthwash. The FTC had issued a cease and desist order to the company requiring it to stop advertising Listerine as a preventive, cure, or palliative for the common cold. The product has been on the market for over 90 years and had been advertised as beneficial for colds and sore throats for years. But the FTC contended that Listerine had no such therapeutic effect as claimed in the advertising, and therefore the advertising was deceptive. The company was ordered to include the following corrective statement in all its future advertising until it had expended $10 million: "Contrary to prior advertising, Listerine will not help prevent colds or sore throats or lessen their severity." The Circuit Court of Appeals for the District of Columbia upheld the Commission's order except for the phrase "contrary to prior advertising."[82] Since the Supreme Court refused to hear the case on appeal, the decision of the lower court stands.[83]

The FTC has promulgated a trade regulation providing for a three-day "cooling off period" in connection with door-to-door selling. Under this regulation a consumer who buys from a door-to-door salesperson can rescind the purchase within three days if it appears that the product or service is not as described.

The Federal Trade Commission's enormous power over business was expanded even further with the passage of the Magnuson-Moss Warranty-Federal Trade Commission Improvement Act in 1975. The act is in two parts, but the second part concerns promotion. Among other things, the act provides for consumer participation in FTC proceedings. It broadens and clarifies the various powers of the commision, including the power to assess penalties on a company as soon as the company breaks a rule.[84]

In the early 1980s, however, there was industry and government concern over the awesome power of the Federal Trade Commission. It was felt that when an agency such as the FTC issues industrywide rules it is exercising the kind of lawmaking power that is vested in Congress by the Constitution. In order to reserve for itself the legislative powers it felt it should have, Congress voted itself a veto power over decisions rendered by the FTC, only to have the power voided two years later by the U.S. Supreme Court.[85]

---

[81]For an excellent discussion of the rationale and legal theory behind corrective advertising see Debra L. Scammon and Richard J. Semenik, "Corrective Advertising: Evolution of the Legal Theory and Application of the Remedy," *Journal of Advertising* 11, no. 1 (1982): 10–20.

[82]See George E. Hartman, "Courts Affirm, Spell Out Rules for Corrective Ads," *Marketing News* 11, no. 8 (21 Oct. 1977): 81–86.

[83]See Richard L. Gordon, "High Court Avoids Listerine Ad Case: FTC Penalty Stands," *Advertising Age* (10 Apr. 1978): 1.

[84]See Gerald G. Udell and Philip J. Fisher, "The FTC Improvement Act," *Journal of Marketing* 41, no. 2 (Apr. 1977): 81–86.

[85]Richard L. Gordon, "Ad Leaders Laud Court Veto Ruling," *Advertising Age* (June 27, 1983): 2, 83.

Bonita Russiff

At the present time the role, the power, and the activity of the Federal Trade Commission are subjects of much debate. It is argued, for example, that the free market should be allowed to work and that clear proof of economic injury should exist before the FTC takes a case.[86] A currently prevailing viewpoint is that the Commission should concentrate on individual companies and not issue industry-wide rules.[87] This is contrary to the stance taken by the FTC for years, but the current approach is felt by some to be effective.[88]

Some people believe the current policies of the FTC are resulting in a strong move toward more self-regulation.[89] But others feel that there is an equally strong push for a revival of more government regulation.[90] The only certain thing at this time is that the outcome is uncertain.

Federal Food, Drug, and Cosmetic Act

The Federal Food, Drug, and Cosmetic Act, passed in 1938, replaced the 1906 Food and Drug Act. Under the Act the Food and Drug Administration (FDA) became the regulatory agency for prescription drug ads which were not allowed in consumer media, while over-the-counter drug ads were under the control of the Federal Trade Commission, although there was some question regarding the authority over animal drugs. With the advent of prescription drug advertising in consumer media, however, Congress is considering the desirability of concentrating the regulation of all drug ads in one agency.[91]

Robinson-Patman Act

The Robinson-Patman Act, passed in 1936 as an amendment to the Clayton Anti-trust Act, affects virtually all marketing activities. Our concern, however, is with those provisions that involve promotion. Under the act, manufacturers who grant advertising or other promotion allowances to any middleman must do so to all such institutions on a proportionate basis. Furthermore, the act prohibits the payment of unearned brokerage fees — that is, paying certain large buyers fees for broker-age services when no such services were provided. The act also prohibits discrimination in price between purchasers of commodities of "like grade and quality" where the effect would tend to injure competition. There are provisions for exceptions, but when price might be used as a promotion tool the law is significant to the promotional strategist.

---

[86]"The FTC's Miller Puts His Faith in the Free Market," *Business Week* (June 27, 1983): 66–70.

[87]"Back to Cases at the FTC," *Business Week* (July 5, 1982): 90.

[88]"A New Approach to Consumer Protection," *Nation's Business* 71 (June 1983): 38.

[89]Stanley E. Cohen, "FTC Tack Veering Toward Self-Regulation," *Advertising Age* (October 4, 1982): 42.

[90]"A Bipartisan Swing Back to More Regulation," *Business Week* (May 30, 1983): 74, 75.

[91]"Congress Eyes Unified Drug Ad Regulation," *Advertising Age* (July 11, 1983): 10.

The Labeling Acts

Since labels and packages are often key factors in promotional strategy, the laws regulating their use for such purposes must be observed. A number of such laws have been passed; but since the names of the acts establishing the laws indicate their purposes, we shall not discuss them. They include the Wool Products Labeling Act (1939), Fur Products Labeling Act (1951), Textile Fiber Products Identification Act (1958), Hazardous Substances Labeling Act (1960), Fair Package and Labeling Act (1966), and the Cigarette Labeling Act (1966).

Other Acts Affecting Promotion

Several other acts have been passed that affect promotion. The Lanham Trademark Act (1946) enables a seller to claim exclusive ownership of trademarks providing certain conditions are met. One case involving an alleged violation of this Act was one in which Parker Brothers, marketer of the board game Monopoly, charged that another company's game, Anti-Monopoly, was an infringement of its trademark. After nine years of litigation, the court decided in favor of Anti-Monopoly.[92] The Consumer Credit Protection Act (Truth-in-Lending) passed in 1968 requires among other things the disclosure of finance charges in credit advertising. The Federal Communications Commission (FCC) is empowered by the Communications Act of 1934 to regulate broadcasters, which has an indirect effect on broadcast advertising.

State and Local Government Regulation

State and local laws regulating promotion vary greatly among the states and cities. A number of states have adopted the Uniform Consumer Credit Code which provides for a three-day cooling-off period for home solicitation sales. Under the Code, the consumer can cancel the purchase by midnight of the third day following the sale. The seller must inform the buyer of this privilege. (The Federal Trade Commission also has such a regulation.)

Many cities have passed so-called "Green River" ordinances requiring that a door-to-door salesperson obtain a license in order to sell house-to-house.

SUMMARY

Legal/ethical considerations are becoming increasingly significant to promotion managers. The attack on various aspects of advertising and other forms of promotion has accelerated in recent years, largely as the result of consumerism. Business has responded to some of the charges, but the actions it has taken are deemed insufficient by most business critics.

Areas of concern include the following: *content* of the advertisement (partic-

---

[92]See Carl E. Person, "Trademarks and the Anti-Monopoly Case," *Advertising Age* (May 16, 1983): 37.

ularly, usefulness of information, deception, obscenity and bad taste, and discrimination); the *product* advertised (including cigarettes, junk foods and candy, energy products, feminine hygiene products, lingerie, contraceptives, liquor, and over-the-counter drugs); advertising directed at *children; excessive* amounts of advertising; advertising in the *professions;* and *comparative* advertising.

With criticism as rampant as it is, the impetus for the regulation of promotional activities is reflected on two fronts. First, the various business institutions involved with promotion have developed effective programs of self-regulation. Second, the federal government has become increasingly active. Through its main watchdog, the Federal Trade Commission, the government has imposed stringent controls over the promotion activities of business and has established severe penalties for violations. Other legislation provides additional teeth in the regulating activities of the government.

QUESTIONS FOR THOUGHT AND REVIEW

1. Why has marketing rather than production generally been the target of business critics? Are there sound reasons for making the distinction?
2. Do you think criticism of business serves a useful purpose? Discuss.
3. How would you characterize the people who are most critical of business? Why are these people more critical than others?
4. Is *consumerism* new? When did it start? When did the current movement start? Do you think it will continue? Discuss.
5. Discuss the contrasting views of consumerism. Attack and defend each point of view.
6. How has business responded to the charges growing out of the consumerism movement? Have the actions been effective? How could the response of business be more effective?
7. Do you think advertisements provide the consumer with helpful information for making decisions? Is information related to emotional reasons for buying justified? Discuss.
8. Is all advertising *persuasive?* Should it be? Discuss.
9. What are your own views on deceptive advertising? For example, to what extent is advertising deceptive? Can you give examples of deceptive ads?
10. Discuss the problem of obscenity and bad taste in advertising.
11. In the light of the criticism that women in advertisements are generally portrayed as homemakers, should advertisers always show women in roles reflecting business and professional careers? Discuss.
12. What should be the advertiser's approach to showing minorities in advertisements?
13. What is the philosophical issue associated with advertising "energy" products? What is your position on this?
14. Discuss the trend toward advertising products historically considered too personal for public promotion.

15. What are some of the criticisms of advertising directed at children? Discuss the pros and cons of restricting such advertising.
16. What is your position on regulating outdoor advertising? Direct mail advertising? Justify whatever position you take.
17. What is *comparative advertising?* Do you think its use adds to the information consumers need in making purchase decisions? Explain.
18. Under what circumstances might advertising be controlled through self-regulation? Could this ever happen? Explain.
19. Explain the role of the Federal Trade Commission in connection with government regulation of advertising.
20. What is *corrective advertising?* Attack or defend its use and justify your position.
21. Do you think there are not enough, too many, or just the right amount of laws regulating advertising? If you think there are too many, which one should be eliminated? If you think there are not enough, what would you add?

PART THREE

MARKET ANALYSIS

The task of planning a specific promotion campaign must begin with a market analysis. Markets are composed of people whose behavior is influenced by and is reflective of the environmental considerations discussed in part 2. With an understanding of the general significance of environmental factors to promotion, we are now in a position to examine more specifically the direct effect of such factors on the development of promotional strategy.

In chapter 6 we consider the factors associated with product perception and the target market. However, the principles are the same for "idea perception and acceptance behavior" when ideas or candidates are being promoted. Chapter 7 deals with purchase behavior and developing the promotion appeal. Chapter 8, then, is devoted to a discussion of the problem of establishing objectives.

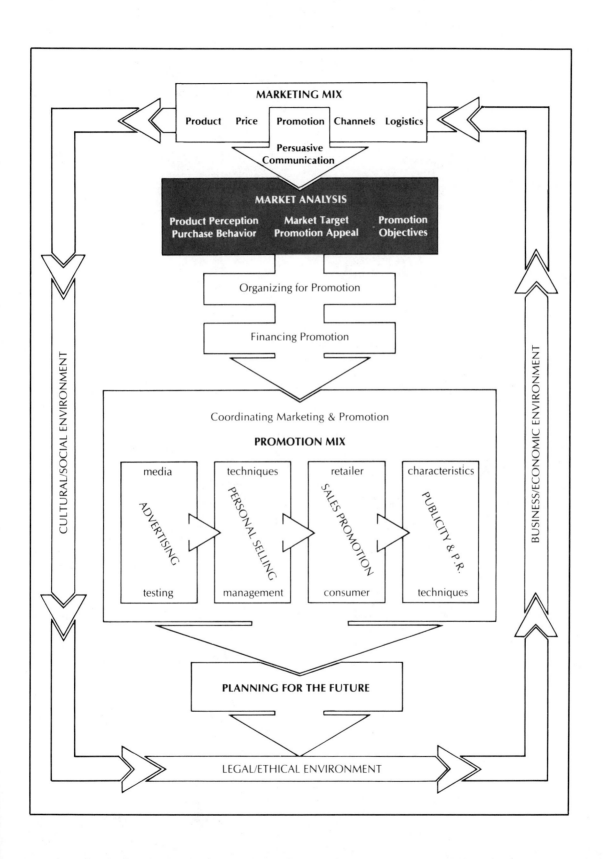

6

PRODUCT PERCEPTION AND THE MARKET TARGET

The *subject* of promotional effort is a product, service, or idea. The *object* of the effort is to communicate information about the subject in a persuasive way to an identified audience. The *arena* in which the activity takes place is a market. With an understanding of promotion's role of communication in the marketing process and how communication works, and recognizing the environmental influences on the process, we can discuss the problem of analyzing the market. Our concern is with such questions as: How do people perceive our product? What has perception of the product to do with defining our market? How can people be grouped into an identifiable target? Can we effectively promote our product or service or idea to these people? How do people make their purchase decisions? How do we induce this? How do we establish objectives? The next three chapters are devoted to a consideration of these and other related questions.

PRODUCT PERCEPTION

A Cadillac is not just a car; nor is a Corvette. A can of Coors beer is more than just a malt beverage, and a package of Marlboro cigarettes has connotations beyond the 20 cigarettes it contains. Blue jeans in Eastern Europe are more saleable if they have the Levi label. Even a can of green beans can be more than just a vegetable when it comes from the Valley of the Jolly Green Giant!

A product is not just a thing. It is a conglomerate of tangible and intangible qualities. It has both intrinsic characteristics and psychological attributes, all of which are potentially want-satisfying to various groups of people.

Some people may view a product primarily in terms of its intrinsic characteristics or its functional aspects, while others may focus more on the product's psychological connotations or its subjective meanings. Some people may be influenced by both kinds of qualities; different people are affected in different ways by different products. However, it is unlikely that any one person perceives a product in terms of its total range of attributes. Certain product characteristics are significant to each of us in product evaluation. It is these "determinant attributes" that are of concern to the promotion manager.[1] Failure to identify these can result in the use of a weak or ineffective promotion appeal.

Product Image

The image most people have of most products is a composite of both the product and the brand, together with other factors consciously or subconsciously associated with them. In some cases, however, the generic product (irrespective of brand) may evoke an image.

Instant coffee and prepared cake mixes, for example, in their introductory years were viewed negatively by many homemakers. Women who purchased instant coffee were considered to be lazy housewives, as the classic Mason Haire

---

[1]James H. Myers and Mark I. Alpert, "Determinant Buying Attitues: Meaning and Measurement," *Journal of Marketing* 32 (Oct. 1968): 13–20.

study showed; and women could take no pride in baking a cake unless they started "from scratch."[2] Oatmeal is considered by some people to be old-fashioned, and others still associate motorcycles with the Hell's Angels. Of course, some products are viewed favorably from the time they are introduced — television sets and ball-point pens were accepted immediately.

The way a consumer "sees" a product depends not only on the stimulus itself but also on such things as the individual's psychological state and his or her cultural background, social groups, and reference groups. The things a person sees are perceived as a part of a total situation, not as fragmented parts.[3]

Thus it would seem that the promotional strategist should concentrate, not on what consumers ask for but rather on "the conditions that lead them to want what they ask for."[4] If we can know the reasons for the image consumers have of our product, we are in a better position to develop a persuasive message than if we are simply aware of how they perceive it.

Whether a product is new or old might make a difference in the image consumers have of it. Old products may be familiar, and the images people have of them are usually the result of impressions developed over the years. The consumer's image of a new product, however, may result from the impact of its effect on life-style.

It has been suggested that there are "two kinds of new products — those which *do not* change a person's life-style and those which *do* change a person's life-style."[5] The images of products that do not change life-styles are probably formed in much the same way as are the images of old products. New kinds of toothpaste, new models of lawnmowers, new table games, canned fruits, and men's socks, for example, are new products that do not change life-styles.

But consider such once-new products as automobiles, radios, television sets, microwave ovens, instant coffee, and prepared cake mixes. Such products do change life-styles; and the images people have of them, whether favorable or not, are affected by their concepts of the changes in their life-styles the use of such products would engender.

Most people tend to resist immediate change, and their images of products that represent radical differences in their ways of thinking and living are initially viewed negatively. Of the products mentioned, the only exceptions to this idea are television sets and possibly radios. When television sets became available to the mass market in the late 1940s and early 1950s they were immediately accepted. People were ready for that particular change in life-style. But we all know the problems the "horseless carriage" had in gaining acceptance; microwave

---

[2]Mason Haire, Projective Techniques in Marketing Research," *Journal of Marketing* 14, no. 5 (Apr. 1950): 651–52.

[3]Herta Herzog, "Behavioral Science Concepts for Analyzing the Consumer," *Proceedings — Conference of Marketing Teachers from Far Western States* (Berkeley: University of California, 1958), pp. 32–41.

[4]Geraldine Finnell, "Consumers' Perception of the Product-Use Situation," *Journal of Marketing* 42, no. 2 (Apr. 1978): 38–47.

[5]Edward Winter and John T. Russell, "Psychographics and Creativity," *Journal of Advertising* 2, no. 1 (1973): 32–34.

ovens are still not universally praised; and we have already discussed the problems encountered in introducing instant coffee and prepared cake mixes.

Product images do change, of course, although the images of new products in the mass market sometimes change gradually. There are always a few people who accept innovations immediately, but the rest of society responds more slowly.

Brand Image

The image people have of many products is tempered or even determined by the brand. A brand is a symbol, and as Sidney J. Levy states, "A symbol is appropriate . . . when it joins with, meshes with, adds to, reinforces, the way the consumer thinks about himself."[6] This notion is a reflection of the significance to promotion of the consumer's self-concept, and is in a way a merging of brand image with self-concept. Since the brand is associated with the product, there is also an intermingling of brand image with product image.

Thus consumers tend to evaluate products and brands of products in terms of the images they have formed; " . . . consumers do not drink beer — they drink their image of beer."[7] Although formation of these images is a complex process involving the influence of many factors associated with human behavior, the catalyst in the image-building can be the efforts of marketing and promotion strategists. In fact, developing a brand image is often the major objective in the promotional strategy for such common products as grocery and drug items, soaps, liquor, and cigarettes since they are not easily distinguished by product characteristics.[8]

Not only is it possible to create a brand image but it is also possible to change it. Perhaps the classic example of changing a brand image is the one effected for Marlboro cigarettes. The image of Marlboro was changed from an extremely feminine cigarette to one that reflects equally extreme masculinity. In its feminine stage the cigarette even had a red tip to camouflage the stain from red lipstick!

Brand image is also a key factor in the purchase decisions for many products because it is identified with product quality. Certain brands of some products denote quality to consumers. In some cases these impressions are the result of actual experience with the brand and are therefore logically developed. In other cases, the impressions evolve in a less rational way. Consumers may simply associate the quality of a brand with their perception of the degree to which it is nationally advertised.[9] They may assume that the more a product is advertised, the higher

[6]Sidney J. Levy, "Symbols by Which We Buy," in Lynn H. Stockman, ed., *Advancing Marketing Efficiency* (Chicago: American Marketing Association, 1959), pp. 409–16.

[7]Kenneth E. Runyon, *Consumer Behavior and the Practice of Marketing,* 2nd ed. (Columbus, Ohio: Charles E. Merrill, 1980), p. 19; Ira J. Dolich, "Congruence Relationships Between Self-Images and Product Brands," *Journal of Marketing Research* 6 (Feb. 1969): 80–84; B. Curtis Hamm and Edward W. Cundiff, "Self-Actualization and Product Perception," *Journal of Marketing Research* 6 (Nov. 1969): 470–73; and Finnell, "Consumers' Perception," pp. 38–47.

[8]See Edward L. Brink and William T. Kelley, *The Management of Promotion* (Englewood Cliffs, N.J.: Prentice-Hall, 1963), p. 158. See also E. John Kottman, "The Parity Product — Advertising's Achilles Heel," *Journal of Advertising* 6, no. 1 (1977): 34–39.

[9]Arch G. Woodside and James L. Taylor, "Consumer Purchase Intentions and Perceptions of Product Quality and National Advertising," *Journal of Advertising* 7, no. 1 (1978): 48–51.

the quality. This may or may not be true, but the fact that some consumers make this assumption is of significance to promotion managers.

It is even possible that testing agencies associate heavy advertising with high quality. In a study of the relationship between the level of advertising and product quality as rated by *Consumer Reports* it was found that products that were heavily advertised were given a higher number of good-quality ratings than products not heavily advertised.[10]

THE MARKET TARGET

Successful promotional strategy usually requires that the target of the effort be carefully defined to isolate those individuals who are potentially receptive to the promotional message. This reduces waste by saving dollars that would have been spent trying to persuade those who cannot be persuaded. More importantly, defining the target figuratively groups people into a collective ''one,'' which provides a concrete basis for developing effective communication in accordance with the tenets of sound communication theory (chapter 2). Furthermore, characteristics of the target group help in design and implementation of specific facets of promotional strategy.[11]

Obviously, a market is composed of people with needs to satisfy, but such people must also be financially able and willing to buy our product, given the proper incentive. How do we identify and isolate such people in terms of their product perceptions and other factors? There are two basic approaches: product differentiation and market segmentation.[12] Both marketing management and promotion management are concerned with this task, and the approach chosen usually reflects *total* marketing strategy of which promotion is a part.

Product Differentiation

The company that chooses to follow a policy of product differentiation views the total market for a product as one fairly homogeneous unit. Such a firm takes the position that there is *a* market for facial tissues, or ball-point pens, or refrigerators, and that the company can generate sales within that total market simply by making its product a little bit different from those of its competitors. The management of such firms does not expect to capture the entire market. Rather, it simply believes that there will be enough people across the entire range of the market who could be convinced of the merits of the product to justify production.

Usually firms that adopt a policy of product differentiation are production

[10]Raymond A. Marquardt and Anthony F. McGann, ''Does Advertising Communicate Product Quality to Consumers? Some Evidence from *Consumer Reports*,'' *Journal of Advertising* 4, no. 4 (1975): 27–31. See also, E. R. Beem and J. S. Ewing, ''Business Appraises Consumer Testing Agencies,'' *Harvard Business Review* (Mar.–Apr. 1954): 113–26.

[11]See Larry Percy, ''How Market Segmentation Guides Advertising Strategy,'' *Journal of Advertising Research* 16, no. 5 (Oct. 1976): 11–22.

[12]For the classic article on this subject, see Wendell R. Smith, ''Product Differentiation and Market Segmentation as Alternative Marketing Strategies,'' *Journal of Marketing* 21, no. 1 (July 1956): 3–8.

oriented; they are less concerned with marketing than they are with production. They may spend less time analyzing the consumer and devote more attention to the problems of production—more or less assuming that the product will sell in sufficient quantities to justify its existence.

Except for certain products such as wheat, natural gas, and other "basic" products, product differentiation as a strategy is risky in the volatile marketplace of contemporary business. The total market for most products today is simply too heterogeneous to be considered as a single unit. The needs of people, their perceptions of products, and their reasons for buying, both real and imaginary, are so diversified that a single product tossed at the total market will usually find few catchers. A notable exception is the Morton Salt Company, which is probably oriented to a product-differentiation policy. "When it rains it pours" has successfully distinguished the company's product from those of its competitors in the total salt market for many years.

Market Segmentation

The other approach to defining a market target is much more common today. Some form of market segmentation is probably used by a majority of manufacturers. It is simply dividing the total market into segments, each of which consist of people with homogeneous characteristics with respect to purchase behavior. Thus, instead of saying there is one market for facial tissues, or ball-point pens, or refrigerators, the firm whose strategy is market segmentation would say there are several markets for each of these products and that the markets are delineated by certain common characteristics of people unique to their respective groups.

The policy is consumer oriented, and is therefore consistent with current marketing theory. In essence, its use requires analyzing consumers to determine the kind of product wanted and possible reasons for buying it and then creating a product accordingly. Promotion's part in the process is to convince the people in the appropriate segment(s) that the product is just what they want.

Market segmentation results in a much more precisely defined target than product differentiation. The firm using the latter strategy simply throws its product up for grabs and hopes there will be some takers, but the firm using market segmentation zeros in on a specific target. Most companies design and promote variations of a product for each of several different market segments. Procter and Gamble, for example, promotes Crest toothpaste to a market segment consisting of families who are concerned about tooth decay problems of their children and promotes Gleam to a different segment. Lever Brothers reaches different market segments with Aim and Close-up as does Colgate-Palmolive with Colgate and Ultra Brite. Automobile manufacturers appeal to many different market segments with the many models and styles of their products.

Market segmentation is significant in the development of promotional strategy for many reasons. At the very outset, of course, it recognizes the differences in the way people perceive the product, as discussed earlier. These differences in product perception affect promotional strategy in many ways, reflecting the basic tenets of communication theory discussed in chapter 2. For example, the nature of the target market segments influences the appeal (the theme of the advertisement or other promotional effort) that will be used to reach people. If the appeal is not consistent with the target consumers' perceptions of the product, they will simply "tune the message out." How many college-age people, for example, would read an advertisement for jeans if the theme of the ad was their ruggedness and durability? Fashionableness is a more likely theme because most people in this market segment perceive jeans as fashionable. A related factor is the language used in expressing the theme. A promotion strategist most certainly would use different language appeals in promoting jeans to working ranchers than to college-age people.

In addition, the characteristics of particular market segments suggest the media appropriate for reaching them. Young women read different magazines than older women; there is a similar difference with respect to young and older men. People with different interests, occupations, and educational backgrounds read different magazines, watch different television programs, and listen to different radio stations. Thus the promotion strategist must choose the media used to carry the message on the basis of their probable exposure to the selected market segments.

Positioning the Product

Essential to approaching the problem of segmenting the market is the proper positioning of the product in the market. A product's position refers to the way it is perceived (or intended to be perceived) vis-à-vis the products of competitors or other products in the company's product mix.[13] The product must be positioned properly. Early correct positioning provides an immediate edge in the marketplace. Scope was successfully positioned against Listerine; Lever's Wisk, while competing with Procter & Gamble's Era and Colgate's Dynamo, was actually positioned as the brand for eliminating tough stains; and M & M candy, positioned in the market to appeal to mothers (who have to wash dirty clothes) and not children (who eat the candy) with the slogan "melts in your mouth, not in your hands," has been very successful.[14]

Sometimes, however, the initial positioning of the product does not result in success, and the company must change the consumer's perception of the product through repositioning. Avis could not successfully position itself against Hertz and changed its position to "Number 2." And 7-Up had to change its position from that of a direct competitor of Coca-Cola and Pepsi-Cola to a different drink — the "Un-Cola."[15] Seven-Up has continued to be an active participant in the ongoing soft drink war as the industry focus has shifted, more recently, to diet drinks, caffeine-free drinks, and drinks with no artificial flavors. Pledge was successfully repositioned from a furniture wax to a dusting aid.

---

[13]See John Holmes, "Profitable Product Positioning," *MSU Business Topics* (Spring 1973): 27–32.

[14]F. Beavin Ennis, "Positioning Revisited," *Advertising Age* (March 15, 1982): M-43–47.

[15]William J. Stanton, *Fundamentals of Marketing, 5th ed.* (New York: McGraw-Hill, 1978), p. 199. See also "A Slow Rebound for Seven-Up, *Business Week* (October 12, 1981): 107–10.

In repositioning their products, however, firms must be careful not to damage an existing image they want to perpetuate. Arby's, for example, has recently entered the children's market with a menu offering appealing to that market and using a robot called "R. B." At first glance this would seem to indicate that Arby's is positioning itself to compete directly with McDonald's and Burger King. But the company emphasizes that it is simply attempting to increase its share of the family market, and that the basic appeal is to the parent purchaser.[16]

Product positioning requires that the firm determine the niche in the array of product offerings that is appropriate for the product in question. It means that the firm must decide on the source from which it intends to carve its market share. The total effort must focus on the perception the consumer has of the product — or should have from the company's point of view.

Bases for Segmenting the Market

There are many bases by which markets can be segmented. It is not the basis itself that is important, however; rather, it is the fact that the people identified by that basis exhibit similar behavior with respect to their purchases. When age is used as a basis for segmentation, for example, it is not the fact that certain people are teenagers that is important, but rather that most teenagers display similar patterns in their purchase behavior. Markets are usually segmented by using a combination of several bases. Although it is not possible to identify all the bases used for segmenting markets, some of the more common ones can be divided into four groups: personal/social, geographic, product-related, and psychographic (see table 6–1).

Table 6–1 is not an exhaustive list of bases for segmentation. Circumstances and conditions may dictate the use of other bases. Moreover, segments determined by any basis are rarely totally discrete. There is some spillover of people from one segment to another. The marketer cannot be sure that all potential consumers of the product are included in any segment or segments, nor that everyone included in a particular segment is a potential consumer. But the objective in segmentation is to arrive at some logical delineation of target groups.

The basis or bases chosen for segmenting the market are determined by the firm's particular promotion situation. The selected basis must also have certain specific characteristics. For example, it must be measurable; otherwise there would be no way of knowing whether the segment was of sufficient size to justify a concentrated effort. Moreover, the segment must be reachable. Its composition of people must be such that the promotion strategist can direct the promotional effort at that group, reaching all or most of it with a minimum amount of costly unproductive exposure to people outside the group who are not potential customers. There must be media available (magazines, newspapers, TV and radio programs, etc.) that are specifically aimed at the chosen segment — or the segment must be accessible to the company's sales force.

---

[16]Scott Hume, "Arby's Aims New Push at Kids' Market," *Advertising Age* (May 30, 1983): 3, 60.

TABLE 6-1
Some bases for segmenting the market

Personal/social	Geographic	Product-related	Psychographic
Sex	Region	Usage rate	Life-style
Age	Population	Brand loyalty	
Race	Climate	Perceived benefits	
Nationality			
Religion			
Education			
Occupation			
Income			
Family life cycle			
Social class			

Personal/social. An obvious basis for identifying separate market segments for some products is sex. Certain products are designed solely for women and others for men. Women's lingerie, men's T-shirts and shorts, and shoes for each are examples, as are countless personal hygiene products. In the latter case, not only are there separate subcategories naturally associated with one sex but also such products as deodorants used by both sexes are separately designed for each. Virginia Slims and Eve cigarettes appeal to women while Marlboro and Camels appeal to men. Yet with the changing values in society today, the distinction may not be as pronounced as it once was. The "unisex" movement is reflected in many items of clothing, sporting equipment, and jewelry.

Another common basis for segmentation is age. The needs of people vary among different age groups. Toys are designed for each of several age brackets among children and are usually so marked on the package. Certain foods are promoted to specific age groups. Gerber Products promotes its baby food to parents of infants and also to older people whose diets call for that kind of food. Ronald McDonald has promoted hamburgers to young people, and cereal companies advertise to kids.

One of the growing age segments, however, is the older market — the "gray market" — which, after many years of neglect, is now being recognized as viable and profitable. American marketers had been obsessed with a youth orientation as symbolized in Pepsi-Cola's slogan of a few years ago, "For those who think young." The accent on youth is still there, but there is increasing recognition of the inexorable changes taking place in the composition and character of the population. Gerber Products now promotes insurance and health care products to older people, and Levi Strauss & Company is marketing a line of clothing for the "mature" figure. Estée Lauder and Elizabeth Arden have introduced lines specifically designed for the older woman.[17] Reaching the older market, particularly the "upper end" of it, may require changes in promotion techniques. People in this group probably differ from other adults with respect to the mass media to which

---

[17]Carole B. Allan, "Over 55: Growth Market of the 80's," *Nation's Business* (April 1981): 25-32.

they expose themselves, the way they learn, and perhaps the way they are influenced.[18]

Other bases used in segmenting the market for some products include *income, education, occupation, race, religion,* and *nationality.* A person's total income determines the amount of disposable income and discretionary buying power available for spending. The amount of such income thus has a bearing on the type, quality, and quantity of product demanded. This is particularly noticeable in connection with the purchase of housing, furniture, clothing, automobiles, food, and sporting goods. Variations in these and other products can also be associated with different stages in the *family life cycle* (discussed in chapter 3) which is another basis for segmentation. *Social class* is another basis for segmentation. Even though the lines between social classes in the United States are somewhat blurred, certain kinds of purchase behavior are associated with each class. Education likewise influences purchase behavior. Generally speaking, more education creates more discerning consumers with respect to both product characteristics and promotion messages. People in certain occupations provide markets for some products and not for others. Race, religion, and nationality are other influences on purchase behavior and responses to promotional efforts.

Geographic.   At the very outset, of course, one would recognize that international marketers segment their markets by countries — even when their marketing activities involve such economic groups as the European Common Market. Each of the countries in the Common Market is actually a separate market. Many domestic marketers, however, also use geographic bases for segmenting their markets. Different regions in the United States comprise different market segments for some products. The Southwest, for example, is a strong market for tacos, enchiladas, pinto beans, and chili peppers; adobe houses are popular in this region. New England and the Deep South are other examples of regions with unique cultural characteristics that influence purchase behavior. Pizza Hut varies the composition of its pizza from one region to another because consumer preferences vary.[19]

Population density and distribution are also geographical bases for segmenting the market. The significance of population certainly goes beyond its association with regions. The concept of the Standard Metropolitan Statistical Area (SMSA), discussed in chapter 4, is used by some firms in identifying their markets. Other companies such as manufacturers of farm equipment, fertilizer, and related products, may define their markets as rural — avoiding the SMSAs. The shifting of the population, reflecting the exodus of people from one area and the resulting influx of people in others redefines market segments geographically.

Climate, too, identifies market segments for some firms. The strongest markets for air conditioners are the areas having consistently high temperatures; peo-

---

[18]Lynn W. Phillips and Brian Sternthal, "Age Differences in Information Processing: A Perspective on the Aged Consumer," *Journal of Marketing Research* 14 (Nov. 1977): 444–57.

[19]Christy Marshall, "Pizza Hut Is Cooking Up Recipe for Future Growth," *Advertising Age* (February 6, 1978): 45.

FIGURE 5–2   An ad comparing the Volkswagen Jetta and the BMW. *Source:* Volkswagen of America.

It's not what you think it is.
(But you're close.)

This Volkswagen Jetta is often confused with another well-known German car.

And not just because their lines are so similar. But because their personalities are so similar.

After all, both were designed for the serious driver.

And both were built to handle the toughest driving challenges Europe has to offer. From Alpine curves with no guard rails to autobahns with no speed limits.

Turn these remarkable cars loose on a really demanding road and they'll both respond: With rambunctious performance. Razor-sharp handling. And a rarely-equalled feel for the road.

All of which brings up a rather obvious question:

Why should you choose Jetta over the other car?

Well, the fact is that Jetta has a feature that makes it considerably easier to handle.

A considerably smaller price tag.

Jetta
Nothing else is a Volkswagen

Gentlemen prefer Hanes

For sheer elegance, sheer
fashion, or the sheer pleasure of
it all, nothing dresses up a pair
of legs like Hanes® Ultra Sheer
pantyhose.
    And for the added benefit of
sheer confidence, Hanes Ultra
Sheer tummy control pantyhose
gives you Ultra Sheer elegance
and a figure flattering hint of hold
where you need it.
    Both are sensuously smooth,
luxuriously silky, unmistakably
Hanes.

ple in the cooler areas of the Rocky Mountain states are not inclined to purchase the product. Manufacturers of winter and summer clothing define market segments based on climate, as do marketers of tire chains, snow skis, umbrellas, rain gear, and different types of recreational equipment.

Product-related.   Markets can be segmented according to the degree to which individuals use a particular product. Thus, segments could be defined as consisting of heavy users, light users, or nonusers.[20] This particular basis can be quite significant to promotional strategy because the question often arises as to whether it is more profitable to concentrate promotional efforts on those people who are already favorably inclined toward the product or on those who are not presently using it. And sometimes it may be wise to try to change light users to heavy users. Beer is generally promoted to users rather than to nonusers, but the promotional efforts associated with the causes of many nonprofit organizations are aimed at the nonusers. The Council on Physical Fitness is an example of the latter. A major objective here is to encourage inactive people to exercise properly.

Brand loyalty is another product-related basis for segmentation. The concept is similar to usage rate except that it applies to brands rather than products. Some people are extremely brand loyal (heavy users of a particular brand) while others may be somewhat loyal (light users of the brand and susceptible to brand-switching pleas). Still others are nonusers. The latter group may deliberately refuse to buy the brand for some reason. As in usage rate as a basis for segmentation, one strategy would be to increase purchase frequency among brand-loyal people or sustain their loyalty through promotional efforts. A better strategy might be to focus on brand switchers and try to make brand-loyal people out of them. A third option would be to concentrate on nonusers—particularly those who have not deliberately avoided the brand but who simply have not tried it.

Benefit segmentation, or the benefits people seek or perceive in a product, has been considered by some as the basis for true market segments.[21] The rationale is that people use products to derive certain benefits; unless they perceive the benefits they are seeking in a product (or brand) they will not buy it. Furthermore, different people see different benefits in the same product, and therefore purchase it for different reasons. Some people buy a car for its power and ruggedness; some buy the most economical car; and some buy a car to impress other people. In each case, the consumer perceives the benefit he or she is seeking in the car purchased. Of course, people generally seek to derive more than one benefit in most of the products they buy. But there is usually one particular benefit they are seeking, and that establishes the basis for the market segment.

Psychographics.   A more recent approach for solving the difficult problems of effectively segmenting the market builds on the concept of psychographics—the

---

[20]A pioneering article dealing with this concept is Dick Warren Twedt, ``How Important to Marketing Is the `Heavy User'?'' *Journal of Marketing* 28 (January 1964): 71–72.

[21]See Russell I. Haley, ``Benefit Segmentation: A Decision-oriented Research Tool,'' *Journal of Marketing* 32 (July 1968): 31–33.

FIGURE 7–2   An effective use of sex appeal. *Source:* Hanes Hosiery.

study of personality traits of individuals. The rationale underlying the approach, which has been referred to as *life-style segmentation,* is that a better understanding of customers results in more effective communication and marketing efforts.[22] Psychographics deals with the attitudes, feelings, and opinions of people as they are reflected in behavior patterns, and thus adds another dimension to demographics in defining the market target. The research associated with it is "intended to place consumers on psychological — as distinguished from demographic — dimensions."[23] For example, a market segment might not be defined simply as middle-aged office workers, but as *party-going* middle-aged office workers.

Thus, the use of certain products can sometimes be identified with particular behavior patterns, and the market can be segmented accordingly. One study showed that the heavy user of eye makeup was an entirely different kind of person than the heavy user of shortening.[24] The problem with using psychographics, however, is that personality characteristics are sometimes difficult to measure because the relationships that exist among them are not absolute. Some traits such as introversion, extroversion, meekness, assertiveness, gregariousness, and unsociableness may vary with circumstances and over time. The life-styles of people are not necessarily consistently reflected in behavior and are therefore difficult to define. Furthermore, they may change as people make adjustments to a changing environment. But when used in conjunction with other bases for segmentation, psychographics can be useful.

Perplexing Aspects

Market segmentation is perhaps the best approach available for defining market targets, but it is not a panacea. Any person may fit into several different market segments during the week, or even a day, because of situations requiring the use of a different product.[25] The same person who uses a compact car for city driving may use a larger car for highway travel. Even more confusing is the fact that different situations may require the use of different brands of the same generic product. The macho man may buy "Old Rotgut" for his everyday highballs, but when he gives a cocktail party for his boss and influential friends, he buys Wild Turkey. It has been suggested that under such conditions a viable approach to market segmentation is to think in terms of the conditions under which the product will be used.[26]

Selecting the appropriate segmentation variable is a related problem. Because there are so many variables, it is often difficult to know which is most relevant to the purpose. Each situation is unique.

---

[22]See Joseph T. Plummer, "The Concept and Application of Life Style Segmentation," *Journal of Marketing* 38 (Jan. 1974): 33–37.

[23]William D. Wells, "Psychographics: A Critical Review," *Journal of Marketing Research* 12 (May 1975): 196–213.

[24]William D. Wells and Douglas J. Tigert, "Attitudes, Interests, and Opinions," *Journal of Advertising Research* 11 (Aug. 1971): 27–35.

[25]See Norman Goluskin, "Every Man a Walter Mitty," *Sales Management* 115 (7 July 1975): 45–46.

[26]*Ibid.*

In a study based on the significance of each of four segmentation variables — income, social class, age, and family life cycle — it was found that a variable significant in one product/market context may not be significant in another.[27] Thus, income might be used effectively to segment the market for off-brands of soft drinks, but age, social class, or peer pressure may be more appropriately used in connection with nationally known brands.

Market segmentation is also aptly used in retailing. Typically, the majority of shoppers attracted to a particular retail store are a fairly homogeneous group in variables associated with their purchase behavior. Indeed, the most successful retailers attempt to identify the most promising of such groups on the basis of appropriate segmentation variables and gear their operation accordingly. It is significant, however, that segmentation studies for one type of retailer do not necessarily provide information relevant to other types.[28]

The problem of market segmentation is also magnified by the fact that often the customer who purchases the product is not the decision maker. Under these circumstances, the question of who really is the market target for promotional effort becomes confusing. The proper target, of course, is the person who *decides* whether to buy or not to buy — not necessarily the one who actually makes the purchase in the store, or even the one who uses the product. But it is sometimes difficult to know who that person is.

For example, who decides on the brand of coffee to buy — the husband or the wife? A price difference among brands may be the decision criterion by consensus. But if the price of most major brands of coffee is about the same, brand choice is determined on the basis of something else. Suppose a husband says to his wife, "Pick up a package of razor blades when you are in the store"; or the wife says to her husband, "Get me some panty hose when you do the shopping today." In either of these cases, the *customer* (the one who makes the purchase) is probably not the *user* and may or may not be the *decision maker* with respect to brands.

It is not by accident that cereals are usually placed on lower shelves in supermarkets. Nor is it unusual for a parent to find a box of "Poopsie Woopsies" in the grocery cart at the checkout stand. When this happens, the typical scene is that the parent chastises the child for picking up the box but buys it anyhow. So, who was the logical target for promotional effort, the customer (parent) or the child?

OPPORTUNITY FOR EFFECTIVE PROMOTION

Among the numerous problems associated with developing a promotional strategy is that of determining the relative potential for success of a particular product/market effort. Resolving the issue would probably be done concurrently with the

---

[27]Robert D. Hisrich and Michael P. Peters, "Selecting the Superior Segmentation Correlate," *Journal of Marketing* 38 (July 1974): 60–63.

[28]William O. Bearden, Jesse E. Teel, and Richard M. Durand, "Media Usage, Psychographics, and Demographic Dimensions of Retail Shoppers," *Journal of Retailing* 54, no. 1 (Spring 1978): 65–74.

task of segmenting the market. The problem is that all products are not equally promotable, nor are all markets equally persuadable. Certain characteristics of each product and market have a bearing on the possible effectiveness of a promotional strategy. If an analysis of such characteristics indicates futility for the proposed effort, perhaps it should either be abandoned or at least be given relatively less support than other more promising possibilities.

Product Characteristics

The classic codification of conditions associated with a product that increase the probability of success in its promotion was suggested by Neil H. Borden a number of years ago.[29] Despite the passage of time, the "laws" paraphrased below still stand. There is a greater chance for success in advertising a product if:

1. There is a favorable primary demand for the product.
2. The product can be effectively differentiated from competing products.
3. There are hidden qualities in the product (as opposed to those which are external and obvious) that are important to the consumer.
4. There are strong emotional buying motives with respect to the product.
5. There are sufficient funds to support the amount of advertising necessary for effectiveness. (This last condition is obviously not associated with the product, but certainly necessary for success in promoting a product.)

Primary Demand

The demand for the generic product is *primary demand.* If the demand is favorable for the generic product, advertising will be easier and more effective. If there is no existing demand for the product, there certainly is no existing demand for a particular brand of the product; under such conditions a major focus of the promotional effort must be on stimulating primary demand. Such advertising would benefit competitors (present and potential) as well as the firm initiating the effort.

This is not to say that a firm should never engage in primary demand advertising. Sometimes it is necessary, as was the case when microwave ovens first appeared on the market. Any new product whose use would result in a major change in living habits will likely require some degree of primary demand advertising. But emphasis on the generic product tends to dilute the effectiveness of brand advertising.

Differentiation

It would be extremely difficult to advertise a product that could not be differentiated from competing products. What could be said about the product? An extension of this notion is suggested in Borden's third condition.

---

[29]Neil Borden, *The Economic Effects of Advertising* (Homewood, Ill.: Richard D. Irwin, 1942), pp. 424–28. © 1942 by Richard D. Irwin, Inc.

Hidden qualities.   If there are hidden qualities in the product, there is something to talk about in the advertising that is not obvious to the consumer but makes the product different from other brands. Toothpastes, for example, are advertised as having special ingredients to make teeth white or to prevent cavities; soaps have special cleansing agents; and pain relievers are made with special formulas.

Emotional Motives

Finally, a product is more advertisable if there are strong emotional reasons for buying it. This is true partly because emotion plays a large part in the purchase of many products, and partly because it is often easier to appeal to emotion than to rationality.

If the foregoing conditions exist, there is a greater opportunity for effective advertising than if they are not present. The absence of any one or all does not mean the product should not be advertised; it simply means that the chances for success are reduced.

Market Characteristics

In this and earlier chapters, we have discussed factors influencing the market's existence, its characterization, and its delineation if it does exist. However, another characteristic of the market could have a more direct bearing on the effectiveness of a particular promotional strategy. This characteristic is *product acceptance.*

People in a market may vary in the degree to which they have accepted a product. In the market for most products there will be some people who have been using the product for quite some time because they began using it when it was first introduced. Others will be trying it for the first time, and still others will not have considered using it. This principle is illustrated very clearly in Everett Rogers' adopter categories for new products.

Rogers' five categories of adopters were based on the rapidity with which people adopt innovations: Innovators, 2.5 percent of the people; early adopters, 13.5 percent; early majority, 34 percent; late majority, 34 percent; and laggards, 16 percent. Thumbnail descriptions of the people in each category (abstractions from empirical cases) portray innovators as venturesome risk-takers, early adopters as respectable people having opinion leadership, early majority as deliberate in their actions and as followers but seldom leaders, late majority as skeptical and requiring pressure of peers for adoption, and laggards as traditional with no opinion leadership who probably do not adopt the product until after it has been superseded by another.[30]

Rogers' work dealt with the adoption and diffusion of innovations, but it is evident that at any given time after a company has introduced a new product there will be at least two adopter categories of people in the market. The significance of

---

[30]Everett M. Rogers with F. Floyd Shoemaker, *Communication of Innovations, A Cross-Cultural Approach,* 2nd ed. (New York: The Free Press—a division of the Macmillan Company, Copyright © 1971), pp. 176–91. See also James W. Taylor, "A Striking Characteristic of Innovators," *Journal of Marketing Research* 14 (Feb. 1977): 102–6.

the notion is that there may be varying degrees of opportunity for successful promotion, depending somewhat upon the degree to which the product has been accepted. Furthermore, the number of people in each category will have a bearing on the *type* of promotional effort (the appeal, etc.) that will be most productive.

SUMMARY

A product is actually a composite of many things, including the psychological attributes associated with it as well as its physical characteristics. All of these are potentially want satisfying, and are factors used by the consumer in evaluating the product.

Since it is unusual for a specific product to be equally acceptable to everyone, it is usually necessary for promotional strategists to identify specific market targets. Not only does this isolate groups of people whose buying motives are similar but it also provides a common ground that makes communication easier and more effective. There are two ways to accomplish this: product differentiation and market segmentation.

Product differentiation is a policy by means of which the firm hopes to tap a portion of the total range of the market. Market segmentation, on the other hand, entails dividing the total market into smaller segments, each of which is composed of people with similar characteristics with respect to their purchase behavior. Bases useful for segmenting the market can be divided into four groups: personal/social, geographic, product-related, and psychographic. Associated with market segmentation is the problem of positioning the product. This is establishing the product in the market in its proper niche — the way it will likely be perceived relative to competitive products and to other products in the company's line.

Opportunities for successful promotion vary. Certain conditions associated with the product and the market are significant in this regard. A favorable primary demand for the product, distinguishing characteristics, and the possibility of using emotional appeals increase the chances for success, as does the degree to which people in the market have adopted the product.

QUESTIONS FOR THOUGHT AND REVIEW

1. Conceptualize *product* and explain your position. Why is it necessary to think of product in this way?
2. How are product images and brand images formed? Explain how they can be "intertwined." Discuss promotion's role with respect to brand image.
3. Relate product and brand image to product perception.
4. Explain why it is usually desirable to identify a particular market target for promotional purposes.
5. Is India a good market? Greenland? Why? What are the characteristics of a market?

6. Carefully distinguish between *product differentiation* and *market segmentation* as marketing strategies.
7. The text states that market segmentation is a strategy that is consumer oriented. Do you agree? Explain.
8. Of what significance is market segmentation to promotional strategy? Identify some products aimed at specific market segments, and explain how promotion is aided as a result.
9. What is meant by *positioning the product?* How would you describe the position of Scope mouthwash? Curtis Mathes television sets?
10. Why would improper positioning of a product be detrimental to its promotion?
11. What is meant by *segmentation base?* Select five brands of consumer products and identify the segmentation bases you think were used in determining the market segments in which they are promoted. Explain why you think they are appropriate.
12. Do you think elderly adults are different from other adults in the way they perceive and react to promotional messages? Do you think they are really a separate market segment for most products?
13. Explain with examples how people at different stages in the family life cycle compose different market segments.
14. What effect does the increasing level of education in American society have on promotion? Do you think promotion messages only appeal to lesser educated people?
15. What is the significance to promotional strategy of segmenting the market according to the degree to which individuals use a particular product?
16. Explain the rationale for the use of psychographics in segmenting the market.
17. Explain how one person can fit into several different market segments at different times. Give a personal example of this.
18. Give examples of the use of market segmentation in retailing.
19. Explain the dilemma of promotional strategists when the purchaser of the product may not be the decision maker. How can it be resolved?
20. How does the presence of a favorable primary demand increase the chances for success in promotion? Does this mean that a product should not be promoted if there is not a primary demand? Explain.
21. Why do people vary in the rapidity with which they adopt new products? Does this also apply to new ideas? How does this affect promotion?

7

PURCHASE BEHAVIOR AND THE PROMOTION APPEAL

Armed with an understanding of how consumers perceive products, and with a clear delineation of the target market or market segments in mind, the promotion strategist can think in terms of a strategy for reaching that market. As indicated in previous chapters, a knowledge of the environmental factors and forces affecting the behavior of the people at whom promotional efforts are directed is an initial requirement. But in crystallizing a specific strategy, it is also important to know how consumers make their purchase decisions and how they relate promotion messages to the associated products. In this chapter we examine certain aspects of purchase behavior that bear on promotional strategy and the resulting effect on the development of the promotion appeal.

BASIC BEHAVIORAL CONCEPTS

Our concern is limited to a few basic concepts directly related to the development of promotional strategy. A number of theoretical models which purport to show the interrelationship of the many variables associated with buying behavior have been constructed. Among the most well-known models are the Howard-Sheth model, including its revisions,[1] The Nicosia model,[2] and the Engel-Kollat-Blackwell model, which also has been revised several times.[3] The models include certain aspects of consumer behavior that relate to promotional strategy, but they also reflect many complicated concepts beyond the scope of this book.[4] Therefore they are not reproduced here.

However, there are certain basic concepts of particular significance to promotion that we shall explore briefly in the next few sections. Among these are needs, buying motives, and self-concept.

Needs

All of us have needs, some of which are innate (biogenic) and some of which are learned (psychogenic). The needs for food, warmth, and protection from the elements, for example, are innate because they are necessary for the life process. Other needs are acquired through experience and contact with one's culture. The need to be accepted in groups, to attract the opposite sex, to impress one's friends, and to feel satisfaction in what one is doing are examples of psychogenic needs. Such needs differ among different societies and among individuals in a single society.

In an affluent society like the United States, the satisfaction of psychogenic

[1]John A. Howard and Jagdish N. Sheth, *The Theory of Buyer Behavior* (New York: John Wiley and Sons, 1969); John A. Howard and Lyman E. Ostlund, *Buyer Behavior: Theoretical and Empirical Foundations* (New York: Knopf, 1973), pp. 3–32; and John U. Farley, John A. Howard, and L. Winston Ring, *Consumer Behavior Theory and Application* (Boston: Allyn and Bacon, 1974).

[2]Francesco Nicosia, *Consumer Decision Process* (Englewood Cliffs, N.J.: Prentice-Hall, 1966).

[3]James F. Engel, Roger D. Blackwell, and David T. Kollat, *Consumer Behavior,* 3rd ed. (Hinsdale, Ill.: Dryden, 1978).

[4]See also Kenneth E. Runyon, *Consumer Behavior and the Practice of Marketing,* 2nd ed. (Columbus: Charles E. Merrill, 1980).

needs is usually the target of more effort than the satisfaction of biogenic needs. The primary reason for purchasing a particular sweater or pair of shoes, for example, usually is not to keep the body warm or the feet dry; rather, it is to be in fashion, impress one's friends, or simply to look nice. In satisfying such psychogenic needs, the individual is at the same time satisfying the biogenic need to keep warm and dry. The same analysis can be applied to food. Most people in the United States do not just seek *food* when they are hungry. They buy hamburger, or steak, or oysters, or pizza depending on their tastes and/or the social circumstances at the time. And they certainly buy houses for reasons other than just to provide shelter.

A long-standing issue has been the question of whether promotion can create needs. It has been argued that people would not have a need for some products, if the need had not been created through the promotional efforts of the manufacturer. The counterargument is that the need was already there. For example, a person might purchase an electric can opener to gain access to food to satisfy the biogenic need of hunger or to impress friends with more of the trappings of society (a psychogenic need). The role of promotion was simply to show how these existing needs might be satisfied better with an electric can opener than with a pocket knife or a Grecian urn.

Buying Motives

A motive is "a stimulated need which is sufficiently pressing to direct the person toward the goal of satisfying the need."[5] Because motives lie within each person, they cannot be observed; they must be inferred from behavior which can be observed. The problem is that behavior may result from any of several or combinations of motives or from something else entirely.

From the standpoint of promotional strategy, it is safe to assert that a *buying motive* is a reason for buying and that it stems from unsatisfied needs. The unsatisfied needs may be biogenic or psychogenic, or both; but unless the person perceives a need of some kind, there is absolutely no reason to buy. A person may have several reasons for buying a particular product or service, but there is usually one dominant reason. The challenge to the promotion manager is to determine what that reason is with respect to the product for which he or she is responsible. Basing the promotion appeal on the wrong motive would be a serious error.

Although buying motives can be classified in a number of different ways, think of them simply as rational and emotional, primary and selective, and patronage.

Rational and Emotional Motives

In 1924, Copeland suggested that buying motives can be considered either rational or emotional.[6] If the motives for purchasing a particular product or brand are the

---

[5]Philip Kotler, *Principles of Marketing* (Englewood Cliffs, N.J.: Prentice-Hall, 1980), p. 246.
[6]Melvin T. Copeland, *Principles of Merchandising* (New York: A. W. Shaw, 1924), p. 162.

result of logical reasoning and are socially defensible, they are considered *rational motives*. But if they relate to some psychological connotations associated with the product that do not necessarily reflect its intrinsic characteristics, they are *emotional motives*. Thus if a person, after carefully analyzing and comparing alternative choices, buys a particular make of automobile because he or she has concluded that it gets good gas mileage, has low maintenance costs, is favorably priced relative to comparable makes, and can be expected to provide years of dependable service, the motives inducing the purchase are rational. Furthermore, the person would not be the least bit embarrassed to use these reasons in explaining the purchase to anyone who asked why that particular make was selected.

On the other hand, if one purchased a particular make of automobile as a status symbol, or because it seemed to be the best means of conforming to a reference group, or because it appeared to be a good device to attract the opposite sex, the motives inducing the purchase would be considered emotional. Moreover, it is not likely that the person would admit to these reasons because they are difficult to defend from a social point of view. Indeed, because of the social stigma associated with such reasons, most people would rationalize and defend their purchase on the basis of rational motives.

Despite its apparent validity there is a bit of inconsistency in the rational/emotional dichotomy. The antithesis of *rational* is *irrational;* and if a motive is not rational, then it must be irrational. Therefore, emotional motives must be irrational motives, reflecting an absence of reasoning. But this is not always true. One could make a conscious, deliberate effort to find the make of automobile that would do the best job of impressing other people. Comparisons would be made with this in mind, and the reasoning process would be vigorously applied. Such effort would have to be considered rational under the circumstances. Nevertheless, the principle underlying the rational/emotional concept is highly significant in the determination of the promotional appeal.

Primary and Selective Motives

Primary motives induce the purchase of a *generic* product; selective motives are the reasons for the purchase of a particular *brand* of the product. Thus a consumer who has been accustomed to cooking the family meals in a traditional gas or electric oven may decide to purchase a microwave oven. The decision at this point is simply to buy a microwave oven, and little thought has been given to any specific brand. Whether the motive for the purchase was to be able to prepare meals faster or to impress friends and neighbors, it would be a primary motive.

The motive that would induce the consumer to buy a General Electric microwave oven, on the other hand, would be a selective motive. The precise nature of the motive is immaterial; if it was instrumental in the purchase of a specific brand, it is a selective motive.

Manufacturers must often convince consumers of the merits of the generic product before attempting to convince them of the superiority of their brand, particularly with new products. For example, many people had reservations about using microwave ovens because of fears of radiation. Until such fears were overcome, it was futile for a manufacturer to engage exclusively in brand advertising. It was necessary to focus on the generic product and make brand advertising secondary.

Patronage Motives

In addition to motives related to the purchase of products or brands, people have motives underlying their decisions to buy those products or brands at particular stores. These are *patronage motives.*

Determining patronage motives is a useful undertaking, but it is difficult because there are so many reasons people might have for preferring a particular store or kind of store. Such things as price, convenience, variety of merchandise, brand names carried, services offered, friendship, reputation, and store image are examples of patronage motives.

In addition, people are not consistent in their preferences. Some people may prefer to do all their shopping in discount houses; others prefer department stores. Some people mix them up, buying certain kinds of products at discount houses and other products in department stores. Other people buy only at one particular discount house or one particular department store.

Patronage motives may also be affected by the way consumers resolve possible idealogical conflicts with respect to chain stores versus independents, supermarkets versus neighborhood grocers, and department stores versus specialty shops. Finally, store preference may change as consumers reorder their individual rankings of patronage motives. The reasons for preference change sometimes have little to do with the stores themselves.

Self-Concept

Every individual has a self-image or self-concept. The concept each of us develops reflects our interpretations of our capabilities and attributes. Sometimes we are pleased with the concept; sometimes we are not. If we are not pleased, we may engage in a bit of fantasy and establish a concept that we like. Thus we may have two self-concepts — one as we actually see ourselves and the other as we would like to see ourselves. This can be illustrated by the man who sees himself as a meek and timid individual in his social relationships; but alone and behind the wheel of his automobile, he is a wild man.

The development of the self-concept is a complex process; but the significant fact to promotion is that every person has a self-concept, which has a bearing on the perception of products and their purchase and use. Consumer behavior is a part of human behavior, and "The basic purpose of all human activity is the protection, the maintenance, and the enhancement not of the self, but the self-concept, or symbolic self."[7]

---

[7]S. I. Hayakawa, *Symbol, Status, and Personality* (New York: Harcourt, Brace, Jovanovich, 1963), p. 37.

Role Playing

Related to self-concept is the notion of role playing. Each of us plays many different roles throughout the day, the week, the month, and throughout our lifetimes. During the day, for example, you may play the role of a student; in the evening you may play a different role entirely. When you go home on holidays, you may play the role of a son or daughter. Strangely enough, it is quite easy to change from one role to another. The roles of mother or father, wife or husband, athlete, musician, "life of the party," and job-holder are various roles that we may play at various times. We may even play some of these roles vicariously such as when we buy Jack Nicklaus golf clubs to play our duffer games of golf.

The significance of role playing to promotion is that certain products or brands are associated with certain roles that people play (or would like to play). Marlboro cigarettes are associated with the macho man; Estée Lauder cosmetics with female youth; and Greek-lettered windbreakers with members of fraternities and sororities. In short, a good deal of purchase behavior is influenced by the perceptions people have of the various roles they play.

THE PURCHASE DECISION PROCESS

Since the ultimate function (not necessarily the immediate objective) of promotional efforts by a business is to sell a product or service, some notion of the way consumers make their purchase decisions is essential to the development of effective promotional strategy. Persuasive communication requires some understanding of those who are the targets of the effort.

Consumer decision-making is a *process* rather than a single act. The decision to buy or not to buy represents the solution to a problem; the solution comes about only after the individual consumer has gone through a series of steps. Furthermore, the process does not end with the purchase of the product. The consumer consciously or subconsciously judges the product and/or the wisdom of the decision for some time after the purchase is made. Such evaluation is significant because it may affect attitudes and beliefs that have a bearing on future purchases.

Perhaps John Dewey laid the foundation for the concept of decision making as a process when, shortly after the turn of the century, he defined five stages in problem solving.[8] Since that time, others have refined and adapted the stages he conceptualized, but his work is still considered the standard.

For purposes of our discussion, consider the five stages as follows:

1. Problem recognition
2. Search for a satisfactory solution
3. Evaluation of alternative solutions
4. Purchase decision
5. Postpurchase evaluation[9]

---

[8]John Dewey, *How We Think* (Boston: D. C. Heath, 1910), ch. 8.
[9]Runyon, *Consumer Behavior*, p. 347.

Figure 7-1 illustrates these stages together with some conditions that generate problem recognition. All consumers do not spend the same amount of time going through any single stage, or all stages, for the same product; nor does any one consumer spend the same amount of time at any one stage, or all stages, for all products.

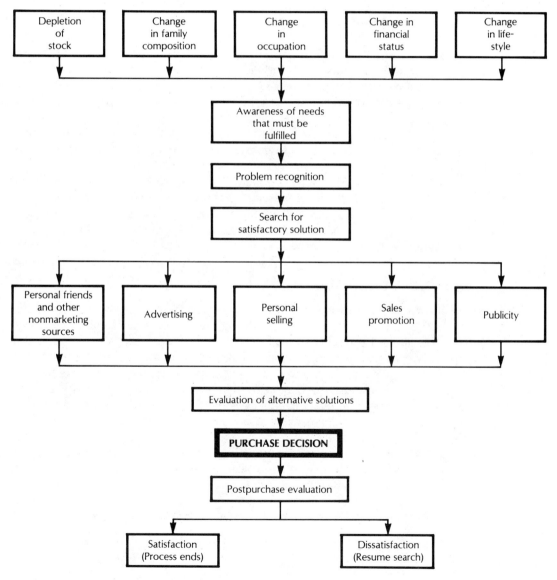

FIGURE 7-1 A diagram of the purchase decision process.

Problem Recognition

Problem recognition occurs when there is "a perceived difference between the ideal state of affairs and the actual situation sufficient to arouse and activate the decision process."[10] As a part of the consumer decision process problem recognition is a complicated process in and of itself.[11] But for our purposes, it is sufficient to consider problem recognition the result of a need the consumer perceives as not being fulfilled, or being inadequately fulfilled. The consumer feels that his or her present situation is not as satisfactory as it might be. If the discrepancy between what is and what might be is great enough, the consumer recognizes a problem; if the problem can be solved by purchasing a product or service, it is of significance to promotion.

Much of a consumer's awareness of unfulfilled needs is brought about by forces and conditions outside of marketing. Running out of coffee or wearing out a pair of shoes, for example, make the consumer aware of needs that must be attended to. A new baby in the family, the departure of the last child, or grandma's moving in to stay generate needs that had not existed before. Even changes in occupation or financial status can produce new and different needs. Promotion's position should usually be that the consumer has already become aware of the need, and the task now is to convince the consumer that the best way of satisfying that need is to purchase "our" product. Of course, promotion can sometimes accelerate the consumer's awareness of a need (either biogenic or psychogenic). Although impulse buying may be partially explained in this way, it is doubtful that promotion created the need. Rather, it simply speeded up the process the consumer goes through in becoming aware of the need.

Search for a Satisfactory Solution

Having recognized a problem that can be solved by purchasing a product, the consumer begins to look for possible solutions. Obviously, the extent of the search varies for different products and different situations. Replacing a depleted can of coffee, for example, may be so routine that the consumer spends little or no time searching for solutions; the brand customarily purchased may immediately provide the answer. But consider the purchase of an automobile, particularly by a family that only buys a new car every five or six years. There may be families who always buy the same model of Buick, or Ford, or Chrysler from the same dealer; but the majority of such consumers will compare products in search of possible solutions to their problems. The amount of time and effort devoted to the search is related to the information the consumer has and is aware of at the outset, the perceived risk associated with the decision, and the consumer's self-confidence in making the decision.[12] The consumer must have enough information about the alternatives to be confident that the decision he or she ultimately makes is the right one. Thus the

---

[10]Engel et al., *Consumer Behavior,* p. 215.

[11]*Ibid.,* ch. 8.

[12]*Ibid.,* p. 239. See also pp. 237–45 for a thorough discussion of this subject.

amount of searching depends in part on the amount of information presently held. Likewise, if the consumer perceives a good deal of risk in connection with the purchase decision the search for information will likely be extensive. Such risks might be financial if the purchase involves a "high-ticket" item, or psychological if it involves either health considerations such as the purchase of over-the-counter drugs or social considerations such as "acceptability" of the product.

Whatever the extent of the search and for whatever reason, the consumer is seeking information that will help solve the problem; that is the cue for promotion. This is not to say that the promotion activities of business firms provide the only source of information. Consumers also look to friends for advice; they pick up ideas from radio and television personalities; they get suggestions from reading articles and stories in newspapers and magazines; and they learn much from their own observations. But certainly among their major sources of information are the four elements of the promotion mix — advertising, personal selling, sales promotion, and publicity.

Advertising

People do read advertisements once they have recognized a problem that may be solved through the purchase of a product.[13] The family that realizes its old refrigerator is no longer efficient, for example, will be very alert to advertising that describes the new models — advertising they would have ignored if they were satisfied with their present unit. Large numbers of grocery shoppers carefully study the food ads that appear in the local newspaper every week.

But unless people have recognized a problem, they are not inclined to even see the ads. It was found that fewer than half the people exposed to thousands of print advertisements included in the Starch readership service notice a particular ad.[14] This is further evidence that it is often futile to attempt to stimulate problem recognition through promotional efforts. Yet it is equally clear that once people have recognized a problem they look to advertising for information that will help them solve it. Moreover, it seems that consumers' attitudes toward specific advertisements greatly influence their purchase intentions and decisions with respect to their choices of brands.[15] The implications of this notion to the advertiser are obvious.

Personal Selling

The importance of personal selling in industrial marketing is generally recognized. Retailers, wholesalers, and purchasing agents in manufacturing firms traditionally

---

[13]See, for example, L. P. Bucklin, "The Information Role of Advertising," *Journal of Advertising Research* 5 (Sept. 1965): 11–15; and George Fisk, "Media Influence Reconsidered," *Public Opinion Quarterly* 23 (1959): 83–91.

[14]Herbert Krugman, "What Makes Advertising Effective?" *Harvard Business Review* 53 (Mar.–Apr. 1975): 96–102.

[15]See Terrence A. Shimp, "Attitude Toward the Ad as a Mediator of Consumer Brand Choice," *Journal of Advertising* 10, no. 2 (1981): 9–15.

rely on information they receive from salespeople to assist them in their decision making. Retail salespeople can be equally helpful with respect to the purchase decisions of ultimate consumers.

Personal selling plays a minor role with product categories identified with self-service retailing, and other sources of information must be used. But in the purchase of such products as automobiles, television sets, major appliances, sporting goods, quality suits and dresses, certain cosmetics, and jewelry, retail salespeople can provide extremely useful information for decision making. Moreover, in the purchase of such intangible products and personal services as insurance, estate planning, corporate securities, dry cleaning, and hair care, salespeople are indispensible for the information they can provide. The key to the quality of the information received in each case, of course, is knowledgeable salespeople who are willing to help.

Sales Promotion

Point-of-purchase materials such as counter cards, displays, shelf stickers, and other items placed near the merchandise often provide the last bit of information the consumer can use in making the purchase decision. Frequently the consumer will have made a tentative decision before exposure to the POP materials; the information obtained at the merchandise location may clinch the decision or sometimes such information changes the previously made decision. Also, with respect to impulse buying and other forms of unplanned purchases (such as menu-planning within the store), POP materials may be the major source of information.

Increasing numbers of consumers use the kind of information now required by law to appear on the package. Nutritional labeling is especially significant in this regard.[16] Giving consumers samples of a product provides first hand information since the consumer actually tests the product personally. The information thus obtained is the result of actual experience.

Publicity

Of the four elements of the promotion mix, publicity is probably the least used for information purposes. The quality of such information is not inferior, but publicity releases are relatively less numerous than other forms of promotion. Releases provide information often considered more credible than information obtained through marketer-controlled sources. A newspaper report of a company's efforts in developing a new product, for example, is useful information for the individual whose needs could be satisfied by that product. A feature story in any news medium that portrays a company's concern with the environment could be the kind of information a consumer is seeking when "social responsibility" is a determining factor in judging the merits of a company and its products.

---

[16]Edward H. Asam and Louis P. Bucklin, "Nutritional Labeling for Canned Goods: A Study of Consumer Response," *Journal of Marketing* 37 (Apr. 1973): 32–37.

Evaluation of Alternative Solutions

When information sufficient to make a decision has been obtained, the various products and brands surveyed must be evaluated in terms of their want-satisfying capabilities. Much of this process takes place concurrently with the search, of course, and the consumer may be eliminating and adding possibilities as product and brand information becomes available. But whether it is done during or after the search is completed, the consumer makes the evaluation on the basis of those product attributes considered essential to the solution of the problem. These attributes may be intrinsic to the product itself, such as its functional characteristics, or they may be psychologically associated with the product, such as prestige. It has been suggested that there are times when as few as one or two attributes may be the determining criteria.[17]

There is a relationship of the evaluation process to buying motives — the consumer judges products in terms of his or her reasons for buying.

Purchase Decision

Making the purchase decision is not always easy, despite the thoroughness with which the product information might have been obtained and evaluated. Not only is it sometimes difficult to rank certain products, particularly if their desirable characteristics are essentially equal, but it can also be hard for the consumer to decide to buy once the choice of products has been made. The decision to buy or not buy may be as difficult as deciding which is the best product.

At this point in the decision process the consumer has weighed the alternatives on the basis of the information obtained and is faced with the problem of making a decision. The decision could be not to buy if the solution to the problem is not urgently required, or it could be to buy. The prudent promotion manager will recognize the possible dilemma of the consumer and attempt to make it easy for the consumer to decide to buy. This can be accomplished most effectively, perhaps, through the sales promotion element of the promotion mix. For example, point-of-purchase materials could include references to product warranties, financing possibilities, service arrangements, and other factors that might provide impetus to the consumer's move to purchase.

Postpurchase Evaluation

The final stage in the consumer decision process is the evaluation of the decision that was made. Sometimes the evaluation is positive and quick; there are no pangs of doubt or dissatisfaction with the purchase. At other times the consumer experiences a good deal of mental agony and questions the wisdom of the decision. The phenomenon is much more complicated than is indicated in this brief discus-

---

[17]Flemming Hansen, ''Psychological Theories of Consumer Choice,'' *Journal of Consumer Research* 3 (Dec. 1976): 133.

sion.[18] For our purposes we can identify two kinds of discontent: that which arises when the consumer believes another brand should have been purchased simply because its attributes now seem more appropriate than those of the brand purchased, and that which is due to actual faulty products.

Who of us has not had the experience of wishing we had bought the other brand or model, or color, or style? It might have been an automobile, a TV set, or a suit of clothes; but in any event we begin to wonder if the decision we made was the right one. How this comes about is beyond the scope of our discussion, but the psychological tension it exemplifies is referred to as *cognitive dissonance*.[19] Among the several methods the consumer has of resolving the doubt is to resume the search for information in an effort to find substantiation for the decision that was made. And that course of action is significant to promotion managers.

When faulty products are discovered in the postpurchase evaluation, the problem is of more concern to marketing or even top management than it is to promotion. There is really no excuse for faulty products; and in today's environment of consumerism and ready critics, people are very conscious of products that fall below their justified expectations.[20] When such a discrepancy exists business must take the obvious corrective measures.

THE PROMOTION APPEAL

The appeal is the basic idea that forms the core of a promotional message. It provides the foundation guideline for constructing the message. It is the source of persuasiveness, if such exists, in the promotional effort. The appeal must be a reflection of the way consumers perceive the product which is a factor in determining the target market, and must be conceived with the purchase decision process in mind.

Choosing the appeal is not as formidable a task as it might seem, if the necessary homework has been done. Much of the discussion so far in this book reflects the kind of analysis needed for the determination of an effective appeal. What is required is a thorough understanding of those who make up the target of the proposed efforts. Persons with a good deal of experience in promotional activity may rely on instinct for ideas, but such instinct is usually the result of numerous experiences with structured formal research.[21] In any event, favorable responses to promotion messages can usually be obtained only if the appeal has been developed with the intended audience in mind.[22] Furthermore, visualizing this audience

[18]See, for example, Engel et al., *Consumer Behavior,* pp. 491–499; and Runyon, *Consumer Behavior,* 2nd ed., pp. 352–54.

[19]Leon Festinger, *A Theory of Cognitive Dissonance* (New York: Harper & Row, 1957).

[20]John O. Summers and Donald H. Granbois, "Predictive and Normative Expectations in Consumer Dissatisfaction and Complaining Behavior," in William D. Perreault, ed., *Advances in Consumer Research,* vol. 4 (Atlanta: Association for Consumer Research, 1977), pp. 155–58.

[21]"Instinct Good Guide: Bloede," *Advertising Age* 44, pt. 2 (June 11, 1973): 81.

[22]W. Feldman, "The Value of Segmented Advertising Appeals: An Exploratory Study," Working Paper, Marketing Science Institute, 1975.

by techniques in the field of psychographics assists in the development of effective communication.[23]

Buying motives, determined by a thorough analysis of the market segment, serve as the point of orientation for establishing the promotion appeal. The buying motive usually suggests the promotion appeal since the intended audience can only be persuaded if it is convinced that the product answers perceived needs. Therefore, it is often convenient to identify promotion appeals in terms of buying motives. Appeals referred to as price, dependability, prestige, or sex, for example, reflect their orientation to their respective buying motives whether the subject of the effort is a product, service, or idea (see figure 7-2). The appeals used in promoting political candidates or social causes, for example, are only effective to the extent that they reflect reasons people might have for "buying" them. The same is true for corporate advertising; the business whose promotion objective is to improve its corporate acceptability should use appeals that reflect reasons for believing it is socially responsible.

A necessary complement to the consideration of buying motives in developing the promotion appeal is an analysis of the characteristics of the product, service, or idea involved. What about the product would satisfy the needs that give rise to the buying motive? It must be remembered that a typical product has both tangible and intangible characteristics, any of which might fulfill the needs of certain people. The promotional strategist must identify those particular product characteristics that relate to the buying motives as determined, whether they are biogenic or psychogenic motives. The appeal can then be developed accordingly. Thus if the reason for buying the product is to impress the opposite sex, sex appeal characteristics of the product would be extolled. If, on the other hand, consumers are looking for durability, those characteristics that indicate this feature should be included in the implementation of the appeal. And so on.

Promotion appeals can be stated in positive or negative terms. Positive appeals emphasize the benefits to be obtained from using the product or accepting the idea; negative appeals warn people of the disadvantages of not doing so. We are urged, for example, to use Camay for a luxurious bath but Dial to avoid offending others — "Don't you wish everyone did?" In any case, the reference is always to the benefits associated with the product. Figure 7-3 (see p. 150) is an example of a humorous use of a negative appeal.

Generally speaking, positive appeals are more effective than negative appeals, but negative appeals are quite effective for some products and product categories. The myriad personal care products — deodorants, mouthwashes, lotions, creams, perfumes, colognes — are often promoted with the focus on the undesirable situation we would be in if we failed to use them. Both kinds of appeals are used in promoting life insurance. If the emphasis is on insurance as as investment for college educations or retirement, the appeal is positive. But playing up disaster that befalls a family without insurance when the breadwinner suddenly dies is a negative appeal and a *fear* appeal. Although the effectiveness of fear

---

[23]Edward Winter and John T. Russell, "Psychographics and Creativity," *Journal of Advertising* 2, no. 1 (1973): 32-35.

appeals has been debated over the years, the fact that it is used successfully in some promotional situations would seem to attest to its usefulness.

SUMMARY

Among the complexities of purchase behavior, certain basic concepts are of particular significance to promotion. These include needs, buying motives, and self-concept.

Everyone has needs. Some of these are innate because they are necessary for the life process; others are learned through experience and social interaction. Most people in an affluent society are able to devote their attention and effort to satisfying the learned (psychogenic) needs and satisfy their innate (biogenic) needs in the process. The primary role of promotion in regard to needs is to show how existing needs can be satisfied best.

Buying motives are reasons for buying. They exist in each person and stem from unfulfilled needs, either biogenic or psychogenic. There are different kinds of motives. Rational motives are the result of logical reasoning and are socially defensible. Emotional motives result in purchases for reasons that may be socially embarrassing. A primary motive induces the purchase of a generic product; a selective motive is the reason for buying a particular *brand* of product. Patronage motives underlie the decisions to buy at particular stores. Self-concept is the interpretation an individual has of his or her capabilities and attributes. Self-concept is significant to promotion because it has a bearing on how products are perceived.

Purchase decision making is a process and not merely a single act. The steps in the process include problem recognition, search for a satisfactory solution, evaluation of alternative solutions, the purchase decision, and postpurchase evaluation.

The promotion appeal is the theme of the message. It is the way the product is interpreted to the intended audience and is based on buying motives. In fact, the appeal is often identified by the buying motives that suggested it.

QUESTIONS FOR THOUGHT AND REVIEW

1. Distinguish between *biogenic needs* and *psychogenic needs*. Give some examples of each.
2. Explain the notion that in an affluent society the focus need not be on the satisfying of biogenic needs, even though such needs must be satisfied for survival.
3. Can promotion create needs? If so, explain how; if not, explain promotion's role with respect to needs.
4. Do you think that people in the developing countries perceive products differently than people in the United States? If so, how would this affect promotion?

5. How do buying motives arise? What is the significance of buying motives to promotion? Explain why a misjudgment of buying motives could lead to ineffective promotional strategy.

6. If a person decides to buy a new electric toaster, is the buying motive primary or selective? What if the decision is to buy a new General Electric toaster? Explain.

7. Are emotional motives irrational? Discuss.

8. Identify some patronage motives you have for buying at certain stores. Under what conditions would you change stores?

9. Explain how an individual can have two self-concepts. How is the self-concept notion related to promotion?

10. Explain how people play different roles and why this is significant to promotion.

11. Why is it usually futile for promotion to attempt to stimulate problem recognition?

12. Discuss fully how each element of the promotion mix — advertising, personal selling, sales promotion, and publicity — can be used as sources of information to the consumer.

13. What is the basis on which consumers evaluate alternative solutions to the problem? Explain.

14. Why is the purchase decision sometimes difficult to make? How can promotion aid the consumer in this regard?

15. What are the two kinds of "discontent" consumers might experience in their postpurchase evaluation? What can promotion do to relieve the consumer of the feeling?

16. Why does the consumer decision process not end with the purchase decision?

17. What is the *promotional appeal?* What is the basis for its determination? How is it related to product benefits?

18. Distinguish between positive and negative appeals. Give some examples of products that are promoted by means of each kind of appeal.

8

PROMOTION OBJECTIVES

Most of us have objectives in life, and the more clearly defined our objectives are, the more directed our behavior is. However, our objectives are often vague, and our behavior is less effective in accomplishing them than it would be if we were more precise in defining them. A college student, for example, whose professed objective is to "get through school" would exhibit much less disciplined behavior than would one who was striving to graduate with a 3.5 grade point average. The more carefully we define our objectives, the more likely we will accomplish them because we can do a better job of directing all relevant aspects of our behavior to that end.

Clearly defined objectives are especially important in organizations. Accomplishment is only possible if all subdivisions of the group or business establish their own objectives in relation to the overall objectives of the organization. If goals are stated in vague terms, the behavior they precipitate can be muddled or counterproductive.

PURPOSES OF OBJECTIVES

Among the many reasons for having objectives, three seem to be particularly significant to organizations: they provide incentive for action; they stimulate coordinated effort; and they facilitate measurement of performance.

Provide Incentive for Action

Having an objective gives us direction as well as enthusiasm. Objectives are really results we expect to achieve. In fact, *results* may be considered to be synonymous with *objectives* but separated by time and cost.[1] (They become results after time and money are spent on their accomplishment.)

Thus, if an objective established for a business is to realize a 15 percent return on investment during the next fiscal year, the expected result is that the firm will earn a 15 percent return. Furthermore, if that objective has been established and communicated to the appropriate personnel and generates enthusiastic acceptance, it will provide incentive for action by those individuals.

Stimulate Coordinated Effort

Since a business, or any other organization is composed of *people,* there will necessarily be a number of individual goals represented in the organization. These personal goals will cause a certain amount of conflict of effort among individuals in the performance of their activities. However, *successful* companies are able to identify objectives to which most individuals in the organization subscribe. There are two possible reasons for this ability: "(1) company goals reflect a consensus of

---

[1]Maurice Mascarenhas, "How to Set Marketing Objectives," *Industrial Marketing* 57, pt. 2 (July 1972): 26-30.

individual goals, or (2) company goals reflect the goals of influential individuals who impose them on noninfluentials.''[2]

In either case or for whatever reasons such objectives can be established, the degree of coordination of effort depends upon the extent to which the objectives are accepted. Acceptance does not just happen. Proper leadership and rapport with subordinates are necessary to achieve coordination of effort toward a goal. In fact, it is the president's duty to first see that objectives are set and accepted and then to provide the necessary resources to reach them.[3]

Facilitate Measurement of Performance

It is impossible to evaluate performance in the absence of objectives. If we do not know where we are supposed to be when we get there, how can we know how much farther we have to go? Thus, one of the major functions of objectives is to provide a benchmark against which we can judge the effectiveness of our actions. If we only realize a 10 percent return on our investment but our objective was 15 percent, we know our performance was not as good as expected. An analagous situation would be a student whose objective was to get an *A* in a course but who only got a *B*. Without the objective, the performance might have been judged satisfactory.

CHARACTERISTICS OF GOOD OBJECTIVES

Objectives are no good unless they are soundly conceived. Poorly conceived objectives often have a more adverse effect on performance than no objectives at all, even to the point of being counterproductive.

Harmony of Objectives

All firms and other organizations have many objectives and many ''layers'' of objectives. At the top, for example, objectives might be established in terms of return on investment, share of market, or growth. In addition to these, each functional area (marketing, production, finance, etc.) will have its objectives. If these functional areas are subdivided in any way, the subdivisions will have objectives.

In view of such a multiplicty of objectives, there must be consistency among them. One way to maximize consistency is to establish subobjectives in such a way that their accomplishment will result in the accomplishment of the overall objectives.[4] A basic condition associated with such a procedure is that the management

---

[2]Jerome B. Kernan, William P. Dommermuth, and Montrose S. Sommers, *Promotion: An Introductory Analysis* (New York: McGraw-Hill, 1970), p. 260.

[3]See Ray Stata, ''In Good Ad Planning, President Outlines Company Objectives,'' *Industrial Marketing* 61, pt. 1 (June 1976): 118, 124.

[4]See Kernan et al., *Promotion*.

in each area for which an objective is established must command the resources necessary to accomplish the objective.[5]

Specific Characteristics

In addition to the underlying requirement of consistency, good objectives have certain specific characteristics.

Stated in Concrete and Measurable Terms

Since one purpose of objectives is to facilitate measurement of performance, they must be stated in such a way as to allow for meaningful measurement and evaluation. This means that such vague statements as ``increase brand awareness'' or ``enlarge our market share'' are unacceptable as objectives. Rather, they should be stated in more specific terms such as ``to increase brand awareness by 20 percent among consumers 18 to 30 years of age in the United States during 198_,'' or ``to increase market share by 10 percent in the first six months of 198_.''

Fair and Reasonable

Objectives should be set high enough to demand the best efforts of the individuals involved, but not so high as to result in discouragement. This characteristic is particularly significant when accomplishment of the objective is dependent upon the efforts of one individual, such as a salesperson. An objective impossible to accomplish does not stimulate incentive but kills it and concomitantly lowers morale. It is not easy to set ideal objectives.

Clearly Stated and Understandable

If a person is expected to work toward the accomplishment of an objective, certainly that individual should understand what is required.

Written

Too many firms fail to write their objectives. Word-of-mouth communication tends to distort the intended message. Moreover, people forget. The only way to make certain that each person affected by the stated objective remembers it correctly is to see that each one has a copy of the objective in writing.

OBJECTIVES IN THE PROMOTION MIX

The promotion mix consists of advertising, personal selling, sales promotion, and publicity. Objectives should be established in each of these areas, and the objectives established for each element of the promotion *mix* should collectively reflect

---

[5] *Ibid.*

the objective established for the promotion *function.* Likewise, the objectives established for the promotion function should, in conjunction with those established for the other elements of the *marketing mix* (product, price, channel, and logistics) reflect the objectives established for the *marketing function,* and so on.

Advertising Objectives

Businesses advertise because management believes that advertising will ultimately increase sales. This belief is generally true. In the long run, effective advertising does act favorably on sales, although it may be, as Ross Garrett suggests, that the effect is to *reduce sales cost.*[6] Nevertheless, an objective expressed in terms of sales may not be logical for advertising.

Advertising versus Marketing Objectives

When sales objectives are established for advertising, they are usually *marketing* objectives. Despite the likely assumption that sales increases occur because of effective advertising, the increases can rarely be attributed *solely* to advertising. The marketing manager responsible for developing the strategy to produce an increase in sales uses every tool in the marketing mix. Such sales increases that may take place may be due to a reduction in price, a change in channels of distribution, a change in the product (or package), or a faster method of delivering the product (logistics) — all in addition to, or instead of, advertising. Thus it would be difficult, if not impossible, to identify any one tool as the only factor producing the sales increase.

If one of the reasons for establishing objectives is to facilitate measurement of performance, how can the effectiveness of advertising be determined if its contribution to the sales increase cannot be isolated? If after an advertising campaign sales did in fact increase by 10 percent, how much of that increase was due to advertising alone? It is simply not possible to know.

Similar reasoning can be applied to the promotion of ideas — or to advertising for nonprofit organizations. Politicians have made extensive use of advertising in recent years in connection with their election campaigns. They advertise to increase the number of voters who support them (analogous to sales for product advertising). But advertising is just one of the tools they use. They also use personal selling (speeches and personal appearances), sales promotion (signs, placards, brochures, business cards), and publicity (published reports on activities, editorials, and other information presented in the media free of charge). Thus, it is not possible to attribute a favorable vote on election day solely to advertising.

Objectives and the Long-term Effects of Advertising

The total effect of an advertising program is not always immediately noticeable. People are not generally persuaded to rush right out to buy a product; this may take several years.

---

[6]Ross Garrett, "What Measure for Media Effectiveness?" *Media Decisions* 11, pt. 2 (Sept. 1976): 190.

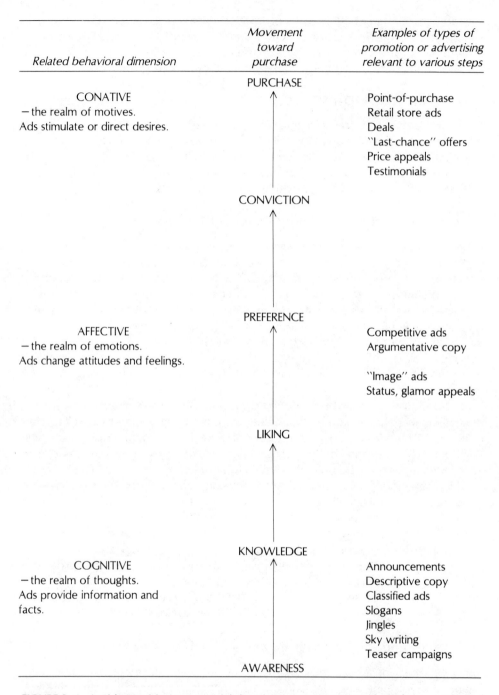

Related behavioral dimension	Movement toward purchase	Examples of types of promotion or advertising relevant to various steps
	PURCHASE	
CONATIVE —the realm of motives. Ads stimulate or direct desires.	↑	Point-of-purchase Retail store ads Deals ''Last-chance'' offers Price appeals Testimonials
	CONVICTION ↑	
AFFECTIVE —the realm of emotions. Ads change attitudes and feelings.	PREFERENCE ↑	Competitive ads Argumentative copy ''Image'' ads Status, glamor appeals
	LIKING ↑	
COGNITIVE —the realm of thoughts. Ads provide information and facts.	KNOWLEDGE ↑	Announcements Descriptive copy Classified ads Slogans Jingles Sky writing Teaser campaigns
	AWARENESS	

FIGURE 8–1 Lavidge and Steiner's model showing movement toward purchase. Adapted from Robert J. Lavidge and Gary A. Steiner, ''A Model For Predictive Measurements of Advertising Effectiveness,'' *Journal of Marketing* (Oct. 1961): 61.

Lavidge and Steiner proposed a number of years ago that people go through a series of steps in arriving at the decision to buy and that advertising can be a force that moves them up these steps.[7] Their model, reproduced in part as figure 8-1, shows this movement together with the appropriate types of advertising for each step.

The implication is that advertising objectives should be related to the steps. If people are unaware of the product, for example, the specific advertising objective should be to make people *aware* and not necessarily to *sell*. The objectives would change, then, as people in a market move up the steps. The final objective may be a sales objective — to "trigger" the sale — since at this point advertising may be somewhat isolated in the marketing mix.

These steps do not constitute an interval scale (they are not equidistant). Furthermore, some consumers may cover two or more steps almost simultaneously, depending upon the nature of the product and their own needs. An additional implication is that it would be logical to consider the money spent on advertising as an investment rather than as an expense. It may take some consumers longer than a year (a typical accounting period) to pass through all the stages, and the results of the advertising may accrue for some time after the end of the campaign. Normally the activities classified as expenses are "consumed" within the accounting period.

Communications Objectives

Advertising objectives should relate to advertising's role in the marketing function. Each subdivision of marketing would be assigned a specific part to play in the total marketing program, and advertising's part should be that of *communication*. Thus, advertising objectives should be stated in communication terms and effectiveness measured in those terms so it is separated from the other variables in the marketing mix.

Russell H. Colley, for example, in *Defining Advertising Goals for Measured Advertising Results* (DAGMAR) suggests that not only should an advertising objective be a specific communications task but also that the audience should be delineated and that time limits be imposed for its accomplishment.[8] Thus, the advertising objective might be to increase by 20 percent during the current campaign year the number of mothers with elementary school children in the Pacific Northwest who know that Brand X toothpaste contains fluoride.

Sales Objectives

The discussion so far suggests that advertising objectives should generally be communications objectives. The rationale is logical when we consider advertising's part

---

[7]Robert J. Lavidge and Gary A. Steiner, "A Model For Predictive Measurements of Advertising Effectiveness," *Journal of Marketing* 25 (Oct. 1961): 59–62.

[8]Russell H. Colley, *Defining Advertising Goals for Measured Advertising Results* (New York: Association of National Advertisers, 1961), p. 6.

in the promotion function and promotion's part in the marketing function. Furthermore, the hierarchy of effects notion embodied in the Lavidge and Steiner model and reflected in the DAGMAR concept suggests the idea. Within this context, the only time an advertising objective should be expressed in terms of sales would be at the last level in the hierarchy of effects — purchase. At each of the other levels (awareness, knowledge, liking, preference, and conviction) the objectives would be expressed in terms of communication because the effort is focused on bringing consumers through the stages preliminary to actual purchase.

As theoretically sound as the concept is, however, many critics argue that it is just as reasonable to state advertising objectives in terms of sales as it is to state them in terms of communication. It is argued, for example, that while advertising may accomplish communication objectives, such accomplishment may have no effect on sales — which is really the ultimate *function* of advertising. Furthermore, implicit in the use of DAGMAR is the assumption that the consumer always passes through the levels of the hierarchy in the order prescribed. But suppose the consumer is ready to purchase immediately? Should the advertising objective then be stated in terms of sales from the very outset of the campaign? To handle such a situation, Aaker and Myers have proposed the use of DAGMAR MOD II,[9] which requires that the hierarchy effects must be adjusted to each situation and not be rigidly applied in every circumstance.

Perhaps there are times when advertising objectives could be stated in terms of sales in a manner consistent with the purposes and characteristics of good objectives including, of course, the facilitation of the measurement of performance. Such times could include those when the consumer's decision to buy is made very quickly — buying an inexpensive item for the immediate satisfaction of needs such as a package of peanuts at a baseball game. Sales objectives could also be appropriate with direct action ads, particularly those involving a coupon which provides an effective device for measuring effectiveness. In most cases involving national advertising, however, communications objectives seem to make the most sense.

Secondary Objectives

An advertising program will likely have several objectives, although one will probably predominate. And accomplishment of the predominant objective usually provides direction for the advertising program with respect to the theme used, the media chosen, and other facets of the program. Thus advertisers attempt to select the media that will result in the least amount of waste circulation in accomplishing the major objective and minimize the number of nonprospects for the product the medium reaches.

In the final analysis, setting advertising objectives is simply crystallizing expec-

---

[9]See David Aaker and John G. Myers, *Advertising Management* (Englewood Cliffs, N.J.: Prentice-Hall, 1975), pp. 99–127.

FIGURE 7–3 A humorous use of a negative appeal. *Source:* Block Drug Co. Poli-Grip Division of Dentco, Inc.

CALIFORNIA WALNUT ATTACKS DENTURE WEARER!

Protect yourself with Super Poli·Grip's occlusive seal.

You wear dentures. You know even tiny nut particles under your denture can feel like boulders. Ouch!

Just one application of Super Poli-Grip® forms an occlusive seal between your gum tissue and your denture...a barrier that helps keep those food particles out while it helps hold your dentures in place for hours.

That's what we mean when we say "Extra Holding Formula." That's the kind of protection you need.

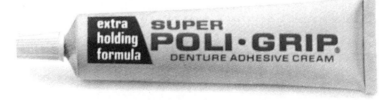

Helps keep food out...dentures in.

"Where's the best fishing in the Gulf of Mexico? Just look for an offshore oil platform."

"If you have any doubts, ask one of the men who run sports fishing boats in the Gulf," says H. E. Braunig, a Manager of Environmental Affairs at Gulf Oil. "When they want to guarantee their customers a good day's fishing, they head straight for the oil platforms.

"Twenty universities and thousands of fish say oil platforms don't hurt the environment."

"What happens around the bottom of the oil platforms is ecologically identical to what happens around any natural reef.

"A food chain starts. Mussels, anemones, starfish, anything that likes to live on a solid underwater surface, all come first. Then the fish that feed on them; and so on, until a whole ecosystem builds up.

"Even with the oil platforms, it's life as usual in the Gulf of Mexico — even for the commercial shrimp and oyster fishermen, whose livelihood depends on clean water.

"That's living proof that offshore platforms aren't ecologically destructive. A two-year study by twenty Gulf Coast universities, concluded in 1974, says the same thing.

"Gulf people are meeting a lot of challenges in getting the oil out while preserving the environment. This problem just seemed to solve itself; and with continual environmental monitoring and sampling, on all current and future offshore sites, we intend to make sure it stays solved."

Gulf

Gulf people: meeting the challenge.

Gulf Oil Corporation

tations into a form that can provide direction for effort and a benchmark for the measurement of effectiveness.[10]

Personal Selling Objectives

Although advertising objectives usually should be communications objectives, the situation is different with respect to personal selling. The interview between salesperson and client is a face-to-face encounter, and the effectiveness of the promotional effort can be identified with sales much more easily than in advertising. However, if a sale results from the interview, it is due largely to the *persuasive communication* of the salesperson. Thus sales, even when established as an objective, may simply be a measure of communication effectiveness.

The foregoing statement notwithstanding, and despite the fact that advertising may have played a part in the purchase decision of the customer, it is entirely logical to state personal selling objectives in terms of sales or sales-related activities. Sales objectives can take several forms, including sales volume in either dollars or units, sales volume less direct expenses, and contribution margin (gross margin less salesperson's direct expenses). Objectives stated in terms of sales-related activities include number of calls made, number of new accounts, and other activities that are not necessarily actual selling.

Sales Volume

The easiest objective to set for personal selling is sales volume or *quota*. There is no inconsistency here because objectives are really results we expect to achieve. For example, objectives (quotas) might be established for each salesperson, the total of which would be the objective for the firm. The process of setting the objectives is complicated. It involves a consideration of salespersons' territories, sales districts and regions, and many other things. In chapter 16 we will discuss the sales management problem of setting quotas.

Sales Volume Less Direct Expenses

The purpose of establishing a sales objective that considers expenses is to strive for some degree of control over the expenses salespeople incur in generating sales. Such expenses include travel, meals, lodging, and entertainment. Greater sales can often be achieved by spending more to get them, but at some point the increasing expenses would nullify any profit. Thus stating the quota in such a way as to recognize the impact of expenses on profit makes the salesperson aware of the need to be careful with expense money.

But there is a danger here. The salespeople must not be so conscious of the

---

[10]See David Corkindale, ``Setting Objectives for Advertising,'' *European Journal of Marketing* 10, no. 3 (1976): 109–26.

FIGURE 12–1 An example of corporate advertising. *Source:* Gulf Oil Corporation.

need to minimize expenses that they unwisely reduce spending. Certain expenses are necessary, and too much budget cutting could reduce sales volume.

Contribution Margin

Contribution margin is equal to the salesperson's gross margin less the expenses over which the salesperson has control.[11] *Gross margin* is essentially the difference between the price the customer pays for the product and the company's cost to produce it. Thus, the difference between the gross margin of the product and the salesperson's expenses in making the sale is the amount that is contributed to the recovery of the overall fixed costs of the firm.

Objectives, or quotas, stated in these terms tend to encourage the salesperson to push the high-margin items. Because the easiest items to sell often carry the lowest margin, objectives stated in terms of sales volume encourage salespeople to ignore those products that earn more money for the company. To emphasize profit instead of units sold, objectives are sometimes stated in terms of contribution margin.

Sales-related Activities

Personal selling objectives are occasionally established for other activities required of salespeople in addition to making sales. An objective may be, for example, for each salesperson in a particular territory to call on a specified number of accounts every day. The rationale for such an objective, of course, is that the more accounts contacted by the salesperson the more sales he or she will make. In addition, such an objective tends to discourage visiting too long with any one buyer.

This kind of objective can have an adverse effect on sales, however. Some buyers enjoy talking with salespeople; and the salesperson's need to hurry through the interview in order to contact the required number of accounts may antagonize those buyers, possibly to the point that they cease to be customers.

Another sales-related objective is calling on a specified number of potential *new* customers to generate new business. Use of this objective depends on the circumstances in the sales territory. For example, if a salesperson is working in a territory where a majority of the potential customers have already been "signed up," a new customer objective would serve no useful purpose.

Other sales-related activities that could be the basis for objectives include such things as increasing order size, increasing the number of service calls, reducing the quantity of merchandise returned, and reducing selling costs — all by specified percentages or amounts.

Sales Promotion Objectives

Sales promotion, the third element in the promotion mix, consists of "those marketing activities other than personal selling, advertising, and publicity that stimulate

---

[11]William J. Stanton and Richard H. Buskirk, *Management of the Sales Force,* 5th ed. (Homewood, Ill.: Richard D. Irwin, 1978), p. 516.

consumer purchasing and dealer effectiveness, such as displays, shows, exhibitions, demonstrations, and various nonrecurrent selling efforts not in the ordinary routine."[12]

Sales promotion efforts are aimed at such diverse groups that it is difficult to generalize objectives. Targets include company employees (particularly salespeople), dealers, and consumers.[13] The role of sales promotion is to provide a direct inducement for response from these targets.[14]

Thus, unlike most advertising, most sales promotion efforts are planned to stimulate *immediate* action. The objective, therefore, can usually be expressed in terms of sales because if action (purchase) does take place in connection with the sales promotion effort it is a measure of communication effectiveness. Although it is rarely possible to *entirely* isolate the effects of the use of one marketing tool from the others, the results of sales promotion activities are the easiest to separate.

When such "nonrecurrent" selling efforts as point-of-purchase materials, contests, premiums, and deals are used to stimulate purchase, the objectives established in connection with their use should be *specific* and *measurable* and usually stated in terms of sales. (Chapters 17 and 18 are devoted to a discussion of sales promotion.)

Publicity Objectives

Objectives for the remaining element in the promotion mix, publicity, should also be stated in communication terms. It is difficult to set objectives logically for publicity since the promotion manager has little control over media use. Because the use of publicity requires the assent of one or more outsiders such as an editor or a reporter, the successful accomplishment of any objective set for publicity is contingent not only upon the reasonableness of the objective but also on the decision of media representatives to publish the material.

Nevertheless, objectives should be set if publicity is to be used. Since a direct relationship between the effects of publicity and sales is difficult to establish, the objectives should be stated in terms of communication, not sales. Publicity can be quite effective in making consumers aware of new products, changes in existing products, and company activities if these things are newsworthy, and a good promotion manager can often persuade the media decision-makers that they are.

THE PROMOTION OBJECTIVE

Although to discuss the promotion mix we must divide it into its elements, it is the *combined effect* of the results from each element of the promotion mix that causes the accomplishment of the objectives established for the promotion *function*.

[12]Committee on Definitions, *Marketing Definitions: A Glossary of Marketing Terms* (Chicago: American Marketing Association, 1960), p. 20.

[13]William G. Nickels, *Marketing Communications and Promotion* (Columbus, Ohio: Grid, 1976), p. 256.

[14]J. F. Luick and W. L. Ziegler, *Sales Promotion and Modern Merchandising* (New York: McGraw-Hill, 1968), p. 4.

Obviously then, objectives should complement one another. Every effort should be made to make certain that the objectives established for any one element of the promotion mix are not only compatible with those set for the other elements but also complement them. Indeed, if the objectives are properly set, the effect will be synergistic — the result will be greater than the sum of the effects of accomplishing each objective individually.

As the maximum efficiency of a system depends upon the effective harmonizing of its parts, the system of marketing is most efficient if all of its parts have specific complementary roles. Each part of the system must carry out its role to reach the system's goal. As one part of marketing, promotion is given its role, and each part of promotion has a specific role and specific objective.

The task of marketing in general is to find out what the consumer wants, develop an appropriate product or service, and see that it reaches as many consumers as possible. Marketing's job is a broad one, but when it is broken down into parts to be accomplished by the subdivisions of marketing the job does get done. Promotion's part in the overall task is communication — making the consumer aware of the existence of the product and informing the consumer of the reasons why it fits his or her needs. The four tools of promotion are utilized for this purpose, and each of them is given a specific part to play in the total process. Objectives are then established.

SUMMARY

The only way any organization can accomplish its purposes is to establish objectives in order to direct behavior. Sound objectives provide incentive for action, stimulate coordinated effort, and facilitate measurement of performance.

Objectives should be established for each element of the promotion mix. Advertising objectives should be stated in communications terms since it is difficult to measure the direct effect of advertising upon sales. Too many variables are associated with generating sales; when a sales objective is stated for advertising it is usually a misplaced marketing objective.

Personal selling objectives are usually stated in terms of sales or sales-related activities because any sales resulting from the use of this tool can be attributed more directly to the salesperson than to other promotion activities.

Sales promotion objectives are usually sales objectives since immediate sales are normally the desired result and sales provide a measure of the communication effectiveness of the devices.

Publicity is difficult to control, but objectives should be established nevertheless. Since it is difficult to relate sales to publicity efforts, the objectives should be communications objectives, dealing with making consumers aware of the existence of new products, changes in existing products, and newsworthy activities.

The objectives established for each element of the promotion mix should collectively reflect the objectives established for the promotion *function*.

QUESTIONS FOR THOUGHT AND REVIEW

1. Do you have objectives in life? How would your behavior patterns differ if you had no objectives?

2. It was stated in the text that *results* may be considered as synonymous with *objectives* but separated by time and cost. Explain what this means. Can you think of a situation in which that would not be true?

3. With so many people in an organization striving toward their own individual goals, how can organizations establish objectives common to all? What if established objectives are not accepted by all individuals?

4. Why are objectives necessary to evaluate performance?

5. Discuss the specific characteristics of good objectives. Why are these characteristics considered essential?

6. The president of a business stated that the firm's advertising objective for the coming year was "to increase sales by 20 percent." Comment and discuss.

7. Explain the DAGMAR concept.

8. Explain the concept of advertising as a force that moves people through a series of steps in arriving at a decision to buy.

9. How do advertising objectives change in response to the movement suggested in question 8?

10. Might an organization ever have any secondary objectives in connection with a particular promotion program? Explain.

11. Why can personal selling objectives be expressed in terms of sales? Is this still a measure of communication effectiveness? Explain.

12. Why would a firm establish a personal selling objective on the basis of sales volume less direct expenses? Do you think such an objective would be effective for its purpose? What is the danger of using such an objective?

13. What is *contribution margin?* How is it used as a basis for setting personal selling objectives? Why?

14. Discuss the reasons for using sales-related activities as the basis for setting objectives.

15. What is *sales promotion?* Why can objectives in sales promotion be expressed in terms of sales?

16. Publicity objectives are usually expressed in terms of communication. Why?

17. Explain the idea that objectives established for each of the promotion tools must complement each other.

PART FOUR

ORGANIZATION AND FINANCE

The promotion function cannot be carried out effectively unless two important aspects of a general administrative nature are properly considered. The company must be organized in a way that fosters the implementation of an effective promotion program, and the program must be adequately financed.

To properly conceptualize the promotion function, therefore, it is necessary to devote some attention to these two aspects despite the fact that they are not in the controllable realm of the promotion manager. Organization is covered in chapter 9, and problems of financing the promotion task are discussed in chapter 10.

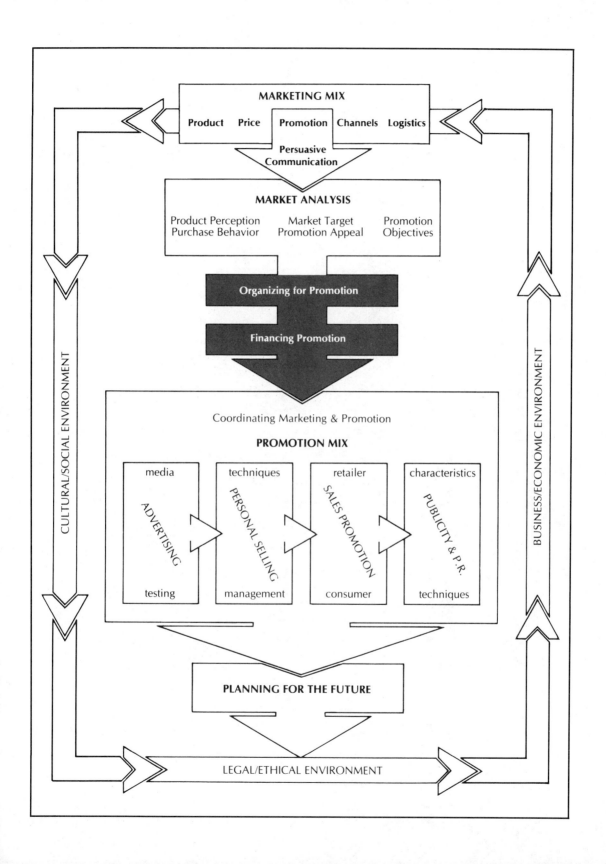

ORGANIZING FOR PROMOTION

In chapter 1 the marketing function was conceptualized as a *system* whose <u>effectiveness is dependent upon the coordination of its components</u>. It was further established that promotion is a system requiring the coordination of its components, that promotion is a subsystem of marketing, and that the entire marketing system is a subsystem of the total business firm — which is, itself, a system.

The key factor in the success of any system is *organization*. It is the purpose in this chapter to discuss organization and its relationship to effective implementation of promotional strategy.

BASIC CONCEPTS

An organization has been defined as ``a social system deliberately constructed to coordinate the activities of people seeking common goals.''[1] Thus, organizations exist wherever there are groups of people with common goals.

The definition of *system* reflects General Systems Theory, which is also the basis for our conceptualization of promotion and marketing as systems in previous chapters. The essence of a system, it will be recalled, is that the whole is composed of a number of parts and that for the whole to work effectively each part must relate properly with the other parts. So it is with organizations.[2]

The idea of coordination was formally recognized in marketing thought with the development of the ``marketing concept.'' Under this concept the focus of managerial activity shifted from the product to the consumer and concern was expressed for profitable sales volume and not just sales volume alone. Also the need for coordinating all marketing activities was established.[3]

Authority, Responsibility, and Accountability

Fundamental to the success of any organization is the proper delineation of authority, responsibility, and accountability. Authority is a right, responsibility is an obligation, and accountability is the need to answer to someone for one's actions.[4]

Authority

In any organization there must be someone in authority. Decisions must be made and orders given for their accomplishment; otherwise chaos would prevail and the very purpose of the organization would be defeated. The degree of authority that any individual has varies among organizations and among different levels in any

---

[1]Robert Albanese, *Managing: Toward Accountability for Performance* (Homewood, Ill.: Richard D. Irwin, 1978), 448–49.

[2]For a discussion of General Systems Theory applied to organizations, see Fremont E. Kast and James E. Rosenweig, ``General Systems Theory: Applications for Organization and Management,'' *Academy of Management Review* 15, no. 4 (Dec. 1972).

[3]See Arthur P. Felton, ``Making the Marketing Concept Work,'' *Harvard Business Review* 37, no. 4 (*July-Aug. 1959*): 55.

[4]See Gerald H. Graham, *Management. The Individual, the Organization, the Process* (Belmont, Calif.: Wadsworth, 1975), p. 115.

organization. But whatever the situation there must be no misunderstanding regarding the nature of the authority.

The natural reaction of one to whom an order is issued is to accept, reject, or question the issuer's authority — the right to give the order. If the authority is accepted, there is no problem. However, rejection indicates dissension, and the firm is in trouble. Questioning the authority generally occurs when the lines of authority are not clearly drawn and there is misunderstanding as to the legitimacy of the order.

The issue often arises when the *source* of the authority is suspect. Over the years, suggested sources of authority have ranged from the Divine at one end of the spectrum to the subordinates of the order-giver at the other end.[5] We shall simply postulate that the authority of executives exists by virtue of the positions they hold and their own expertise.

Responsibility

Responsibility has both contractual and ethical dimensions. Obviously, those who have the right to do something in connection with the functioning of the organization have the responsibility to judiciously exercise that right. If they are given the right to manage a particular function, they are responsible for its success; it would be unfair to make a person responsible for the success of an activity unless the person also had the required degree of authority to see that it is done.

From an ethical point of view, however, each individual in the organization should feel a responsibility for contributing to its *total* success. This means that each individual should not only assume the "contractual responsibility" associated with his or her job, but should also recognize the impact of job-related decisions on other aspects of the organization or on the organization as a whole. There are no isolated decisions in business for a decision in any one function area affects and is affected by decisions in other areas.

Accountability

It has probably always been true that everyone is accountable to someone for his or her actions. But the concept of accountability has become increasingly significant in recent years. Not only is one accountable for on-the-job performance but also for peripheral relationships with affected publics.

For example, in contemporary thinking business is accountable in a general way to society for *all* its actions. Business must be alert to the effect of its actions on such areas of common social concern as the environment, education, poverty, health, and even morality. More specifically, business is accountable to stockholders, employees, and customers as three of the publics affected by its actions. Since the activity of business is only possible through the efforts of *people,* to say that

---

[5]For discussions of sources of authority see Albanese, *Managing,* pp. 471–74; David C. Limerick, "Authority Relations in Different Organizational Systems," *Academy of Management Review* 1, no. 4 (Oct. 1976): 57.

"business is accountable" is to say that "the people in business are accountable." Thus the *individuals* in a business firm must be held accountable for their actions.

Increasing emphasis on accountability prevails with people in all organizations. This is particularly true for those whose operations affect the public in any way, such as charitable groups, civic clubs, and the myriad of government bureaus and agencies.

Centralized versus Decentralized Authority

All firms are decentralized to some extent for such is the very purpose of organization. Authority and responsibility must be distributed in such a way as to maximize the effectiveness of the organization in the pursuit of its goals. No one person can manage an organization single-handedly if the size of the organization is of any consequence at all. But the degree of decentralization depends upon the needs of the organization and the philosophy of those who structure it.

Decentralization requires delegation of authority to make decisions. And some delegation is essential in virtually all organizations. In fact, as Albanese suggests, "decision-making authority should be delegated to the lowest organizational level having the required competence and knowledge and consistent with organizational needs for coordination and control."[6]

This is easier said than done. Many executives find it extremely difficult to relinquish any authority for fear it will diminish their status in the firm. More charitable is the idea that some executives sincerely believe that lower level personnel simply are not capable of making the decisions that, realistically, they should make. Given the required degree of competence, however, routine operational decisions are generally more appropriately made by those immediately responsible for the outcomes than by higher level executives whose positions separate them from the action.

It should be understood, of course, that delegation of authority does not relieve the executive of accountability for the actions of those to whom the delegation is made. But it does relieve the executive of the necessity of devoting time to a consideration of problems that could be handled effectively by someone else. More time is thus made available for dealing with major problems that are unquestionably those of the executive alone.

Line and Staff Authority

The terms *line* and *staff* describe the kinds of authority associated with certain positions in an organization and exercised by those occupying those positions.

Line authority refers to the right of an executive to demand accountability from those persons under his or her supervision. If there are several levels in the organizational hierarchy, line authority flows down from the chief executive to the first subordinate and then through each successive subordinate, as indicated in figure 9–1.

---

[6]Albanese, *Managing*, p. 544.

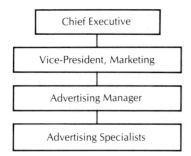

FIGURE 9-1 The flow of line authority.

Staff authority, on the other hand, does not demand accountability. Rather, it describes an *advisory* relationship between executives. The Vice-President, Research and Development, for example, may make suggestions to the Vice-President, Marketing, or the Vice-President, Finance, or to other executives. This relationship is shown by the dotted lines in figure 9-2.

The notion of *authority* in the staff concept exists in the sense that those executives to whom the suggestions are made are expected to consider the advice very carefully, although compliance is not mandatory.

Executives in departments having staff authority vis-à-vis other departments may also have *line* authority with respect to subordinates in their own departments. Furthermore, staff authority as depicted by the dotted lines in figure 9-2 can exist in a similar manner at succeeding levels in the hierarchy of the organization or between levels.

Coordination

In the light of General Systems Theory referred to earlier, each component of the goal-oriented organization must work harmoniously with all other components for maximum effectiveness. There must be coordination.

Most of us tend to be ''empire builders'' to some degree, and our behavior in organizations is subject to that tendency. For an organization to be most effective, it must be organized to minimize conflict and self-aggrandizement and to maximize the coordination of effort.

ORGANIZATION STRUCTURES

The purpose of a formal organization structure is to identify and label the divisions or units and the relationships among them for the most effective operation of the

FIGURE 9-2 Staff authority.

organization. In almost all formal organizations there eventually exists within the designed structure an informal organization, which is not necessarily detrimental to the proper functioning of the intended arrangement. Although the formal arrangement is based on such things as functions, products, territories, and activities, it can only be implemented by *people;* and people develop effective relationships on their own that may not always coincide with those indicated in the formal structure. It is both foolish and futile to discourage informal organization.

Types of Structures

We shall orient our discussion around a brief consideration of four basic forms of structure: functional, geographic, product, and matrix. Not only do these forms represent the kinds of organization structures most common today but they also reflect the evolutionary changes taking place in structure. Between 1949 and 1969, for example, the percentage of the *Fortune* 500 companies having a functional structure declined from approximately 63 percent to 11 percent, while the product-manager form increased from about 20 percent to 76 percent during the same period.[7] In another study it was found that 85 percent of the package-goods companies surveyed used product managers.[8] In recent years there has been a trend toward adoption of the matrix form.[9]

We shall focus on the place of promotion in each structural form and shall include in the discussion other areas of the organization only to show their relationships to promotion.

Functional

The functional type of organization structure reflects an arrangement based on the nature of the activities that must be performed. Related activities are grouped together in the functional areas with which they are most clearly identified. The chief executive of each area occupies a position on the second level of the organization and generally has the title Vice-President. The subdivisions of the area report to that person. Figure 9–3 illustrates one version of a simplified functional organization structure; all functional areas are not shown or subdivided.

The functional structure allows for coordination of related activities, thereby reducing the risk of empire building by specialized areas and resulting in greater efficiency. The structure's most distinguishing feature is that staff managers may have line (functional) authority for their particular activities. For example, the advertising manager may want the field sales force to explain a forthcoming advertising campaign to the retailers on whom they call. In an organization characterized by strict adherence to line and staff authority the advertising manager could only *ask* the sales people to perform that duty. But in a functional structure the request

---

[7]Robert W. Ackerman, "How Companies Respond to Social Demands," *Harvard Business Review* 51 (July-Aug. 1973): 88–98.

[8]Association of National Advertisers, *Current Advertising Management Practices* (New York: Association of National Advertisers, 1974), p. 4.

[9]"How to Stop the Buck Short of the Top," *Business Week* (16 Jan. 1978): 82–83.

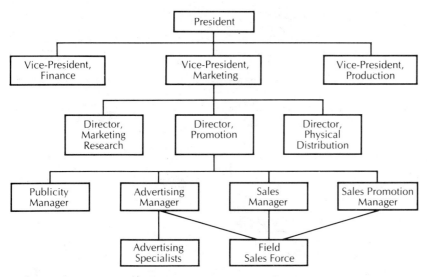

FIGURE 9-3 A simplified functional organization structure.

could be an *order.* Similarly, the sales promotion manager may want the sales force to check on some promotional displays in the retail stores on which they call. The sales promotion manager with line authority could order this done.

A disadvantage of the structure is that unless caution is observed in delineating line authority, some personnel may be subject to the orders of too many bosses. Thus contradictory directives could be given.

Figure 9-3 is just one example of a functional organization structure. The position Director, Promotion, is often absent from organizational charts. It was included here to call attention to the fact that promotion is a *total* function consisting of the four elements of the promotion mix as conceptualized in chapter 1 and into which the function is subdivided in figure 9-3. The inclusion is theoretically sound, yet it adds an additional level in the hierarchy. The four subdivisions of promotion may be more commonly found immediately under Vice-President, Marketing, on the level occupied by Director, Promotion, in the figure.

An organization's structure should be consistent with its own unique requirements and resources. As Hurwood and Bailey suggest, there are many common organizational arrangements. Advertising can be a subfunction of marketing, some other functional department, or even a separate function reporting directly to general management. Similarly, sales promotion can be handled in any number of ways.[10] The same is true for the specialized areas.

Geographic

The geographic organization structure is particularly useful in connection with the personal selling part of the promotion function. Decentralization of authority is

---

[10]David L. Hurwood and Earl L. Bailey, ''Organizing the Company's Promotion Function,'' *The Conference Board* 5, no. 2 (Feb. 1968): 36–43.

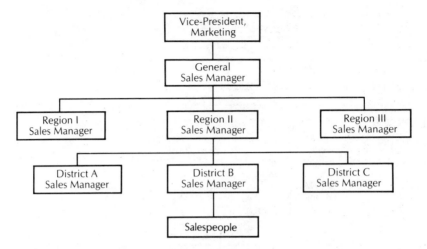

FIGURE 9-4   A geographic organization structure (personal selling function).

virtually mandatory in managing salespeople, although it can be adapted to the entire organization if circumstances suggest such an arrangement. Figure 9–4 illustrates a geographic organization of the personal selling function.

Figure 9–4 shows the entire market of a company divided into three regions; each region has a sales manager who reports to the general sales manager. Each region is divided into districts as indicated for Region II, and each district has a sales manager whose immediate superior is the regional manager. The salespeople in each district are directly responsible to their respective district sales managers.

A geographical structure reflects decentralization and pushes authority and responsibility close to the scene of action. Such an arrangement provides for better relationships with customers in handling their problems and adjusting complaints.

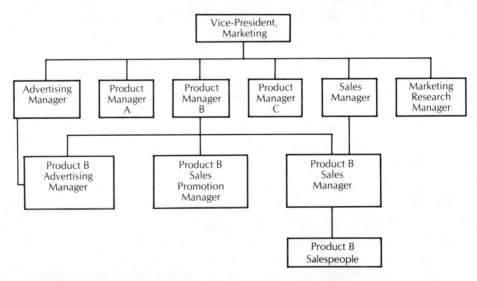

FIGURE 9-5   Simplified product-manager structure.

Product (Brand)

Among the major firms that shifted from the functional organization structure to the product- (or brand-) manager structure are Procter and Gamble, PepsiCo, Eastman Kodak, Levi Strauss, Lever Brothers, and H. J. Heinz Company.[11]

The same principles apply to the product-manager system and to the brand manager system. The essence of the product-manager organizational structure is that the effort associated with the marketing of a particular product or group of products is coordinated and made the responsibility of a product manager. This form of organization is suggested when a multiproduct firm becomes so large as to result in excessive dilution of management expertise with respect to the expanded number of products in the firm's offerings.[12]

Despite the popularity of the product-manager system, there have been many problems associated with its use.[13] Some firms such as PepsiCo, Eastman Kodak, and Levi Strauss have abandoned it after using it for a number of years.[14] It is argued, for example, that many product managers have had very little advertising experience and therefore have only a halfhearted interest in that function. Moreover, it is said that many lack the creativity and risk-taking characteristics considered necessary for complete marketing success.[15] As a result, the system has undergone numerous changes over the years, and it is not possible to illustrate a universally accepted structure. Figure 9-5, however, represents the ideas embodied in the system.

Figure 9-5 incorporates some elements of a functional structure into the product-manager system (all functions are not shown). For example, the advertising manager, who occupies a position on the same level as the product managers and who coordinates all the company's advertising, has line (functional) authority over the advertising manager for Product B. Similarly, the sales manager has line authority over the Product B sales manager. The same structure and relationships would prevail for Products A and C.

An alternative arrangement is to eliminate the specialization under the product managers and have, for example, the corporate advertising manager and sales manager *directly* responsible for their respective activities in all product categories. Such a structure would solve the built-in problem exemplified in figure 9-5 of two bosses — the advertising manager or sales manager and the product manager —

---

[11]Albanese, *Managing,* p. 524.

[12]See Victor P. Buell, "The Changing Role of The Product Manager in Consumer Goods Companies," *Journal of Marketing* 39 (July 1975): 3–11.

[13]See Stephens W. Kietz, "The Product Manager System is in Trouble," *Advertising Age* (2 June 1969): 43–44; David J. Luck and Theodore Nowak, "Product Management — Vison Unfulfilled," *Harvard Business Review* 43, no. 3 (May–June 1965): 143–44; and Victor P. Buell, *Changing Practices in Advertising Decision-Making and Control* (New York: Association of National Advertisers, 1973).

[14]Peter S. Howsam and G. David Hughes, "Problems with Brand Management? Consider Product Strategist System," *Marketing News* 14, no. 26 (June 26, 1981): Section 2, 1–2; see also "The Brand Manager: No Longer King," *Business Week* (9 June 1973): 58–66.

[15]See Merle Kingman, "Product Manager: Adman's Friend or Foe?" *Advertising Age* (August 17, 1981): 43–44.

over the comparable areas in each product division. But it would also reduce the responsibility of the product manager and somewhat defeat the purpose of the system.

This reduction of responsibility may not be as bad as it seems. Indeed, the concept of product manager as "little president" with total responsibility and accountability for profits is being abandoned. Buell reports that the executives interviewed in his study agreed that most product managers lack the ability to make creative decisions in advertising, although they should be involved in planning and coordination.[16] Undoubtedly, changes will continue to be made in the product-manager system as efforts to improve its efficiency are implemented.

Matrix

A form of organization structure that combines some aspects of both the functional and the product-manager types is the matrix structure. This form, adopted by such firms as General Electric, Equitable Life Insurance, TRW Systems, Citicorp, Dow Corning, and Shell Oil, reflects the notion that sometimes there should be equal influence by different lines of authority over the same resources.[17]

Companies using some variation of the matrix structure generally have a product or project manager, who coordinates all the activity necessary for the successful completion of a particular endeavor. In fact, the matrix form is particularly useful in connection with specific project contracts.[18]

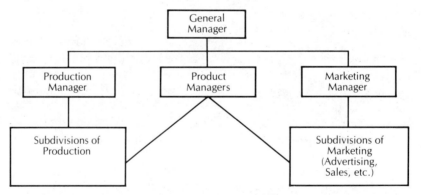

FIGURE 9-6 A simplified matrix organizational structure.

The unique feature of the matrix structure is that the personnel in the company's functional divisions report to two or more superiors on the same level. Thus, complete line authority (perhaps "negotiated") may exist horizontally as well as vertically as indicated in figure 9–6.

The personnel in the functional areas of marketing and production are under the authority of two bosses — the heads of their respective areas and a product

[16]Victor P. Buell, *Changing Practices.*

[17]See "How to Stop," 82-83.

[18]John F. Mee, "Matrix Organization," *Business Horizons* 7, no. 2 (Summer 1964): 71.

manager. Thus the product manager must negotiate with the marketing and production managers for the services of the personnel in those divisions. Such a system creates problems not found in the more traditional organization structures, but the advantages of increased flexibility and a meld of specialization and coordination are considered by many to be compensating factors.[19] Furthermore, when the system is properly implemented, conflicts are resolved before they get to the top.

Guidelines for Structuring an Organization

The structure of any organization should be a dynamic thing, adaptable to changing circumstances. This is true regardless of the structural form prevailing at any one time — whether it is some variation of those discussed in this chapter or something else. As far as promotion is concerned, the important thing is that its inclusion in the structure reflects its significance in the organization as a key factor in the marketing function and vital to the success of the company.

In addition, the structure should be organized and the assignments of authority and responsibility made on the basis of activities and positions, not people. Spans of control should be carefully considered, and the total structure should reflect coordination among its various divisions.[20]

Although circumstances peculiar to any specific organization will determine the type of structure best suited for the accomplishment of its goals, the guidelines indicated should be observed in building or modifying that structure.

ADVERTISING AGENCIES

The advertising agency is so significant to the promotion function for many organizations that it is sometimes shown as a kind of staff function to the advertising department on organization charts.[21]

Whether or not it is that important to all organizations, an agency is used by virtually all major advertisers; its role as an industry is vital in a free enterprise economy such as we have in the United States.

Historical Development

The advertising agency as an institution is over one hundred years old, but its method of operation has changed considerably over the years. The forerunner of the modern agency was the *newspaper agent* who simply sold space for newspapers in the mid-1800s. Apparently it was a promising field because competition developed among the agents to the point that they became *space wholesalers,*

---

[19]See "How Ebasco Makes the Matrix Method Work," *Business Week* (June 15, 1981): 126–31; and "Trust: The New Ingredient in Management," *Business Week* (July 6, 1981): 104–5.

[20]See Thomas F. Stroh, *Managing The Sales Functions* (New York: McGraw-Hill, 1978), pp. 113–14; and William J. Stanton and Richard H. Buskirk, *Management of the Sales Force,* 5th ed. (Homewood, Ill.: Richard D. Irwin, 1978), pp. 54–59.

[21]See, for example, Buell, *Changing Practices.*

buying space in large quantities from publishers and reselling it to advertisers in smaller lots.[22]

But it was in 1876 that the modern agency really got its start when N. W. Ayer & Son agency began to contract with advertisers for all the space they would use, thus discouraging the practice of brokering space. The result was to stabilize prices at the publishers' established rates. As time went on and competition among agencies became more severe, agencies began to offer their client advertisers more of the services now considered standard.[23]

But the Curtis Publishing Company set the stage for the development of the full-service agency of today. In 1901 Curtis conceived its *agency recognition policy,* designed to eliminate the prevailing practice of rebating a part of the commissions received from publishers to the advertisers. That practice had evolved as a result of the competition of the space brokers for clients. Under the new policy Curtis refused to deal with agencies who were rebating commissions to their clients; they recognized as agencies only those who would quote Curtis' established price to advertisers for space in their publications. Furthermore, Curtis would not grant commissions to advertisers attempting to bypass the agencies and deal directly with the publisher, but would only pay commissions to "recognized agencies."[24]

The agency recognition system was further advanced under the leadership of the American Association of Advertising Agencies (Four A's), founded in 1917. One of the early purposes of that organization was to discourage certain developing business practices considered to be detrimental to the advertising industry. Anyone could be an advertising agency, and the commissions paid by the media (newspapers and magazines) to the agencies for the contracted space could be arbitrarily set. Moreover, many agencies rebated or split the commissions they received with their advertiser clients. Some advertisers insisted on receiving the commissions themselves when they did not use an agency. These kinds of activities had an adverse effect on the "traditional" agencies.[25]

Such problems were eliminated, however, under the "recognition system" started by Curtis and strengthened by the Four A's. Not only was the practice of rebating or splitting commissions discouraged but the commission was fixed at 15 percent. Furthermore, an agency had to meet certain requirements to be a recognized agency, and only recognized agencies received commissions from the media. If the aspiring organization qualified, then, its name was added to the list of recognized agencies distributed to all association members. Media managers could then immediately identify an unrecognized agency by checking the list.[26]

The impact of the policy was that advertisers could gain nothing by avoiding the use of recognized agencies, and their only viable course of action was to choose the agency that provided the most efficient service. The result was that

---

[22]See Albert W. Frey and Kenneth R. Davis, *The Advertising Industry* (New York: Association of National Advertisers, 1958), pp. 207–8.

[23]See John S. Wright, Daniel S. Warner, Willis L. Winter, Jr., and Sherilyn K. Zeigler, *Advertising,* 4th ed. (New York: McGraw-Hill, 1977), pp. 159–61.

[24]*Ibid.*

[25]See Donald R. Holland, "The Great Tradeoff," *Advertising Age* (July 6, 1981): 41–42.

[26]*Ibid.*

competition among agencies was necessarily focused on the number and quality of services they offered. The performance of all agencies was thus improved, ultimately leading to the development of the full-service agency.

But in 1955 the Anti-Trust division of the U.S. Department of Justice filed a civil action against the Four A's and certain associations of publishers involved with the recognition system, charging that the system was in violation of the Sherman Anti-Trust Act. The suit was never brought to trial, but in 1956 the defendants signed consent decrees resulting in the virtual elimination of the recognition system. Today the policy is implemented by the media individually, with much less severity than before.

Organizational Structure

Most large agencies in the United States today are full-service agencies, which developed as a result of the process just described. Full-service agencies are capable of providing their clients with professional advice and service relative to the client's total advertising program. They have the necessary personnel and expertise to handle all the planning, research, creation, execution, placement, coordination, and other related activities essential to the success of the client's advertising program. The two basic forms of structure are group and department.

Group Form

In the group form of organization a senior account executive (in charge of the account) and perhaps one or more junior account executives, together with copywriters, artists, media buyers, and other specialists are assigned specifically to one large account or to several small accounts. The big advantage in this form of organization is that the specialists, working only with a particular account or accounts, become quite knowledgeable about the problems of their clients. Presumably, they can do a better job for them than if they were also working on other agency accounts from time to time. Figure 9–7 illustrates the basic idea of the group form.

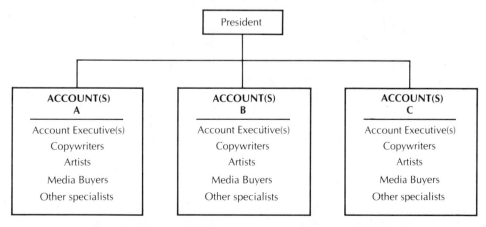

FIGURE 9–7   The group form of agency organization.

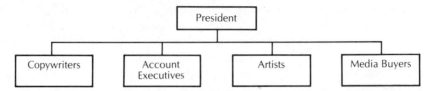

FIGURE 9–8 The department form of agency organization.

The group organization form is generally used only by the larger agencies since it is a rather expensive use of personnel. Workloads may be uneven throughout the year, and shifting of personnel to compensate is not consistent with the organization form.[27]

Department Form

Instead of grouping their personnel according to their assigned accounts, agencies using the department form organize by groups of specialists. All the copywriters are in one department, all the artists in another, and so on. Individuals in these departments are assigned to accounts as needed. Thus they are potentially available for work on all accounts. Figure 9–8 illustrates the basic idea of the department form of organization.

The specialists in the department form do not become as familiar with the problems of the clients as they do under the group form, which may be a disadvantage. But the form does provide for a more economical use of the specialists' time because personnel can be shifted wherever needed. The department form is thus more appropriate than the group form for smaller agencies.[28]

Agency Compensation

For many years one of the most controversial issues with respect to advertising agencies has been the method by which they are paid for their services. There are two basic methods: the commission method and the fee method.[29]

Commission Method

The commission method is the traditional one. The agency receives a commission (historically set in the United States at 15 percent) based on the cost of media space or time. For example, a client authorizes the agency to place a full-page advertisement in a magazine for which the cost of the space is $60,000. After the advertisement has appeared, the magazine bills the agency for the $60,000 less a discount of 15 percent ($9,000). The agency is obliged to pay the magazine $51,000.

[27] Richard E. Stanley, *Promotion: Advertising, Publicity, Personal Selling, Sales Promotion,* 2nd ed. (Englewood Cliffs, N.J.: Prentice-Hall, 1982), p. 129.

[28] *Ibid.,* p. 131.

[29] For a comprehensive discussion of agency compensation, see Herb Zeltner, "Sounding Board: Clients, Admen Split on Compensation," *Advertising Age* (May 18, 1981): 63–76.

The agency, then, bills the client for the list price of space, or $60,000, retaining the $9,000 as payment for its services to the advertiser-client.

There are some additional factors associated with the system, such as the fact that the media generally allow a 2 percent cash discount for prompt payment by the agency; this is usually passed on to the client. Furthermore, special costs incurred by the agency beyond the standard ones arising from such routine activities as designing and preparing the advertisements are charged to the client. But the basic payment is the commission allowed the agency by the media.

There are several arguments against the commission method, beginning with the philosophical question of the logic whereby the *media* seemingly pay the agency for services the agency performs for the *advertiser.* The best explanation seems to be that the system is rooted in the origin of the advertising agency as a seller of space for the media.[30]

But there are at least two additional arguments made against the system: it either underpays or overpays the agency for its services, and it discourages the use of noncommissionable media.

It would seem fairly obvious that remuneration based on the cost of the space or time has little bearing on the work required to design and produce the advertisement. Consider, for instance, the example mentioned earlier where the cost of space in a particular magazine was $60,000 and the agency's commission for its services to the client using the space was $9,000. Suppose that instead of wanting to use that particular magazine the client wanted the same kind of advertisement placed in a magazine whose cost of space for a full page was $10,000. In the latter case, the agency would receive $1,500 (15 percent of $10,000) for the same work it would have done had the advertisement been placed in the first magazine and the commission $9,000. Certainly there is no logic here.

The system also discourages the use of certain media that might be the most logically recommended under certain circumstances. What agency, for example, would recommend the use of direct-mail advertising for which there is no way to determine a commission? The use of noncommissionable media is not likely to be suggested by agencies being paid by the commission method.

Fee Method

Because of these and other reasons, there has been a movement in recent years toward the use of the fee method. Under this system the agency does not receive a commission based on the cost of the space or time; rather, it is paid a fee for the work it does for the client. The fee is based on the costs incurred by the agency plus a fair markup and is negotiated with the client. Media commissions — the agency's compensation under the commission method — are returned to the client.[31]

It is hard to break from tradition, however, and the rapidity of the change in compensation methods is difficult to predict. But change is taking place. For exam-

---

[30]See Sid Bernstein, "Commissions: End of the line?" *Advertising Age* (March 28, 1983): 16.

[31]See Stephens Dietz and Rodney Erikson, "How Agencies Should Get Paid: Trend Is to 'Managed' Systems," *Advertising Age* 48, pt. 1 (17 Jan. 1977): 41–42.

ple, in 1976, 83 percent of advertisers used the commission system. This figure declined to 75 percent in 1978, and to 71 percent in 1983.[32]

The fee system does seem to make sense. In view of the developments discussed in the next section, the fee method is the only method of agency compensation that can be used logically. Although the cause and effect relationship between the fee method and the developments indicated is not clear, there is a relationship.

Departures from the Full-Service Agency

The full-service agency would seem to represent fruition in the evolution of advertising agencies. But very few things are static, and the evolutionary process continues. As firms become more dependent upon advertising agencies for the services, the liaison between the two becomes more difficult to maintain. It is not easy to engage experts in their fields to do a job and still retain some degree of control over their actions. Since they are experts, understandably they resist being told how to do their jobs. On the other hand, the advertising manager is justifiably concerned that the company's *total* promotional plans be harmonized; sometimes the account executives of the advertising agency are not fully cognizant of the whole picture.

For this reason and others, some advertisers are avoiding the use of full-service agencies.[33] They have found there may be better ways of accomplishing their purposes. Some advertisers are doing more of their own work in their own advertising departments and "shopping" for what they feel they cannot do effectively themselves. Others have established in-house agencies — agencies whose only clients are the advertisers who established them. These in-house agencies perform all the creative work and media services normally associated with the full-service agency. But since they are owned by the advertiser, they are under the advertiser's direct supervision. There is no need for a liaison person between advertiser and agency. A major purpose in establishing an in-house agency, of course, is to reduce the cost of advertising; the in-house agency receives the media commissions. It is argued by some, however, that this advantage is overshadowed by the loss of the outside, objective viewpoint provided by a full-service agency. Nevertheless, in-house agencies are becoming more prevalent among large advertisers.

The increasing tendency of advertisers to seek specialized areas of assistance in lieu of the total package of services provided by the full-service agencies has led to the development of institutions providing limited service. For example, there are "creative boutiques" (which only perform the creative function), media-buying services, and consulting firms; each of these agency types does the one thing it does best. Obviously, the commission method of compensation does not lend itself to the contractual arrangements necessary for these services.

The full-service agencies have found it necessary to consider making adjust-

---

[32]"Clients Continue Shifting from 15%," *Advertising Age* (April 25, 1983): 3, 73.
[33]See, for example, M. E. Ziegenhagen, "Advertisers Continue Trend from Full Service Agencies," *Advertising Age* (26 Dec. 1977): 32–33.

ments to their traditional modes of operation. Some are offering their services a la carte, whereby the advertiser can pick and choose the services needed and pay a commensurate fee. Others are establishing subsidiaries within their own organizations to handle such special activities as media buying, research, and new product development.[34] And it has been suggested that there is a declining need for the ''account executive'' — the traditional person in charge of an advertiser client's account with a full-service agency. Clients now tend to deal directly with the media or the creative personnel.[35]

Although the full-service agency is certainly not finished, it must be prepared to change to meet the changing demands of the clients it expects to serve.

SUMMARY

Effective management of the promotion function requires an organization structure designed for that purpose. In designing such a structure, certain basic concepts relative to organization theory must be observed. These include the fundamental notion of *system* applied to organizations; the proper delineation of authority, responsibility, and accountability; the pros and cons of centralization versus decentralization; the effective division between line and staff authority; and the coordination of all elements of the structure.

The purpose of a formal organization structure is to provide meaning and understanding to the interrelationships within the organization. There are at least four basic types of structures: functional, geographic, product, and matrix. Each type of structure should reflect a recognition of the significance of promotion to the overall success of the organization.

The advertising agency is sometimes considered an arm of the organization's advertising department. Whether or not it is considered in that light, it is an important adjunct to an organization's promotional team. A full-service agency is usually organized into groups or departments. In the group form, specific agency specialists are ''permanently'' assigned to specific accounts, and they work only with those accounts. In the department form all personnel in one specialty compose a department; thus there is a department for every group of specialists. Personnel in these departments are potentially available for service on all the agency accounts.

The two basic methods of paying agencies are commission and fee. Under the commission method the agency receives 15 percent of the cost of media space or time. Under the fee system fees are negotiated between agency and client. The commission method appears to be losing ground to the fee method because of the allegedly greater logic of the fee method.

In recent years the full-service agency has experienced competition from limited-service institutions, each of which may offer only one service in a specialized area. The full-service agency, however, is adapting to the changing conditions.

---

[34]See Dietz and Erikson, ''How Agencies Should Get Paid.''

[35]Alvin Eicoff, ''The 'Death' of Account Execs,'' *Advertising Age* (October 19, 1981): 68.

QUESTIONS FOR THOUGHT AND REVIEW

1. Define an *organization* and relate your definition to the promotion function.
2. What is *authority?* Does it exist automatically? Under what conditions will one accept authority?
3. Discuss the ethics of responsibility. What is the relationship of responsibility to authority?
4. Explain how a business is accountable to its various publics.
5. Describe a situation that would call for (a) centralization of authority, (b) decentralization of authority.
6. How is decentralization related to delegation of authority? Why is it sometimes difficult to delegate authority?
7. Distinguish between *line authority* and *staff authority*. Given the concept *authority,* is it inconsistent to say "staff authority?" Explain.
8. What is the purpose of a formal organization structure? What is informal organization? Should it be discouraged? Why or why not?
9. How can a geographic structure be utilized in conjunction with a functional structure? When is it particularly useful?
10. Explain the concept of the *product* or *brand* manager. What is the rationale for structuring an organization around a product manager?
11. What is the unique feature of the *matrix structure?* What are its advantages and disadvantages?
12. It is suggested that in structuring an organization activities should be considered, not the individual people currently employed. Why?
13. How did advertising agencies get their start? What major change with respect to the identity of their "clients" has occurred?
14. Explain *agency recognition.* How did it improve the performance of agencies? How did the Justice Department change the conditions for agency recognition? What was the basis for its ruling on the issue?
15. Discuss the advantages and disadvantages of the group and department organization in large agencies.
16. Explain the *commision method of* compensating advertising agencies. What are the arguments against it?
17. Explain the *fee method of* compensating advertising agencies. How does it overcome some of the disadvantages of the commission method?
18. Discuss the reasons why limited-service agencies have developed.
19. What changes do you foresee in the advertising agencies of the future?

10

FINANCING THE PROMOTION TASK

No one ever knows precisely how much money should be spent for promotion. It is quite likely that those people responsible for *submitting* requests for funds will feel the amount approved is insufficient. It is equally likely that those people in charge of *approving* requests for funds will feel the amount requested is too much. There is usually agreement only to the extent that *some* money should be spent on promotion.

It is the purpose in this chapter to examine the problem and to discuss some of the methods used for determining the amount of the promotion appropriation and other related ideas.

GENERAL CONSIDERATIONS

Promotion, especially advertising, is both glamorized and criticized. It is held in awe and is considered a blotch on society. But in any event, "a moment of truth comes to advertising at least once a year when the budget is drawn up."[1]

As with everything else, requests for promotion funds necessarily reflect the erosion of the dollar due to inflation. Media costs have continually risen the last few years, and advertising budgets have had to be increased accordingly to maintain even a constant impact.[2] The cost of using television as an advertising medium has been particularly noticeable in this regard. This is not to say, however, that television costs are out of proportion to the costs of using other media. Its value to advertising must still be at least equal to its cost since there certainly has been no abandonment of it as an advertising medium.[3]

Two important terms related to funding of promotion are *appropriation* and *budget*. The promotion appropriation is the total amount of money approved for financing the function. The promotion budget is the distribution of the appropriated funds to the elements of the promotion mix — advertising, personal selling, sales promotion, and publicity.

Similarly, the advertising appropriation is the total amount of money allocated to that element of the promotion mix, and the advertising budget is the proposed distribution of those monies to the appropriate facets of advertising (such as salaries, space and time costs, testing, and research) relative to the requirements for advertising different products and brands in different territories and market segments. Likewise, there are sales promotion, personal selling, and publicity appropriations and budgets.

Thus the theoretically sound approach in arriving at a request figure is to establish the amount needed to perform the *total promotion function*. The amount of money approved should then be distributed appropriately to the individual elements of the promotion mix. If the approach orientation is, instead, individual ele-

---

[1] "The Advertising Budget: Moment of Truth," *Sales Management* 93, pt. 1 (3 July 1964): 86–92.

[2] See, for example, "Media Costs Will Rise 11.1% in 1978," *Media Decisions* 12, pt. 2 (Aug. 1977): 57–59, 102.

[3] See "David McCall: He Feels TV's Value Outweighs Its Increased Costs," *Broadcasting* 93, pt. 2 (Oct. 17, 1977): 81.

ments, one impressive project for any one of the elements of the promotion mix could use up all the funds leaving little or nothing for the other promotion tools. The overall promotion budget should reflect the relative strengths of each individual component of the promotion mix with respect to its purpose.[4] No single element of the promotion mix should receive a disproportionate amount of funds.

Despite the soundness of the foregoing approach, most organizations do not think in terms of a promotion budget. Rather, they simply have a budget for each component of the mix — advertising, sales, sales promotion, publicity, etc.[5]

Advertising as an Investment

The question of whether advertising expenditures should be considered an expense or an investment could have a bearing on the size of the appropriation management might approve. If corporate executives viewed the money spent for advertising as an investment, they might support a larger request for funds than if they considered it an expense.

To consider advertising an investment is not unrealistic. Because the effect of all advertising is cumulative to some degree, the expenditures made for it are in the nature of investments.[6] An investment is associated with the future, and an expense relates to the present. If the benefits resulting from a cash outlay today are not immediate but come in the future, the outlay is an investment rather than an expense.[7] Thus when advertising is considered an expense, the supposition is that the results from the expenditures of money on advertising for any one fiscal year will cease at the end of that year. And that hardly seems logical.

To be sure, the cumulative effect and future benefits of advertising expenditures is not the same for all products. A study reported in 1976, for example, showed that there was no "lagged effect" of advertising for the following products: bakery products, cutlery and hand tools, dairy products, newspapers, books, jewelry, watches, wines, women's apparel, beer and malt liquors, costume jewelry, drugs, and tobacco. Expensing advertising for such products is therefore logical. On the other hand, the study showed some lagged effect associated with canned and frozen foods, meat products, distilled liquors, household appliances, photographic equipment, radio/television, cosmetics, and soft drinks. Capitalizing advertising expenditures for these products, therefore, may be justified.[8]

The problem with considering advertising expenditures as an investment is that the future benefits are difficult, if not impossible, to measure. If they are not measurable, accounting for the expenditures that produced them would be awk-

---

[4]See Marion Harper, Jr., "The Marketing Communications Budget," *Printers' Ink* 267 (26 June 1959): 86–94.

[5]William G. Nickels, *Marketing Communications and Promotion* (Columbus, Ohio: Grid, 1976), p. 354.

[6]Joel Dean, *Managerial Economics* (Englewood Cliffs, N.J.: Prentice-Hall, 1951), p. 355.

[7]Joel Dean, "Does Advertising Belong in the Capital Budget?" *Journal of Marketing* 30 (Oct. 1966): 15–21.

[8]Stanley R. Stansell and Ronald P. Wilder, "Lagged Effects of Annual Advertising Budgets," *Journal of Advertising Research* 16, no. 5 (Oct. 1976): 35–40. Reprinted from the *Journal of Advertising Research* © Copyright 1976, by The Advertising Research Foundation.

ward and imprecise. Treating advertising expenditures as a capital investment may never be accepted until it is possible to measure the carry-over effect.[9]

Nevertheless, it makes sense philosophically to think of the money spent for advertising as an investment, even though it is treated as an expense. People who submit requests for funds should emphasize this to those who must approve the requests.

Expenditures made for publicity and personal selling can be considered in the same light within the same constraints. In fact, sales promotion (whose objective is to generate *immediate* response) is the only element of the promotion mix for which at least some of the expenditures made could not be considered an investment. Who knows, for example, when the information presented in a publicity release will produce a reaction? Since publicity releases are newsworthy items about a firm or its products or personnel, their basic purpose is to create or magnify favorable attitudes; sometimes it takes the cumulative effect of repeated exposures to the ideas presented to achieve success.

With respect to personal selling, it is often necessary for a salesperson to call on a prospect several times before actually making the sale. This is especially the case when a salesperson is assigned to a new territory formerly covered by a salesperson who was disliked. The selling costs incurred during the ''dry'' period are thus an investment in future sales. But actually, of course, such costs are considered expenses.

Marginal Analysis and the Appropriation

The theoretically ideal approach to setting the appropriation is marginal analysis — equating marginal revenue with marginal cost. As far back as 1951, Joel Dean suggested that advertising expenditures should be increased to the point where the cost of getting more business just equals the profits resulting from the additional business thereby generated.[10]

There can be no argument conceptually with using marginal analysis. But the problem is that in order to use it, it is necessary to know the advertising/sales ratio. It is necessary to know how many sales are due to advertising, or what the exact effect of advertising is on sales. Such data are only obtainable if the effects of advertising can be isolated from those of the use of other marketing tools. Who can say, for example, that an increase in sales was due to advertising and not to our price or that of our competitors? Perhaps sales increased because we reduced our price or because our competitors raised theirs. Or perhaps we changed our product or the size of the package. Maybe we changed channels of distribution by selling our product through discount houses instead of or in addition to department stores. There may be many reasons why sales increased, and to attribute the increase solely to advertising may be giving advertising credit for something for which it was not entirely responsible.

Using marginal analysis is difficult for another reason: it fails to recognize the

---

[9]See ''Long-term Benefits of Advertising,'' *The Accountant* 178 (Apr. 13, 1978): 492. See also Nariman K. Dhalla, ''Assessing the Long-term Value of Advertising,'' *Harvard Business Review* 56 (Jan. 1978): 82–95.

[10]Dean, *Managerial Economics*, p. 357.

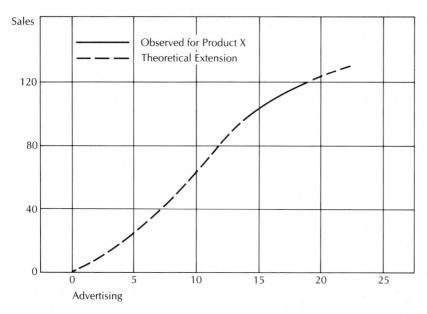

FIGURE 10-1 Generalized relationship of advertising to sales for product X. *Source: Reprinted by permission of the Harvard Business Review. The exhibit from "A rationale for advertising expenditures" by Sidney J. Hollander, Jr. (Jan.-Feb. 1949). Copyright © 1949 by the President and Fellows of Harvard College; all rights reserved.*

cumulative effect of past advertising on future sales.[11] There is a cumulative effect of advertising from one year to the next, and it is extremely difficult to determine the marginal effect of increasing "units" of advertising.

The foregoing constraints notwithstanding, efforts continue to be made to find ways of using the concept of marginal analysis. One suggested approach involves the use of a sales-response model developed from historical data combined with controlled experiments with various facets of advertising after making necessary adjustments for uncontrollable factors.[12]

But it is difficult to determine the precise effect of advertising on sales, although the shape of the response curve might be generalized. The return per dollar spent for advertising would probably be plotted as an S-shaped curve for nearly all products. That is, as advertising is increased, sales would increase to a point where the increase in sales would begin to diminish and finally level off completely.

A study made a number of years ago suggested such a curve.[13] Product X was a nationally advertised proprietary drug product sold through wholesalers without the use of missionary salespeople. The generalized response curve is shown in figure 10-1.

---

[11]*Ibid.*

[12]See Nariman K. Dhalla, "How to Set Advertising Budgets," *Journal of Advertising Research* 17, no. 5 (Oct. 1977): 11-17.

[13]Sidney J. Hollander, Jr., "A Rationale for Advertising Expenditures," *Harvard Business Review* 27 (Jan. 1949): 79-87.

The solid portion of the curve reflects the empirical observations made in the study (consistent with the constraints established in the research design), and the dotted portion of the curve represents its theoretical extension.

Obviously one cannot arbitrarily apply the results of this study to all products. But the shape of the curve would probably be common to all products, except for an adjustment made for products that would show some sales without any advertising.

Classifying Promotion Expenses

Since the promotion budget really consists of at least four separate budgets (advertising, sales, sales promotion, and publicity), the various expenses associated with promotion must be identified with their appropriate areas. Some expenses fall neatly into place and are very easily categorized. For example, media costs are quite obviously a part of the advertising budget. Likewise, the salaries of salespeople are sales expenses; the costs associated with in-store demonstrations are sales promotion expenses; and the costs incurred in generating newsworthy items for publicity purposes should be in the publicity budget. But there are some promotional expenses that are not so easily classified.[14] Are advertising aids for salespeople advertising costs or sales costs? Should point-of-purchase promotional material be charged to sales promotion or to advertising?

Although there would never be a consensus on classifying charges, some kind of agreement should be reached so each promotion budget gets its fair share of the total promotion appropriation. Even more serious than honest disagreement is the deliberate charging of inappropriate expenses to a particular budget. A common complaint of advertising managers, for example, is that various kinds of sales expenses are often erroneously charged to advertising.[15] A sales representative may offer a customer a special promotional allowance and charge it to advertising, although it should be considered a sales expense.

An important part of the problem associated with appropriation and budgets is getting approval for the requested funds. This in itself can be a major promotion task since someone must be convinced of the merits of the request. One approach is to use the technique employed by many people in asking for money — ask for more than you think you will get. The amount finally approved, then, might approximate what you actually expected.

A variation of this technique is to prepare two budgets — one reflecting the sum really needed for an effective program as viewed by the advertising manager and the other totalling a lesser amount. If the first budget is not approved, the second one is ready for submission. Having two budgets ready for submission could expedite the budget approval process.[16]

---

[14]See "Is Your Ad Budget up to Date?" *Printers' Ink* 273, no. 11 (Dec. 16, 1960): 27.

[15]Ovid Riso, "Ad Managers Must Protect Ad Budgets Against Marauders from Sales Side," *Industrial Marketing* 60, pt. 2 (Sept. 1975): 72.

[16]See Lawrence W. Mahar, "Set Ad Budget Priorities by Sorting out 'Visible' vs. 'Invisible' Elements," *Industrial Marketing* 60, pt. 1 (June 1975): 70–72.

SPECIFIC CONSIDERATIONS

With the foregoing general considerations in mind, we are in a position to approach more specifically the problem of determining the promotion budget.

Key Factors Affecting Budget Size

Several specific factors are significant to the problem of budgeting. Among these factors are objectives, the nature of the product, the nature of the market, and the channels of distribution.

Objectives

One of the purposes in establishing objectives is to provide direction for behavior, and the greater the objective, the greater the amount of effort required to accomplish it. This relationship applies to the expenditure of funds as well as to other facets of goal-oriented behavior. One method of determining the size of the budget is based almost entirely on the objective.

In organizations that do not have promotion objectives or that have only vague objectives, the significance of the objective to the size of the budget is less obvious and often overlooked entirely. But it should be considered. Clearly, the objective of making 30 percent of a carefully defined audience in a precisely delineated area aware of a product would require more funds than an objective set at 10 percent. Similarly, if a sales objective were established for the sales force, a larger sales volume objective would require more salespeople and therefore a greater expenditure of funds than would a more modest sales objective.

Thus, regardless of the method used to determine the budget figure, it would seem desirable to relate it to the established objectives before it is finalized.

Nature of the Product

Different kinds of products require different amounts of promotion. Convenience goods — those purchased at the most convenient location and without search — must generally be advertised vigorously. Consumers are often quite fickle with respect to brand preferences for these items and can often be persuaded by active advertisers to try their brands. Thus a manufacturer of convenience goods who minimizes promotional effort is quite likely to experience a declining sales volume. Moreover, a retailer handling these products is not inclined to help a particular manufacturer promote them. The retailer really does not care which brand sells.

At the other extreme is the manufacturer of specialty goods — those goods consumers make a special effort to find. Brand loyalty for these products is much more pronounced than for convenience goods. Thus the manufacturer who has created such brand loyalty has a smaller promotion problem than does the manufacturer of convenience goods. In addition, retailers who handle these products and whose survival depends upon the sale of a particular manufacturer's brand will help promote them.

New products, whether they are convenience, specialty, or "in-between" shopping goods, usually require more promotion than established products. As pointed out in chapter 8, people go through a series of steps in arriving at the decision to buy or accept an idea, and the first two steps are awareness and knowledge. Obviously, people must be aware of a product before they buy it. But this is an important point to keep in mind when promoting a new product, particularly when considered in the light of communication theory. It usually requires considerable promotional effort to generate mass awareness of a new product and to effectively transmit sufficient information about it to induce a favorable reaction.

Nature of the Market

The required intensity of the promotion effort is also related to certain characteristics of the market. If a firm is promoting in an established market where consumer attitudes toward the product are favorable, less promotional effort may be necessary than if the attitudes were negative. The latter situation could exist if a firm were attempting to gain a foothold in a market dominated by a strong competitor.

Often promotion strategists must decide whether to promote to the nonusers of the product or to the users. If they choose the latter, they must decide whether to promote to heavy, medium, or light users. Heavy users likely have favorable attitudes toward the product, and the strength of such attitudes probably decreases progressively among medium and light users and perhaps becomes negative among nonusers.

Channels of Distribution

The size of the budget can also be affected by the channel of distribution used in getting the product to the consumer. The channel includes all flows related to the goods (physical, title, negotiations, etc.) from producer to consumer. It is composed of various institutions of which middlemen are the most significant. A relatively long channel might include wholesalers, retailers, and some type of agent middlemen. The manufacturer who uses a long channel must usually promote more vigorously than one who uses only retailers in the channel. The more institutions in the channel, the less likelihood any of them will supplement the manufacturer's promotional efforts. To do so would help their competitors as much as it would help themselves, and thus the promotional burden is entirely on the manufacturer. Manufacturers of convenience goods usually find themselves in this position because in order to have their products conveniently available to all consumers they must have their products in every possible retail outlet. Their policy must be one of intensive distribution, and this requires the use of wholesalers and other middlemen in the channel to reach the myriad of retailers necessary.

But the manufacturer who follows a policy of exclusive distribution carefully selects a minimum number of strategically located retailers to handle the product. These retailers are given the exclusive privilege of handling the manufacturer's brand in their assigned areas, and the manufacturer can usually reach these retailers without the use of other middlemen in the channel since there are relatively fewer of them. Specialty goods and some shopping goods are often sold in this manner.

Therefore, the promotional problems of the manufacturer who follows a policy of exclusive distribution may be less severe than the problems of the one who follows a policy of intensive distribution. Retailers handling exclusive brands will likely promote the manufacturer's brand themselves since their efforts would not be helping their competitors; in addition, they want to retain the exclusive right to sell the brand. They know the manufacturer could easily change retailers if their performance were unsatisfactory.

Methods of Determining the Budget

The budget period is usually 12 months, although some advertisers believe that a shorter period would be more logical to keep marketing and promotion plans current.[17]

Regardless of the length of the budget period, several methods can be used independently or in some combination for determining the budget figure. Among these are arbitrary determination; percent of sales, either past or future; competitive parity; objective and task; payout planning; and various mathematical models and quantitative methods.

Ideally one should think in terms of determining the total promotion budget figure (appropriation) and then allocate it to the various elements of the promotion mix. The methods used in determining the appropriation, therefore, would be directed to this purpose. In reality, however, most firms think in terms of individual budgets identified specifically with each element of the mix. Thus the methods used can be aimed specifically and separately at the determination of the budget for each element.

Arbitrary Determination

Some companies determine the amount of money to use for promotion budgets in a seemingly arbitrary manner. However, many firms using this method contend that their method reflects the intuitive knowledge coming from budget-making experience and the impracticality of more sophisticated methods.[18]

The budget-setters in many firms have had a good deal of experience in dealing with the problem. Such experience is extremely valuable, regardless of the method used in determining the appropriation figure. Yet their suggestion that the more sophisticated methods are impractical is a rather broad generalization. The objective and task method is an example of a more complex yet practical approach.

Nevertheless, one survey of 25 firms in *Advertising Age's* annual list of 100

---

[17] Andre J. San Augustine and William F. Foley, "How Large Advertisers Set Budgets," *Journal of Advertising Research* 15, no. 5 (Oct. 1975): 11–16.

[18] *Ibid.*

leading advertisers and 25 firms as listed annually by the American Business Press, Inc., showed that the percentage of these advertisers using the arbitrary approach was greater than the percentage for any other method.[19]

Percent of Sales

A widely used method of determining the promotion budget is the percent of sales method. This approach is popular because of its simplicity and ease of implementation and not because of the soundness of its logic. All that is required is the determination of a sales figure and the use of a fixed percentage applied to that amount. If the sales figure is $100 million and the percentage applied is 2 percent, the promotion budget for the coming 12 months would be $2 million. The two possible bases are past sales and future sales.

Past Sales.   If past sales are used, the figure can be the sales volume for the previous year only, or it can be the average yearly sales for the last, say, three years. Using an average of several years may be preferable since the budget for the coming year is predicated on past sales and a decline in sales the preceding year would result in a reduction of the budget for the coming year. Getting a yearly average sales figure for several preceding years would tend to minimize the reducing effect.

Perhaps the major weakness of using past sales is that it confuses the cause and effect relationship between advertising and sales (if a precise relationship can be established). Presumably, it is advertising or promotion that determines sales. Yet the percent-of-sales method, by definition, uses sales to determine advertising or promotion. Thus if advertising budgets increase, it is because sales have increased.

It is quite likely that advertising budgets will increase as sales increase regardless of the method used in determining the appropriation. Most companies continue to advertise products that sell, and the better the products sell, the more they are advertised.[20]

Finally, using past sales as a basis for future budgets is looking backwards. What has happened in the past has no necessary significance to conditions in the future.

Future Sales.   Using future sales may be an improvement over using past sales. At least it is forward looking. The technique here is to forecast sales for the coming year and then apply a fixed percentage figure to the anticipated volume to get the promotion budget. Thus the budget is based on future conditions and not on past events. But there is a flaw in this method, too. Anticipated sales volume is used to determine the promotion budget, but the size of the promotion budget affects the sales volume. Thus we have circular reasoning.

Nevertheless, many firms in the United States and in Western Europe use this

---

[19]*Ibid.*

[20]See Kenneth Mason, ''How Much Do You Spend on Advertising? Product is Key,'' *Advertising Age* (12 June 1972): 41–44.

TABLE 10-1

1981 advertising expenditures of the leading U.S. advertiser in each of twelve categories expressed as a percent of sales

Company	Category	Advertising[a]	Sales	Advertising as percent of sales
RCA Corporation	Appliances, TV, radio	$208,798,300	$8,004,800,000	2.6
General Motors Corp.	Automobiles	401,000,000	62,698,500,000	0.6
Richardson-Vicks	Drugs	149,000,000	1,088,100,000	13.7
General Foods Corp.	Food	456,800,000	8,351,100,000	5.5
Mars, Inc.	Gum, candy	78,400,000	1,350,000,000	5.8
Eastman Kodak Co.	Photographic equipment	101,000,000	10,337,500,000	1.0
Sears, Roebuck & Co.	Retail chains	544,104,500	27,360,000,000	2.0
Procter & Gamble	Soaps, cleansers (and allied)	671,757,400	11,944,000,000	5.6
PepsiCo	Soft drinks	260,000,000	7,027,443,000	3.7
Phillip Morris, Inc.	Tobacco	432,971,400	10,885,900,000	4.0
Warner-Lambert Co.	Toiletries, cosmetics	270,400,000	3,379,092,000	8.0
Anheuser-Busch Cos.	Wine, beer, and liquor	187,228,500	4,409,600,000	4.2

[a]Total 1981 Advertising expenditures, including measured and unmeasured media.
Source: Reprinted with permission from the September 9, 1982, issue of *Advertising Age.* Copyright 1982 by Crain Communications, Inc.

method. In one study in Western Europe, 58 percent of the advertising executives with nonconsumer goods companies and 56 percent of those with consumer goods firms stated that they determine their advertising budgets on the basis of anticipated sales.[21]

Whether firms use the percent-of-sales method (past or future) for determining their promotion budgets or not, most convert their budgets to a percent of sales for accounting purposes and analytical reasons. Table 10-1 shows advertising budgets as a percent of sales for the leading advertiser in each of twelve different categories. However, one should not necessarily infer that these firms used the percent-of-sales method for determining their budgets. *Advertising Age,* the source from which this information was extracted, shows the figures for the 100 largest advertisers.

Most of the companies listed in table 10-1 are consumer goods companies. A study by the Association of National Advertisers and MIT's Sloan School of Management showed that for industrial goods marketers the median advertising/sales

[21]Steve E. Permut, "How European Managers Set Advertising Budgets," *Journal of Advertising Research* 17, no. 5 (Oct. 1977): 75-79.

ratio was 0.6 percent. The study indicated further that marketing budgets are 6.9 percent of the sales of industrial firms and that advertising gets 9.9 percent of those budgets.[22]

Competitive Parity

Some firms use the promotion expenditures of their competitors as a model for their own budgets. Colgate spends on a level between Lever Bros. and Procter and Gamble, and Celanese Company's budget is similar in amount to those of other companies of the same rank in the industry.[23]

There are arguments against the use of competitive parity as a method for determining the promotion budget. The budget setter cannot necessarily assume the marketing situation of competitors is the same as that of the company in question. Promotion objectives may differ, and the effect of environmental conditions may not be the same. Furthermore, the method is based on historical data because it is impossible to know what competitors are planning for the coming year.

Even if a firm's dollar expenditures are the same as those of a competitor, however, there is no assurance that the effectiveness of the promotion will be the same. Heavy advertisers may be able to make the best media buys with respect to both the selection of media and preferred positions within the media. As a result, the impact of their promotional efforts could be greater than those of the weaker firm even with the same dollar outlay.

Nevertheless, businesses like to know what their competitors are doing and to predict what they will be doing in the future. Services that provide this information can be used in this regard. Publishers Information Bureau in the consumer magazine field is a source; for business publications there is *Media Records* (the business publications part of *Media Records* was formerly the *Rome Report*), although at the time of this writing it was considering discontinuing the service on business publications because of the increasing costs.[24]

Information about competitors' activities is useful, regardless of whether a company uses competitive parity in its strict sense for determining the budget. Since consumers often make their decisions on the basis of their reactions to competing advertisements, it is logical and even necessary that promotion managers be aware of the advertising "tonnage" generated by their competitors.[25]

Objective and Task

Of all the methods available for determining the promotion budget, probably the most defensible is the objective and task method, which assumes nothing. With

---

[22]"Budget Norms for Industrial Advertisers," *Sales and Marketing Management* 115–16 (8 Mar. 1976), p. 22.

[23]"The Advertising Budget," 86–92.

[24]Frank Carvell, "How Much Does Competition Spend in Business Media," *Media Decisions* 12, pt. 2 (Oct. 1977): 136–38.

[25]See Jeffrey A. Lowenhar and John L. Stanton, "Forecasting Advertising Expenditures," *Journal of Advertising Research* 16, no. 2 (Apr. 1976): 37–42.

this method, the managers establish precise objectives, then determine the nature and magnitude of the task necessary to accomplish the objectives.

It is essentially a build-up method; that is, each element of the promotion mix is analyzed with respect to its contribution to the accomplishment of the overall promotion objective. This analysis requires thinking of subobjectives for each element (advertising, personal selling, sales promotion, and publicity) and then determining the specific activities necessary for their accomplishment. Thus the total of the anticipated costs associated with the delineated activities becomes the budget figure for that element; the total of the budget figures for the several elements is the promotion budget.

The build-up method can also be used to determine the budget figure for each individual element of the promotion mix. In advertising, for example, an analysis can be made of the necessary performance of each medium used (newspapers, magazines, television, radio, etc.) in accomplishing the advertising objective. The required amount of money can then be established in each case; this, added to other funds necessary for implementing the advertising program becomes the advertising budget figure. Budget figures for the other elements can be determined similarly.

A major problem in the method is that it is difficult to know how much promotion will be required to accomplish a given objective. How much advertising does it take, for example, to increase awareness of a brand in a given market by 10 percent in the budget year? History is useful here; perhaps even more helpful is the advice from advertising agencies who can rely on the collective experience from a number of completed campaigns. The same problem exists, of course, in personal selling. It is sometimes difficult to know how much selling effort is required to accomplish a given sales objective.

Despite the obvious rigor required for complete effectiveness in the use of the method, many firms are using it. Even as far back as the late 1960s, the method was being adopted by a number of firms.[26] Subsequent studies indicate that the trend is continuing. One such study showed that even though budgeting is considered to be a series of judgmental decisions, some form of the task method was favored by most companies.[27]

Adoption of the method was given additional impetus by President Carter's well-publicized support of zero-base budgeting in government. The basic principle is that all budgets should be started from zero and that they should not simply be built up from the previous year's figures. The method would reduce much of the waste built into many budgets through continued allocation of funds for activities that should no longer be supported.

Zero-base budgeting may not be exactly analagous to the objective and task method, but it is close. Starting from zero and justifying all expenditures in terms of objectives is common to both concepts.[28] Companies that use zero-base bud-

---

[26]David L. Hurwood, "How Companies Set Advertising Budgets," *The Conference Board Record* 5, no. 3 (Mar. 1968): 34–41.

[27]"How Many Ad Dollars are Enough?" *Media Decisions* 12, pt. 2 (July 1977): 59–61.

[28]See Louis J. Haugh, "Carter-Style Zero-Base Budget Planning Attracts Promoters," *Advertising Age* (9 May 1977): 58–60.

geting include Westinghouse Corporation, Xerox Corporation, Allied Van Lines, Texas Instruments, Playboy Enterprises, and Ford Motor Co.[29]

Payout Planning

Payout planning is really an extension of the objective and task method and is especially useful in connection with determining the appropriation and budget for a new product. It is simply extending the planning period beyond the typical budget year. The rationale is that it often takes more than a year's promotional effort to successfully introduce a new product and generate sufficient sales to make the venture profitable. Payout planning, therefore, is an attempt to establish an objective whose accomplishment is not expected to take place until two, three, or even five years beyond the fiscal year. The necessary expenditures for accomplishment, then, are determined, and their total would obviously exceed what would be spent in one budget year.

The method recognizes the frequent futility of trying to launch a new product successfully in one year. It provides the necessary funds from the outset to plan the promotional effort required for success in the time needed to do the job.

Mathematical Models

In the 1950s and the 1960s, various mathematical models and quantitative techniques were proposed for use in solving certain problems associated with the promotion budget, but acceptance of the methods by practitioners has been slow. The data required for using many of the techniques is sometimes difficult to get, and the complexity of most of the models tends to discourage their extensive use.

These mathematical models hold promise for the future. Their use would add a scientific dimension to budget making that is not present to the same degree in the use of other methods.[30]

Reserve Funds

The promotion budget should be flexible for no one can accurately anticipate the future, and there will always be changes in the promotion environment that require changes in promotional strategy. A rigid budget that prevents accommodation to such environmental changes will lead to a less effective strategy. Since changes often require unexpected expenditures, some reserve funds should always be built into the budget.

An interesting question has arisen relative to the tax accounting for such

---

[29]*Ibid.* See also Don Korn, ``Industrial Advertising Warming up to Zero Base,'' *Sales and Marketing Management* 118 (13 June 1977): 54–59.

[30]See David B. Montgomery and Glen L. Urban, *Management Science in Marketing* (Englewood Cliffs, N.J.: Prentice-Hall, 1969), pp. 115–37; Leonard S. Simon and Marshall Freimer, *Analytical Marketing* (New York: Harcourt, Brace & World, 1970), pp. 200–207; Paul E. Green, Patrick J. Robinson, and Peter T. FitzRoy, ``Advertising Expenditure Models: State of the Art and Prospects,'' *Business Horizons* 9, no. 2 (Summer 1966): 73–80.

funds. *Advertising Age,* in an editorial, suggested that as a part of a tax reform effort, reserve funds should be tax free even though they are not spent in one year. For example, a company could set up a contingency fund of, say, $500,000 at the start of the fiscal year. The Internal Revenue Service would allow a tax deduction as a normal business expense for that fiscal year. But as long as the money was spent on advertising, it would not have to be spent entirely that year (which is the requirement under present law). Such a policy would increase advertising, and thus consumer spending, which would stimulate the economy.[31]

In rebuttal to the editorial, Peter W. Allport, then President of the Association of National Advertisers, took a different position. Although he, too, stated that there is much wrong with the tax system, he contended that the change suggested in the editorial would pose problems. There would be questions relative to the buildup of reserves during a succession of good years; the requirement or nonrequirement of firms to spend the entire accumulated reserve in a bad year; and the application of the policy to other business functions.[32]

The tax question notwithstanding, reserve funds should be included in the promotion budget. The uncertainty of the future demands it.[33]

ALLOCATION OF THE FUNDS

Once the total budget figure is determined, or being determined if the build-up method is used, decisions must be made regarding the division of the money. If we are dealing with the total promotion budget figure, for example, we must decide on how it should be apportioned among the four elements of the promotion mix. The initial consideration here is the relative importance of each of the elements in accomplishing the promotion objective. Each situation is unique. However, it is safe to generalize, for example, that in promoting industrial goods, personal selling would receive the largest share of the appropriation, but in promoting convenience goods to consumers, advertising would be the major ingredient in the mix.

But the allocation problem does not end there. Decisions need to be made as to how the money will be distributed to the various facets of each element of the promotion mix. In each case, for example, a portion of the respective budgets must be allocated for administrative costs. Beyond that, there are many alternative distribution ratios. Advertising managers must decide on how much to spend in each of the media used, each market covered, and on each product or product line. Sales managers must allocate funds to finance salespeople in each of a number of different sales territories (compensation, travel expenses, etc.), to reach each of various customer groups, and to the different product lines in a multiproduct com-

---

[31]Reprinted with permission from the September 14, 1977, issue of *Advertising Age.* Copyright 1977 by Crain Communications, Inc.

[32]Reprinted with permission from the October 10, 1977, issue of *Advertising Age.* Copyright 1977 by Crain Communications, Inc.

[33]See T. Kirk Parrish, "How Much to Spend for Advertising," *Journal of Advertising Research* 14, no. 1 (Feb. 1974): 9–11.

pany. Sales promotion managers must provide funds for materials appropriate to the purpose such as coupons, samples, or point-of-purchase materials and in the selected target markets. Publicity managers must allocate funds to the various efforts required in developing material for publicity releases.

Specific approaches to solving these allocation problems are difficult to generalize because each situation is different. But they are based on objectives — which emphasizes further the need for establishing objectives. The objective and task method is relevant in detemining the amount of funds needed, particularly if it is applied at each step in the build-up method of determining the total budget figure.

SUMMARY

Financing the promotion task has always been difficult, especially in today's inflationary economy. Conceptually there are two notions associated with the problem: the *appropriation,* both in terms of the total promotion function and the individual elements of the promotion mix, and the *budget,* similarly for the total function and for its individual elements. The appropriation is the amount of money approved, and the budget is its distribution to the respective subdivisions.

The theoretically ideal approach to determining the advertising appropriation is marginal analysis — that is, equating marginal revenue with marginal cost. The difficulty in using marginal analysis is the requirement of an advertising/sales ratio and dealing with the effect of advertising on future sales. A major problem in establishing specific budgets for the various elements of the promotion mix is the determination of the expenses appropriate to each.

There are several key factors that have a bearing on the size of the budget. These include objectives, the nature of the product, and the channels of distribution. These factors should be considered in the process of establishing the budget.

Specific methods of determining the budget include arbitrary determination, percent of sales, competitive parity, objective and task, payout planning, and various mathematical models. Although the simplest method is percent of sales, the best method is probably the objective and task. Regardless of the method used, there should be some reserve funds built into the budget.

The total funds appropriated must be allocated to the various subdivisions of promotion — either after the total figure is determined or during the process of determining, if the build-up method is used. These subdivisions include not only the four elements of the promotion mix but also the different facets in each element.

QUESTIONS FOR THOUGHT AND REVIEW

1. Distinguish between *appropriation* and *budget.* Explain how the two terms are applied to the total promotion function and to the various elements of the promotion mix.

2. Should the appropriation figure be established before the budgets are constructed? Discuss.
3. Do you think the expenditures for advertising should be considered an investment? Present arguments both defending and attacking the concept.
4. Explain the concept of *marginal analysis* in connection with determining the advertising appropriation. Why is it not used?
5. What is the general shape of the curve representing the relationship of advertising to sales? Why is it so shaped?
6. Explain the problem of classifying promotion costs. Should consumer contest awards be considered advertising or sales promotion costs? Why?
7. How do promotion objectives affect the size of the budget?
8. Which kind of product would seem to require the largest promotion expenditures for a manufacturer — convenience goods or specialty goods? Why?
9. Would a manufacturer who uses a relatively long channel of distribution have greater or less promotion costs than one who uses a shorter channel? Why?
10. Why do some companies use the arbitrary method of determining the budget? Do you think it is justified?
11. What are the major weaknesses of using the percent of past sales method? the percent of future sales? Why are these methods used?
12. Do you think competitive parity is a defensible method of determining the budget? Is there any other reason for knowing what competitors are doing? Explain.
13. Explain the rationale for using the objective and task method of determining the budget. How is zero-base budgeting related to the method?
14. Why should all budgets include some reserve funds? Do you think they should be tax free? Argue both sides of the issue.

PART FIVE

THE PROMOTION MIX

The purpose in this section is to examine each element of the promotion mix. We begin, in chapter 11, by taking a general look at the relationship of the marketing effort to the promotional mix. We then discuss each element separately in succeeding chapters in the section.

Chapters 12, 13, 14, and 15 are concerned with advertising media—their nature, the advantages and disadvantages of each, and methods of measuring the effectiveness of their use. Personal selling is examined in chapters 16 and 17, and the various aspects of sales promotion activities are explored in chapters 18 and 19. Chapter 20 is devoted to a discussion of publicity.

MARKETING MIX

Product Price **Promotion** Channels Logistics

Persuasive
Communication

MARKET ANALYSIS

Product Perception   Market Target   Promotion
Purchase Behavior   Promotion Appeal   Objectives

Organizing for Promotion

Financing Promotion

Coordinating Marketing & Promotion

PROMOTION MIX

media	techniques	retailer	characteristics
ADVERTISING	**PERSONAL SELLING**	**SALES PROMOTION**	**PUBLICITY & P.R.**
testing	management	consumer	techniques

PLANNING FOR THE FUTURE

CULTURAL/SOCIAL ENVIRONMENT

BUSINESS/ECONOMIC ENVIRONMENT

LEGAL/ETHICAL ENVIRONMENT

THE MARKETING EFFORT AND THE PROMOTION MIX

Before we begin a detailed analysis of the elements of the promotion mix to be discussed in chapters 12–19, it is necessary to devote some attention to the interrelationships among certain aspects of the marketing effort and promotional strategy. Only then can we see each promotional tool, as we discuss it, in its proper perspective.

THE MARKETING EFFORT

Persuasive communication is easier to accomplish if the marketing program of which it is a part is soundly conceived and properly implemented. It has been suggested that successful marketing case histories indicate the presence of at least one of three conditions: a product advantage, a marketing advantage, or a creative advantage.[1] Innovative products such as Polaroid cameras with the once-unheard of capability of developing pictures in the camera, Xerox machines that would copy anything in seconds, and Shake 'n Bake that introduced a new way to cook chicken exemplify product advantages. A marketing advantage exists for Avon with 500,000 women selling the company's products to friends and neighbors and for the Barbie doll with its countless items of clothing and costumes. The "Marlboro Man" was a creative advantage for the cigarette as was the "Pepsi Generation" for Pepsi-Cola, and Jell-O was number two behind Royal in the gelatin field before the creativity associated with Jack Benny.[2]

The marketing effort can be described in terms of the nature of the marketing mix — product, price, channel of distribution, logistics, and promotion — and the way it is implemented. Our concern here is with the influence of each of the first four components mentioned on promotion. Of course all five components must work together as a system.

Product

The consumer should be the focal point in the development of any marketing strategy — whether it is for the marketing of a product, service, or idea. But beyond that the foundation for success is the product service, or idea. The increasingly discerning contemporary consumer simply will not be fooled very long by an unworthy product; no amount of promotional effort can perpetuate its acceptance. A good product, on the other hand, such as Tide detergent, Wrigley's gum, Campbell's soup, or Heinz ketchup, can achieve a certain "momentum of the marketplace" and continue to be successfully promoted, even if the creativity in the effort drops occasionally.[3] Thus while the consumer should receive first consideration in the development of promotional strategy, the product is a close second.

---

[1] Harry Wayne McMahan, "All-Time Ad Triumphs Reveal Key Success Factors Behind Choice of 100 Best," *Advertising Age* (Apr. 12, 1976): 72–75, 78.

[2] *Ibid.*

[3] *Ibid.*

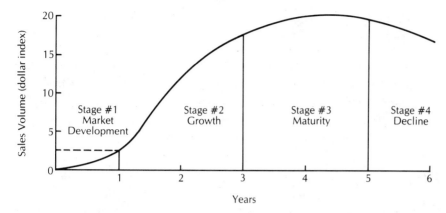

FIGURE 11–1 Product life cycle — entire industry. *Source:* Reprinted by permission of the *Harvard Business Review*. The exhibit from "Exploit the product life cycle" by Theodore Levitt (Nov.-Dec. 1965). Copyright © 1965 by the President and Fellows of Harvard College; all rights reserved.

Promotion and the Product Life Cycle

Most successful products have a life cycle. The cycle may be completed in a few weeks or months or it may take decades. The "Pet Rock" phenomenon was very short-lived, but Coca-Cola is still going strong, and it has been around for several generations. Figure 11–1 shows the stages in the life cycle of a product.

Throughout the process of product life cycle the nature and magnitude of promotional effort should change with the transition from one stage to the next. For one thing, demand elasticities change over the product life cycle, and marketing effort should be greater in the early years of the cycle.[4]

But it is more than that. The purpose and form of promotional effort must be consistent with the conditions associated with each stage. When the product is first introduced and is in the market development stage, for example, the emphasis should be on informing and educating the consumer on the merits of the product. It may even be necessary to engage in primary demand stimulation (demand for the generic product) if the product is truly innovative. All elements of the promotion mix may be utilized in this stage — advertising, personal selling, sales promotion, and publicity.

In the growth stage, the majority of consumers will know of the product, and many will be buying it. Advertising will assume a relatively more important role in the promotion mix and will be aimed at stimulating selective demand — demand for the manufacturer's brand. Because there is an increasing demand, with a corresponding increase in potential profit, retailers will assist in the promotional effort.

By the time the product reaches the maturity stage, competition will have entered the market in force. Advertising will have to be increased by the manu-

---

[4]Leonard J. Parsons, "The Product Life Cycle and Time-Varying Advertising Elasticities," *Journal of Marketing Research* 12 (Nov. 1975): 476–80.

facturer, and retailers will be less inclined to promote the manufacturer's brand since they are not particularly concerned about which brand they sell. When the product reaches the decline stage, promotional effort should be reduced because the product will have been superseded by new and better offerings, and further promotion under the circumstances would be futile. The question of what to do then is a marketing problem rather than promotion.[5]

Promotion and the Introduction of New Products

Because most products do have life cycles, a company's survival often depends upon periodic introductions of new products or improvements in existing ones. Even when survival is not the issue, new products provide a means of remaining competitive and improving market position, and the introduction of new products always requires intensive promotional effort. Examples abound. Thomas J. Lipton introduced flavored tea bags with a strong magazine ad campaign together with couponed newspaper and Sunday supplement ads.[6] Colgate-Palmolive, after a brief period of concentrating on established products, again devoted attention to the introduction of new products such as Experience complexion soap, Irish Spring in blue and yellow colors, and Respond shampoo.[7]

In the fast foods line, Arby's came out with a barbeque sandwich and a beef and cheddar cheese sandwich.[8] Burger King, with its Magical Burger King promotion aimed at the 9–12-year-old group competed effectively with McDonalds.[9] And in still another field, Coca-Cola introduced its new brand of wine, Taylor California, on the East coast using television and other major media, although it has now sold the line to Joseph E. Seagram and Sons.[10] Parker Brothers has added video games to its board game lines.[11] Low-calorie, high-price frozen foods have been introduced by Pillsbury, General Mills, ConAgra, Campbell Soup, and Van de Kamp.[12] Gillette Company came out with "Foamy Gel" — a gel version of its successful Foamy shaving cream — to challenge Edge, manufactured by S. C. Johnson & Son.[13]

The Brand and New Products. Should a new product be introduced under the umbrella of a "family" brand or should a different brand be attached to the new product? There are logical marketing arguments supporting the latter view under

[5]For further discussion of the product life cycle, see William J. Stanton, *Fundamentals of Marketing* (New York: McGraw-Hill, 1978), pp. 203–6, 419.

[6]John J. O'Connor, "Lipton Dips into Gourmet Tea Market," *Advertising Age* (21 Aug. 1978): 1.

[7]"New Colgate Chief Takes over Amid New Product Binge," *Advertising Age* (22 Jan. 1979): 1, 80.

[8]Christy Marshall, "New Products Add Flavor to Arby's Marketing Effort," *Advertising Age* (9 Oct. 1978): 50.

[9]"Managing Marketing Growing Industry Priority," *Advertising Age* (4 Sept. 1978): 26.

[10]Margaret LeRoux, "Coke Adds Life to Wine Field with Taylor California Line," *Advertising Age* (21 Aug. 1978): 1, 70; and Ruth Stroud, "Coke's Wine Spectrum Sale Sets Stage," *Advertising Age* (October 3, 1983) 3, 85.

[11]Gay Jervey, "Parker Bros. Puts Its Chips on New Boards," *Advertising Age* (August 22, 1983): 4, 52–53.

[12]Janet Neiman, "New Frozen Foods Shape Up," *Advertising Age* (August 22, 1983): 2, 59.

[13]Gay Jervey, "Gillette Readies Gel-Style Foamy," *Advertising Age* (August 1, 1983): 2, 45.

certain conditions. For example, if the new product is totally unrelated to the firm's existing products, it could be a mistake to identify it by the family brand, particularly if it confuses the consumer in any way. If Procter and Gamble's Crisco shortening and Jif peanut butter were identified by the same brand, the peanut butter sandwich in the lunch bucket might be made with shortening!

From a promotional point of view, the question of whether to use a family brand for a new product might never arise. If the new product is *chosen to fit the brand,* instead of conceiving the product first and then wondering about the brand, there would be no problem.[14] If the brand is well established and one that consumers associate with quality products and the firm that owns it, the new product would be more easily promoted if it is identified by the familiar name. The halo of an established brand can be quite pervasive. When Johnson's Wax considered entering the shoe polish field, it found that many consumers assumed that the company already was producing that product, and some even had a favorable impression of the nonexistent product's characteristics! Thus, a brand's successful acceptance with consumers is largely due to previous promotional effort. Why waste all that?

However, such an approach is not always successful, and frequently firms must resort to other means of broadening their product mixes. Pillsbury, whose basic products are flour, cake mixes, and refrigerated biscuits, has struggled in that regard. Among several attempts at introducing new products, the company came out with a new cake mix called Pillsbury Plus in 1977. It was initially successful but soon dropped behind similar products of General Mills and Procter and Gamble. Pillsbury has had greater success in broadening its base by acquiring such firms as Burger King, Speas (apple juice and vinegar), American Beauty macaroni, Totino's Pizza, Steak & Ale restaurants, and the Green Giant Company.[15] It has recently added ice cream to its product offerings by acquiring Häagen-Dazs Co.[16]

Comparative Advertising and New Products.   If the product is in the introductory stage, the promotional strategy should center on informing and educating the consumer. One way of achieving impact is through the use of comparative advertising, discussed in chapter 5. The question of its effectiveness with established products is still moot, particularly if the products are among the leaders in the field. But using comparative advertising to introduce new products may be worthwhile.[17]

For example, as a newcomer in the rent-a-car field, Olins has vigorously compared itself with the two leaders. Among other things, its advertising has stated that Hertz and Avis rent the car and then charge twenty-nine cents per mile driven, while Olins rents the car and charges nothing for each mile driven. Such a head-to-head approach may be effective because of the shock value of an upstart taking

[14]See Frederick Buggie, ``Let Brand Inspire New Products,'' *Advertising Age* (23 Oct. 1978): 72.

[15]See ``Pillsbury's Ambitious Plans to use Green Giant,'' *Business Week* (5 Feb. 1979): 87–88.

[16]Jennifer Alter and Gay Jervey, ``Pillsbury Gets Into Ice Cream,'' *Advertising Age* (June 13, 1983): 3, 63.

[17]For a discussion of this and related issues, see Michael Etgar and Stephen A. Goodwin, ``Planning for Comparative Advertising Requires Special Attention,'' *Journal of Advertising* 8, no. 1 (Winter 1979): 26–32.

on two leaders. A confrontation between two leaders, on the other hand, may lack credibility because of the tendency of consumers to view the claims made as suspect.[18]

Promotion and No-Brand Products

One of the most recent innovations in the field of grocery products marketing is the sale of no-brand products (also referred to as no-frills products or generics). These products carry no brand name on their labels and are identified only by their generic names. They are presumably sold at prices considerably below those of nationally advertised brands and somewhat less than the private brands of supermarket chains. The first major chain to offer such items was Jewel Cos. in its Chicago stores in 1977.[19]

The trend caught on rather quickly. The following year, Big Bear Stores introduced its Un-Brand items in Ohio and West Virginia; Pathmark and Waldbaum's came out with similar products in the New York metropolitan area; and Waldbaum's introduced the items in New England.[20] Other chains followed suit; even liquor has not escaped. Harry Hoffman's Liquors, one of Denver's largest retail liquor stores, began selling generically labeled liquor in 1978.[21] Generic beer is now available in virtually all liquor stores and supermarkets. Generic cigarettes are also increasingly common.

An issue that has developed in connection with generic marketing — especially in drugs — arises from their similarity in appearance to branded versions. Is it an infringement of trademark rights when the colors and shapes of the generics are identical to those of the branded products for which they can be substituted?

Such pharmaceutical firms as Hoffman-La Roche, Ives Laboratories, and Pfizer have filed law suits charging that it is an infringement. Arguments defending the practice center around the notion that copying the colors and shapes assures the consumer that the generic is indeed a correct substitution for the branded product. Although the issue is presently not resolved, some courts have ruled in favor of the brand name pharmaceuticals.[22]

The generic product trend raises the question of how to promote such products. If the trend spreads to other product lines, the question will be even more significant. It has been argued that the reason prices of generics are so much lower than those of nationally advertised brands is that there are no manufacturers' advertising costs or fancy packaging. The counterargument is that the packaging appears to be the same as the name brand products and that the costs of developing such packaging have already been amortized and recovered over the years

---

[18]See William D. Tyler, ''New Product Intros Can Challenge the Goliaths By Meeting Them Head on,'' *Advertising Age* (17 July 1978): 39, 42.

[19]''Newcomer Generics Get Growing Consumer Interest,'' *Advertising Age* (30 Oct. 1978): 84, 86.

[20]''No-Brand Products Enter Chains in New York and Ohio Markets,'' *Advertising Age* (6 Mar. 1978): 2.

[21]''Booze Goes Generic at Harry's Place,'' *Advertising Age* (24 July 1978): 8.

[22]See Sidney A. Diamond, ''Generic Drugs: Colors, Shapes Protected Property,'' *Advertising Age* (June 8, 1981): 58; and ''Ives Takes 'Look-Alike' Generics to High Court,'' *Advertising Age* (March 1, 1982): 49.

in connection with the heavily promoted brands. The packaging for generics may cost *more* than that for name brands because of the lesser quantity involved. Furthermore, the generics *are* advertised.[23]

But the promotion problem is that the natural market for no-brand products is made up of low-income consumers; many people in this category are reluctant to publicize their plight in supermarkets by obviously buying what might be construed as "cheap" products. Since in most cases the no-brand products are as nutritional as the name brands, albeit not as attractive (containing "pieces" instead of "wholes," for example), middle-class shoppers might be persuaded through advertising that the products represent good buys. Acceptance by the middle class could reduce the stigma felt by the low-income group in purchasing the products.[24]

An interesting sidelight to the no-brand phenomenon was the introduction by Safeway of its Scotch Buy line in 1978. This line, perhaps Safeway's response to the generics of other chains, has a more attractive label than the generics, but the prices of the products are comparable to those of the no-brands. There was an intensive promotional campaign associated with the introduction of the line, estimated at the time at $10,000,000 in television, print, and in-store activities.[25]

An increasing consumer acceptance of no-brand products in the next few years could have an enormous impact on the marketing activities of the firms involved and particularly on their promotional strategies. Many firms with traditional brands are attempting to convince skeptical consumers that the brands are worth the extra price. In an ad for Glad plastic bags, for example, a generic bag was shown rupturing, spilling garbage all over.[26]

Promotion and Planned Product Obsolescence

Historically, business has been accused of deliberately shortening the life cycles of products by following polices of planned obsolescence — making last year's model obsolete to sell this year's model. The practice has been adamantly attacked and defended. Product obsolescence can be viewed from many perspectives, including technology, style, and even inferior quality. If planned obsolescence is practiced, it has a great impact on promotional strategy because of the continual introduction of new products.

However, the requirements of promotional strategy may now be more in the nature of perpetuating the acceptance of existing products than in the introduction of new products. As far back as 1974, the managements of some companies began to consider eliminating marginal lines, consolidating higher profit items in their product mixes, and "re-marketing" existing products.[27] The trend now seems to be toward encouraging the development of longer-lasting products.[28]

[23]Dick Jackson, "Ads Unneeded? Pathmark's No-Frills Brand May Need this Frill for Market Survival," *Advertising Age* (20 March 1978): 50–51.

[24]*Ibid.*

[25]John Revett, "Safeway's Scotch Buy Line: Upscale Generics," *Advertising Age* (11 Sept. 1978): 1, 133.

[26]See "No-Frills Food. New Power for the Supermarkets," *Business Week* (March 23, 1981): 70–80.

[27]"Toward Higher Margins and Less Variety," *Business Week* (14 Sept. 1974): 98–100.

[28]"Planned Obsolescence May be Obsolete Idea," *Advertising Age* (15 May 1978): 24.

If the trend continues, the number of new product offerings may be reduced. In any event, promotional strategy is bound to be affected.

Price

Price affects promotional strategy and the promotion mix in at least two ways. First, the price of the product must be high enough to provide a gross margin sufficient to finance the desired promotional effort. Stated differently, the size of the gross margin has a bearing on the number of ingredients used in the promotion mix and the degree to which they are used. This is a budget factor, and would be considered in connection with determining the amount of money appropriated for promotion.

Second, the use of price in the marketing effort is governed by the image consumers have of the product and the market at which it is directed. When price connotes either quality or status, for example, it tends to be minimized in the promotional effort. People who purchase products for either of these reasons are rarely price-conscious; they may even dislike talking about it. On the other hand, if the market at which the product is directed is more concerned about price than quality or status, price would be emphasized in the promotional effort and would be the basis for the major appeal.

Channel of Distribution

Most firms do not sell just one product through one channel of distribution to one type of customer.[29] Many companies are multiproduct firms and use several channels of distribution. Or a firm may sell the same product under different *brands* through different stores. For example, if a company grants an exclusive franchise to a particular retailer in a specific area but also wants to sell through another retailer in the same area, the company can develop a second brand for the additional store.

Multiple channels of distribution are often used for the same product. The Great Atlantic and Pacific Tea Company, for example, sells to its own stores and to independents. Oil companies, likewise, sell through their own outlets and to independent dealers.[30] Also a firm may have more than one kind of market for the same product, such as when paint companies sell to both retailers and contractors.[31] Such varied channel situations require different promotional strategies.

Intensive versus Exclusive Distribution

A firm may follow a policy of intensive distribution that requires the use of every possible retail outlet, or its policy may be one of exclusive distribution. In the latter,

---

[29]Robert E. Weigand, ''Fit Products and Channels to Your Markets,'' *Harvard Business Review* 55 (Jan.– Feb. 1977): 95–105.

[30]*Ibid.*

[31]*Ibid.*

the firm carefully selects a minimum number of retail outlets to handle its product in each market area. The chosen few are given the exclusive right to sell the brand in their respective areas. An intermediate policy is referred to as *selective distribution.*

Intensive distribution requires the heavy use of advertising in the promotion mix. Because competition is keen and the target is a mass audience, the only feasible way of reaching the target is through advertising by the manufacturer. Retailers cannot be relied upon to assist in the promotional effort because, with so many retailers handling the product, promotional effort by any one outlet would benefit all manufacturers and be of little direct use to that single retailer. No retailer is inclined to spend money with so little reward. In addition, because there are so many retailers involved, it would be impossible for the manufacturer to have its salespeople call on them for the purpose of promoting the product. So personal selling is not a viable tool.

But carefully chosen and wisely used sales promotion techniques can be effective in intensive distribution. Couponing and sampling can sometimes stimulate purchases by consumers, and promotion deals offered to all retailers may generate their interest in the product. Publicity, to the extent that it can be used, is always good.

Exclusive distribution presents a different situation. In this case, each retailer wants to retain the brand franchise and is willing to assist the manufacturer in its promotional efforts. Failure to do so could result in the loss of the franchise. Under such circumstances, the manufacturer can adjust the promotion mix accordingly, perhaps by reducing national advertising somewhat and allowing the retailer to pick up the slack. Because fewer retailers are involved, the manufacturer may be able to use personal selling advantageously by having salespeople call on the retailers.

The Length of the Channel

Short channels usually require different promotion mixes than long channels. With respect to personal selling in the mix, for example, the shorter the channel the greater the need for personal selling. Avon and Tupperware use the shortest channel possible in selling directly to the consumer. Their success is largely due to the effectiveness of their salespeople (in addition to the quality of the products, of course). Advertising and sales promotion are important in the mixes used in short channels, but personal selling seems to be the key factor. In longer channels involving the use of several stages of middlemen, the relative importance of advertising as compared to personal selling in the promotion mix is usually the opposite of that in the short channels.

Multiple Markets for the Same Product

Selling the same product to different markets usually requires the use of different channels of distribution and promotion mixes. The paint manufacturer may use relatively more advertising and less personal selling with the retailer market and reverse the ratio to reach the contractors. The same situation may prevail with plywood, wallboard, and other building materials purchased by both contractors and do-it-yourself homeowners. Pharmaceutical firms selling their products through various kinds of retailers may employ different kinds of promotion mixes. Drug stores, variety stores, department stores, and supermarkets may respond differently to promotion efforts, and the strategy must be adjusted accordingly. And in industrial marketing the manufacturer of items such as certain automobile parts that retain their identity (sparkplugs, for example) will use a different promotion mix to reach the replacement market than to sell to the original equipment manufacturer. Promotion in the replacement market must be heavily weighted with advertising, while the original equipment market requires a greater use of personal selling.

Push Versus Pull Strategy

The manufacturer sometimes has the problem of deciding whether the dominant promotional strategy should be "push" or "pull." Use of a _push strategy_ implies that the manufacturer is attempting to push the product through the channel. Each successive institution in the channel must be convinced of the merits of the product by the preceding institution, as well as by the manufacturer. In a typical channel the manufacturer pushes the product to the wholesaler, the wholesaler to the retailer, and the retailer to the consumer. Success of the strategy requires the cooperation of all institutions in the channel. Of course, such cooperation is possible only if each institution can be persuaded that there is something to be gained.

The push strategy calls for a relatively heavy use of personal selling and sales promotion. The personal contact of salespeople at each level is usually required to generate the necessary conviction. Furthermore, the proposal can be more persuasive if trade sales promotion devices such as trade allowances and price-off deals are used in conjunction with the salespeople. Advertising plays a lesser part in the strategy and is directed primarily at the institutions through trade publications and direct-mail.

A _pull strategy_ requires a different approach. The manufacturer appeals directly to the consumer — in effect, ignoring the intermediate institutions in the channel. The hope is that consumers will become so "sold" on the product that they will insist retailers carry it in stock, the retailers will therefore demand it from the wholesalers, and the wholesalers will buy it from the manufacturer. The analogy is that the manufacturer is pulling the product through the channel. Consumer advertising is the predominant element in the promotion mix, supplemented perhaps by such consumer sales promotion devices as coupons, premiums, and deals. Personal selling plays a relatively smaller role in the mix.

Most manufacturers use a combination of the two strategies. Not only do they advertise to the consumer but they also attempt to get cooperation from the middlemen in the channel in promoting the product. But convincing middlemen to promote a product is difficult because they are only interested in helping themselves. If they feel it is more profitable to promote a particular manufacturer's brand or product than to promote another's or not to promote any they will do so. The feeling is particularly strong if the retailer is large enough to have an established private brand.

Logistics

The major influence of logistics on promotion is on the timing of the promotional effort. There must be sufficient coordination of these two elements of the marketing mix to assure that the products are available to consumers when they hear about them. It would be self-defeating if a product or a product offer were vigorously promoted, and consumers were unable to respond because the product was unavailable.

THE PROMOTION MIX

The promotion mix refers to the specific combination of promotion tools and their relative importance as they are used in a particular promotional strategy. Of the possible components of the mix (advertising, personal selling, sales promotion, and publicity), no single tool can be judged more important than the others since the relative importance of each depends upon the circumstances. Furthermore, some situations do not require the use of all the tools.

Advertising would very likely be the major component if the market is widespread, particularly if it is national in scope. But if the product requires demonstration, or if it has a high unit value, personal selling would probably be the main ingredient in the mix — especially of the market is sufficiently concentrated to minimize the required number of salespeople and their travel expenses. Sales promotion devices should probably always be used to some degree in promoting consumer goods; publicity is always appropriate when it can be implemented. But each situation is different, and the mix depends upon the prevailing circumstances.

However, there seems to be a trend in the relative use of certain components of the mix. For example, although the figures are difficult to evaluate because it is uncertain as to what exactly is included, it is estimated that expenditures for sales promotional activities were $38 billion in 1978, while national advertising expenditures were $25 billion; the annual growth rates were 9 percent for sales promotion and 7 percent for advertising.[32] Other reported figures show that of the total advertising and promotion spending, 53 percent was spent on sales promotion in 1968, and 59 percent was spent in 1975.[33]

But there is nothing sacred about any particular promotion mix. Changing situations necessitate a corresponding change in the mix. Constant monitoring of conditions is required to maintain a consistently superior promotion mix and a viable marketing mix. There has been such a drastic change in the eating habits of

---

[32]Louis J. Haugh, "Professional Managers Do Promotion Planning," *Advertising Age* (23 Oct. 1978): 74, 80.

[33]Roger A. Strang, "Sales Promotion — Fast Growth, Faulty Management," *Harvard Business Review* 54 (July–Aug. 1976): 115–24.

people that food marketers and promotional strategists are sometimes hard put to maintain effective programs. As recently as 1940 families ate at least two meals a day together at home; today we spend about thirty-five cents of each food dollar away from home and have as many as 20 "food contacts" per day.[34]

The enormous growth of fast-food outlets reflects the change. McDonald's grew at an average rate of 23 percent in the years 1975–1978 and had sales of $2.7 billion in 1977. Kentucky Fried Chicken had sales of $1.16 billion the same year—second only to McDonald's.[35] Other chains have experienced similar growth. Even convenience stores such as 7-Eleven often provide some sort of fast food items now. Such changes in the methods of food consumption have had a tremendous impact not only on the manufacturers of "traditional" food items but also on the retailers who sell them. The promotion mix must be sufficiently flexible to adjust to such changes.

THE FRAMEWORK FOR PROMOTIONAL STRATEGY

Strategy refers to the procedure for accomplishing objectives. The development of promotional strategy requires the judicious selection of suitable promotion tools and the design of effective mixes for the prevailing conditions.

The framework for establishing objectives and developing promotional strategy essentially consists of the following:

1. Creating awareness
2. Arousing interest
3. Generating acceptance
4. Inducing action

The specific promotional strategy at any given time is influenced by the relative emphasis given to each of the listed elements. Not only would the promotion mix vary with the circumstances but the creative aspects associated with each element would be different.

In the next nine chapters, we will examine each element in the promotion mix and the submixes.

SUMMARY

The basic tools of promotional strategy are found in the promotion mix, and they must be implemented with the consumer in mind. But in addition to being oriented to the consumer, promotional strategy must be closely tied to the marketing effort.

All elements of the marketing mix affect promotional strategy. The introduction of new products is a constant influence because it happens so frequently. A fairly recent phenomenon associated with the relationship of product to promo-

---

[34]Leo J. Shapiro and Dwight Bohmback, "Eating Habits Force Changes in Marketing," _Advertising Age_ (30 Oct. 1978): 27, 65–66, 68.

[35]Christy Marshall, "Supermarkets Fight Fast-Foods Challenge," _Advertising Age_ (30 Oct. 1978): 30, 34.

tional strategy was the introduction of no-brand food products. Planned obsolescence is receiving increasing attention. The price of the product affects profits and thus influences the size of the promotion budget. Price is also related to product image and determines the nature of the promoting effort.

Whether a firm has an intensive or exclusive distribution policy makes a difference in its promotional strategy. The length of the channel — the number of different kinds of institutions in the channel — is also important. And a firm selling the same product to different kinds of markets must use different promotion mixes. The nature of the channel also helps determine the wisdom of using a push or pull strategy as the predominant method. Logistics is significant in the timing of the promotion effort; products must be available to consumers at the appropriate time.

The promotion mix is composed of advertising, personal selling, sales promotion, and publicity. Each of these can be further delineated by its own mix, designed for specific situations in accordance with a general framework for developing promotional strategy.

QUESTIONS FOR THOUGHT AND REVIEW

1. The consumer should be the focal point in the development of promotional strategy. Why? Why not the product?
2. For each stage of the product life cycle — introduction, growth, maturity, and decline — name two products you think are representative of that step. Explain your choices.
3. For each product you identified in question 2, describe the appropriate promotion mix and justify your contentions.
4. Why is it often necessary for firms to continually introduce new products? Do you think circumstances will eventually prevent them from doing this?
5. Procter and Gamble uses individual brands for its products instead of a "family" brand. Why do you think they do this? Under what conditions is the use of a family brand appropriate?
6. Explain the notion that a company should choose a product to fit the brand rather than design a new product first and then fit a brand to it. Can you think of examples that might illustrate this approach?
7. If you were a manufacturer of a no-brand product, how would you promote it? What would be your promotional mix?
8. What is comparative advertising? Why is it possible that the use of comparative advertising may be more feasible in the introduction of new products than in competitive rivalry between two leaders in the field? How do *you* react to comparative advertising?
9. Present arguments both attacking and defending the practice of planned obsolescence. Do you think its use will decline in the future? If so, what will companies replace it with?
10. Distinguish between intensive and exclusive distribution. Which would generate more support by the retailer for the manufacturer's promotion program? Why?

11. Explain how the length of the channel affects the promotional strategy of a manufacturer.
12. Explain how a manufacturer of plywood might develop promotion mixes to reach the two separate markets of contractors and home owners.
13. Carefully distinguish between a *push strategy* and a *pull strategy*. Under what conditions would a manufacturer favor one over the other? Explain.
14. Describe some of the effects on promotion of the changes in eating habits of the American people. Be specific and use examples.
15. What do you think would be an appropriate promotion mix for each stage indicated in the framework for developing promotional strategy?

12

ADVERTISING— AN INTRODUCTION

Advertising has been defined by the Committee on Definitions of the American Marketing Association as ''any paid form of nonpersonal presentation and promotion of ideas, goods, and services by an identified sponsor.''[1] It also usually involves the use of mass media.

The words ''paid form'' distinguish advertising from publicity. Advertising requires the purchase of space or time in the medium in which it appears; publicity notices do not require such purchases. Although the numerous public service appeals concerning the United Fund, prevention of forest fires, and reduction of litter have all the characteristics of advertising, they are not paid for in the usual sense. ''Nonpersonal'' distinguishes advertising from personal selling, and ''ideas, goods, and services'' establishes that such effort is not restricted to products alone. Finally, a presentation is not advertising unless the sponsor is identified.

Advertising often occupies a dominant position in a promotion mix since it is an important source of product information for many consumers. But advertising can never provide the consumer with *total* information about a product. What it can do is to present sufficient information in a persuasive way to get the consumer to try the product.[2]

One study showed that consumers may evaluate products by *averaging* attribute information rather than *adding*. Given one bit of pertinent information about a product along with one less useful fact the consumer might average the two, and the resulting impression would be less favorable than if only the one piece of quality information were presented. Quality of information would seem to be more important than quantity.[3]

TYPES OF ADVERTISING

Selecting the right type of advertising to accomplish a particular objective is significant in the selection of media and the development of promotional strategy. The following three pairs of concepts describe different types of advertising: Product versus corporate advertising, primary demand versus selective demand advertising, and national versus local advertising.

Product versus Corporate Advertising

Most advertising is product advertising, and when used in this sense, the term *product* includes services and ideas. Corporate advertising, however, is becoming increasingly prevalent in today's business environment.

---

[1]Ralph S. Alexander and the Committee on Definitions, *Marketing Definitions* (Chicago: American Marketing Association, 1963), p. 9.

[2]See ''Too Much Info in Ads Hurts Consumer, Advertiser: Wells,'' *Advertising Age* (4 Mar. 1974): 57.

[3]C. Michael Troutman and James Shanteau, ''Do Consumers Evaluate Products by Adding or Averaging Attribute Information?'' *Journal of Consumer Research* 3 (Sept. 1976): 101–6.

Product Advertising

The subject of product advertising is the product itself (or service, or idea), and the advertising is aimed at informing people about the product in a persuasive way. It is often subdivided into direct-action and indirect-action advertising. _Direct-action advertising_ attempts to generate an immediate response from the consumer by such methods as including a coupon in the advertisement or distributing a flyer to residential doorsteps advertising a five-day sale.

With _indirect-action_ advertising, it is assumed that people are not going to rush right out to buy the product but can be persuaded to retain the information presented in the advertisements and use it when the time comes to make a buying decision.

Corporate Advertising

Corporate advertising (also known as institutional, or image) is concerned with enhancing the image of the company. Such advertising may not even mention the product, or at least the major product, but strives instead to create favorable impressions about the company (see figure 12-1, p. 151). It is often a moot question, however, as to whether such image enhancement can produce a lasting effect that will result in public support for the company in some future public issue.[4]

If a company is known at all, it always has an image. People form such images from company-initiated and company-controlled information and also from favorable or unfavorable information from other sources. The question of "high profile" or a "low profile" often arises. Should a company actively engage in promoting itself, or should it not call excessive attention to itself?[5]

A number of business executives have a high regard for corporate advertising. In a survey of top management executives of _Fortune's_ 500, 72 percent expressed favorable opinions about such advertising. The themes they considered appropriate and worthy of emphasis in the advertising included, in descending order, quality products/services, company philosophy, research and development, corporate leadership, ecological concerns, public issues, and corporate growth/profits.[6]

An increasingly sensitive issue associated with corporate advertising is _advocacy advertising_. The term is used to describe advertising in which businesses take positions on various social issues, usually at odds with the positions taken by influential critics of business, and usually in defense of their own actions.

In justifying such advertising it is argued that there are two forces involved with respect to such issues — the system (industries, businesses, financial institutions, etc.) and the adversary culture (certain facets of the intellectual and aca-

[4]See "Success of Corporate Ads Examined," _Advertising Age_ (August 24, 1981): 63.

[5]See Katherin Marton and J. J. Boddewyn, "Should a Corporation Keep a Low Profile?" _Journal of Advertising Research_ 18, no. 4 (Aug. 1978): 25-31.

[6]William S. Sachs and Joseph Chasin, "How Top Executives View Corporate Advertising," _Public Relations Journal_ (Nov. 1976): 20-22.

demic community, some political activists, and a few consumer-interest groups). Since the press is usually, by nature, on the side of the adversary culture because both question established institutions, advocacy advertising is said to be the only voice of the system. Moreover, such advertising provides the consumer with the other side of the issue, particularly if the advertising presents facts and is not restricted to flag-waving and extolling the virtues of the free enterprise system (commendable though that may be).[7]

But some people fear that allowing businesses to freely engage in advocacy advertising will lead to an imbalance of ideas because of the large financial resources businesses can put into the effort. Both sides are concerned about the "imbalance of ideas." Furthermore, critics of business see problems related to First Amendment considerations. Some critics would prefer that businesses classify advocacy advertising as commercial speech. Although companies would save taxes this way, they could be subject to the Federal Trade Commission's ad substantiation requirements for proof of accuracy. Otherwise the advertising would be considered political speech, tax deductions would not be claimed, and the company's right to state its opinions without proof would be protected under the First Amendment.[8]

In any event, many executives feel increasingly compelled to make use of corporate advertising, including advocacy advertising. The feeling is particularly strong in industries such as oil and lumber that have been the special targets of ecological critics. Yet there is no universal agreement as to the wisdom of engaging in advocacy advertising. Some contend that since such advertising says the things the company wants the audience to know, it is rarely successful because of the skepticism of an increasingly sophisticated audience.[9]

Primary Demand versus Selective Demand

In the concepts primary and selective motives and primary and selective demand, *primary* is related to generic products and *selective* to specific brands of products.

Primary Demand Advertising

The use of advertising designed to stimulate primary demand is often essential when introducing truly innovative products, especially if such products imply changes in life-styles or routine behavior. Because the objectives of such advertising are usually related to enhancing the consumer's knowledge of the generic product, the advertising must be more descriptive than argumentative. Most firms are somewhat reluctant to use primary demand advertising, except when it is nec-

---

[7]John E. O'Toole, "Advocacy Advertising Shows the Flag," *Public Relations Journal* 31, no. 4 (Nov. 1975): 14–16. See also Gertrude I. McWilliams, "Corporations Have Facts Vital to Public so Why Hide Them?" *Advertising Age* (Feb. 21, 1977): 54–58.

[8]S. Prakash Sethi, "Institutional/Image Advertising and Idea/Issue Advertising as Marketing Tools: Some Public Policy Issues," *Journal of Marketing* 43 (Jan. 1979): 68–78.

[9]See Tony Thompson, "Group Raps Advocacy Ads," *Advertising Age* (November 16, 1981): 82.

essary in the early stages of the product life cycle, because it benefits competitors as well as the initiating firm.

It might be worthwhile for firms to reconsider their traditional positions in this regard and continue primary demand advertising beyond the time they would normally abandon it. If they were to continue such generic advertising but adjust it to include the brand while maintaining the emphasis on the product, they might increase per capita consumption of the product and, in addition, prolong the product life cycle. All firms in the industry would benefit, of course; but the deserving companies should be able to retain their respective shares of the expanding market and be better off for the effort.[10]

Selective Demand Advertising

The purpose of selective demand advertising is to stimulate demand for the company's brand. This is the most common type of advertising, probably because there appears to be a more immediate pay-off with its use than with the use of primary demand advertising. However, some selective demand advertising probably stimulates primary demand, too. It is quite possible, for example, that the advertising for Scotch brand transparent tape increases the sale of all brands of such tape and that advertising Kleenex increases the sale of all brands of facial tissues.

National versus Local Advertising

The terms *national* and *local* identify the level of the advertiser. National advertising (also called *general*) is advertising placed by a manufacturer or other producer. Even if a manufacturer restricts an advertising effort to a single city, it is called national advertising. One explanation for the use of the term is that if the advertised brand has the potential of being sold nationally the advertising can be considered national.

Local advertising (also called *retail*) is advertising placed by retailers and other local businesses such as banks and service businesses, in local media. Some large retail chains actually engage in both local and national advertising. Retailing giants such as Safeway and Sears Roebuck & Company not only advertise locally, but also advertise on a national scale to the extent that their private brands become, in effect, national brands with sales restricted to their own outlets.

The objectives of national and local advertising are usually different. The national advertiser is promoting the product and does not really care where it is purchased as long as it is purchased. The local advertiser is not promoting products as much as he or she is promoting the store and does not really care which products are purchased as long as they are purchased at the store. Such differences in objectives are reflected in the respective promotional strategies.

---

[10]See Hershey H. Friedman and Linda Friedman, ''Advertising Myopia,'' *Journal of Advertising* 5, no. 2 (Spring 1976): 29–31.

CREATIVE ASPECTS OF ADVERTISING

Although promotion managers are usually not responsible for creating advertisements themselves, they are often required to evaluate proposed efforts, and intelligent evaluation requires a rudimentary knowledge of advertising creativity. In the following sections, therefore, we shall examine a few basic ideas in that light.[11]

Creativity has been defined as "the ability to formulate new combinations from two or more concepts already in the mind."[12] While creativity in this sense can be applied to any activity, in advertising it refers to designing and constructing advertisements. It should be mentioned, too, that not everyone can be a truly creative person. But everyone can be a critic of the creative efforts of someone else.

Initial Considerations

Creativity in advertising must begin with a consideration of many of the ideas already discussed. A consumer analysis, for example, provides an indication of the needs (biogenic or psychogenic) consumers may seek to satisfy with the purchase and use of the product. Moreover, such an analysis may thus serve to isolate appropriate groups of people with common buying motives and purchase behavior, thereby identifying the target markets. On the basis of the information thus obtained, the advertising appeal or the theme that will form the basis for the advertisement or advertising campaign can be determined.

An analysis of the product, then, indicates the want-satisfying characteristics of the product, either intrinsic or attributed. The characteristics associated with the needs determined in the consumer analysis can thus be selected, becoming "talking points" in the advertisement.

The foregoing analysis, plus a thorough understanding of the marketing, promotion, and advertising objectives, forms an effective information base for the creative effort.

Hierarchy of Effects

Objectives in the creation of advertisements are significant in connection with the hierarchy of effects concept of advertising. The discussion of objectives in chapter 8 of this concept suggests that advertising moves people up a series of steps beginning with awareness of the product and culminating in its purchase, and that advertising must be created consistent with the objectives at each step. The model used to describe the process was the Lavidge and Steiner model.[13] However, since that

---

[11]For a thorough discussion of creative aspects, see John S. Wright, Willis L. Winter, Jr., and Sherilyn K. Zeigler, *Advertising,* 5th ed. (New York: McGraw-Hill, 1982), Chapters 12–13; Maurice I. Mandell, *Advertising,* 3rd ed. (Englewood Cliffs, N.J.: Prentice-Hall, 1980), Chapters 25–27; or Kenneth E. Runyon, *Advertising and the Practice of Marketing* (Columbus: Charles E. Merrill, 1979), Chapters 11–15.

[12]John W. Haefele, *Creativity and Innovation* (New York: Reinhold, 1962), p. 5.

[13]Robert J. Lavidge and Gary A. Steiner, "A Model for Predictive Measurements of Advertising Effectiveness," *Journal of Marketing* 25 (October 1961): 59–62.

model was published in 1961 there have been at least fourteen other such models.[14]

Equally significant is the notion of the hierarchy of effects *within a single advertisement.* Since advertising and all of promotion is persuasive communication, each advertisement must reflect the steps through which one goes in being persuaded. A realistic model that portrays these steps is one with an unknown origin — AIDA (Attention, Interest, Desire, and Action). This model has been used historically in developing sales presentations in personal selling. The salesperson must first attract the attention of the prospect, then create interest in the product, then generate desire for the product, and finally induce action (purchase). Since persuasion is the goal in advertising as well as in personal selling, the essence of the model is equally appropriate in creating an advertisement.

Attention

Obviously, an advertisement cannot persuade until it attracts attention. Yet attracting attention is often difficult to do because of the influence of the forces of selective perception (discussed in chapter 2). So what can be done in creating an advertisement to make it attention-getting?

One needs to think in terms of the consumers' interests. Potential receivers of the message will simply "tune it out" if it is not consistent with their interests at the time. Beyond that, the creative artist uses dramatic headlines, bold colors, extensive white space, contrast, provocative illustrations, and musical jingles to attract attention.

But the advertisement will not accomplish its purpose if all it does is attract attention. So the device used should be associated in some way with the rest of the advertisement. The persuasion process will not be complete until the other three components in the model have done their work. Therefore, for example, the use of scantily clad females in inappropriate situations is not only sexist but irrelevant. An illustration of a woman in a bikini in an advertisement for earth-moving equipment will attract attention, but it will not sell bulldozers.

Other devices used to attract attention such as size and position of the ad are not a part of the creative process. Large ads attract more attention than small ones, and an advertisement on the back cover of a magazine gets more attention than one on the inside pages. In addition, some advertisers use fold-outs in magazines and inserts in newspapers to make their ads stand out.

Interest

An effective device used to attract attention will lead the reader or viewer into the rest of the advertisement. Persuasion will rarely be accomplished without moving the target audience beyond the attention-getter. The headline in a State Farm Insur-

[14]Charles Raymond, *Advertising Research: The State of the Art* (New York: Association of National Advertisers, 1976): 15.

ance advertisement, for example, states, "Claims aren't all alike, so State Farm has five different ways to get you action." The ad then explains the five ways.

The best way to create interest is to appeal to the self-interest of the reader or viewer. In general this requires thinking in terms of the consumer. Specifically it requires an understanding of the consumer's needs in purchasing and using the product.

Desire

Interest must be developed into desire if the persuasion process is to be completed. The reader or viewer must be convinced that the product will indeed be the solution to a need or problem. This can be accomplished by associating the appropriate product characteristics (benefits) with the needs the consumer is seeking to satisfy — relating talking points to buying motives.

Action

Finally, the advertisement should induce action by asking the reader or viewer to do something. But action does not necessarily mean the purchase of a product. If the objective of the advertisement is to generate knowledge about the product, for example (the second stage in the Lavidge and Steiner hierarchy), the action may simply be to "see it at your nearest department store." For example, the headline in an advertisement reads, "Get a free sample of Unisom and see why it's the #1 sleep aid," and a coupon to get the sample is included in the ad. The advertisement should suggest some action by the reader or viewer.

Also, since most people rarely read an entire print advertisement or devote complete attention to an entire TV commercial, the major thrust of the advertisement should be indicated in the early part of the ad. The headline cited not only attracts attention but also stimulates interest and induces action.

Unique Selling Proposition

Consumers are only interested in what the product will do for them. They have absolutely no reason to purchase any product or accept any idea unless they believe they will derive some benefit from doing so. Therefore, product benefits must be matched with consumer needs. Usually one or two benefits stand out from the others, and these form the basis for the central idea presented in the advertisement.

This central idea was referred to as a "Unique Selling Proposition" (USP) by the late Rosser Reeves of the Ted Bates advertising agency in the early 1940s. It suggests finding a particular selling point of a product that clearly distinguishes the product from its competitors in a unique way.[15] A single advertisement should con-

---

[15]Rosser Reeves, *Reality in Advertising* (New York: Alfred A. Knopf, 1961): 46–49.

tain one good USP and very few additional selling points because the minor points will tend to dilute the impact of the USP.

Visualization

Once the seeds of an idea have begun to germinate in the creative mind, a mental picture of what the idea will look like and how it will be presented must be formed. This activity is called *visualization*. Usually an idea or concept can be visualized in a number of ways. To visualize "golf," for example, one person might see a golfer teeing off; another might picture the golfer putting; and a third might simply imagine an entire golf course. The creative artist or artists must imagine how the idea can be conveyed best to the intended audience, using the most effective combination of words and illustrations and/or whatever else is appropriate for the medium considered before it is put on paper. Thus, visualization would include some or all of the possible elements of the advertisement.

Elements of a Print Advertisement

A print advertisement could include the following elements: headline, subheadlines, illustrations, body copy, and the standard items which might consist of a slogan, a trade character, seals of approval, and the logotype. Although many advertisements do not contain all of the elements, some do.

Headline and Subheadlines

The headline not only serves as an attention-getting device but it also identifies the audience to whom the advertisement is directed. "Fisher-Price Riding Toys rack up more mileage," for example, attracts the attention of parents or grandparents interested in toys. In addition, a good headline should generate interest in reading further into the ad. However, it should be a "selling" element itself because five times as many people read the headlines as read the body copy.[16]

In some cases, subheadlines are useful, particularly if they can serve as a bridge between the headline and the body copy, or if they can elaborate on the headline in an informational way. In an advertisement for Libby's salt- and sugar-free canned vegetables, for example, the headline is "Libby's Natural Pack Tastes Fresh," and the subheadline is "There's no salt or sugar added."

Illustrations

Most advertisements contain illustrations, which, like headlines, are designed to attract attention, select the audience, and generate interest in the body copy. But the illustration should also contribute to an understanding of the idea. An irrelevant

---

[16]David Ogilvy, *Confessions of an Advertising Man* (New York: Atheneum, 1964): 104.

illustration may attract attention, but unless it reinforces the idea in the advertisement, the attention may actually be diverted from the real meaning of the ad.

Body Copy

Although the word *copy* is sometimes used in advertising to refer to all the reading matter in an advertisement — headline, subheadlines, text, etc. — the term *body copy* refers only to the copy in the body of the advertisement. Most advertisements contain an element of body copy which is the major thrust of the ad. It is the *clincher* to the attention and interest generated by the headline and illustration. It provides the information intended to create desire and stimulate action.

Since many people do not read body copy, the headline and illustration should carry some of the selling burden. But if the headline and illustration are completely effective, they will lead the reader into the body copy, and if the copywriter has done a good job, the copy will be read.

Standard Items

Some firms include certain elements in all their advertisements. If a firm has a slogan, for example, it will be used most of time. "Like a good neighbor, State Farm is there," or "When you care enough to send the very best" (Hallmark) nearly always appear in their advertisements. Trade characters such as Ronald McDonald, the Jolly Green Giant, and the Pillsbury Dough Boy are consistently used if they have been established as symbols. When appropriate, seals such as the seal of the Underwriters' Laboratories or the Good Housekeeping Seal of Approval are included. Finally, the *logotype* (logo), a special design that identifies the advertiser and often is the same as the trademark, always appears in the advertisement.

Mrs. Butterworth
IBM's Groucho Marx

Elements of a Broadcast Commercial

The elements of a broadcast commercial are essentially the same as those of a print advertisement, with a few additional constraints and complexities. Radio commercials, for example, must appeal to the ears instead of the eyes, and television commercials must be designed for both eyes and ears.

One of the problems with radio commercials is the importance of the announcer. Since the impact of the commercial is determined by the delivery style of the announcer, and since delivery styles differ among announcers, the copy should be written with a particular delivery style in mind. If the commercial is presented by means of a dialogue or playlet, the copy must be written to fit and appropriate actors chosen to read the parts. Singing commercials require the combined efforts of a copywriter and a music composer.

Since television commercials must contain both video and audio components, their creation is the most complex of all. A television commercial is more than simply the combination of a print advertisement and a radio commercial. Properly conceived, its effect is synergistic. But the basic elements of both must be considered and incorporated into a TV format, including dramatization and demonstration.

Layout and Storyboard

The layout for a print advertisement and the storyboard for a television commercial are the physical manifestations of visualization. They are the means by which the creative idea is initially put on paper. The task in their construction is difficult, requiring uniquely creative talents.

The *layout* includes all the elements of the advertisement as visualized in the earlier process and combined in a way that purports to resemble the finished advertisement. It is used as a guide in developing the finalized product, both by the creative personnel and the client whose approval is sought.

The *storyboard* for a TV commercial is analogous to the layout for a print advertisement. It is a portrayal of the visualized commercial and is shown to the client for approval. It is then used as the basis for the production of the commercial. The storyboard consists of a series of illustrations (stills) with detailed instructions for camera techniques and action. The storyboard is not quite as functional as the layout, however, because the completed commercial will involve action which can only be suggested in the storyboard. Nevertheless, it plays a vital part in the development and production of a television commercial.

The Advertising Campaign

Advertising creativity generally extends beyond the design and construction of a single advertisement or commercial. Usually the effort must be directed toward the creation of a series of advertisements and/or commercials combined around a central theme into an advertising campaign. Thus the crux of the campaign is the theme, often called the *copy platform.* Individual advertisements or commercials, then, may vary in both specific creative aspects and media used. But the theme provides the direction. Examples of effective themes in recent years include Virginia Slims cigarettes' "You've come a long way, baby," Pepsi's "Take the Pepsi Challenge," and Folger's "Mountain Grown" coffee.

Sometimes a campaign may be planned so the series of advertisements builds toward the accomplishment of an ultimate objective, in the manner of Lavidge and Steiner's hierarchy of effects model. For example, early presentations may be aimed at creating awareness, with successive ads designed to lead the consumer through the subsequent steps of knowledge, liking, preference, conviction, and purchase.

Morris in Nine Lives

Coke "Catch The Wave"

ADVERTISING MEDIA

To the average person not associated with the business side of advertising, *media* refers to those devices by means of which people are informed or entertained. To the advertiser, *media* refers to the vehicles used to carry the advertising message to its intended target. In some cases both are referring to the same things — newspapers, magazines, television, and radio. But the advertiser includes in the concept other devices as well, such as direct mail, outdoor (billboards), transit, and various other communication methods not generally thought of as media by lay people.

Each medium has its own role to play in the advertising scheme of things, and the relative importance of each medium to any single advertiser depends upon the advertiser's particular objectives, target market, and resources. Media can be classified as follows:

billboards?

A. Print media
  1. Newspapers
  2. Magazines
B. Broadcast media
  1. Television
  2. Radio
C. Direct mail
D. Out-of-home media
  1. Outdoor advertising
  2. Transit advertising
E. Specialty advertising
F. Other media
  1. Directory advertising
  2. Free-circulation shoppers' guides
  3. Motion picture advertising

In the next two chapters we shall discuss each medium in detail.

SUMMARY

Advertising differs from other elements of the promotion mix in that it is a nonpersonal, paid form of presentation, with the sponsor being identified; but it is similar to other elements in that it involves products, services, or ideas.

Product advertising is often subdivided into direct-action and indirect-action categories. Corporate advertising is aimed at enhancing the image of the firm, and its focus is not directly on promoting the product. Identified with corporate advertising is the practice of advocacy advertising, which can be loosely defined as promoting the business side of certain controversial social issues.

Primary demand advertising is designed to stimulate demand for the generic product; selective demand advertising is concerned with the demand for a particular brand. National (general) advertising is usually considered that which is placed by a manufacturer or other institution at that level. Local (retail) advertising is placed by retailers and other local advertisers in local media. The objectives of national advertising are usually relatively more product oriented than those of local advertisers, which are usually more ''store'' oriented.

Promotion managers are not usually responsible for creating advertisements or commercials, but they must often evaluate the creative efforts of others. In order to do this it is necessary to understand the basic process involved. Creating advertisements or commercials begins with a thorough analysis of the consumer and the product to find the match between the product and the market. This should generally include the use of a "Unique Selling Proposition," or major selling point associated with the product. The advertisement must then be developed to lead the target audience through the successive steps of attention, interest, desire, and action.

Visualization is the process of forming a mental picture of the finished advertisement and must incorporate all the elements of the advertisement or commercial. The elements may include a headline, subheadlines, illustrations, body copy, and certain standard items that always appear. The basic elements are the same for both print and broadcast advertisements but differ in their adaptation. The layout and storyboard are the physical manifestations of visualization for print and broadcast media, respectively. The entire process must usually be applied to a series of advertisements which, taken together, comprise an advertising campaign.

Advertising media carry the advertising message to its intended target. They can be conveniently classified into print, broadcast, direct mail, out-of-home, specialty, and miscellaneous media.

QUESTIONS FOR THOUGHT AND REVIEW

1. Carefully distinguish advertising from the other elements of the promotion mix. How do "public service" announcements fit into the concept?

2. What is meant by the statement that consumers may *average* attribute information rather than *adding?* What is the significance of this to advertisers?

3. What is *primary demand* advertising? How can selective demand advertising also stimulate primary demand? Relate argumentative versus descriptive copy to primary and selective demand advertising.

4. What is *institutional advertising?* What justification is there for its use? Discuss in terms of the current business environment.

5. What is *advocacy advertising?* Present arguments both attacking and defending its use.

6. Discuss the basis for distinguishing national advertising from local advertising. What is the logic?

7. Explain why the creative process must begin with an analysis of the consumer and the product. What use is made of the information?

8. Compare the concept of the *hierarchy of effects* as discussed in chapter 8 with the concept applied to a single advertisement.

9. Since getting attention is the first step in the persuasion process, the creative artist should use whatever device necessary to accomplish the purpose. Do you agree? Discuss.

10. Explain, using examples, the best way of creating interest in an advertisement or commercial.

11. What is meant by *inducing action?* Does this always mean purchasing the product? Explain.

12. What is a *Unique Selling Proposition* and why is it important?
13. Explain the concept of *visualization.* What is its use?
14. What are the elements of a print advertisement? Are they the same for a broadcast commercial? Explain.
15. The headline should not only attract attention but should also be a selling element itself. Why?
16. Discuss considerations in selecting or designing an illustration for an advertisement.
17. What is the *layout?* The *storyboard?* How are the two related? What are their uses?
18. What is an *advertising campaign?* Discuss the creative problems associated with it.
19. How are media classified?

13

ADVERTISING—
PRINT AND
BROADCAST MEDIA

I. Print media
   A. Newspapers
   B. Magazines
II. Broadcast media
   A. Television
   B. Radio

With this chapter we being a discussion of the specific media used in advertising, devoting our attention to the print and broadcast media. We will consider the remaining media in chapter 14.

PRINT MEDIA

The predominant print media used by advertisers are newspapers and magazines. The advertiser in a sense buys an audience because these media create their audiences through their editorial content of news, stories, and features.

Newspapers

More advertising dollars are spent in newspapers than in any other medium. Furthermore, by far the heaviest users of newspaper advertising are local advertisers. This is understandable because most newspapers have a local audience. They are often confined to a single city or, as in the case of metropolitan newspapers, to a state or region. Moreover, the readership in the area a newspaper serves is selected geographically rather than qualitatively in contrast to magazines, which appeal to nationwide special-interest groups such as men, women, hunters, or photography buffs and are not usually confined to one geographical area.

But geographical selectivity can often make newspapers useful to national advertisers. When a particular city or region offers unusual profit opportunities, the advertiser can reinforce the overall program with additional concentration in the newspaper serving the area. In view of the increasing pressure for the presentation of more facts in advertising, newspapers offer an excellent medium since they lend themselves to this purpose so well.[1]

Newspapers may also become more attractive to national advertisers because of a relatively new service under experimentation called *target market coverage*. The service, a sort of newspaper — direct-mail mix, involves the dissemination of preprinted advertising flyers supplied to the newspaper by the advertiser. Traditionally, such flyers are inserted into the newspapers as they come off the press and are delivered with the newspapers for a fee. But the flyers only reach those people who buy the newspaper.

The objective in the experimental target market coverage is to assist the advertiser in getting the flyers into the hands of the people who do not see the newspaper. The approach is to identify the nonsubscribers of the newspaper and then provide direct-mailing assistance to the advertiser in reaching those people. The net result is that theoretically everyone in the market will receive the advertiser's flyer, either in the newspaper or by direct mail.[2]

---

[1]John Consoli, ``Leading Users of Newspaper Ads Praise Medium's Effectiveness,'' *Editor and Publisher* 109, part 3 (24 July 1976): 7–8.

[2]``Now It's `Target Market Coverage,''' *Media Decisions* 11, pt. 2 (Sept. 1976): 64–65; 148. See also Stuart Emmrich, ``Papers Start to Cash in on Shared Mail,'' *Advertising Age* (August 11, 1982): 14, 70; and Renee Blakkan, ``Strength Among the Week,'' *Advertising Age* (May 30, 1983): M–11–14.

Classification of Newspapers

Newspapers are typically classified according to their frequency of publication – daily, weekly, etc. In addition many daily newspapers publish Sunday editions. Weekly newspapers are usually associated with small towns or with otherwise homogeneous communities.

Traditionally, newspapers have also been classified by paper size, either standard size or tabloid. The standard size consisted of eight 2-inch columns about 21 inches deep, and the tabloids were about half that size. The current standard size may vary from 6 to 9 columns with varying page lengths; there is also variation in the size of tabloids. Advertisers often criticize the lack of standardization.

Newspapers may also be divided into morning or evening papers, although there is a declining trend in the number of evening papers published, even in markets where one company publishes both morning and evening papers. From 1978 to 1982, for example, at least fifty-seven evening papers in the United States have converted to morning editions.[3] It is predicted that in the 1980s half the cities in the United States with two or more independently owned newspapers will lose one of their papers.[4] However, newspapers are not on the way out. On the contrary, most existing papers have high hopes for the future – particularly those established as the leaders in their markets.[5] Suburban newspapers and special interest papers appeal to certain ethnic groups, business people, and other specialized groups.

Classification of Newspaper Advertising

Newspaper advertising is usually divided into four categories: display, classified, classified display, and special. Display advertising is of most concern to most business advertisers since it involves the use of more components such as illustrations, headlines, variations in type, and white space and is usually considered more effective. Classified advertising is typically referred to as "want ads." With the exception of a few types of businesses such as real estate agents, used car dealers, and builders, it is used predominantly by individuals. There does seem to be the possibility, however, that its use will increase in the future.[6] Today many publishers are aggressively marketing their classified sections. For example, some print the classified sections separately and insert them into the body of the paper; others offer to readers free two-line ads which seem to be so successful they stimulate purchase of this space for other items.[7]

Classified display describes advertisements that appear in the classified section but contain some elements of display ads, such as an illustration. Special adver-

---

[3]"A Newspaper Shoot-Out in Dallas," *Business Week* (September 27, 1982): 113.

[4]Jennifer Alter, "Competitive Dailies Vanishing," *Advertising Age* (June 1, 1981): 32.

[5]Stuart Emmrich, "Newspapers Hold Hope for '83 Rebound," *Advertising Age* (November 29, 1982): 28; also "What's Feeding the Popularity of the Press," *Business Week* (May 2, 1983): 118.

[6]For an excellent discussion of an expanded use of classified advertising see E. S. Lorimor, "Classified Advertising: A Neglected Medium," *Journal of Advertising* 6, no. 1 (Winter 1977): 17–25.

[7]Craig Endicott, "Publishers Put Class into Classifieds," *Advertising Age* (May 30, 1983): M-24.

tising includes such things as legal advertising — the required publication of certain legal actions — and political advertising. The advertising purchased by candidates running for public offices must be paid for in advance. Historically, losing candidates have not been inclined to want to pay for advertising that obviously failed to get them elected!

Newspaper Supplements and Tabloid Inserts

Until recently nearly all Sunday editions of newspapers have had at least one supplement. The comic section is one such supplement. Others include such syndicated publications as *Parade* and *Family Weekly,* which are produced by publishing companies who sell them to the newspapers. Still others may be locally edited. The supplements are printed on paper comparable to that used in magazines, and the physical quality of the advertisements is thus superior to those in the newspapers. Moreover, the advertising rates for four-color advertisements in the supplements are very close to the black-and-white rates for magazines. Unlike magazines, the selectivity of audience is the same as that for the newspapers in which they are included — geographical and not qualitative.

Many newspapers, however, are scrapping the supplements. There seems to be a trend among retailers to use more inserts, and the advertising pages in the supplements have suffered as a result.[8]

Tabloid inserts are preprinted usually multiple-page advertising supplements provided to the newspaper by the advertiser to be inserted into the newspaper. The newspaper's charge for the inserting and delivery service is usually comparable to that for the same amount of space for black-and-white advertisements in the newspaper.

Newspaper Rates

Newspaper rates are quoted in terms of either *agate lines* or *column inches.* An agate line is a measurement of space equal to $\frac{1}{14}$ inch deep and one column wide, whatever the width of the column. A column inch is a space 1 inch deep and one column wide — again, regardless of the width of the column. Thus, a column inch contains 14 agate lines.

Typically, newspapers quote lower rates to local advertisers, expressed in terms of column inches, than to national advertisers whose rates are usually computed in agate lines. Such a dual rate structure is attacked by national advertisers as being unjustified; but it is defended by newspapers on the grounds that local advertising is their basic livelihood, and since agency commissions are not involved, the lower rates are appropriate. Furthermore, they argue that the greater amount of space purchased by retailers simply because of the lower rates is substantial; whereas a lower rate would make little difference to national advertisers.

The basic rate applies to advertisements placed ROP (run-of-paper). This means that the advertisement may appear on any page, or at any place on the

---

[8]Stuart Emmrich, "Future Cloudy for Sunday Supplements," *Advertising Age* (March 14, 1983): 3, 6, 62.

page. There are preferred positions, such as next to reading matter, or at the top of the page, or on a specific page; if an advertiser wants to be assured of a specified preferred position, the newspaper usually charges extra. In addition to this adjustment to the basic rate, newspapers also charge more for color in advertisements and require the purchase of a certain minimum amount of space for such advertisements. Another adjustment to the basic rate is often found in the use of *open* rates. If the rate is quoted open, it is increasingly lower as additional space is purchased, resulting in substantial discounts for large amounts of space. If no rate differential is allowed for quantity purchases, the rate is said to be *flat*.

Compounding the rate structure further is the use of *combination rates*. These occur when a single publisher owns, say, both the morning and evening newspapers. In such cases the rate for advertising in both papers is substantially less than the sum of the basic rates quoted for advertising in each of the two newspapers alone.

Comparison of Two or More Newspapers

An advertiser may be faced with the problem of deciding which of two or more newspapers to use. The important criteria are *cost* and *circulation* because the objective is to reach the largest number of potential customers at the lowest cost. Therefore, the first consideration with respect to any newspaper or other medium is that its circulation comprise people in the advertiser's market. Anyone else whom the newspaper reaches is *waste circulation,* and the number of such people should be minimized.

Having established that the newspapers under consideration have appropriate circulations, the procedure is to determine the cost of reaching such people in light of the advertising rates of the respective newspapers. But comparing rates alone without circulations can be misleading because the newspapers with the highest circulations usually have the highest rates. To accomplish the purpose, a hypothetical rate called the *milline rate* is employed. The milline rate is the cost of reaching an assumed one million people with one agate line of advertising and is reflected in the following formula:

$$\text{Milline rate} = \frac{\text{Agate line rate} \times 1{,}000{,}000}{\text{Circulation}}$$

The milline rate's only function is in comparing the cost efficiency of newspapers. Its use allows the advertiser to analyze newspapers in terms of both agate line rates and circulation. The following example illustrates its use:[9]

$$\textit{Tulsa World:} \quad \frac{\$2.64 \times 1{,}000{,}000}{99{,}603} = \$26.50$$

$$\textit{Daily Oklahoman:} \quad \frac{\$4.50 \times 1{,}000{,}000}{187{,}352} = \$24.02$$

[9]Rates and circulation figures from Standard Rate and Data Service, Inc., *Newspaper Rates and Data,* (June 12, 1983): 639–40, 643.

Notice that the newspaper with the highest rate per agate line ($4.50 as opposed to $2.64) has the lowest milline rate. The difference is a reflection of the difference in circulation.

Standard Rate and Data Service, a service listing rates, circulation figures, and other information for all major media, utilizes two versions of the milline rate — *maximil rate* and *minimil rate*. The maximil rate is computed from the open or flat rate; the minimil rate is figured from the lowest rate available (after deducting all space or frequency discounts).

Magazines

Despite the demise of a number of old friends that will forever remain in the hearts of those who knew them, the magazine industry is not dead. It is true that *Collier's, The Saturday Evening Post, Life,* and *Look* are no longer with us — at least in their original form. But the void created when they left the scene is being filled by new and different publications designed to appeal quite effectively to our changing culture.[10]

Among the latest magazine trends is the increasing prevalence of city, regional, and statewide publications, referred to by the umbrella term *local magazines.*[11] These magazines are found in virtually every section of the country and are devoted to promoting the areas they serve. They feature activities and stories about their areas and include discussions of noteworthy events. The readership is apparently excellent, and the concept must have appeal to advertisers wishing to magnify their impact in special markets.

Another relatively new development is the use of in-flight magazines on airlines. Traditional magazines have always been available for passengers, but these magazines are published for or by the airlines themselves and are placed in the seat pockets in front of the passengers. Their appeal to advertisers is in reaching the businesspeople described as "frequent fliers."[12]

There are many reasons why magazines rank high as a major medium for many advertisers. The exceptionally good selectivity of audience possible with magazines minimizes waste circulation. There is a magazine designed for almost every special-interest group, as well as magazines that appeal to general audiences.

Magazines have a longer life than most other media. A monthly magazine often remains on the coffee table for an entire month, and the members of the household may be exposed to a firm's advertisement several times during that period; but there is nothing more stale than a day-old newspaper. Moreover, magazines are usually read in a leisurely way, whereas the average time spent in reading a daily newspaper is 20 to 30 minutes (see figure 13–1).

Color reproduction in most magazines is superior to that in newspapers. The main reason is the lower quality of paper used by newspapers, which affects the

---

[10]See Section 2 in *Advertising Age,* October 19, 1981, and *Advertising Age,* October 25, 1982, pp. M-9–60 for an extensive discussion of magazines.

[11]For an in-depth discussion of local magazines, see Section 2 in *Advertising Age,* Jan. 22, 1979.

[12]See Robert Reed, "Flying Those Not-Always-so-Friendly Skies," *Advertising Age* (July 5, 1982): M-2–3.

The double exposure factor.

Two advertising exposures are better than one. And two advertising exposures for the price of one are even better.

The question is, where can you find such a bargain? And the answer isn't a television commercial. Once it runs, it runs its course. And nobody gets another look unless you pay the price all over again.

A magazine is a different proposition. It doesn't disappear before the reader's eyes. It waits for him to come back to the same magazine and the same ad.

The result is, the average reader of the average magazine is exposed to your ad twice. And what's that worth to you?

The three classic Politz research studies on the subject will all tell you that a reader's second exposure causes a significant increase in the one result every advertiser wants: willingness to buy. And it's all yours at no extra cost.

Make this your year to re-evaluate the balance of power between television and magazines. And ask the MPA for an IMS computer run based on the Media Imperatives* and your prospects, your data, your dollars.

Magazine Publishers Association, Inc.
575 Lexington Avenue, New York, N.Y. 10022. (212) 752-0055
*Simmons Media Studies

Magazines.
The balance of power.

FIGURE 13–1   An advertisement for magazines as an advertising medium.   *Source:* Magazine Publishers Association, Inc.

quality of color. A certain amount of prestige is associated with advertising in some magazines, too. In the heyday of *Life* magazine, for example, one would often see counter cards in retail stores proclaiming that a particular product was "as advertised in *Life.*" Another factor is the secondary or *pass-along* circulation enjoyed by most magazines. Secondary circulation is not as valuable as the primary circulation, but it can add to the total reach.

However, magazines are not as flexible as newspapers, spot radio, and even television in some instances. Most magazine deadlines for the insertion of advertising are from three weeks to two months in advance of publication; whereas newspaper advertisements can be placed with as little as two or three days' notice. Moreover, nationally distributed magazines do not lend themselves to advertising tailored for local areas, although in recent years improvements have been made. Most national magazines now offer regional editions, and the advertiser is not obliged to contract for national distribution when a single region will suffice. Some magazines offer a *partial ad,* whereby the advertiser chooses the states where the ad will appear; but the cost is usually the same as for full circulation.

Classification of Magazines

There are several ways to classify magazines. For example, they can be viewed according to their frequency of publication. On this basis there are weeklies, semimonthlies, monthlies, bimonthlies, and quarterlies. Monthly magazines outnumber all other types, and weeklies are the second most important. The frequency of publication is sometimes a significant factor in the development of promotional strategy. If the strategy calls for repetitive impact in a short period of time, for example, weekly publications may be more appropriate than monthlies.

Magazines can also be classified on the basis of page size, as exemplified by the size differences among such magazines as *TV Guide, National Geographic, Newsweek,* and *Ebony.* But the most important method of classifying magazines is in terms of the audiences they reach; there are consumer magazines, business publications, and farm magazines.

Consumer magazines are read by people who purchase products for personal consumption. The category is so broad that it must be subdivided to be useful to the advertiser. A logical way to divide consumer magazines initially is to separate them into general magazines and those appealing to special interest groups. General magazines include such publications as the *Reader's Digest* whose appeal is to both men and women from various age, occupational, and income groups. Special interest magazines are not designed for the public in general but are edited for people whose interests lie in the areas by which the magazines are identified. Such magazines range all the way from men's magazines *(Playboy)* and women's magazines *(Cosmopolitan)* to the much narrower interest groups served by such magazines as *Hot Rod, Field and Stream,* and *Popular Photography.* The advent of home computer magazines, some of which are designed especially for people who know very little about computers, is a recent departure from the traditional.[13] In

---

[13]Stuart J. Elliott, "Computer Books for Novices Go On-Line," *Advertising Age* (June 27, 1983): 32, 74.

addition, magazines such as *Avenue* and *Parkway* aimed at the "very wealthy" are delivered without charge to affluent residents in New York City and Dallas, respectively. Other cities are following the trend.[14]

Business publications appeal to people in various trades and identifiable groups of publications are associated with each of several categories. General business magazines, such as *Fortune* and *Business Week,* are of interest to managerial people at many levels in all kinds of businesses. Trade magazines are primarily aimed at retailers and wholesalers; they include such publications as *Progressive Grocer, Supermarket News,* and *Hardware World.* Industrial magazines such as *Iron Age* appeal primarily to manufacturers, and professional magazines are edited for people in such professional fields as medicine, dentistry, and law. The list of special interest business publications is almost endless.[15]

Business publications may serve their markets vertically or horizontally. Vertical publications, such as *Iron Age* in its field and *Advertising Age* in a different field, are aimed at people in their entire respective industries. Horizontal magazines, on the other hand, deal with specific functions across many industries. *Sales and Marketing Management,* for example, appeals to people in those positions in any type of business and is not restricted in interest to any single industry.

Farm magazines as a group, too, reflect interests as varied as those in the other fields. General farm magazines such as *Successful Farming* are designed for all categories of farming; some farm magazines appeal to people in specific types of farming or ranching. The latter includes such diverse publications as *Hoard's Dairyman, Beef, and Poultry Tribune.*

Farm magazines are generally family magazines. They are often concerned with the many aspects of farming as a way of life and provide an excellent medium with generally high readership to an advertiser for use in reaching this particular market segment.

Magazine Rates

The base unit in a magazine's rate structure is the page. Thus the cost of advertising in magazines is usually expressed in terms of pages, half-pages, or quarter-pages. A sliding scale in the determination of rates is applied to the size of the advertisement and also to the frequency of insertion and quantity of space purchased over a contract period. Thus a full page costs less than two half pages; the cost of a half page is less than twice the cost of a quarter page; and the rates decrease with increasing amounts of space purchased. The decision regarding the appropriate size of advertisement can be more difficult than it seems. It has been found, for example, that a large advertisement attracts more attention than a small one, but not proportionately so. That is, a full-page ad will be noticed by more people than a half-page ad, but not by twice as many. So the question might be whether the additional attention generated by the larger advertisement is worth the additional cost.

---

[14]See "Magazines that Zero in on the Super-Rich," *Business Week* (May 23, 1983): 47.

[15]For an extensive discussion of business publications, see Section 2 in *Advertising Age,* May 11, 1981.

In addition to the discount structure already mentioned, adjustments to the base rate are also made for other reasons. For example, a *four-color* advertisement may cost from 15 percent to 40 percent more than a black-and-white (B/W) page, depending upon the magazine. A *bleed* page (one on which the color runs to the edge of the page and there is no white border around the advertisement) may cost more, although some magazines make no additional charges for bleed pages.

A premium is also charged for *preferred positions.* The most significant preferred positions in magazines are the cover pages — second, third, and fourth and first, when it is sold. The first cover is the outside of the front cover; the second is the inside front cover; the third is the inside back cover; and the fourth is the back cover. Other positions may be considered preferred under certain conditions, and additional charges may or may not be assessed. The center spread in some magazines, bound in such a way that the magazine naturally falls open at that point, may be considered preferred. In addition, some advertisers want their insertions to appear adjacent to certain feature sections of the magazine dealing with subjects related to their products. Other than these positions, however, it does not seem to make much difference where the advertisement appears. Unless preferred positions are specified, the advertisements are usually placed ROP, as in the case of newspapers. However, magazine advertisers are beginning to insist on more attention to ad positioning.[16]

Comparison of Two or More Magazines

The space rate for advertising in magazines is not necessarily significant by itself. Also to be considered is the magazine's circulation. As with newspapers, the objective is to reach the largest number of people at the lowest cost and with the least amount of waste circulation. So the first consideration in establishing alternatives is to make sure their respective circulations comprise the right people. Then, the problem is to determine the relative costs of using each of the alternatives in reaching a specified number of people.

Several factors complicate circulation comparisons. A magazine's secondary or pass-along circulation adds to the total number of people included in the primary circulation figures as shown by the magazine itself and audited by the Audit Bureau of Circulations, an independent organization providing reliability to the published figures. But no one knows how much it adds. There seems to be evidence that the primary readers are considerably more responsive to advertising than the secondary readers. Despite this evidence, advertisers have been making media decisions on the basis of a total audience concept by which they lump primary and secondary readers together.[17]

Another complicating factor is the difference between a magazine's *delivered* circulation and its *guaranteed* circulation. The rate structure is based on circulation figures, and a portion of the circulation comes from newsstand sales. But

---

[16]See Stuart Emmrich, "Magazines Pressed on Positioning of Ads," *Advertising Age* (September 28, 1981): 3, 92.

[17]Bernice Kanner, "Dozen Magazines Study Primary Readers," *Advertising Age* (12 Feb. 1979): 2.

since one is never certain how many copies will be sold in the newsstands, to avoid overstatement magazines may guarantee a figure less than the delivered circulation it actually expects.

In comparing two or more magazines for possible use in the media mix, the basic factors to be considered are space cost and circulation. The procedure is to use a formula analogous to the milline rate associated with newspaper comparisons, except that instead of indicating the cost of reaching one million people with one agate line of advertising, it indicates the cost of reaching 1,000 people with one full-page advertisement. The rate is called the *cost-per-thousand,* usually expressed as CPM (M is the Roman numeral for 1,000), and is determined by the following formula:

$$CPM = \frac{\text{1-page rate} \times 1,000}{\text{Circulation}}$$

Use of the formula enables an advertiser to compare the rates of the magazine alternatives despite the differences in their circulations, as indicated in the following example (page rates are for a 1-page, four-color advertisement):[18]

$$\textit{Reader's Digest} \qquad \frac{\$91,300 \times 1,000}{17,900,290} = \$5.10$$

$$\textit{National Geographic} \qquad \frac{\$97,970 \times 1,000}{10,613,599} = \$9.23$$

The cost-per-thousand for *Reader's Digest* is considerably lower than for *National Geographic.* There may be factors that serve to temper such disparity. The circulation of one magazine may be more definitive than that of another, for example, and therefore potentially more productive as far as a particular advertiser is concerned. Then the higher cost-per-thousand can be worth the difference.

BROADCAST MEDIA

Television viewing and radio listening are almost as much a part of American life as eating and sleeping. Virtually every family in the United States has at least one TV set. It has been said, perhaps facetiously, that more people own TV sets than bathtubs. And an increasing number of American families have two or more sets. The market saturation is even greater with radios. The average home in the United States contains several radios — perhaps as many as 5 or 6 — located throughout the house, in the car, and in the barns and on farm vehicles of farm and ranch families. In addition, portable radios can be taken anywhere.

With a mass market so saturated with broadcast receivers, it is no wonder that television and radio offer enormous opportunities to advertisers.

---

[18]Rates and circulation figures from Standard Rate and Data Service, Inc., *Consumer Magazines and Farm Publication Rates and Data* (May 27, 1983): 203–4, 214–15.

Television

The growth of television has been phenomenal. It took no more than 25 years from the time TV sets really became available to the mass market in the early 1950s to reach near saturation of the market. No other medium can claim that distinction, and its unique qualities have made it the leading medium for national advertisers.

Advantages

Because a typical family has its TV set on several hours each day, the potential for exposure to an advertiser's message is quite high. With print media, the reader uses the self-selection process to determine what advertisements to read; the television viewer uses the same process to determine what commercials *not* to watch.[19] This habit may be an advantage to the advertiser because the viewer is less likely to "tune out" a commercial to which exposure is imminent than a reader is to ignore an advertisement to which exposure is simply latent.

The impact of a combined oral and visual presentation of an advertisement is potentially greater than when one or the other is lacking; the target audience is doubly stimulated. Moreover, the target audience is usually quite large even for those programs that fail to make the top ten. Even strategically placed *spot advertising* reaches sizable audiences.

Repetition sometimes to the point of nausea is characteristic of television advertisers. But repetition is an important part of most effective advertising campaigns, and the success of many campaigns is largely due to its use.

Television is as personal as a "nonpersonal" medium can be. Because it brings familiar faces into the living room as if they were old friends, it is a natural medium for the use of well-known personalities in presenting messages. However, the product endorsement or testimonial is not restricted to and did not start with television. The first woman to endorse a product was Lily Langtry, an English actress who endorsed a product of the Pears' Soap company around the turn of the century.

When entertainers read commercial messages on television, they may not necessarily be giving testimonials in the strict sense of the concept. However, they are doing so by implication. Since the effect is the same, legal sanctions prevent such people from creating an identification with products they do not use.

Properly chosen, famous personalities can add credibility to an advertiser's message. But those who are selected should be easily associated with the product. For example, Karl Malden, because of his detective roles, has been quite readily associated with American Express traveler's checks in their emphasis on the risk of losing cash while traveling. Full-figured Jane Russell has been identified with an 18-hour bra, and Bill Cosby has successfully promoted Jell-O because of his identification with kids. But unless there is some association between the individual and

---

[19]"Advertiser Says TV Commercials Capture Attention Print Can Miss," *Broadcasting* 92, pt. 1 (21 Mar. 1977): 55–56.

the product, the use of well-known personalities in television commercials is usually ineffective.[20]

Limitations

Some characteristics of television limit its effectiveness. The life of a TV commercial is over the moment the commercial ends. The viewer who misses it cannot go back later for the message as is possible with print media. The fact that television reaches such a mass audience can be a limitation as well as an advantage. Unless the product advertised is used by everyone, for example, there is no way to avoid paying for some waste circulation. The choice of programs and stations can provide only a limited degree of audience selectivity.

Unlike print media wherein advertisements can be added by simply increasing the number of pages, the number of television commercials that can be added is limited by the number of hours a station is on the air. This inherent limitation has been a major cause of one of the biggest criticisms of television by both viewers and advertisers and is called *TV clutter*.[21] Viewers resent having to watch 6–10 successive commercials; advertisers dislike their messages blurred by sheer numbers and fear they will lose much of their impact. Remote control channel switchers often referred to as *commercial zappers* allow an increasing number of TV watchers to avoid commercials by switching the set off or to another channel when the commercial comes on.[22]

Despite the possibility of reasonably low costs in reaching a thousand homes, television is an expensive medium, and the costs have been steadily rising. Since the late 1960s the cost of a commercial minute on certain network programs has risen from around $60,000 to well over $200,000. The cost of a 30-second commercial on the 1983 Super Bowl was $400,000, and on the final episode of M*A*S*H, a 30-second commercial cost $450,000. Spot announcements (those not identified with any program) also entail high out-of-pocket costs. A 30-second spot during Class AA time (7–10 P.M.) may cost several thousand dollars. It should be emphasized, however, that the cost figures alone are not necessarily significant. When one considers the number of potential receivers of the message, the costs become quite reasonable.

Types of Television Advertising

Three basic alternatives are available to an advertiser using television: program sponsorship, participation shows, and spot advertising. (A fourth type of advertising is local advertising, which is primarily of concern to retailers and some manufacturers who share the cost with their retailers.)

---

[20]Bourne Morris, "Will a Personality Sell a Product Better? Pros & Cons," *Advertising Age* (5 Feb. 1979): 43–44.

[21]Colby Coates, "TV Clutter Rankles Public Most, Survey of Media Shows," *Advertising Age* (12 Feb. 1979): 4.

[22]Susan Spillman, "Is TV Spot Zapping Zooming?" *Advertising Age* (June 27, 1983): 1, 82.

Program sponsorship.   In the early years of television, program sponsorship was the predominant method; it is a rarity today. With this type of advertising, an advertiser sponsors an entire show and does not share commercial time with anyone else. Although a few specials each year are identified with a single company, rising costs have caused the demise of the single-sponsor program.

In the years of the single sponsor, the advertisers had a good deal to do with the development of the programs they sponsored. The responsibility is now almost entirely that of the network or of the local stations in nonnetwork shows.

Participation shows.   Most shows today are participation shows; several noncompeting sponsors share the costs and the commercial time for a particular show. Sponsors have little or nothing to do with the development of the show and "buy in" to those shows most compatible with their products and images. The network and local stations attempt to broadcast programs that attract large audiences that will, in turn, attract the advertisers. The popularity of a show is fleeting, with the exception of a few shows such as the long-lived "Gunsmoke," and a new show is always a bit of a gamble.

In addition to programs designed strictly for network television, Hollywood motion pictures are available to networks and local stations after their initial run in the theaters. Commercial time on these shows, too, is sold on a participating basis. And syndicated programs are becoming increasingly significant. These include reruns on local stations of previously successful network programs as well as a number of new programs produced independently and sold to individual stations. Two extremely popular recent shows of the latter type are "Entertainment Tonight" and "People's Court."[23]

Spot advertising.   The term *spot advertising* is confusing because it can refer to two different concepts. It is used in a time sense to refer to *spot announcements* placed by either a national or a local advertiser. Such announcements appear between regular programs, and the advertiser cannot establish any identity with the programs.

As a strategy, however, the term is used in a geographic sense to refer to *spot broadcasting,* which is a method whereby a national advertiser picks the geographical areas in which to air commercials. Spot advertising in this sense is nonnetwork broadcasting by a national advertiser and originates in the station from which it is telecast. It is particularly valuable to advertisers who do not need network coverage, who cannot afford it, or who simply want to increase their coverage in particular markets. The biggest problem is that it requires working arrangements with a large number of stations instead of a single network.

Cable TV

Satellite and cable TV are now very competitive with traditional television, with cable expected to have exposure to 80 percent of the population in the mid-

---

[23]See "TV Syndication," *Advertising Age* (March 14, 1983): M-9-25.

1980s.[24] The number of cable networks and the variety of programs they offer, enormously increase the number of alternatives available to advertisers. Advertisers have found they can experiment with different marketing techniques not possible on network TV — such as sponsoring a daily 2-hour program, sponsoring 5- or 10-minute interviews, or giving 80-second commercials.[25]

The cable networks providing such opportunities include Entertainment Sports Programming Network (ESPN), Cable News Network (CNN), Cable Health Network (CHN), USA Network (USA), and Public Affairs Network (C-Span). The success of cable TV has even resulted in cable listings in *TV Guide;* Time, Inc., experimented unsuccessfully with a publication called *TV — Cable Week.*[26]

Television Rate Structure

The rate structure for television advertising is usually quite complicated. The basic unit is the minute, and it is further broken down into seconds. Thus time is sold in periods of 10-, 20-, 30-, and 60-second lengths; the 30-second commercial is the most common, although 10-second commercials are becoming popular because of rising costs.

Under the discontinued NAB code discussed in chapter 5, the 30-second time slot had to be used to advertise a single product. However, since the code was declared unconstitutional, recent developments have led to the growing practice of *piggybacking* — adjoining 15-second spots for unrelated products of a single sponsor. But there is a good deal of controversy over the practice. It is argued that it is entirely defensible because of rising costs. Furthermore, it allows small advertisers who were formerly unable to use network TV to do so. Counterarguments include the charge that it adds to the existing clutter of commercials, that it lessens the impact of a commercial that runs adjacent to the piggyback ads, and that it makes it more difficult for local stations to sell their own spots. Some fear that the practice will eventually make the 15-second spot the standard selling unit. Nevertheless, piggybacking presently appears to be on solid ground.[27]

The basic factors determining the rate are the quality of the program, the quality of the audience, and the size of the audience, usually determined by the time of day the commercial is aired. Whether it is produced and developed (comedy, variety, or detective show) or whether it is "purchased" (major sporting event), a high-cost show commands higher prices for commercial time than a low-cost show. Also, the quality of the audience can affect the time rates. If a particular program attracts a well-defined homogeneous audience, the commercial time rates may be higher than if the audience is more diversified.

---

[24]See Section 2 in *Advertising Age,* November 16, 1981. See also "Cable Programming Catches Up with Demand," *Business Week* (February 22, 1982): 130–32.

[25]"Why Advertisers are Rushing to Cable TV," *Business Week* (November 2, 1981): 96.

[26]See "Time, Inc. Takes on TV Guide," *Business Week* (April 18, 1983): 64–67; and "Some Top Products of '83 Won't See '84," *Advertising Age* (Jan. 2, 1984): pp. 3, 26.

[27]See "Judge Tosses Piggyback Rule," *Advertising Age* (March 8, 1982): 1, 67; Diane Mermigas, "NBC Opens Piggyback Gate," *Advertising Age* (April 11, 1983): 1, 68; "Alberto Will Ride CBS' Piggybacks," *Advertising Age* (May 16, 1983): 12; and Craig Reiss, "Split–30s Worrisome," *Advertising Age* (June 6, 1983): 3, 70.

The size of the audience is always relevant to the establishment of rates; larger audiences usually command higher commercial time rates than small audiences. Most television stations establish different rates for commercial time at different times of the day to reflect different audience sizes. A typical division in the Eastern time zone is shown in the following listing. Class AA time is the most expensive, and each succeeding time period is progressively lower in cost.

Class AA	*Monday through Saturday:*	7:30–11 P.M.; *Sunday:* 6:30–10:30 P.M.
Class A	*Monday through Friday:*	noon to 7:30 P.M.; 11 P.M. to sign-off; *Saturday:* 1:00–7:30 P.M.; *Sunday:* 2:00–6:30 P.M. and 10:30–11 P.M.
Class B	*Monday through Friday:*	7 A.M. to noon; *Saturday:* 7:30 A.M. to 1 P.M. and 11 P.M. to sign-off; *Sunday:* 11 P.M. to sign-off.
Class C	*Monday through Friday:*	sign-on to 7 A.M.; *Saturday:* sign-on to 7:30 A.M.; *Sunday:* sign-on to 2 P.M.
Class D	*All other time.*	

As with print media, adjustments to the basic rate in television advertising are often made for quantity purchases and frequency of advertising.

Cost Comparisons

The basis for considering advertising alternatives in any medium, including television, is the number of "right" people the message reaches relative to the cost of reaching them. But the problem is somewhat more complicated in television than with other media because of the general nature of the assumed viewers. Somehow broadcast audiences must be measured, and the televised programs or stations thereby rated.

Program (station) ratings. Several methods are used for collecting data, but the method referred to most is one developed by the A.C. Nielson company, which utilizes the *Audimeter*. This is a small metal box attached to the television sets of a statistically determined sample of viewers in the United States. The device records every minute the set is on and the channel to which it is tuned. The tapes on which the information is recorded are sent to Nielson every week and are compared with the programming schedules of the stations identified with the respective areas of each set owner. The information compiled from all the tapes provides the basis for determining national program ratings. The Nielson company also uses a diary method to obtain certain other information not provided by the Audimeter, particularly pertaining to the composition of the audience.

Audience data are compiled and analyzed to provide several figures of interest to advertisers and network and station executives. Since the sample used in obtaining the data is presumed to be representative of all television viewers in the United States, the figures apply to nationwide viewers. *Sets in use* is the percentage of homes where the set was turned on during a particular time period. *Program rating* is the percentage of homes where the set was tuned to a particular program. *Share of the audience,* the percentage of homes where the set was tuned to a particular station, is based on the sets in use at the time. *Audience composition* identifies the audience in terms of demographic factors.

Cost-per-thousand. Cost comparisons in television advertising are usually made on the basis of the cost of reaching a thousand viewers. The formula for computing the figure is, with the necessary adjustments for the nature of the medium, analogous to the one used in comparing magazine alternatives.

$$CPM = \frac{\text{Cost of a commercial} \times 1{,}000}{\text{Program (station) audience}}$$

As with print media, comparisons are made using the factors cost and "circulation." Since the cost is always available, if the audience size for alternative stations or programs is known, comparisons can be made effectively.

Gross rating points. A fairly recent development in the purchase of television advertising is the gross rating point. One rating point is equal to an audience of one percent of the households with television sets in a given area. Thus 100 gross rating points means the average home in that area would receive one message. Ratings are established for programs and spot announcements, and the advertiser can purchase the number of gross rating points deemed necessary to accomplish the purpose. For example, if the advertiser wants to buy 150 gross rating points (so the average household will receive 1.5 messages), the option may be to purchase 10 spot announcements each with a rating of 15, or 15 spots each with a rating of 10, and so on.

Radio

The medium that many people thought would die with the advent of television did not; it just changed its programming.[28] Radio is stronger now than it ever was. There are about 4,554 AM stations and 3,993 FM stations on the air, and the Federal Communications Commission wants more.[29] Radio takes in more advertising dollars than the magazine industry, and its dollar volume was exceeded only by newspapers, television, and direct mail in 1978. It was estimated that advertising expenditures in radio would approach $3 billion in 1979, with $2 billion of that from local advertisers.[30] The radio audience increased by 37 percent between 1968 and

---

[28]For a nostalgic look at radio in the early days, see Section 2 in *Advertising Age,* September 13, 1982.
[29]"Striking It Rich in Radio," *Business Week* (5 Feb. 1979): 58–62.
[30]*Ibid.*

1976, compared to a 14 percent increase for television and 4 percent for magazines.[31]

Advantages

Radio is an excellent, sometimes overlooked, medium for advertisers.[32] Despite the somewhat broad delineation of broadcast audiences, radio segments its listeners. There are enough stations, each offering its own brand of programming, that almost any group can enjoy listening.[33] Some stations do have a mixed bag of programming, but most concentrate on one segment of the population. Any single station will likely develop its programming around rock, pop, country and western, easy listening, big band, gospel, or classical music; or on news, audience talk shows, or sporting events; or around certain ethnic groups. Furthermore, the disc jockeys themselves often have appeals of their own.

Radio is an immediate source of information or entertainment. In many homes the radio goes on as soon as a family member gets up in the morning, gets home in the evening, or comes into the house. People expect the latest news items and announcements to be broadcast immediately, and they usually are. The fact that most people have radios in several rooms of the house and in the car, and also have a portable radio, perhaps magnifies this expectation.

Radio is a flexible medium for advertisers as commercials can be aired with very little lead time, and the advertiser can pick the regions needing a boost from additional promotional effort. Furthermore, the costs are exceedingly low, particularly compared to television. A 30-second spot on radio station KVOO, Tulsa, Oklahoma, in Class AAA time was only $72 in 1983.[34]

Radio is innovative. Stations are constantly experimenting with new formats. One station transmits simulcasts of HBO musical specials, airs live rock concerts, and has a number of regular features such as a weekly one-hour country music concert. Another station is all comedy. And many stations, including about 200 AM stations, are broadcasting in stereo.[35]

Limitations

As in television, the message has no life but is gone the moment it is spoken; the print media have an advantage in this regard. People are inclined to do other things while listening to the radio, and this may tend to dilute their attention. The fact that radio is essentially local may make it less attractive to some national advertisers. Yet radio seems to be an excellent supplemental medium for most advertisers.

---

[31]Walter Staab, "Your True Media Alternative? Improved Television Buying," *Advertising Age* (25 Oct. 1976): 46, 49-50.

[32]Cyril C. Penn, "Marketing Tool Underused," *Advertising Age* (25 Sept. 1978): 122, 126, 130.

[33]See *Advertising Age* (June 7, 1982): Section 2.

[34]Standard Rate and Data Service, Inc., *Spot Radio Rates and Data* (June 1, 1982); 578.

[35]"Radio. New Tools, New Tunes," *Advertising Age* (July 11, 1983): M-9-32.

Types of Radio Advertising

The alternatives available to radio advertisers are the same as for television — network, spot, and local. Unlike television, however, local radio is the most important of the three. But network radio is expanding. RKO Radio Network, Enterprise Radio Network, and Satellite Music Network are examples of networks expecting growth; and of course Mutual Broadcasting system, CBS, ABC, and NBC are well entrenched.[36]

Radio Rate Structure

The basic unit in radio rate structure is the minute. Thus time is sold in blocks of 10-, 20-, 30-, or 60-second periods, and the rates are determined, in part, by the size of the audience at various times of the day. Information on radio listening is available from RADAR (Radio All-Dimension Audience Research), and from Arbitron, a service provided by American Research Bureau.

Time divisions are different for radio than they are for television. Whereas prime time (the most expensive) in television is usually 7:30 to 11:00 P.M. in the Eastern time zone, it is morning and evening driving hours to and from work for radio. Thus radio time might be classified as follows:

Class AAA   6:00 A.M. – 10:00 A.M.
Class AA   3:00 P.M. – 7:00 P.M.
Class A   10:00 A.M. – 3:00 P.M.
Class B   7:00 P.M. to midnight

Discounts are usually built into the structure for increasing frequency and quantity purchases, as is the case with most media. To compare radio alternatives, the cost-per-thousand formula used in comparing television alternatives is frequently applied.

SUMMARY

The major print media are newspapers and magazines; both deliver a potential audience to the advertiser when space is purchased.

Newspapers are selective geographically and not qualitatively; that is, they appeal to many special-interest groups who are located in a particular area. They can be classified according to frequency of publication, size, and morning/evening. Newspaper advertising is usually divided into four categories: display, classified, classified display, and special; display advertising is of most concern to promotional strategists. In addition, newspaper supplements and tabloid inserts are becoming increasingly important. Newspaper rates are quoted in either agate lines or column

---

[36]See Colby Coates, "Network Radio Poised for Growth," *Advertising Age* (April 13, 1981): 38, 48.

inches and are usually lower for local advertisers than for national ones. In comparing two or more newspapers for possible use, consider both the cost of the space and the respective circulations. Comparisons are made by means of the milline rate which takes into account both factors.

Magazines are still strong as advertising media; their importance is becoming greater with the increasing prevalence of local magazines. They can be classified according to the frequency of publication, page size, and the audiences they reach; the last is perhaps the most important. On that basis there are consumer magazines, business publications, and farm magazines, each of which can be further subdivided. The basic unit in terms of which magazine rates are quoted is the page; there are discounts for the purchase of increasing quantities of space. Different magazines can be compared by the use of the cost-per-thousand formula, which is analogous for the milline rate used for comparing newspapers and considers both space cost and circulation.

Television and radio are the two types of broadcast media. Television's combined impact of both oral and visual presentations makes it particularly effective and although it is expensive in terms of out-of-pocket costs, it is quite competitive when reduced to cost-per-thousand viewers. Comparisons of the cost of using various alternative networks, stations, or programs are made on the basis of cost-per-thousand viewers reached.

Radio can be an effective medium for several reasons, the most important of which is the degree to which it segments its audience. Nearly everyone listens to radio; it is flexible; and the costs are reasonable. It has disadvantages, some of which are the same as those for television. Comparisons of alternatives are made the same way as they are in television.

QUESTIONS FOR THOUGHT AND REVIEW

1. Why is the medium with the largest dollar advertising volume newspapers and not television?
2. Explain the notion that newspapers are selective geographically rather than qualitatively. How does an advertiser use that fact in making media decisions?
3. Do you think the "total market coverage" concept, involving a newspaper–direct-mail mix, has merit? Why or why not?
4. Discuss the relative advantages and disadvantages to an advertiser of the use of the newspaper supplements and tabloid inserts compared to the newspaper itself.
5. Explain the newspaper rate structure, including reference to agate lines, column inches, ROP, open rate, flat rate, and combination rates.
6. Do you think newspapers are justified in quoting lower rates to retail advertisers than to national advertisers? Why or why not?
7. Explain the milline rate and how it is used. Why does it consider both space cost and circulation?
8. What do you think of the future of local magazines? Explain.

9. Explain why magazines are usually selective qualitatively rather than geographically.
10. Discuss some of the advantages to an advertiser that magazines have over other media. Are there disadvantages to using magazines? Explain.
11. What is the rationale for classifying magazines according to the audiences they reach? What are the categories when they are so classified?
12. Explain the magazine rate structure, including reference to the basic rate and adjustments. Does a full-page ad attract twice as much attention as a half-page ad? Explain.
13. Explain the cost-per-thousand rate. Why does it consider both space cost and circulation?
14. What is a magazine's *secondary circulation?* Discuss its value to an advertiser.
15. Explain the notion that people choose the advertisements they want to look at in print media, but they choose the television commercials they want *not* to look at. Do you agree with this?
16. Think of the television commercial you dislike the most. Is it because it is repeated so much? Do you buy the product? Discuss.
17. Discuss the use of noted personalities in presenting television commercials. Include in your discussion the conditions necessary for their most effective use. Give some examples.
18. Discuss selectivity of audience in television advertising. Include both geographic and qualitative selectivity.
19. Distinguish among program sponsorship, participation shows, and spot advertising. Discuss the advantages and disadvantages of each.
20. How are television advertising rates established? Discuss the factors involved in their determination.
21. Explain how cost comparisons are made in television advertising, including the signficance of program ratings to the problem. What are gross rating points?
22. Discuss the advantages and disadvantages of using radio as an advertising medium. Give some examples of companies that use radio in their advertising programs.

14

ADVERTISING— OTHER MEDIA

Advertising media were classified in chapter 12 as print, broadcast, direct mail, out-of-home, specialty, and other media. Print and broadcast media were discussed in chapter 13, and the remaining media are examined in this chapter.

DIRECT MAIL

Technically direct mail is a form of print media and could be considered in that classification. There are enough differences between it and newspapers and magazines, however, to consider it in a separate category. For example, as an advertising medium, direct mail must win a reading on its own; there is no editorial content to attract an audience as with newspapers and magazines.

Direct mail ranks third among the media in terms of advertising dollar volume, exceeded only by newspapers and television. The rank is surprising because a recent study showed that 51 percent of consumers said they would prefer not to receive such mail, and the percentage was even higher (64 percent) among people 50 years of age and older. Yet the same study showed that an estimated 29,000,000 Americans receive at least one piece of direct-mail advertising every day. Furthermore, 37 percent had bought one or more products within the past six months as a result of the advertising[1]. Also 60 percent of a number of executives, when asked, said they preferred to hear about new office products through direct mail; half of another 21 percent who felt that direct mail was annoying said, "Send it to me anyway."[2] So a considerable number of both ultimate consumers and business executives are responsive to direct-mail advertising.

Because of the similarity of certain terms and concepts, it is necessary to distinguish among them. *Direct advertising* refers to all types of printed advertising not employing a medium such as a newspaper or magazine but which reaches the consumer directly. This may be accomplished through counter "pick-ups" in retail stores, door-to-door delivery by ambitious youths, handouts at conventions, and sending the advertising through the mail. If it is sent through the mail, it is *direct-mail* advertising.

Direct mail must also be distinguished from *mail-order selling,* which is really a total method of marketing the product without the use of middlemen or salespeople. Sometimes referred to as *direct marketing,* it may involve the use of any medium, including direct mail that may induce the consumer to order the product directly by mail.

Direct marketing has ballooned in recent years. Not only are there hundreds of catalog mail-order houses but some of the old standbys are appealing to different markets than they once did. Spiegel, for example, no longer positions itself as a price-oriented store of last resort, but now aims designer clothes and department store merchandise at "working women from 25–54 years old with household income of $34,000 and up."[3] Sears, J. C. Penney, and Montgomery Ward, too,

[1]"Direct Mail Ads Reach 1 in 5 Daily: Study," *Advertising Age* (21 Aug. 1978): 56.
[2]Ann Helming, "Direct Mail Leaves Its Indelible Stamp," *Advertising Age* (June 14, 1982): M-12-15.
[3]Robert Ebisch, "Just What the Customer Ordered," *Advertising Age* (January 17, 1983): M-10.

have changed and upgraded their merchandise. Perhaps we are experiencing a modern version of an era when catalog shopping from Sears and Wards was the common practice of Western families.

A relatively new procedure involving direct mail is called *marriage mail* or *network mail*. Two or more advertising pieces for large retailers such as J. C. Penney Co. and K-Mart Corp. are wrapped around each other and sent through the mail. The mailings consist of ads and coupon offerings designed to generate store traffic. Thus it is a "marriage" between national advertisers, such as General Foods, Colgate-Palmolive, and Johnson & Johnson in direct couponing campaigns, and retailers who handle the products.[4]

Characteristics of Direct Mail

Several things about direct-mail advertising make it unique among the media. Perhaps among its most notable characteristics is the degree to which it allows the advertiser to select an audience. Given an effective mailing list, an advertiser can virtually eliminate any waste circulation; theoretically, every person on a mailing list can be a prospective customer.

Direct mail is extremely flexible. It has few physical limitations, and the advertiser is free to use anything from inexpensive advertising inserts in monthly statements to elaborate catalogs, with numerous alternatives between the two.

Despite the opportunity to minimize direct-mail costs, however, the cost per reader is still high, and includes the rising postal rates and the cost of producing each piece. Inherent in direct mail, too, is the fact that it must generate readership on its own because it is not accompanied by any editorial content, as are newspapers and magazines. The pervasive term *junk mail* connotes negativism by the consumer, who discards a portion of the mail without reading it.

The Mailing List

The mailing list is the key to success in direct mail. It must be right to begin with, and it must be kept up-to-date. Some firms compile their own lists, using various sources both inside and outside the firm. But more often than not mailing lists are rented from firms in that business. Such lists are available in extremely narrow product categories, ranging from rubber earplug buyers to purchasers of two-masted yachts. Once the list is obtained, it should be kept current. New people should be added as they join that market. People who are deceased, or have moved, should be removed from the list if the cost of doing so is less than paying for the return of undelivered mail. Complicating the whole problem are the sometimes difficult-to-implement provisions of the Privacy Act of 1974 which addresses itself to the rights of individuals with respect to having their names appear on mailing lists.

---

[4]See Gay Jervey, "Blair, ADVO to Debut 'Network Mail' Plan," *Advertising Age* (May 16, 1983): 37; "Marriage Mail: A Letter-Perfect Match," *Advertising Age* (May 30, 1983): M-15, and "A Smorgasbord for Advertisers," *Business Week* (July 19, 1982): 142.

OUT-OF-HOME MEDIA

The term *out-of-home media* is somewhat misleading because it does not refer to all advertising to which people are exposed away from home. Rather, it is concerned with only two kinds of such advertising, both of which are well-defined media — outdoor and transit. These media are also sometimes referred to as *position media* because their "circulations" revolve around them, in a sense, while they remain in position. This is unlike newspapers and magazines, whose circulations reflect the dissemination of the media themselves.

Outdoor

Outdoor advertising is more familiarly known as *billboard advertising*. But in the advertising industry outdoor advertising includes only those signs that meet the standards established by the Outdoor Advertising Association of America (OAAA). Thus many of the signs along the highways, such as those urging travelers to "Eat at Joe's Place," or stating "Cabins for rent," are not outdoor advertising. They are simply nonstandardized signs. Outdoor advertising is subject to some degree of control by the industry, which serves to lessen the adverse criticism often leveled at billboards, whereas the nonstandardized signs are beyond any such control.

The use of outdoor advertising is growing. In 1982, $887 million was spent in the medium, which was a 10.9 percent increase over 1981 spending.[5] Many major advertisers in such industries as food, drugs, cosmetics, and automobiles are returning to the medium.[6]

Advantages

The usefulness of outdoor advertising is increasing because of the high mobility of American consumers. In addition, the fact that people are eating out more than they ever have makes for less opportunity to reach them with "armchair" media because they are at home less during prime time.[7]

Target Group Index (TGI) is a well-known private research firm that provides media information. In its first product and demographic study of outdoor advertising, TGI found that a 50 national showing (half the billboards presumed necessary for complete coverage of the market) reaches more than 80 percent of all adults over 13 times in 30 days.[8] Furthermore, it will reach 87 percent of the 18- to 34-year-olds 15 times, and 84.5 percent of the college graduates 15 times.[9]

Outdoor advertising is natural for motels and restaurants. Travelers look for posters indicating the presence and location of such businesses and would be dis-

---

[5]Gay Jervey, "Outdoor Ad Field Urged to Look Down the Road," *Advertising Age* (March 14, 1983): 12.

[6]Frank Carol, Jr., "Outdoor Is Alternative," *Advertising Age* (26 Sept. 1977): 72, 76.

[7]Richard Briggs, "Outdoor — the Logical Alternative Medium as Housewives Go Out-of-Home," *Media Decisions* 12, no. 1 (Jan. 1977): 74.

[8]R. Dana Barnes, "Outdoor Sees New Role in Media Mix," *Advertising Age* (25 Sept. 1978): 86.

[9]"Outdoor Study Shows More Women are Exposed," *Advertising Age* (24 July 1978): 44.

turbed if such indicators were absent. But it is also useful to other advertisers, particularly as a supplementary medium. Outdoor advertising is an excellent way to remind consumers of the advertiser's brand and to impress the picture or image of the package upon them. Furthermore, it adds to the repetitive effect of a firm's total advertising, and it provides this service 24 hours a day.

Limitations

Because a traveler's exposure to any single panel is quite brief (perhaps as little as 5 or 6 seconds), the message must be short. That the medium can be selective geographically is perhaps an advantage, but outdoor advertising is nonselective in its circulation in general. Thus except for products that are universally used, there is some waste circulation.

Perhaps one of the biggest drawbacks is the criticism from environmentalists and certain aesthetic groups. They contend the posters are eyesores in the environment and interfere with travelers' enjoyment of the countryside. The negative pressure in the early 1960s was one of the forces that led to the passage of the Highway Beautification Act in 1965. The impact of that act is felt in the restrictions placed upon the use of outdoor advertising on the interstate highways. Federal enforcement is accomplished through withholding highway subsidy funds from states that fail to comply.

Types of Outdoor Advertising

The three main types of outdoor advertising are posters, painted bulletins, and electric spectaculars. The most important type is the poster.

Posters. The finished poster is a printed paper pasted on a 12-foot high by 24-foot long panel. But the finished poster is not one single sheet; it is usually ten sections printed separately and put together like a jigsaw puzzle.

There are two common sizes of posters, each of which is pasted on the same size panel. They are referred to by the names that originally indicated the number of sections in them. There are 24-sheet posters, which are 8 feet, 8 inches high and 19 feet, 6 inches long, and 30-sheet posters, which are 9 feet, 7 inches by 21 feet, 7 inches. There are also bleed posters on which the color runs to the edge of the panel (analogous to bleed pages in magazines). In addition, some panels are illuminated.

A third size poster is growing in popularity, however. Sometimes referred to as a small outdoor board or a miniboard, it is an 8-sheet poster which is 6 feet by 12 feet, conforming proportionately to the larger posters, thus allowing easy reduction of a large outdoor ad to fit the smaller format. Reasons cited for its growing popularity include economy of both space and money, and versatility — it can often be placed between two buildings, for example.[10]

---

[10]Anna Sobczynski, ''Eight-Sheet Industry Growing in Stature,'' *Advertising Age* (March 10, 1980): S-2, 31–32.

Painted bulletins.   A painted bulletin resembles a poster except that it is painted directly on the panel. Furthermore, such panels are usually of a different size than the poster panels; the common size is 14 by 48 feet. Since they are painted they can be tailor-made. Moreover, various unusual effects can be achieved, such as animation, three-dimension, and multivision.

Painted bulletins are a subdivision of *painted displays,* which also include advertisements painted on walls. However, the last are more difficult to control, because of the obvious impossibility of standardizing them.

Electric spectaculars.   Although not standardized, electric spectaculars are usually considered a part of outdoor advertising. They are elaborately constructed electric signs found in heavy traffic areas and usually associated with the downtown areas of large cities. Perhaps the first electric spectacular (so named because it was spectacular at the time) was a Camel cigarette sign. The sign portrayed a man blowing smoke rings over Times Square in New York City. There are many others now, and they are not considered as spectacular by today's standards.

Variations.   Mobile billboards and moving signs are two of the numerous ''departures from the traditional'' that have been tried. A *mobile billboard* is a brightly colored automobile or van on which an advertising message is placed. Companies that provide this service act as middlemen between the advertiser and the car's owner. Advantages include the facts that they do not fall under the legal restraints associated with stationary billboards and that otherwise inaccessible markets can be reached.[11]

Moving signs are simply animated billboards. The type of movement incorporated into the sign is limited only by its cost and one's imagination, and has included such things as water falling, propellers spinning, bread being sliced, and cigarettes glowing. Such signs are hybrid because they do not fall neatly into established categories. They are not simple posters, nor are they true electric spectaculars. But they do attract attention.

Outdoor Rate Structure

Advertisers do not own the structures on which outdoor posters are placed (except in the case of nonstandardized signs). Instead, they purchase the space for a specified time from organizations known as *plant operators,* who have leased or purchased the sites on which the structures are placed. A *plant* consists of all the structures owned by the plant operator, who has determined the most strategic spots to erect them.

The basic unit of purchase for posters has traditionally been the *showing.* An advertiser who buys a 100 showing is assured of having a sufficient number of posters to provide exposure to the message to 100 percent of the mobile population of the area in a 30-day period. A 50 showing guarantees that half the population will see the message in the same period; in some areas a 150 or 200 show-

---

[11]Jim Hammett, ''Mobile Billboards Pave Unique Path,'' *Advertising Age* (March 10, 1980): S–28–29.

ing is available. Actually, the delivered population may be slightly less than 100 percent for the 100 showing and slightly more than half for the 50 showing for there will be a number of repetitions. A 100 showing does not mean 100 panels. One or two panels may constitute a 100 showing in a small area, and in a large city it might take as many as four or five hundred.

Instead of selling outdoor posters in terms of showings, the trend now is to sell them on the basis of *gross rating points.* Under this system, the basic unit of sale is 100 gross rating points daily. Purchase of the basic unit provides the advertiser with enough posters to produce daily exposures (whether repeat or not) equal to 100 percent of the population of the area. As in the case of showings, the advertiser can purchase 75, 50, or 25 gross rating points daily. The standard time period for either method is 30 days, and discounts are included in the rate structure for purchases covering longer periods.

There is considerable variation in the costs of using outdoor advertising. The cost depends upon the area desired, whether the attempt is to reach the top 10 markets or the top 50, and whether illuminated signs are included. A 100 showing (posters) in the Dallas-Fort Worth market cost $44,552 per month in 1982.[12] The costs of using painted bulletins and electric spectaculars depend entirely on the whims of the advertiser.

Transit

Transit is that advertising to which exposure is achieved in conjunction with the operation of mass transportation facilities in urban markets. Thus it includes messages appearing on or in the vehicles themselves and in the stations of certain systems. Transit advertising is associated with all forms of public transportation, including buses, subways, elevated trains, streetcars, and commuter trains.

It is not a major medium in the context of overall advertising expenditures. But it is an important supplementary medium for many advertisers and is considered quite significant to some. Wrigley (chewing gum), for example, is legendary in its use of the medium and has always considered it a very important part of an overall advertising program.[13]

Advantages

Transit advertising is said to be one of the least expensive of all media; the cost-per-thousand has usually been considerably less than 20 cents. It is a flexible medium in that the advertiser can choose the geographic location and elect one of several options of coverage. Moreover, the riding audience is somewhat captive and often reads the messages through sheer boredom.

---

[12] *The Buyers' Guide to Outdoor Advertising, 82/83* (Searsport, Main: F. R. Cawl & Associates, 1981).

[13] See Theodore J. Gage, "Transit Advertising on Verge of Boom." *Advertising Age* (March 10, 1980): S–8, 25.

Limitations

The greatest limitation to its effectiveness is that it fails to reach the large segment of the population who drive to and from work. The increasing pressure on people to reduce their automobile driving and make more use of public transportation because of the impending gasoline shortage and concern with exhaust pollution may increase the percent of the population exposed to transit advertising.

Types of Transit Advertising

Transit advertising is classified into three groups: car cards, outside displays, and station posters.

Car cards.   Advertising messages placed inside the vehicle appear on car cards, whose standardized size is 11 × 28 inches, although they are also found in other sizes. These cards are mounted above the windows next to the ceiling and sometimes also in other locations and resemble very miniature outdoor posters. They can contain longer messages than outdoor posters because of their longer exposure time to the riding audience.

Outside displays.   The posters placed on the outside of vehicles (sides, front, or rear) also have standardized size. The most common outside displays are *traveling displays* which are 21 × 44 inches, and *king size,* which are 30 × 144 inches. The copy traditionally put on paper is pasted on a panel, then is mounted on the vehicle. But a recent development may change this procedure. The public transit industry has generated a new kind of bus called *advance design buses* (ADBs) on which the displays will be mounted directly on the skin of the bus using adhesive-backed vinyl posters instead of paper.[14]

Station posters.   Station posters are very similar to outdoor posters except they are smaller, usually found in one-sheet and two-sheet sizes. Usually they are only available in the stations of the systems in large cities, particularly in those that have subways or elevated systems, and in airline terminals.

Transit Rate Structure

Advertisers do not, as a rule, deal directly with the transportation system itself. They deal with firms somewhat analogous to outdoor industry plant operators who have contracted with the system for all the space.

Car card advertising is sold in terms of showings (or services). The advertiser can buy a *full showing* which gets a card in every vehicle in the system, or a *half showing* or a *quarter showing,* which provides a card in half or a quarter of the vehicles, respectively. The basic unit in the purchase of outside displays is a 100 showing; or the advertiser can purchase a 75, or 50, or 25 showing. Each of the

---

[14]B. J. Batchelder, ''Transit Attracts New Ad Categories,'' *Advertising Age* (25 Sept. 1978): 84, 88.

various showings provides a sufficient number of displays to reach a specified percentage of the population in that particular area in a 30-day period.

SPECIALTY ADVERTISING

An often-overlooked medium is *specialty advertising*. The term refers to the practice whereby firms give away free to present and potential customers products bearing the company's name and, perhaps, a brief advertising message. Specialty advertising sales volume was expected to exceed $2.7 billion in 1979, according to Specialty Advertising Association International, and it has been the sixth largest advertising medium since 1977.[15] Moreover, the results of a study conducted for SAAI indicated that 43 percent of the qualified respondents among the general public prefer to buy from companies using the medium, and 59 percent of the business respondents indicated such preference.[16]

Contrary to appearances, however, just "any product" will not do the job. It is not the product but rather the *creative strategy* that should be of first concern, and the selection of the product should be based on that strategy. Such things as the demographic characteristics of the intended recipients, the goals of the advertiser, the advertiser image desired, and the role of the specialty in the total advertising program are important in this regard.[17] (See figures 14–1, 14–2, and 14–3.)

Once the creative strategy has been determined, the product should be selected on the basis of at least three underlying criteria: it should be of good quality, it should be familiar to the recipient, and it should be useful to the recipient.[18] If the product is of inferior quality, giving it might even be counterproductive. This does not mean that it must be made out of expensive materials. A coffee measure does not have to be made of stainless steel, for example; plastic is entirely sufficient as long as it does not appear cheap. A product requiring detailed instructions as to its use is self-defeating, and certainly it should be useful to the individual receiving it.

Specialty advertising is a good supplementary medium if it is used wisely. Because advertising specialties have a long life, they are excellent reminders. Calendars, key ring tags, ballpoint pens, and thermometers, for example, may be looked at every day. Not to be ignored either is the psychological feeling of obligation by the receiver to the firm that provided the specialty. There is no obligation, of course, but the feeling may be there nevertheless. Furthermore, the medium is flexible in that the advertiser can select whatever "audience" is appropriate and also spend as little or as much on the items as circumstances dictate.

Specialty advertising has its disadvantages. The message must be brief. A

---

[15]Henry R. Bernstein, "Specialty Ad Industry Forecasts Large Growth," *Advertising Age* (19 Feb. 1979): 72–73.

[16]*Ibid.*

[17]Walter A Gaw, *Specialty Advertising* (Rolling Meadows, Ill.: Specialty Advertising Association International, 1972), p. 19.

[18]*Ibid.*, p. 20.

FIGURE 14–1   Use of advertising specialties in a program to stimulate the interest of sales-people in a sales contest.   *Source:* American United Life Insurance Company.

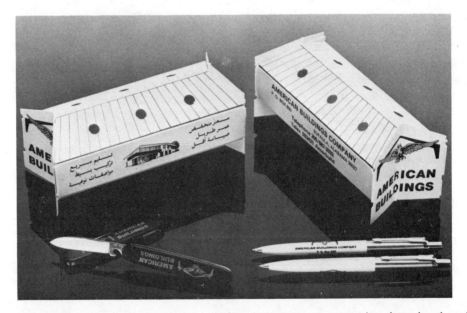

FIGURE 14–2   Use of advertising specialties in a program promoting the sale of prefab metal buildings in the international market.   *Source:* American Buildings, International Division.

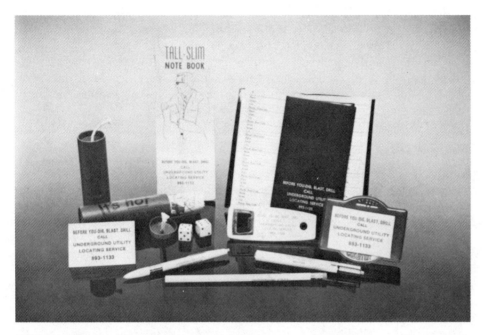

FIGURE 14-3 Use of advertising specialties for nonprofit promotion. *Source:* Underground Utility Locating Service.

lengthy message is not suitable on advertising specialties, even if there is room for it, which there usually is not. Moreover, it is an expensive medium to use, even with inexpensive items.

Types of Advertising Specialties

Since there are probably between 10,000 and 20,000 products used as advertising specialties, it is convenient to group them into three categories: ad specialties, calendars, and executive gifts.[19]

Ad Specialties

Included in this category are such items as ash trays, yardsticks, balloons, key cases, ballpoint pens, buttons, fly swatters, cannister scoops, caps and items of clothing. Most of these are relatively inexpensive but useful. Matchbooks are also included in this category, although they are slightly different in that they are "used up."

Calendars

Although it is difficult to determine the origin of it, or its precursor, specialty advertising as we know it today probably had its start in 1845 when a salesman got the

---

[19]George L. Herpel and Richard A Collins. *Specialty Advertising in Marketing* (Homewood, Ill.: Dow Jones-Irwin, 1972), p. 12.

idea of attaching a calendar to his advertising message.[20] The practice ballooned to enormous proportions. Today there are pocket calendars, desk calendars, and wall calendars. There are calendars showing pastoral scenes, patriotic illustrations, family activities, and scantily clad women and men. Furthermore, calendars are used by manufacturers, wholesalers, retailers, banks, insurance companies — virtually every kind of business. As with advertising specialties, they should be appropriately designed and chosen to fit the purpose of the firm.

Executive Gifts

Items are given to business men and women — usually executives — for the purpose of expressing appreciation and generating future good relationships. The items included in the executive gift category are usually more expensive than those in the other groups. They include such things as desk sets, briefcases, wallets, jewelry, and even consumable items such as fancy cheeses, fruits, and wines. They differ from the other two categories in that usually the advertiser's name or message does not appear on them. They are given ostensibly in appreciation of past relationships and also with the hope of generating future business.

There is an increasingly sensitive issue associated with the use of executive gifts. When does a gift cease to be an expression of appreciation for past business and become an actual bribe for future business? A desk set, for example, could be considered a token of appreciation for past business, but what about expensive golf clubs presented to a purchasing agent? In the contemporary environment of accelerating demands for moral accountability of business and industry, the practice of gift giving to executives must be approached with extreme caution. Of course, proven bribery is illegal.

Organization of the Specialty Advertising Industry

If the management of a firm wants to include specialty advertising in its promotional program, it first contacts a distributor who in turn deals with a supplier. The channel of distribution of a specialty item is normally supplier to distributor to advertiser to recipient. There is also some vertical integration in the channel, as exemplified by an institution known as a *direct-selling house* which combines the functions of the supplier and the distributor.[21]

Supplier

The *supplier* is a company that manufactures advertising specialties. Some suppliers are small family-owned firms, and others are corporate giants. Each supplier usually

---

[20]*Ibid.,* p. 27.

[21]For a more complete discussion of the specialty advertising industry, see *Ibid.,* pp. 19–23, and *Careers in Specialty Advertising* (Rolling Meadows, Ill.: Specialty Advertising Association International), pamphlet, pp. 4–6.

specializes in a product made of a particular material — paper, plastics, glassware, or any of several other materials. In addition to the manufacturing or sometimes acquiring of the items, the supplier also imprints the advertiser's message and/or name on the items.

Distributor

Sometimes called a *counselor,* the *distributor* is the advertiser's contact for specialty advertising. The distributor works with the advertiser to develop the appropriate creative strategy and convinces the advertiser of the merits of a particular idea. Distributors must maintain contact with suppliers to know what kinds of items are available. Only with such knowledge can distributors be completely effective in recommending appropriate items. They maintain no stock other than samples, and, like suppliers, they may be very small or very large operations.

Direct-selling House

There are relatively few direct-selling houses, but they are usually large. They combine the operations of the supplier and the distributor by manufacturing the item and also establishing direct contact with the advertisers, doing the selling and necessary creative work otherwise done by the distributor.

OTHER MEDIA

Newspapers, magazines, direct mail, television, radio, out-of-home advertising, and specialty advertising are the major advertising media, but there are a few additional media that are of some importance. Three of these are: directory advertising, free-circulation shoppers' guides, and motion picture advertising.

Directory Advertising

The most familiar directory advertising is the Yellow Pages of telephone directories. However, thousands of other classified directories are published in the United States, many of which are individual city directories.

Directory advertising is particularly valuable to businesses that depend upon the periodic or nonrecurring search by consumers for particular products or services. It is also useful for companies dealing in emergency services, such as plumbers, heat and air conditioning service firms, and electricians. Other kinds of firms can also benefit from directory advertising. The best-known directory in the industrial market is probably the *Thomas Register of American Manufacturers.* But other directories also serve this market.

Free-Circulation Shoppers' Guides

The shoppers' guide seems to be growing in both prevalence and importance, particularly in small towns and rural areas. Although it could never become a major medium, the shoppers' guide is of some significance to advertisers.

Shoppers' guides have some of the characteristics of both weekly newspapers and direct advertising. They are published every week and use a format resembling newspapers, except that they usually contain no news. They are usually distributed free to consumers, either by direct mail or through strategic *pick-up placement* in shopping centers and other consumer traffic areas. Their coverage of the markets for which they are intended is fairly complete.

Motion Picture Advertising

Motion picture advertising resembles the commercials shown on television, except it is shown in theaters. Although some companies use advertising on film in other ways, such use of film is more in the nature of public relations than advertising; our concern is with advertising film shown in theaters.

The medium is used by both local and national advertisers. Its effectiveness lies in the repetitive nature of the messages and the fact that they are presented to captive audiences. The medium's biggest disadvantage is perhaps the fact that some people resent having to watch advertising messages shown in theaters. They feel that although television commercials may be an intrusion on their time, they have not had to pay to see them, and the price of a ticket to a movie should not include having to watch commercials.

Motion picture advertising was quite common a number of years ago, and it was shown in nearly all theaters. Then most of the larger theaters stopped accepting it, and it was found only in drive-ins and in some theaters in small towns. Its use seems to be increasing again, however, but its future remains to be seen.[22]

An idea somewhat related to this is the use of in-flight advertising on airplanes. Airlines have been considering the possibility of in-flight audiovisual presentations for some time, but the idea is quite controversial, and at the time of this writing the decision is still unresolved. It is argued that well-educated, affluent people fly, and that this is a good way to reach them. In addition, of course, the practice would contribute to the revenue of the airlines. Arguments against the practice include those associated with motion picture advertising — the captive audience and its resentment, and the question of taste. Nevertheless, some airlines are experimenting with 30-minute feature films with standard TV commercial breaks.[23]

---

[22]See for example, "Tests Set for Ads in 1,000 Film Theaters," *Advertising Age* (10 Oct. 1977): 1, 112; "Patrons Are Buying In-Theater Ad Idea, Sellers Maintain," *Advertising Age* (28 Nov. 1977): 2, 71; and "Tonight at the Movies: The Latest National Ads," *Business Week* (24 Oct. 1977): 39.

[23]See Richard Kreisman, "Airlines Deciding on In-Flight Ad Formats," *Advertising Age* (June 28, 1982): 10, 89.

SUMMARY

Direct mail consists of advertising pieces sent through the mail directly to the consumer. It provides a high selectivity of audience and is quite flexible with respect to cost and physical limitations. Of particular significance is the fact that direct mail must create its own audience and cannot rely upon any kind of editorial content to accomplish this.

Out-of-home media consist of outdoor and transit. Outdoor advertising, commonly known as billboard advertising, is particularly useful for motels and restaurants, but it is also a good supplementary medium for other advertisers as reminder advertising and package identification. Transit advertising is advertising associated with the mass transportation systems of municipalities and commuter areas. Its cost-per-thousand is quite low, although its coverage is somewhat limited. The rate structures of both outdoor and transit advertising are based on showings, which reflect market coverage.

Specialty advertising is the practice of giving away products to show appreciation for past relationships and to build goodwill for the future. If creatively used, it provides excellent reminder advertising to a limited audience.

Directory advertising, free-circulation shoppers' guides, and motion picture advertising are among the numerous types of minor media available to advertisers. There are certain advantages to some advertisers in using them as supplementary media.

QUESTIONS FOR THOUGHT AND REVIEW

1. Distinguish among the terms *direct advertising, direct mail,* and *mail-order selling.*
2. What are some of the characteristics of direct mail that make it unique among media?
3. Discuss the importance of the mailing list to direct-mail advertisers.
4. What are *out-of-home media?* Why are they so called? Are they likely to increase, or decrease in importance? Why?
5. Why is outdoor advertising distinguished from nonstandardized signs? Do you think the distinction is important?
6. Discuss the advantages and disadvantages of outdoor advertising, and give some examples of companies that could use it effectively.
7. Present arguments both attacking and defending outdoor advertising from a social point of view. Do you have an opinion about it?
8. Explain the types of outdoor advertising available to an advertiser, and explain how rates are established and quoted for each.
9. What is *transit advertising?* Under what circumstances can it be used effectively? Discuss selectivity in transit advertising.
10. Distinguish among the various types of transit advertising, and explain how rates are established and quoted for each.

11. What is *specialty advertising?* How can creative strategy be applied in using it?
12. What basic criteria should be used in selecting the products for specialty advertising? Explain why these criteria are basic.
13. How are the products used in specialty advertising classified? Explain.
14. Discuss the moral problem involved with the use of executive gifts. Do you have an opinion about this?
15. Explain the functions of suppliers, distributors, and direct-selling houses in the specialty advertising industry.
16. When is directory advertising advantageous? Free-circulation shoppers' guides? Give examples of firms that might use each.
17. Discuss the advantages and disadvantages of using motion picture advertising. How do you feel about buying a ticket to a movie and having to watch commercials?

15

ADVERTISING-MEDIA PLANNING AND MEASUREMENT OF EFFECTIVENESS

Deciding on the most appropriate media for particular purposes is usually the responsibility of the advertising agency, but the promotion manager should have some understanding of the problems involved to be able to intelligently approve the agency's decisions.

Related to the problem of selecting the media and developing plans for their use is the task of measuring the effectiveness of advertising, both as it is proposed and as it is actually used. The information thus obtained can be helpful in the media decision-making process. (Although tests and measures are used more often in connection with the evaluation of alternative *creative* efforts, for our purposes we shall deal with them as they relate to media planning.)

MEDIA PLANNING

The underlying purpose in media planning is to select those media most appropriate for the purpose and to develop the most effective methods of using them. These are not easy tasks. The dissimilarities of media make comparing them difficult. Even though certain numerical concepts are used in common with all of them, such numerical analysis ignores the creative aspects of the advertisements themselves. For example, the relative effectiveness of a magazine advertisement or a television commercial could be completely contrary to anything the calculations might show with regard to the respective media. Nevertheless the comparisons must somehow be made.

Complicating the problem further is a notion that any single medium might be able to adequately cover the primary markets for many product categories in which the classic "80-20 principle" prevails — a single medium could reach the 20 percent of the customers who provide 80 percent of the business. In cases where this is possible, a media mix may not be necessary.[1]

However, most advertisers think that the use of one medium is usually insufficient to cover all bases. An interesting analogy has been made of media planning to military operations. Effective military strategy calls for the use of several different weapons; no single weapon is best for everything because each has a specific role to play. Furthermore, battlefield conditions vary, and enemy activity changes. In media planning, basic to the selection of the weapons (media) is a proper perspective of the battlefield (market) and a knowledge of the enemy (competition — what it is spending and where). Television is the air force that provides maximum shock in a given time; print is the infantry that occupies and holds a territory; radio is the armor that provides a surprise attack; outdoor is the artillery that hits everyone but lacks precision; and direct mail is the parachute drop that gives pinpoint precision against specific targets.[2]

Budget constraints often prevent the use of more than just a few media. In fact, reducing expenditures in any one medium to spread them into several different media may reduce the effectiveness of the total media plan. Perhaps the very

---

[1]John J. Meskil, "The Media Mix," *Media Letter* 5, no. 1 (Jan. 1979): 1–2.
[2]Al Ries, "Military Guide to Media Planning," *Media Decisions* 12, pt. 1 (Feb. 1977): 76–78, 114.

reason media planning is so important is that because most firms do limit their advertising expenditures, the media must be carefully selected and wisely used to get the most value for the dollars spent. One creative approach might be to limit the mix to television and newspapers and either use one as the major medium supported by the other or use them both equally.[3]

A media plan cannot be static but must be ongoing. A completely effective plan under given conditions could be a disaster when conditions change. And they *do* change. Sometimes a drastic change in the media mix is called for, particularly if the firm is at the bottom in market share and has nothing to lose.[4]

Components of the Media Plan

There is no standard form for a media plan; the relative importance of any single component in any particular plan depends on the circumstances and on the perspectives of the people involved. But all media plans should include comprehensive statements of the media proposed, justification for their selection, and suggestions for, and implications of, their use. The key components of a media plan might include the following:

1. *Objectives* — stated in terms of reach, frequency, etc., and specifically tied in with marketing objectives.
2. *Strategy* — the primary medium chosen, the secondary medium and other supplementary media, and explanations for the choices.
3. *Recommended plan summary* — including tables showing the breakdown of media and costs.
4. *Rationale for the recommendations* — including detailed justification.
5. *Discussion of possible alternatives.*
6. *Competitive activity.*
7. *Supporting documents.*[5]

Significant Factors in Media Planning

The many factors that have a bearing on the development of a media plan may be divided into three groups — basic, marketing (mix), and media factors.

Basic Factors

Foremost among the basic factors affecting the media plan is perhaps the budget constraint. Media planners must be extremely analytical in order to maximize results with the funds available. Also basic to the development of the media plan are the delineation and composition of the market. Not only does knowledge of

[3]See Chaman L. Jain, "Broadcast Support to Newspaper Ads," *Journal of Advertising Research* 15, no. 5 (Oct. 1975): 69–72.

[4]Ed Papazian, "Mediology," *Media Decisions* 13, pt. 1 (April 1978): 12, 14.

[5]Herbert Zeltner, "How to Write (and Recognize) a Good Media Plan," *Advertising Age* 48, pt. 3 (26 Sept. 1977): 31, 59, 60, 62.

the market provide geographical clues as to which media are appropriate, but it indicates the kinds of media, both generic and specific, to which its component people are most likely to respond. Ignoring market characteristics would result in a considerable amount of waste circulation.

The final basic factor is competition. Since a firm does not want to lose its share of the market, knowledge of competitors' advertising effort is essential. Both the magnitude of the competitor's effort and its characteristics are important bits of information. If competitors are gaining at "our" expense, perhaps it is because either they are spending more than we are or they are using different media. Media planners should not blindly duplicate the media plans of competitors, but they should know about the plans and use the information in developing their own strategies.

Marketing (Mix) Factors

Advertising and other forms of promotion *must* be designed and implemented in a manner consistent with the total marketing program of the firm.[6] Thus each element of the marketing mix must be considered in designing a media plan.

Product.   Certain media are more appropriate than others for advertising some products. If the product is catsup and the strategy calls for picturing a big, red, ripe tomato, magazines can probably do the job better than other media because of their superior color reproduction. On the other hand, if product use must be dramatized to get the desired effect, television may be the right medium. Old, established products may be advertised effectively in outdoor and transit media if all that is necessary is to remind people that the products are still around. But if the product is just being introduced, print media may be required in order to allow for lengthy descriptions. Of course, broadcast media are required to sell such products as musical instruments on the basis of sound.

Price.   Rarely does one find expensive furs and jewelry advertised on outdoor posters. Not only would the use of the medium result in a tremendous amount of waste circulation, but it would tend to nullify the products' prestige value. On the other hand, if price is the major appeal in promoting the product, the media selected should reflect consistency with that appeal. Newspaper ads, for example, often emphasize price appeals.

Channel of distribution.   The product's channel of distribution can affect media planning in several ways. If the nature of the channel is such that the middlemen feel obliged to advertise the manufacturer's product themselves, the manufacturer can reduce the amount of advertising from that which otherwise would be required. This situation could prevail if the manufacturer is following a policy of exclusive distribution and the retailers want to perpetuate their franchise privilege.

---

[6]See Jack Z. Sissors and E. R. Petray, *Advertising Media Planning* (Chicago: Crain, 1976), ch. 4; and Arnold M. Barban, Steven M. Cristol, and Frank J. Kopec, *Essentials of Media Planning: A Marketing Viewpoint* (Crain, 1976), ch. 2.

Sometimes the channel situation requires the use of a push strategy using media that reach the retailers and wholesalers rather than the consumers. At other times such a strategy is inappropriate. Geographical considerations are also significant to media planning in that media must be selected to coincide with the areas reached by the channels used.

Logistics. The movement of goods to their proper destinations and the timing thereof may also influence media planning. For example, it would be counterproductive to develop a media plan that would promote the sale of products not available to the consumer. This could happen if the media planner did not keep up-to-date on the firm's logistic plans and progress.

Promotion. As a task of the advertising function, which is a part of promotion, media planning must be carried out in light of the total promotion program. For example, if sales promotion activities (yet to be discussed) are to occupy a dominant position in the promotion mix, often they must be advertised heavily. Consumers must be well informed if coupons, premiums, deals, contests, and other such sales promotion devices are to be effective. Sometimes advertising must be designed to support the efforts of personal salespeople. If the entire promotion program is to be a coordinated effort, the media plan must be designed accordingly.

Media Factors

The third group of factors affecting media planning are those qualitative and quantitative factors associated with the media themselves. The qualitative factors of the major media that were discussed in chapters 13 and 14 must be considered in relation to the market as media plans are developed. In addition, the media planner must consider that the editorial content of certain media appeals to the people in some markets and not to those in others. Each specific medium has an image, and the images should be matched with the markets.

Quantitative considerations related to the accomplishment of media objectives are primarily based on three concepts—reach, frequency, and gross rating points; the last is a method combining the reach and frequency figures.

Reach. Reach is the number of different people, or homes, that will be exposed to a particular media mix at least once during a specified period of time (usually four weeks). The concept is applicable whether there is a mix of several different media or whether there is but a single medium, and reach can be expressed either as a numerical value or as a percentage. If there were 1,000 homes in a particular market area and 900 would be exposed to the advertiser's message at least one time (in any of the media used in the media mix) during the four-week period, the reach would be 900, or 90 percent.

Frequency. Frequency is the average number of times during the given period that each person or home reached would be exposed to the message. Some of the 900 people in the previous example could be exposed more than once. If the media mix included magazines, television, and radio, for example, some people might see the message in a magazine ad, in a television commercial, and hear it in a radio commercial; or they may see it three times in television commercials; or they may be exposed to the message three times in some other media or media combinations. Perhaps the 900 people would be exposed as follows:

600 people exposed to 1 TV commercial	=	600 exposures
150 people exposed to 1 TV commercial and 1 magazine ad	=	300 exposures
150 people exposed to 2 TV commercials and 1 radio commercial	=	450 exposures
900 people		1,350 exposures

The frequency, determined by dividing the total number of exposures by the total number of people reached (1,350 divided by 900), would be 1.5.

Gross rating points.   The multiplication of reach times frequency determines gross rating points (GRP), which indicate the total impact of a particular media proposal. The GRP for the example above would be 135, obtained by multiplying 90 by 1.5.

The media planner could obtain the same figures in the computation of gross rating points by increasing or decreasing the reach and frequency figures respectively. The 135 GRP in the example was the result of a reach of 90 and a frequency of 1.5, but the same 135 GRP could be obtained if the reach were 45 and the frequency 3.0. A reach of 45 would mean that 450 people in the market of 1,000 would be exposed to the message at least one time; a frequency of 3 would mean that the average home reached was exposed to the message three times. It could be as follows:

225 people exposed to 3 TV commercials	=	675 exposures
225 people exposed to 2 magazine ads and 1 radio commercial	=	675 exposures
450 people		1,350 exposures

The frequency is 3 (1,350 divided by 450), and when combined with the reach of 45 results in the same 135 GRP's.

Thus the media planner must decide whether the appropriate strategy is to strive for *extensive* coverage among a large audience (relatively greater reach) or *intensive* coverage among a limited number of people (relatively higher frequency). One study showed, for example that the probability that a viewer will perceive a television commercial three times increases up to 12 exposures.[7]

Other complicating factors in these decisions include problems relative to duplicating the audience with different media, the continuity of media insertions, and the relative effectiveness of larger print advertisements. If the objective is to achieve extensive coverage, for example, the different media in the mix should

[7]Howard Kamin, ``Advertising Reach and Frequency,'' *Journal of Advertising Research* 18, no. 1 (Feb. 1978): 21-25.

reach different people for the most part. But if frequency is the objective, it can be accomplished by using different media that reach the same audience.

Continuity refers to the idea that people must be frequently exposed to the advertiser's message. The degree of exposure necessary to achieve continuity affects the timing in the placement of advertisements and/or commercials. Continuity should be maintained because people tend to forget the advertiser's message and must be reminded of it often. But the degree of exposure depends upon the situation and the media planner's perception of it.

The size of a print ad is significant because it may have a bearing on the number of people who notice the ad and are thus actually exposed. Larger ads attract more attention than small ads but not proportionately so. It was found, for example, that a two-page spread in a magazine attracted only slightly more than 6 percent more readers than a full-page ad.[8] The media planner must decide whether the additional readership is worth the additional cost.

Reach versus frequency.   The question of whether the major emphasis should be placed on reach or on frequency must be resolved in developing a media plan. The initial consideration should be objectives. If the objective is simply to create awareness, perhaps introduce a new product, reach is most important because the advertiser wants as many people in the market as possible to know that the product is available. On the other hand, if the objective is to generate interest, desire, and purchase, the focus should be on frequency. A study by Jos. E. Seagrams & Sons and Time, Inc., for example, showed that a consumer's response builds as frequency increases, although perhaps at a decreasing rate (the incremental value may decrease).[9]

But the question of just what the frequency should be is still difficult to answer. Some prospects are more valuable than others and therefore should be reached more frequently than those less inclined to respond favorably. Furthermore, the common use of *average frequency,* as described in the earlier discussion, is often misleading. As is so often the case, average figures do not reflect a realistic situation, like the man with his head in the oven and his feet in the freezer who was said to be comfortable because his average temperature was normal. An average frequency of 4 does not necessarily mean that everyone who was reached was exposed to the message 4 times. Some might have been exposed 7 or 8 times and others only once; but the "average" could be 4.

A better approach is to use a *frequency distribution analysis* which enables the media planner to determine how many people reached will be exposed to however many messages are to be included in the media plan. The resulting figures provide a better base than does the average frequency figure.[10]

---

[8]See Lawrence W. Mahar, "How to Get Greater Market Impact Faster with Right Ad Sizes, Frequency," *Industrial Marketing* 61, pt. 2 (Aug. 1976): 66.

[9]See Stuart Emmrich, "Major Study Details Ads' Effect on Sales," *Advertising Age* (June 21, 1982): 1, 80; and Stuart Emmrich, "Ad Impact Study Stirs Questions," *Advertising Age* (June 28, 1982): 2, 86.

[10]See Joseph W. Ostrow, "What Level Frequency?" *Advertising Age* (November 9, 1981): S-4–8.

The Media Schedule

The media schedule is a crystallization of media planning. It reflects resolutions to the questions, problems, and considerations developed in the process of media planning. It delineates precisely the media proposed, the timing of the advertisements and/or commercials, their size, and their cost in the proposed campaign.

Media schedules tend to follow certain patterns, particularly with respect to the use of print media. There are, for example, schedules described as even, staggered, step-up, and step-down.[11] An *even* schedule connotes regularity. Such a schedule might require the placement of advertisements of the same size at regular intervals, such as a full-page ad in *Cosmopolitan* every month. A *staggered* schedule maintains the same insertion regularity as the even schedule but requires alternating sizes of advertisements — for example, a full-page ad in the January, March, and May issues and a half-page ad in the alternate monthly issues. A *step-up* schedule begins light and progressively increases its impact throughout the period; a *step-down* schedule is the reverse of that. The patterns are not absolute, for geographical market considerations and the seasonality of the product temper them.

Two scheduling strategies are *pulsing* and *flighting*. Pulsing refers to the somewhat regular intermittent bursts of advertising separated by short periods of relative, or sometimes complete, inactivity. Flighting is similar to pulsing except that it may lack the regularity usually associated with pulsing. These techniques are used when funds are considered inadequate to maintain a strong continuous effort or when it is believed that periodic extensive reach and/or intensive frequency are desirable strategies. Of course, continuity is sacrificed when they are used.

Computer Models and Media Planning

In the 1960s computer use accelerated rapidly. During that time, numerous models were developed for use in media planning. The typical model contains an objective function, a set of constraints, and some selection mechanism. Objective functions may be established to minimize costs, maximize reach, maximize frequency, or to accomplish some other purpose. Constraints are reflected in the assumptions associated with the use of the model, such as the relationships among variables, the size of the audience, and the time period. The selection mechanism provides the means by which the "solution" emerges.

Linear programming models, such as one developed by the advertising agency Batten, Barton, Durstine, & Osborn, are based on the assumption that the relationships among variables are linear. For example, one relationship assumption might be that the response to each successive exposure is the same as for the first exposure.[12] By artificially duplicating an audience, simulation models provide information relative to the possible impact of different media schedules on proposed targets. The High Assay Media Model of Young and Rubicam advertising agency is

---

[11]John S. Wright, Daniel S. Warner, Willis L. Winter, Jr., and Sherilyn K. Zeigler, *Advertising*, 4th ed. (New York: McGraw-Hill, 1977), pp. 601–2.

[12]For a discussion of linear programming in this respect, see David B. Montgomery and Glen L. Urban, *Management Science in Marketing* (Englewood Cliffs, N.J.: Prentice Hall, 1969), pp. 143–47.

an adaptation of a simulation model. Another simulation model is one developed by the Simulmatics Corporation.[13]

Many other models have been developed, including some that are quite comprehensive such as MEDIAC, created by Little and Lodish.[14] Continued experimentation should improve the usefulness of computer models to media planning. At the present time, however, their effectiveness is limited by the many assumptions necessary in their use. Furthermore, they ignore the creative element in advertising and focus entirely on the dissemination of the message — whatever it is and in whatever form it appears.[15] Therefore, complete reliance on the models can be misleading. They can be of value in reducing irrational subjectivity in media planning, provided that their solutions are harmonized with rational subjective thinking.

MEASUREMENT OF ADVERTISING EFFECTIVENESS

Copy testing is the term for the measurement of advertising effectiveness. The term is used to describe all such tests and measurements, not just those concerned with the copy itself. The underlying purpose in all testing, of course, is to "cull out the duds and run with those believed to do the most efficient selling job."[16] But measurement is necessarily somewhat imprecise. Advertising often produces results much beyond the life of a particular advertisement or campaign.[17] Therefore, it is extremely difficult to isolate the effect of any single advertisement or campaign from the lingering effects of previous efforts.[18]

In addition, advertising affects consumer behavior in more ways than simply triggering sales. The effects include persuasion, reinforcement, reminding, and precipitation. The multiplicity of effects magnifies the problems of measuring effectiveness.[19] Although the *ultimate* goal of all business advertising is to increase sales, other aspects of behavior must be affected before the decision to buy is made. In fact, the use of sales to measure advertising effectiveness could be grossly misleading. For example, a consumer might become convinced of the merits of a brand by the advertising for it, go to the store to buy it, but have to settle for another brand because the store was out of the advertised brand. In such a situation the advertising would have been effective but the sales would not show it. Thus the measure should usually be concerned with the psychological effects

---

[13]See Philip Kotler, *Marketing Management: Analysis, Planning, and Control,* 3rd ed. (Englewood Cliffs, N.J.: Prentice-Hall, 1976), p. 353.

[14]John D. C. Little and Leonard M. Lodish, "A Media Planning Calculus," *Operations Research* 17, pt. 1 (Jan.-Feb. 1969): 1–35.

[15]Leo Bogart, "Media Models: A Reassessment," *Journal of Advertising* 4, no. 2 (Spring 1975): 28–30.

[16]David C. Leach, "Should Ads Be Tested?" Advertising Age (October 20, 1980): S-28–29.

[17]See Chapter 8. See also Richard T. Hise and Robert H. Strawser, "Advertising Decisions and the Long Run Effects of Advertising," *Journal of Advertising* 5, no. 4 (Fall 1976): 20–23, 41.

[18]See Donald S. Tull, "The Carry-over Effect of Advertising," *Journal of Marketing* 29 (Apr. 1965): 45–53.

[19]Jagdish N. Sheth, "Measurement of Advertising Effectiveness: Some Theoretical Considerations," *Journal of Advertising* 3, no. 1 (1974): 6–11.

which the advertising was designed to create on the customer and not on the sales that may or may not result.[20]

Because of the vagueness historically associated with testing procedures, twenty-one of the nation's largest advertising agencies endorsed a set of principles that can serve as guidelines for copy testing methodology and practices.[21] The nine principles are referred to by the acronym, PACT (Positioning Advertising Copy Testing), and have been distributed to all members of the American Association of Advertising Agencies. The nine principles state that a good copy testing system does the following:

- Provides measurements which are relevant to the objectives of the advertising;
- Requires agreement about how the results will be used in advance of each specific test;
- Provides multiple measurements, because single measurements are generally inadequate to assess the performance of an ad;
- Is based on a model of human response to communications — the reception of a stimulus, the comprehension of the stimulus, and the response to the stimulus;
- Allows for consideration of whether the advertising stimulus should be exposed more than once;
- Recognizes that the more finished a piece of copy is, the more soundly it can be evaluated and requires, as a minimum, that alternative executions be tested in the same degree of finish;
- Provides controls to avoid the biasing effects of the exposure context;
- Takes into account basic considerations of sample definition; and
- Demonstrates reliability and validity.

A number of tests have been devised for copy testing purposes. Such tests are usually divided into pretests and posttests.[22]

Pretests

The purpose of pretests is to ascertain, if possible, the potential effectiveness of each of several alternatives. Pretests are made before major advertising is run and before large sums of money are committed. Many advertisers believe pretests are absolutely essential.[23] To the extent that the tests are effective, they reduce the risk of making the wrong decision. However, even if the best alternative is chosen, only rarely could one expect a direct correlation with sales.[24]

Pretests can be used to determine the best of several entirely different adver-

[20]Alfred Politz, "The Function of Advertising and its Measurements," *Journal of Advertising* 4, no. 2 (Spring 1975): 10–12.

[21]*PACT — Positioning Advertising Copy Testing. A Consensus Credo Representing the Views of Leading American Advertising Agencies* (New York: J. Walter Thompson, 1980).

[22]See John D. Leckenby, "An Empirical Approach to the Multiple Criteria Problem in Copy Testing Research," *Journal of Advertising* 7, no. 1 (Winter 1978): 19–27.

[23]See "Europeans Insist on Pretesting," *Advertising Age* (August 24, 1981): 38.

[24]Derek Bloom, Andrea Jay, and Tony Twyman, "The Validity of Advertising Pretests," *Journal of Advertising Research* 17, no. 6 (Apr. 1977): 7–16.

tisements. They can also be used to test several alternatives all of which are identical with the exception of one element — the headline, or the copy, or the illustration, for example. Our discussion will deal primarily with print advertisements because TV and/or radio commercial testing is both difficult and expensive.

The two most common procedures for testing TV commercials are *on-air exposure* with a 12- to 24-hour recall measure and *forced exposure* with an immediate measure of buying intentions. An example of the latter is the Schwerin test.[25] This test is designed to measure changes in consumer product preferences as a result of exposure to television commercials. Respondents are invited to view new television shows presented in theaters in selected cities. In a drawing held before the showing, each consumer can select a gift from a number of different products and their choices are recorded. The show is then presented with the commercials appearing in their appropriate places. After the show is finished, a second drawing and offer of gifts is made and changes in brand preferences are then recorded. Presumably, the changes result from exposure to the commercials.

Another testing procedure for TV commercials is a *day-after recall* test in which advertisements are placed in regular programming and viewers are telephoned the next day to determine the degree to which they recall the commercial. A different approach is to contact a target audience ahead of time and ask that they watch a low-rated show in which an advertisement is placed. The respondents are contacted the next day to determine the degree of recall.[26]

However, fine distinctions among alternatives in television commercials are difficult to make, and the reliability and validity of tests purporting to measure their effectiveness is somewhat questionable.[27]

The simplest pretest for print advertisements is really not a test at all. It is simply a checklist of the desirable attributes of a good ad to which a proposed advertisement is compared. It probably should be used whether or not additional tests are included. The most complicated tests are in a group of rather sophisticated laboratory techniques whose usefulness is somewhat suspect. These include tests that measure pupil dilation, sweat gland activity, and other bodily reflections of emotional changes. The rationale for their use is that an individual's reaction to an advertisement will be indicated by changes in certain functions of the body.

Several specific tests of a more "practical" nature are used by some firms with varying degrees of success. These include the order-of-merit, paired comparisons, portfolio, dummy magazines, rating scales and inquiry tests. Because all of these tests involve the opinions or reactions of *consumers,* the results are less biased than if the alternative advertisements were compared solely by professionals. The rationale is that since consumer response will be elicited by the advertisements ultimately used, consumer reaction to the test ads is more indicative of an advertisement's potential effectiveness than are the judgments of advertising practitioners.

[25]See Patrick J. Kelly, "The Schwerin Model: How You Can Use It to Build Your Share of Market," *Printers' Ink* (8 May 1964): 31.

[26]See "Evaluative Pre-testing of Advertising," N. W. Ayer Advertising Agency, pamphlet.

[27]See Kevin J. Clancy and Lyman E. Ostlund, "Commercial Effectiveness Measures," *Journal of Advertising Research* 16, no. 1 (Feb. 1976): 29–34.

Order-of-Merit Test

A panel of consumers is used to make the evaluation in the order-of-merit test. The panel usually consists of from 50 to 150 users or potential users of the product advertised. It is not a true random sample of people because nonusers of the product are excluded. Their opinions would not necessarily be indicative of those of the people at whom the advertising will be directed. Each panel member is given all the advertisements being considered and asked to rank them in the order of their relative effectiveness. If six ads are being evaluated, for example, the "best" ad would be ranked Number 1 and the "worst" Number 6. The evaluations of all the panelists are then summarized, and the potentially most effective advertisement is thereby determined.

The method has several limitations. It is frequently difficult to rank a number of advertisements in that manner. It is somewhat like trying to decide on which single necktie to buy off a rack containing several dozen. Perhaps more serious is the fact that the test assumes there is one good ad among the alternatives; maybe none is any good.

Paired-Comparisons Test

The paired-comparisons test is similar to the order-of-merit test except that it differs in the method used to determine the best ad. Instead of receiving all the alternative advertisements at one time to rank, each panel member is first given two ads and asked to pick the best of the two. When the choice has been made, the rejected ad is removed and replaced by a third ad. Again the panel member is asked to pick the best of the two. The process is continued until the panel member has evaluated all the alternatives being tested.

The method overcomes the difficulty of ranking a number of ads all at once since it is easier to pick the best of two than the best of six. Otherwise, the method has the same limitations as the order-of-merit test.

Portfolio Test

In the portfolio test each consumer respondent is handed a folder containing the test ads as well as a number of control ads. The control ads are not being tested, but the respondents are not told that some ads are in this category. Control ads are included in order to make the results of the test more indicative of the perceived effectiveness of the test ads. The respondents are asked to look through the folders. They are given some time to do so and then are questioned by an interviewer. The questioning is designed to determine which ad produced the greatest impact on the respondent. If the test goes as planned, one of the test ads will emerge as the "best" ad.

Dummy Magazines

A test that eliminates much of the artificiality of the testing environment necessarily associated with the previously described tests involves the use of a dummy magazine. In this test a magazine having all the characteristics of a "real" magazine (editorial content, advertisements, etc.) is sent to a representative sample of homes. Of course, the test ads are incorporated into the magazine. The respondents are asked to read the magazines as they normally would; and then at an appropriate later time an interviewer questions the respondents to determine their recall of the test ads.

The advertising agency Young and Rubicam has employed the technique for many years using a magazine that they publish called *New Canadian World.* Batten, Barton, Durstine, & Osborn, another agency, uses a variation of the technique, in which they use two national weekly magazines. Through arrangements with the publishers, the agency gets some advance copies of certain issues, removes some of the legitimate ads, and replaces them with ads they want to test. The altered copies are then distributed to sample homes at the time the regular copies are distributed, and subsequent interviews are conducted.[28]

Rating Scales

Rating scales of various kinds are often used in pretesting advertisements. These can take many forms; a common form is the *semantic differential* developed by Charles E. Osgood and his associates.[29] The method was not conceived specifically for testing advertisements, but it is quite effective as a rating scale. Its use reflects the feelings or attitudes respondents have toward each of the specific advertisements being tested. The technique uses a series of *polar adjectives* (strong/weak, noninformative/informative, etc.) to define possible feelings people might have toward the advertisements. Each pair of adjectives is separated by seven underscored blank spaces, and the respondent is asked to place an "X" in the space representing the degree of feeling he or she has toward the advertisement. Each pair of adjectives in the series would appear to the respondent as follows:

Strong __ __ __ __ __ __ __ Weak

The middle space indicates a neutral feeling, and each successive space in either direction represents progressively stronger feelings toward the respective polar adjective. When the results are tabulated, a profile of feeling toward each advertisement tested can be constructed and the "best" ad selected. An advantage claimed for the use of rating scales is that the respondent is judging each ad on its own merits and is not, theoretically, making comparisons among the advertisements.

---

[28]S. Watson Dunn and Arnold M. Barban, *Advertising: Its Role in Modern Marketing,* 4th ed. (Hinsdale, Ill.: Dryden, 1978), pp. 290–91.

[29]C. E. Osgood, G. J. Suci, and P. H. Tannenbaum, *The Measurement of Meaning* (Urbana: University of Illinois, 1957).

Inquiry Test

The inquiry test is conducted in a more realistic testing environment than any of the other pretests. It is also used for testing during a campaign. The test involves running two or more advertisements for a limited time under normal conditions in selected print media for the purpose of determining which one to use in the major advertising effort. The basis for evaluation is returned coupons. Each ad being tested contains a coupon which the reader is asked to return for more information about the product, a sample, or whatever. The coupons are coded to identify them with the specific ad from which they were clipped. A count is made, and the ad from which the most coupons were clipped and returned is deemed to be the best ad. Usually two ads are tested; the technique for implementation is the *split run.*

One authority has suggested that there are four kinds of splits, only one of which is ideal:

1. *The A-B split.* This is the ideal split. The publisher (usually a magazine but it can be a newspaper) designs the press run in such a way that ad A appears in every other copy, and ad B appears in the alternate copies. Every region in which the magazine is distributed gets half the copies with ad A and half with B.
2. *Clump splits.* Some publishers who are unable to provide the A-B split may offer the clump split. Clumps of copies, say 50 or 100, in every lift will be evenly split.
3. *Flip-flops.* The tester uses two comparable publishers offering no splits, places ad A in one and ad B in the other for the first phase and then reverses their placement in a second phase.
4. *The split that isn't.* In this method all the copies distributed west of the Mississippi (for example) would contain ad A, while those distributed east of the river would contain ad B.[30]

The major weakness of the inquiry test is that the results may show nothing more than the number of people who return coupons. There may be some people who read the ad but did not return the coupon, and there may be some people who were attracted to the ad only because of the coupon. In either case, the results may not indicate the effectiveness of the advertisment itself.

Posttests

Posttests are conducted after the advertising has been run or sometimes while it is being run, in which case *post* refers to the *start* of the major effort. Their purpose is to determine the effectiveness of the advertising effort as it has been designed. The major kinds of posttests are recognition, recall, and sales results.

---

[30]Gerald Schreck, ''How to Test Your Print Ads with Four Kinds of Splits,'' *Advertising Age* (12 July 1976): 68–69.

Recognition Tests

The most widely used recognition test today is the Starch Readership Survey conducted by Starch Inra Hooper, Inc.[31] Its results reflect readership of the advertisements tested; the basic premise is that an ad has to be read before it can have any effect at all. The Starch organization surveys the readership of advertisements in hundreds of publications annually. Each advertiser-subscriber receives a report containing survey results for the pertinent magazine(s), together with a copy of the magazine in which stickers have been placed on various individual elements of the advertisements providing additional readership information. Figure 15-1 is a sample of the Starch Readership Report.

Appropriately timed after the on-sale date of the magazine, carefully planned interviews are held with sample respondents across the country to provide the information necessary to determine the readership of both men and women. The interviews are conducted in the respondent's home or place of business. The interviewer goes through the magazine with the respondent and asks questions about each ad in the survey. As a result of the questioning, three degrees of readership are determined: noted, associated, and read most. The respondent who remembers having seen the ad becomes a statistic in the "noted" column. If the respondent not only noted the ad but was able to associate it with the brand or the advertiser, that person is an "associated" reader. Finally, those respondents who read at least half the ad are put in the "read most" column. The summarized figures from all interviews are then expressed as percentages of all primary readers of the magazine.

The Starch service is particularly useful to the advertiser-subscriber because of the many kinds of comparisons that can be made with the information it provides. For example, the advertiser can compare the current campaign with the campaigns in previous years or with the current campaigns of competitors. Moreover, readership comparisons can be made between months throughout the current campaign.

Recall Tests

Recall tests can be either *unaided* or *aided*. Unaided tests are rarely used; they involve asking such questions as "What advertisments have you seen?" The information received from the use of such tests is usually too vague to be of much value. Among the most important aided recall tests are the Gallup-Robinson Impact Test and the triple-associates test. As the term *aided* implies, the respondent is given some assistance in remembering the advertisements being tested. But even with such help, it is sometimes difficult for respondents to remember the medium in which they saw the advertisement. They may know that they saw it, but they do not remember where.[32]

---

[31]See "Scope, Method, and Use," Daniel Starch & Staff, Inc., Mamaroneck, New York, pamphlet.

[32]See, for example, Michael Perry and Arnon Perry, "Ad Recall: Biased Measure of Media?" *Journal of Advertising Research* 16 (June 1976): 21-25.

STARCH
READERSHIP REPORT

PAGE 2

66 ADS 1/2 PAGE AND OVER
SPORTS ILLUSTRATED OCTOBER 9 1978

MEN READERS

PRODUCT CATEGORIES			COST	RANK IN ISSUE		PERCENTAGES			READERS PER DOLLAR			COST RATIOS		
PAGE	SIZE & COLOR	ADVERTISER	PENNIES PER READER	BY NUMBER OF READERS	BY COST PER READER	NOTED	ASSOCIATED	READ MOST	NOTED	ASSOCIATED	READ MOST	NOTED	ASSOCIATED	READ MOST
		RESORTS/TRAVEL ACCOMMODATION												
89	1P4	LAS VEGAS NEVADA RESORT PROM	3.7	7	3	60	50	13	32	27	7	168	180	350
		HAIR PRODUCTS												
114	1P4	GILLETTE $1,000,000 WORLD SERIES BONUS OFFER	6.7	43	29	32	27	6	17	15	3	89	100	150
		MEDICINES/PROPRIETARY REMEDY												
129	1P B	STRESSTABS 600 VITAMINS/IRON	8.3	57	47	24	17	*	18	12	*	95	80	*
		CONFECTIONERY/SNACKS												
77	V2/3P4	SUN GIANT ALMONDS	11.1	61	60	26	13	1	18	9	1	95	60	50
		SOFT DRINKS												
69	V2/3P4	SQUIRT BEVERAGE WORLD SERIES POSTERS	11.1	61	60	22	13	6-	15	9	4	79	60	200
		LIQUOR & WHISKEY												
12	V2/3P4	OLD GRAND-DAD BOURBON	5.0	36	13	33	29	5-	22	20	3	116	133	150
41	1P4	SEAGRAM'S EXTRA DRY GIN	4.3	14	8	56	43	5-	30	23	3	158	153	150
51	1P4B	RONRICO RUM	4.8	11	11	45	45	2	21	21	1	111	140	50
59	1P4B	BURNETT'S WHITE SATIN GIN	7.1	36	36	38	29	2-	18	14	1	95	93	50
60	1P4B	SEAGRAM'S 7 CROWN WHISKEY	5.0	17	13	51	42	2	24	20	1	126	133	50
97	1P4B	WOLFSCHMIDT GENUINE VODKA	7.1	33	36	41	30	2	19	14	1	100	93	50
98	1P4B	SEAGRAMS V O CANADIAN WHISKY	5.0	14	13	49	43	7-	23	20	3	121	133	150
108	1P4	PUERTO RICAN RUMS	9.1	51	54	28	21	6	15	11	3	79	73	150
136	H1/2P4	GILBEY'S LONDON DRY GIN	5.3	47	16	26	23	1-	22	19	1	116	127	50
145	1P4B	JOHNNIE WALKER BLACK LABEL	5.9	23	22	52	36	20-	24	17	9	126	113	450
		TOBACCO/TOBACCO PRODUCTS												
4	1P4B	SALEM CIGARETTES	7.7	41	44	29	28	2-	14	13	1	74	87	50
52	1S4B	BENSON & HEDGES CIGARETTES SWEEPSTAKES	16.7	46	65	34	24	2	9	6	1	47	40	50
111	1P4	DECADE CIGARETTES	10.0	55	59	23	18	*	12	10	*	63	67	*
131	1P4B	WINSTON CIGARETTES	7.1	36	36	36	29	10-	17	14	5	89	93	250
139	1P4	TAREYTON CIGARETTES	8.3	49	47	26	22	*-	14	12	*	74	80	*
4C	1P4B	CAMEL CIGARETTES	6.7	19	29	41	40	3	15	15	1	79	100	50
		JEWELRY/WATCHES												
81	1P4B	CITIZEN WATCHES	7.1	36	36	45	29	6	21	14	3	111	93	150
		CAMERAS/PHOTOGRAPHIC SUPPLIES												
21	1P4B	KODAK EXTRAMAX CAMERA	5.6	21	19	46	38	3	22	18	1	116	120	50
44	1P4	VIVITAR CAMERAS FOCUS ON VICTORY SWEEPSTAKES	9.1	52	54	29	20	3	16	11	2	84	73	100
92	1P5B	PENTAX ME CAMERAS	6.7	27	29	45	33	6	20	15	3	105	100	150
		RETAIL &/OR DIRECT BY MAIL												
82	1S	TRUE VALUE HARDWARE STORES	5.9	18	22	44	41	2	19	17	1	100	113	50
		MISC. HOUSEHOLD FURNISHINGS												
126	V2/3P4	SEARS GLASS DOOR FIRESCREEN	9.1	58	54	24	16	5	16	11	3	84	73	150
		RADIO/TV/PHONO COMPONENTS												
6	1P B	TECHNICS LINEAR-DRIVE HEADPHONES/PANASONIC	4.2	27	6	42	33	8	31	24	6	163	160	300
18	1S	RCA SELECTA VISION VIDEO CASSETTE RECORDER	6.7	23	29	42	36	9	18	15	4	95	100	200
67	1P4B	SONY BETAMAX VIDEO RECORDER	4.0	6	4	60	53	14	28	25	7	147	167	350
		BLDG. EQUIP./FIXTURES/SYSTEMS												
73	1P4B	STANLEY TOOLS	6.3	27	25	39	33	2	18	16	1	95	107	50
137	1P	PPG SOLARCOOL BRONZE GLASS	12.5	65	63	24	10	*	20	8	*	105	53	*
		PROTECTIVE COATINGS/FINISHES												
87	1P4	RUST-OLEUM RUST PREVENTIVE	6.7	43	29	34	27	*	18	15	*	95	100	*

* LESS THAN 1/2 OF ONE PERCENT.
- FEWER THAN 50 WORDS IN AD.

MEDIAN READERS/DOLLAR   19   15   2

READERS PER DOLLAR ARE BASED ON 2,014,000 MEN READERS AND PUBLISHED ONE-TIME SPACE RATES. READER FIGURES ARE OBTAINED FROM 2,189,143 U.S. A.B.C. CIRC. TIMES MEN PRIMARY READERS PER COPY FROM STARCH ESTIMATES.

Gallup-Robinson Impact Test.   In this test the respondent is first asked to describe at least one editorial feature in the magazine to determine if the magazine has been read. If the respondent has read the magazine, he or she is handed a group of cards, each of which has the name of an advertised brand. Some of the brands were advertised in the magazine, and some were not; the respondent is asked to indicate the brands that were advertised in the magazine. Through a series of questions, then, the interviewer attempts to determine the degree of impact an advertisement had on the respondent.

Triple-associates test.   This test is used primarily to determine the degree to which people remember copy themes or slogans. Three elements are involved in the test—the generic product, the theme or slogan, and the brand. The respondent is given two of the "associates" and asked to supply the third. The question might be, for example, "What brand of credit card (credit card company) advertises 'Don't leave home without it'?" If the theme has penetrated, the respondent would reply, "American Express."

Sales Results Test

Unlike most of the other tests, the sales results test is an attempt to establish a direct relationship between advertising and sales. The test can be used in several ways. It can be used to compare the sales-producing effects of two or more campaigns; it can be used to compare sales figures in areas where there was no advertising with those in areas where the product was advertised; or it can be used in other ways.

In any case, two sets of cities are involved—test cities and control cities—and three of each are normally used for each factor being tested and for control. The test could be conducted using only one of each, but in order to minimize any possible distortion of results due to some unforeseeable event such as a labor strike, or a flood, or even competitors' actions more than two cities are typically used. All the cities must be as comparable as possible in population, composition of the population, and industry. Furthermore, the test cities for each campaign must be remote enough from the control cities and from the other test cities to prevent any advertising effect on the people in the cities not supposed to be exposed to it.

Usually, sales are checked for a two-month period in all the cities. The advertising is then run in the test cities for at least a two-month period, after which sales are again checked in all cities and the results compared with the initial figures. If the test were set up to compare sales generated by advertising with sales occurring without advertising, we would have six cities—three test and three control; there would be no advertising in the control cities. If, over the period of the test, sales had increased in the test cities more than in the control cities, we could assume

FIGURE 15–1   (See opposite page.) Sample page from a Starch Readership Report. Source: Starch Inra Hooper, Inc.

that advertising was the reason. This would only be an assumption because unknown variables might have had more influence on the result than advertising.

The raw figures that emerge must be adjusted. If the cities used were indeed comparable, we would have to assume that sales in the test cities would have increased even without advertising by the same amount as in the control cities. The total increase in the test cities, therefore, would have to be reduced by the percentage of increase in the control cities to determine the net effect of advertising on sales.

SUMMARY

Media planning and the measurement of advertising effectiveness were discussed in this chapter. The objective in media planning is to select and plan the use of those media most appropriate for the purpose.

There is no standard format for a media plan, but any plan is influenced by basic factors, marketing mix factors, and media factors. Among the basic factors are budget limitations, the nature of the market, and competitive activity. All elements of the marketing mix also influence the media plan, as do various factors associated with the media themselves. The media schedule is, in a sense, a concise summary of the media plan.

The measurement of advertising effectiveness, or copy testing, is a difficult task because of the impossibility of really isolating the effects of one advertisement or one campaign. Pretests and posttests are the two basic kinds of tests. Pretests are conducted before the major advertising effort is launched; posttests are made at some time after the effort has been started, usually after it has been completed. The major pretests include the order-of-merit, paired comparisons, portfolio, inquiry tests, and the use of dummy magazines and rating scales.

The major posttests fall into three categories—recognition tests, recall tests, and sales results tests. The most commonly used recognition test is that of Starch Inra Hooper, Inc. Major recall tests are the Gallup-Robinson Impact Test and the triple-associates test. The sales results test is used in an attempt to establish a direct relationship between advertising and sales.

QUESTIONS FOR THOUGHT AND REVIEW

1. What is *media planning?* What is its purpose? What major facet of advertising does it ignore? Is this a serious problem? Why?
2. If media planning is the responsibility of the advertising agency, why is it important for the promotion manager to know something about it?
3. Explain the analogy of media planning to military operations. Would you say that this analogy reflects the characteristics of media as discussed in chapters 12 and 13? Explain.
4. What are the major components of a media plan? Is there a standard form? Why is this so?

5. Discuss the basic factors significant to the development of a media plan.

6. What is *reach?* How is it significant to media planning?

7. What is *frequency?* Explain how the duplication of audiences with the use of several different media affects frequency. If you were a media planner, how would you approach the problem of using different media in this respect?

8. How are gross rating points computed? Explain how varying the relative degrees of reach and frequency can result in the same number of gross rating points. How does media strategy (extensive versus intensive coverage) affect the resolution of that issue?

9. What is *message continuity?* How does it affect media planning? Discuss some of the matters of strategy that bear on the question of continuity.

10. What is the *media schedule?* Distinguish among the schedule patterns of even, staggered, step-up and step-down schedules. Explain the circumstances under which each would be used. Give examples.

11. What are *pulsing* and *flighting?* Under what circumstances might they be used?

12. How are computer models particularly valuable to media planning?

13. Discuss some of the reasons the measurement of advertising effectiveness is so difficult. If so, why is it done?

14. Distinguish between pretests and posttests, and explain why both kinds of tests are used. What part of the ad is tested?

15. In what ways is the order-of-merit test different from the paired-comparisons test? In what ways are they alike? What are the major weaknesses of both? Is the portfolio test similar to these?

16. Do you think the use of dummy magazines is a valid test? Why or why not?

17. Explain the use of rating scales for determining the potential effectiveness of alternative advertisements. What advantage is claimed for them over other methods?

18. Explain the rationale in the use of the inquiry test. What does it measure, and what are its weaknesses?

19. What is a *split run?* Explain the several ways of implementing it. Why is only one of the ways ideal?

20. What kind of test is the Starch Readership Survey? Is this a pretest or a posttest? What does it measure?

21. Explain and distinguish among *noted, associated,* and *read most.*

22. Describe the two recall tests.

23. What does the *sales results test* measure? What is the purpose of using control cities? Explain how a sales results test might be implemented.

24. Explain why, when the final sales are determined in connection with the sales results test, adjustments must be made to get the net effect of the advertising effort.

16

PERSONAL SELLING— THE SALESPERSON AND THE SELLING TASK

Personal selling is unique among the four elements of the promotion mix. The other three elements (advertising, discussed in the four preceding chapters, together with sales promotion and publicity, discussed in chapters 18, 19, and 20) are *mass* communication forms; personal selling is *interpersonal.* But the background material covered in earlier chapters is equally applicable to personal selling. We are still dealing with *persuasive communication,* and the factors that bear on the effectiveness of mass communication bear also on the interpersonal form. Although much of the discussion in this chapter is applicable to retail selling in retail stores, most of it relates to salespeople dealing with business and industry and manufacturers' salespeople selling directly to the consumer.

Personal selling is "the process whereby the seller ascertains, activates, and satisfies the needs or wants of the buyer to the mutual, continuous benefit of the buyer and the seller."[1] This definition is relevant whether the subject of the effort is a product, a service, or an idea. Continuous satisfaction of both buyer and seller is the desirable outcome. This point separates the modern *professional* salesperson from the shady character who is the stereotype in the minds of many people today.[2]

Personal selling is the major ingredient in the promotion mixes of many firms. Insurance companies, for example, rely heavily on personal selling as a promotion tool because most insurance programs must be tailored for each individual or family. The situation is similar with real estate. In the marketing of packaged consumer goods, too, personal selling may play an important role. House-to-house selling of course, epitomized by Avon, is the extreme example. But even those firms that, because of the ubiquity of self-service merchandising, employ a pull strategy with advertising and sales promotion aimed at the consumer, sometimes find personal selling a necessary part of their promotion mixes. Salespeople are indispensable, for example, in promoting and selling expensive products, or complex products requiring demonstration. In addition, many firms find it necessary to use salespeople to call on large-volume wholesalers and retailers to maximize their promotional effort.

Not to be overlooked either is the use of personal selling in the marketing of services and ideas. Political candidates and their supporters certainly use personal selling in their promotional efforts, as do fund-raising organizations. Even the government, with recruiting programs for the military and other government services, uses personal selling.

But personal selling has the starring role in the realm of industrial marketing. Industrial buyers are generally professional buyers and do not respond quickly to advertising appeals alone. Furthermore, industrial products are often expensive and complex, requiring detailed explanation and demonstration; they are often evaluated in terms of pre-established specifications. Can you imagine a company buying IBM equipment without talking to a company representative?

---

[1]Carlton A. Pederson and Milburn D. Wright, *Selling: Principles and Methods,* 6th ed. (Homewood, Ill.: Richard D. Irwin, 1976), p. 4.

[2]See Donald L. Thompson, "Stereotype of the Salesman," *Harvard Business Review* 50, no. 1 (January–February 1972): 20–30.

For firms in general, however, the costs of personal selling are higher than the costs of advertising.[3] In 1980, costs reached an average per industrial sales call of $137.02, and no doubt they have continued to rise.[4] But even more significant is the cost of closing a sale, which often requires as many as 4 or 5 calls. In 1981, the average cost of closing an industrial sale, requiring an average of 4.3 calls, was $589.11.[5] Thus, while we may not hear as much about personal selling as we do about advertising, it is a major element in the promotion mix.

THE EVOLVING PROFESSIONAL SALESPERSON

Personal selling has always been an important part of American business. From the days of the Yankee Peddler to the present time, business has relied heavily on the ingenuity and enthusiasm of salespeople to promote and distribute its products. The fact that society has benefitted from these efforts is perhaps not readily apparent to consumers. The high standard of living enjoyed by the American people today is due in some measure to the activities of salespeople. They are disseminators of innovations; they are catalysts of consumption; and they are perpetuators of growth. Without the efforts of salespeople consumers would not only be unaware of the continuous offering of new items that make life and living easier, but they would lack the enthusiasm for trying them. Personal selling is and always has been a part of the American way of life.

But the nature of salespeople and their methods of operation have changed and will continue to change. The days of the back-slapping, glad-handing salesman are gone. The high pressure tactics and exaggerated claims that once characterized selling methods are no longer effective, and the salesperson today who expects to be around long enough to cash in on his or her pension plan must avoid using them. The salesperson is expected to do homework – writing reports and planning for the next day.

But change is evolutionary; certainly not all salespeople today have seen the light. The vision of some may be blurred by the short-run effectivenesss of their outdated methods. They fail to project the consequences of their actions into the future. But more and more salespeople, and the firms for which they work, have come to recognize the need to reevaluate the selling situation and how it should be handled.

Factors Causing Change

It would be naive to suggest that the changes taking place are due entirely to an aroused compassion for the human race. People are becoming more concerned

---

[3]Thayer C. Taylor, "Selling Costs Climb a Record 15.5 Percent," *Sales and Marketing Management* 124, no. 3 (February 25, 1980): 12.

[4]"Marketing Briefs," *Marketing News* 14, no. 3 (August 8, 1980): 2.

[5]"Industrial Sales Call Tops $137, but New 'Cost to Close' Hits $589," *Marketing News* 14, no. 22 (May 1, 1981): 1.

about other people, but not that concerned. However, certain identifiable factors are instrumental in the change.

The Demand for Accountability

Business is presumed accountable to society for all its actions; with the accelerating clamor for public manifestations, executives are becoming more and more sensitive to actions and methods that may be considered suspect. High-pressure selling and false claims by salespeople fall into the suspect category. Persuading people to buy products they do not need or extolling nonexistent product attributes does not generate goodwill. Furthermore, voluntary or government-dictated product recall policies require restitution to disgruntled customers, and the wrong kind of selling magnifies this problem.

Higher Level of Education

As people become more educated they become more discriminating, both with respect to the products themselves and to the selling efforts stimulating their purchase. The educated person is not likely to be influenced by high-pressure tactics, nor to accept statements of the salesperson without some probing for substantiation of claims.

But highly educated people are susceptible to persuasion; the salesperson is completely justified in directing his or her efforts to that end, provided that the conditions required by the contemporary environment have been met.

Consumer Orientation of Business

One requirement of the "marketing concept" is that business be consumer oriented. Critics argue that the term *marketing concept* camouflages the real intent of business — consumer exploitation. Business counters with the argument that it has always been consumer oriented because the consumer's dollar vote in the marketplace determines the success or failure of a business. The arguments notwithstanding, business in recent years has become more aware of the implications of consumer orientation, or the lack of it. Whether this increased awareness is due to the activities of consumerist groups, government edicts or threats of such, or a spontaneous reaction of business to a changing environment does not matter. The fact remains that business is finding it increasingly necessary to concentrate on building consumer goodwill. This includes directing its salespeople to avoid antagonizing those people with whom they deal.

The Resultant Salesperson

As a result of the factors just discussed, and others, the modern salesperson is not the same individual who bore the title in earlier years. The modern salesperson is a professional in his or her field. Some salespeople even place service to others above their self-interests; this is one of the historic marks of a true profession.

Among the numerous qualifications of the salesperson today that reflect professionalization are education, knowledge, and ethics.

Education

Although many sales positions are filled effectively by people with no more than a high school education, the trend today is for companies to seek college graduates for their sales forces. Promotional strategy requires creative selling, and higher education is increasingly important in creative positions. In order to communicate effectively with the people with whom they deal, salespeople must have commensurate education. Persuasion is the goal, and one cannot be persuasive if the target of the effort is more perceptive and discriminating, and the level of education in the United States has been steadily rising for a number of years.

In addition to the changes occurring in the market (people) that require a high level of education in the sales force, conditions on the other side (business) push in the same direction. The information avalanche from the sophisticated marketing information systems used by most firms today affects salespeople and requires a good deal of formal education to understand and assimilate. In fact, the enormous impact of all of our dynamic technology is felt by everyone; certainly those involved in selling should understand its implications.

Knowledge

Classroom exposure to philosophy, sociology, psychology, social psychology, and other disciplines in the arts and sciences enhances one's ability to understand behavior and to deal with people; courses in business administration generate a conceptual understanding of the problems and perspectives of business. Such background information is increasingly essential for the salesperson today, but it is not enough. In addition to academic knowledge, the professional salesperson today must possess a high degree of knowledge not obtainable in the college classroom. Without a thorough understanding of the product, the customers, and the competition, for example, the modern salesperson would flounder in the competitive marketplace of today. The pursuit of such knowledge never ends for the professional salesperson, but becomes a continuous learning effort.

Ethics

It is the area of ethics, perhaps, that presents the most severe challenge to the contemporary professional salesperson.[6] At the very outset, for example, if the consummation of a sale is to result in mutual benefits for the salesperson and the customer, the salesperson must not attempt to persuade a potential prospect to buy the product if it became apparent that the prospect would not be better off for having done so. This does not mean that just because the prospect shows

---

[6]For a discussion of ethical problems, see Frederic A. Russell, Frank H. Beach, and Richard H. Buskirk, *Selling: Principles and Practices,* 11th ed. (New York: McGraw-Hill, 1982): pp. 442–58.

initial resistance the salesperson should abandon the effort. If the salesperson really believes it would be beneficial to the prospect to buy (even though the prospect does not think so), the effort should be continued. But in the absence of such conviction, it should not.

Ethical behavior has many dimensions in addition to the foregoing fundamental principle. Some questionable practices are illegal. Most are unethical if not used with discretion. They involve relationships with customers, employers, and competitors.

Relationships with customers.   Bribes and kickbacks, of course, are to be avoided by the professional salesperson. The two are similar in that they both involve "paying the customer" to get the sale. They are different in that a bribe is anything, especially money, given to induce the sale, while a kickback is returning money (usually a part of the commission) to the buyer — again to induce the sale in the first place. The temptation to engage in this activity can be quite strong. The giving of gifts to buyers is somewhat related, but is generally considered an acceptable practice, if it constitutes a token of appreciation for past business and not a bribe for future business. Entertainment, a standard practice to establish a congenial relationship, is acceptable as long as it cannot be construed as a bribe. Ethical behavior toward customers also includes, of course, maintaining the confidentiality of any sensitive information about the business, freely or unintentionally provided by the customer.

Relationships with employers.   Among nonprofessional salespeople, the padding of expense accounts is probably the most common violation of ethical behavior towards employers. The temptation to do this is particularly strong if the compensation plan is unsatisfactory, or if "everyone else does it." Nevertheless, the professional salesperson refrains from such practice. Related to this is using a company car for personal use, unless such use is a part of the agreement with the company. Moonlighting — carrying another company's line — is generally considered unethical unless the salesperson is an agent middleman known as a "Manufacturers' Rep" who, by definition, carries a number of noncompeting lines. The temptation to moonlight presents an ethical dilemma. The company can rightly expect its salespeople to devote full attention to its line; if the salespeople have time to work for someone else, they are not doing their jobs satisfactorily for the company. The salespeople, on the other hand, can argue that if they are working on a straight commission and paying their own expenses, their time is their own.

Relationships with competitors.   Ethical behavior toward competitors generally involves comparison with a competitor's product. Behavior can range all the way from simply staging a product demonstration to make the competitor's product look comparatively inferior to secretly and deliberately inflicting damage on a competitor's product. The latter is obviously unethical and illegal, but what about the former? Desirable shelf space in supermarkets can also generate unethical behavior by sales reps who deliver and stock their products on the shelves. The temptation is strong to "rearrange" competitors' products on the breadrack, in the dairy case, and on the soft drink display. Such activity not only incites anger among the competitors but also creates ill will with supermarket managers.

The professional salesperson is honest and aboveboard in all his or her dealings. Such a philosophy is not only self-satisfying but it is also bound to have a long-term financial payoff. Continuing relationships are only possible if there is mutual respect between the parties involved.

THE SALESPERSON AND THE JOB

There are many kinds of selling jobs and many ways to classify them. People on routine delivery routes for such products as milk, bread, soft drinks, beer, and laundry services are considered salespeople. At the other extreme are the sales engineers or engineering salespeople who sell expensive, highly technical products to industrial buyers. And there are dozens of kinds of jobs between the two extremes.

Although each job requires a different kind of person, salespeople in all jobs have some things in common. The astute sales manager is alert to the common characteristics as well as to the unique requirements associated with the jobs for which he or she is responsible.

Types of Selling Jobs

For purposes of conceptualizing personal selling as an element of the promotion mix, it is convenient to think of the many different kinds of selling jobs as falling loosely into one of three categories: order taking, missionary selling, and creative selling. The three types of jobs are not mutually exclusive, nor can they be directly compared. The salespeople in each category may do some of what is required of the people in the other two categories, but because the goals and objectives are different in each of the three kinds of selling, work performance that is effective in accomplishing the objectives in one category may not be effective in the others.

Order-Taking

The primary function of salespeople who are order-takers is just that — taking orders for the products they sell. In some order-taking jobs the salespeople also deliver the products; in others the products are delivered by someone else at a later date. In any event, the emphasis is not on creative selling but rather on simply taking the order of the customer.

Although order-takers can be found in many kinds of selling situations, they are probably most predominant among route salespeople, wholesaler representatives, and retail salespeople. Route salespeople include those who sell and deliver bread, milk, soft drinks, beer, and other products to retailers and milk, laundry services, and other items to consumers. Such salespeople either take orders at each call for the products or services they sell or have standing orders for each routine visit. Order-takers are frequently given the latitude to determine the proper orders themselves if they are regulars on the routes and the buyer has confidence in them. The major objective in route selling is regular and efficient service. Good route salespeople can also occasionally engage in some creative selling. The soft drink representative, for example, can persuade retail buyers to stock and promote a new flavor in the line. Even on milk delivery routes to consumers (where they still exist), the salesperson can "sell" cottage cheese or ice cream or some other dairy product not on the customer's standing order.

Wholesaler representatives are usually more order-takers than creative salespeople, although they may have more opportunity to suggest new things than route salespeople. Their primary objective is to generate and maintain a continuing good relationship with their retailer customers. This can usually be done best by simply asking the retail buyer, in effect, "What's on your want list today?" Furthermore, most wholesaler salespeople have thousands of items to sell, and it is sometimes difficult to select a specific item that can be appropriately "sold" to a particular retailer. Despite possible problems in this regard, a good wholesaler salesperson can usually find some products in the line that can be brought to the buyer's attention in a creative way.

Missionary Selling

Missionary selling is really a kind of indirect selling; that is, missionary salespeople rarely take orders but serve as advisors and sources of information for customers and prospects of the companies they represent. They are "goodwill ambassadors," performing a function in the field of selling somewhat analogous to that performed in the field of theology. Called *detail men and women* in some fields, such as the pharmaceutical industry, the main objective of missionary salespeople is to make converts of potential buyers who have not yet seen the light, and to retain the loyalty of those who have.

The activities performed to accomplish their goals depend upon the nature of the products, companies, and industries involved. Among the activities are keeping customers and prospects abreast of new product offerings, providing appropriate market information, helping with displays, solving unusual problems encountered by customers, and generally helping in any way they can. The efforts of missionary salespeople are directed at attitudes and feelings rather than *immediate* sales. Their successful performance should result in an *ultimate* increase in sales.

Creative Selling

Creative selling is the art of generating a sale that would not likely happen without the efforts of the salesperson. The ingenuity of the people involved in this kind of selling is often put to test. Not only must prospects be carefully selected and qualified, but each prospect must be studied individually to determine buying motives that might lead to purchase. When there is resistance, which there usually is, the salesperson must often have a good deal of creative ability to overcome the negative position. Creative selling is a real challenge, and if the salesperson approaches it with a professional attitude, success can be extremely self-satisfying.

Creative selling exists at manufacturing, wholesaling, and retailing business levels, and in all major product categories. There are creative salespeople representing manufacturers of consumer goods and industrial products who call on wholesalers, retailers, distributors, suppliers, and consumers. Although wholesaler salespeople often serve as order-takers, they can be creative in their relationships with customers. There are creative salespeople in retailing. In fact, the better retail stores attempt to employ creative individuals as salespeople.

Product categories requiring creative selling are unlimited. New consumer products in any field must often be promoted creatively to persuade middlemen to carry them. When dealing directly with the consumer, manufacturer sales representatives must often use creative selling for such products as cosmetics, encyclopedias, kitchenware, and insurance. Building improvements, advertising, and insurance must often be "sold" to business executives. And the list goes on. It can probably be said that creative selling is required in all situations where the prospective buyer is not aware of a possible need that can be satisfied with the product or service in question.

Essential Characteristics

The old saying that salesmen are born and not made is nonsense. It may be true that some individuals can learn the art of selling more quickly than others, just as some people can learn to play the trumpet more easily than others. But both can be learned. Moreover, the individual who feels so strongly in possession of some innate ability to sell that training is unnecessary is likely doomed to failure.

The practice of selling is the art of dealing with people in a persuasive way while retaining their goodwill. It is not easy. It requires not only a thorough knowledge of the product and the company and of selling techniques, but an understanding of people.

Not everyone could be a good salesperson. The most successful people in any position like their jobs; if a person does not like selling, he or she will probably not do well, regardless of the amount of training received.

In the extensive literature about the qualities necessary for success in selling, the prominent characteristics are positive attitude, determination, empathy, ego-drive, and self-motivation. Most successful salespeople have a positive attitude toward their work and a high degree of determination.[7] They must believe each time they call on a prospect that "this one is it." They know they are not going to be successful in every interview, but they must believe that each one as it comes up is not going to be the one that fails. Furthermore, they are determined to succeed in more interviews than they fail, and they have the necessary confidence to go with their determination.

Good salespeople have a high degree of empathy and a particular kind of ego-drive.[8] They must be able to identify with their prospects or clients or customers. It may be that one could have too much empathy to be a good salesper-

---

[7]Fred Tibbitts, Jr., "What It Takes to Make It in Selling," *Sales and Marketing Management* 117 (13 Dec. 1976): 79–80.

[8]David Mayer and Herbert M. Greenberg, "What Makes a Good Salesman?" *Harvard Business Review* 42, no. 4 (July–Aug. 1964): 119–25.

son; with too much empathy the salesperson would be unable to proceed with the presentation if the prospect indicated early refusal. The counterargument is that the salesperson could not have too much empathy because he or she would not only understand the situation from the prospect's point of view, but would have knowledge the prospect did not have.

Successful salespeople seem to have the necessary drive to complete a sale simply for the self-fulfillment that results. It is perhaps this characteristic that keeps them enthusiastic even after a series of unsuccessful interviews. A related characteristic particularly essential for salespeople ''on the road'' is being a self-starter. Since the typical salesperson is not under direct day-to-day supervision, it could be tempting to take an afternoon off. Too many afternoons spent in this manner, of course, would be reflected in sales performance, and the salesperson who is inclined to yield to such temptations is probably in the wrong field.

Opportunities and Rewards

Few fields of endeavor offer more opportunities and rewards than selling. Not only do the challenges met and problems solved every day provide an enormous amount of self-satisfaction, but the potential financial rewards are superior to those in many other career fields. Obviously, not everyone who sells will be a high scorer. But for those determined people who like selling, the field holds tremendous promise. Furthermore, it is somewhat like being in business for yourself with little or no investment. The rewards are commensurate with the effort put forth, and it is up to the individual as to how much effort to make.

There is probably no better stage on which to be observed for possible movement into management than selling. The performance of other jobs in a business often goes unnoticed; but selling is so conspicuous that superior performance is immediately recognized and attention drawn to the aspiring manager.

An interesting, and perhaps unfortunate, paradox exists in this connection. Because companies are in constant need of good salespeople, they encourage young people to go into selling by telling them of the advantages of being a salesperson. Then as a clincher to their arguments they inform the prospective salespeople that they will probably not have to stay in sales very long because in a few years they will be moved into management.[9]

The professional salesperson today views selling as a challenging, financially rewarding, and personally fulfilling job that benefits society as well as the salesperson and the firm for which he or she works. Moreover, as the field of selling becomes more professionalized, the opportunity for such rewards is even greater. Consequently, one may feel successful as a salesperson without moving into management.

---

[9] Robert MacGrayne, ''What Kind of Career Do We Really Offer Salesmen?'' *Sales Management* 115 (8 Sept. 1975): 100–2.

THE SELLING PROCESS

Each organization selling anything has its own methods of handling personal selling situations. Prescribed techniques of selling must be adapted to the unique circumstances associated with each organization. However, certain activities must be performed in sequence by the salespeople of any organization to implement the selling process.[10] These activities include prospecting, pre-interview effort, the approach, the presentation and demonstration, responding to objections, and closing the sale.

Prospecting

The term *prospecting* is another example of terms used in marketing that have been borrowed from other areas or disciplines. Its original meaning is the search for gold or other minerals, and the analogy in selling is fairly direct — the search for potential buyers of the product or service.

Effective prospecting is basic to the success of the entire selling process for there can be no selling without buyers. The difficulty of prospecting varies among different selling situations. In retail selling, for example, salespeople must do most of their prospecting within the store, although they can inform friends of the arrival of new merchandise. But the store management has done the initial prospecting by advertising and by creating a store image attractive to the kinds of people management wants as customers. At the other extreme, perhaps, are people who sell life insurance and other products and services and whose livelihood depends almost entirely on their own efforts in prospecting. Between the extremes are selling situations requiring varying degrees of effort in performing the prospecting task; some salespeople do no prospecting in the true sense of the word, but simply knock on doors ("cold canvass") in the neighborhood or business area.

Prospecting is really a two-fold task: obtaining the names of individuals who *might* be prospects and evaluating such people to determine if they are indeed prospects. The process is really an extension of the concept "defining the market" discussed earlier in connection with marketing and promotion in general.

Obtaining Prospect Names

Prospecting is an ongoing process. The salesperson without a perpetual prospect list can never realize an increase in sales; in fact, total sales will gradually decrease because of the inevitable occasional loss of existing accounts. At the very minimum, these lost accounts must be replaced, and good salesmanship requires more than that.

Each salesperson and/or firm should devise a system for obtaining the names of people who might be prospects. The kind of system devised would depend upon the nature of the salesperson, the kind of product involved, its market, and

---

[10]For an interesting conceptual model of the selling process see Rosann L. Spiro, William D. Perreault, Jr., and Fred D. Reynolds, "The Personal Selling Process: A Critical Review and Model," *Industrial Marketing Management* 5, no. 6 (Dec. 1976): 351–63.

the firm producing the product. Several universally used techniques might be considered.[11]

Personal observation.   The good salesperson will always be alert to possible prospects in day-to-day associations and activities. Daily contacts with friends and acquaintances, business and professional people, clubs, meetings, and entertainment events can often suggest prospects. Items in the local newspapers, radio, and television can sometimes provide clues to potential buyers. Information in news magazines and trade publications can even suggest possibilities; not to be overlooked are public records, directories, and other lists. In fact the ambitious salesperson will always use the personal observation method of prospecting whether or not any other more formally structured system is used.

Spotters.   Spotters (also called "bird dogs") are people in a position to notice possible prospects for certain products or services, either by overhearing or participating in conversations or by observation. Barbers, cosmetologists, utility meter readers, parking lot attendants, service station attendants, and clerical workers in offices are examples of the kinds of people who can be helpful. The particular spotters used depend upon the product or service the salesperson is selling. Meter readers are particularly useful in connection with prospects for home repair and construction products. Clerical workers in business offices could be aware of certain needs in their offices. Some spotters, such as barbers, who are in contact with many different kinds of people may be helpful to the salespeople of many different products. Spotters are compensated for each productive lead provided to the salesperson.

Centers-of-influence.   Centers-of-influence are respected people in their social or business environments who are in a position to recommend possible prospects to particular salespeople. They may be doctors, dentists, lawyers, bankers, ministers, or executives, for example. Cooperative relationships with such people can be of invaluable help in the prospecting task. Members of this group can not only provide names of potential buyers but often assist the salesperson in arranging for interviews and even influencing the prospects in a favorable way. They usually are not compensated for their efforts because that is not the kind of relationship they have with the salesperson. However, the salesperson usually expresses gratitude in some way.

Endless chain.   The endless chain is a commonly used method of prospecting. It simply involves asking each person interviewed for the names of people who might be interested in the product or service. The method is particularly good if the person supplying the names has purchased the product. But even if that is not the case, the interviewee may be willing to suggest some names if the salesperson has not been offensive in the interview.

---

[11]See Pederson and Wright, *Selling,* pp. 219–31; and Russell, Beach, and Buskirk, *Textbook of Salesmanship,* ch. 7.

The salesperson successfully using the endless chain method will never run out of prospects because the method is self-perpetuating. Furthermore, it has the advantage of resulting in a "referred" lead because the implication to the new prospect is that the friend is recommending the salesperson, even though that may not actually be the case.

Party plan.   Although the use of the party plan for prospecting is limited to certain kinds of products, it has proven quite successful. Kitchenware (utensils, pots and pans, etc.), jewelry, and cosmetics lend themselves particularly well to this system. The procedure is for the salesperson to prevail upon a customer to have a "party" to which a number of friends are invited, and at which the salesperson presents his or her line. Appointments are then made with interested people to interview them in their own homes at a later date. The host or hostess is presented with a gift for having the party, and sometimes with remuneration for sales that are made as a result of the party.

Evaluating Tentative Prospects

Every person on a list of potential prospects is not necessarily a true prospect. Thus the second phase of prospecting is to identify those individuals who, in addition to being apparent prospects in the first phase, actually possess the necessary characteristics to qualify them as real prospects. Such characteristics include a want or need that can be satisfied with the salesperon's product or service, the ability to pay for the product or service, the authority to buy, accessibility to the salesperson, and the eligibility to buy.[12]

The want or need can be biogenic or psychogenic, as discussed in chapter 6; if the product or service can satisfy it, the individual has passed the first test. But if the price of the product or service is beyond reach, no matter how intense the want or need, the individual cannot be considered a prospect. Furthermore, the person on the list must have the authority to buy. It does no good for a salesperson to conduct a sales interview with a junior executive of a business firm if that individual has no authority to purchase the product. Accessibility must be considered because some people, particularly senior executives in some companies, instruct their receptionists and secretaries to screen visitors so thoroughly it is virtually impossible for the average salesperson to gain an audience. Finally, if the first four conditions are met, the salesperson must still determine the tentative prospect's eligibility to buy. Eligibility may relate to the person's physical condition (for insurance, for example), the area of residence in relation to the salesperson's territory, and the selling firm's possible policy of exclusive distribution (selecting certain retailers to handle the product).

A tentative prospect who meets all these requirements is placed on the *genuine prospect* list. This type of prospecting minimizes the amount of time lost on fruitless interviews, some of which are inevitable, and maximizes the effectiveness of the salesperson's selling time.

---

[12]See Pederson and Wright, *Selling,* p. 217.

Preinterview Effort

If the prospecting phase of the selling process has been done effectively, each person upon whom the salesperson calls is a candidate for a successful sale. But the salesperson can lose the interview at the start if certain information about the prospect is lacking or is incorrect. At least a minimum amount of research is required to prevent this possibility, and some situations require more research than others.

At the very least, the salesperson should know exactly how the prospect's name is spelled and pronounced. Errors in this regard can be disastrous. Beyond this, the salesperson should find out about the prospect's family — the names, ages, and activities of the children and the spouse — and the prospect's interests, hobbies, club affiliations, and even any personal peculiarities and mannerisms. Not only does such information reduce the possibility of embarrassing moments in the interview, but it also provides topics for discussion if the occasion should arise.

If the prospect is a business with which the salesperson's company has dealt previously, the computer can often furnish additional helpful information. Many companies, for example, have programmed their computers to provide information as to who the buying influences are within the prospect firms, the firms' purchase records, credit ratings, and personnel changes.[13]

Armed with this kind of information, the salesperson is ready to interview the prospect.

The Approach

The initial contact and the first few minutes of the interview are referred to as the *approach.* This step is always important, especially when the salesperson is calling on the prospect for the first time. What is said in the approach, and how it is handled, can often either turn the prospect on or off.

It is usually advisable to make an advance appointment to see the prospect. Most people are busy, and the likelihood of gaining an interview is considerably increased if the salesperson has an appointment. Moreover, the salesperson should always remember that receptionists and secretaries are often gatekeepers for the inner office. It is frequently their jobs to screen visitors, and even express opinions to the "boss." Secretaries and receptionists are important people, so the salesperson should establish a good rapport with them from the outset.

The approach must accomplish two objectives: attract the prospect's attention, and stimulate interest in the product. There are many ways to do this; the good salesperson learns through experience the proper approach for different kinds of prospects. A single interview will often require a combination of several approaches. An approach *not* to use is one that is so trite or "slangy" it is actually offensive. "Hi, what's up?" for example, will probably end the interview before it

---

[13]B. G. Yovovich, "Willy Loman Never Had It So Good," *Advertising Age* (June 14, 1982): M-22–23.

starts. But a few basic approaches have become fairly standard. Some of these are discussed briefly in the next few paragraphs.[14]

The most frequently used technique is the *introductory approach,* and simply requires doing that which the name implies. But unless it is combined with one or more of the other approaches, it is not very effective. "Hello, I'm Jim Johnson representing the Magic Carpet Company" may get a response such as, "That's good, but what can you do for me?" It is better to combine it with another approach such as the *consumer-benefit approach,* and follow the introduction with something like, " . . . and I would like to show you how you can increase your carpet sales."

If the product is unique, the *product approach* might be effective. In this approach the salesperson, without saying a word, places the product in the hands of the prospect and waits for him or her to respond – perhaps by asking what it is. A *curiosity approach* can sometimes be used if it does not border on trickery. "What do you think I have in my hand?" may make the prospect curious, but it may also offend.

Some salespeople use a *dramatic or showmanship approach,* such as dropping an unbreakable plate on the floor or having the receptionist take a "surprise package" into the prospect. Others use the *compliment approach* wherein the salesperson greets the prospect with a compliment such as, "I just heard about your promotion. That's great!" The salesperson must adapt one or more approaches to each situation, in his or her own style.

The Presentation and Demonstration

The core of the selling process is the presentation and demonstration. It is during the presentation and demonstration that the sale is or is not made, so it should be carefully planned. The planning of the sales presentation is somewhat analogous to that required in planning an advertising communication. Both involve persuasive communication, and the concepts discussed in earlier chapters apply in both cases.

Numerous theories have been developed over the years purporting to describe the sales process and the framework within which the presentation should be fashioned. Three of these as described by Nash and Crissy are stimulus-response, selling formula, and need satisfaction.[15] In the *stimulus-response* theory the assumption is that the prospect will respond favorably if exposed to the right stimuli (words, actions, etc., of the salesperson); if this does not happen, it is because the salesperson failed to present the right stimuli. The *selling formula* discussed in chapter 12 in connection with the creative aspects of advertising suggests that the prospect moves through the stages of attention, interest, desire, and action (AIDA). *Need satisfaction* is based on the notion that prospects only buy to

---

[14]See Ralph D. Shipp, Jr., *Practical Selling* (Boston: Houghton Mifflin, 1980): 218–23; and Russel, Beach, and Buskirk, *Selling,* pp. 206–14.

[15]Harold C. Nash and W. J. E. Crissy, "Ways of Looking at Selling," *The Psychology of Selling,* vol. 1 (New York: Personal Development Associates, 1958): 9–14.

satisfy unfulfilled needs, and that the salesperson should uncover a particular prospect's needs and plan the presentation accordingly. A fourth theory is Lavidge and Steiner's *hierarchy of effects* model which was discussed in earlier chapters.[16]

Richard D. Nordstrom has developed an interesting blend of theories which he calls MONEY (Motivate, Overcome objections, Needs, Easy to buy, and Yes).[17] His theory does not presuppose that buyers have a need awareness as they enter the purchase decision process as do the others; rather, it suggests that the salesperson is an influence throughout the entire presentation — that there is no "automatic" movement of the prospect through the stages in the purchase process. His theory recognizes the important role the salesperson has in the entire decision-making process of the prospect.

In any event, a sales presentation must be carefully planned. Good sales do not just happen; it is a rare salesperson who can successfully "wing" it through an interview. The fundamental rule is to relate the product benefits to the prospect's needs whether he or she is aware of them or not, and present the product in this light. If the product lends itself to demonstration, it is always more effective if the presentation can appeal to as many of the five senses as possible. Even memorized or "canned" presentations — those that have been prepared by professionals and given to the salesperson to use verbatim with all prospects — are constructed around this principle.[18]

Responding to Objections

Objections are bound to arise throughout the course of the interview, and the salesperson must respond to them effectively. In a well-planned presentation many of a prospect's objections have been anticipated and are answered before they are voiced. But some cannot be foreseen, and these may give the salesperson trouble.

Theoretically, if the individual has been duly qualified as a genuine prospect, his or her only *real* objection would stem from a lack of information, and this could be overcome by expanding on the product benefits. Such *apparent* objections as lack of money, no need for the product, or wrong time to buy are simply efforts of the genuine prospect to get rid of the salesperson. Nevertheless, all objections, real or apparent, must be handled some way, usually as soon as they are made.

Two principles are basic to handling objections effectively: maintain a positive attitude, and avoid arguments. A positive attitude is absolutely essential because prospects often voice objections that not only belittle the product but also the salesperson. The salesperson, therefore, must thoroughly believe in himself or herself and the product in order to deal with such put-downs, and overcome the objections in a confident manner. Arguing with the prospect is never advised. The

---

[16]Robert J. Lavidge and Gary A. Steiner, "A Model for Predictive Measurments of Advertising Effectiveness," *Journal of Marketing* 25 (Oct. 1961): 59–62.

[17]Richard D. Nordstrom, *Introduction to Selling: An Experiential Approach to Skill Development* (New York: Macmillan, 1981): 192–97.

[18]See Marvin A. Jolson, "The Underestimated Potential of the Canned Sales Presentation," *Journal of Marketing* 39 (January 1975): 78.

salesperson may win an argument because, despite the old adage, the customer is not always right. But when this happens, the sale will not likely be made.

The salesperson should listen to an objection very carefully, perhaps even restate it. This not only assures the prospect that the salesperson has heard the objection and understands it, but it also flatters the prospect by attaching some importance to it. The response, then, can take any one of a number of forms depending upon the objection, the personality of the prospect, and the circumstances in which it arises. Sometimes the salesperson should use a *direct denial* — simply stating in a tactful way that the objection is not true. At other times an *agree and counter,* or "yes, but" response is better. The salesperson agrees that the objection may have some validity, but immediately points out something about the product that more than compensates for the alleged weakness. If the prospect says, "These bags are not made of genuine leather," the response could be, "Yes, but vinyl is almost as durable and much lower in price." The *boomerang* method is somewhat similar to the agree and counter technique, except that it turns the objection itself into a reason for buying. If the prospect says, "This wrench is so light," the salesperson could say, "Yes, it makes it easier to handle."

Whether the salesperson uses one of these methods, one of numerous other standard methods, or one personally created, the objection should not be magnified, but should be minimized in its importance and eliminated from the prospect's list of considerations in making the purchase decision.

Closing the Sale

Closing the sale can take place at any time during the interview. It should occur whenever the prospect is ready to buy. Strangely enough, sometimes closing the sale is as difficult for the salesperson as it is for the prospect. The prospect is usually at least a little reluctant to "sign on the dotted line." But some salespeople, because of a fear of rejection or of losing the sale, find it equally difficult to ask for the order.

If the prospect is qualified, and if the sales presentation has been effective, the close should be the natural culmination of the interview. Usually the prospect drops clues, directly or indirectly, that the time to close has arrived; the salesperson must be alert to such signals. Sometimes the salesperson must steer the prospect to a close by asking questions that point in that direction. It may be necessary to attempt several "trial closes" to determine if the prospect is ready to buy. Under such circumstances, the good salesperson will always keep a few selling points in reserve to use as additional persuasive thrusts.

As with the other steps in the selling process, certain standard techniques have been identified for closing the sale. Sometimes, for example, it is expedient to use a *direct close* — simply asking for the order directly. "Shall I write up the order now?" may get an easy "yes" answer. *Assuming the close* is a technique in which the salesperson takes for granted from the outset that the sale will be made. The presentation is structured around the idea that purchase is inevitable, and at the end of the presentation the salesperson simply says, "I'm sure you'll like this. I'll send it out tomorrow."

Sometimes it is effective to *imply ownership*. In the presentation, the salesperson discusses the product as if the prospect already owned it, using the words *you* and *yours* consistently. "Your new computer will really do the job for you." *Continued affirmation* is a method whose purpose is to get the prospect to respond with a "yes" answer to a series of questions that lead up to the buying decision. "Are you looking for a machine that is durable?" "Are you interested in a machine that operates economically?" "Would you like a machine that is easy to handle?" The theory is that having answered "yes" to such questions as these, the prospect will find it easier to say "yes" when asked for the order. Any one of these techniques, or others, may be appropriate depending upon the circumstances, and should be held in readiness for use at the proper time during the interview.

Closing the sale should not be considered the end of the relationship between salesperson and prospect because a *satisfied* customer is the goal. To assure success in this regard the salesperson should maintain a continuing relationship with the customer, at least until the customer's satisfaction has been verified.

SUMMARY

Personal selling is unique among the four elements of the promotion mix in that it is interpersonal rather than mass communication. It reflects a mutually beneficial relationship between seller and buyer.

The field of personal selling is becoming more professionalized than it has been historically. High-pressure tactics are giving way to more reasoned approaches. The effect has been to produce salespeople whose backgrounds and methods of selling are different from what they were a few years ago. The average salesperson today has more formal education and more nonclassroom training than before. Perhaps one of the most noticeable effects is the increasing concern of the professional salesperson with a code of ethics.

There are many types of selling jobs, but they can be broadly classified into three categories — order-taking, missionary selling, and creative selling. The primary objective in order-taking jobs is simply to take the orders of the customers and not necessarily attempt to create sales. The emphasis in missionary selling is on building goodwill through service and advice. Creative selling reflects the ingenuity and creative ability of the salesperson in generating sales.

The good salesperson must have a positive attitude, a high degree of determination, and confidence in his or her ability. In addition, the good salesperson must be empathic and have a special kind of ego-drive that stimulates effort.

The selling process is essentially the same in principle for all kinds of selling. The sequence of activities is prospecting, preinterview effort, the approach, the presentation and demonstration, responding to objections, and closing the sale. Prospecting is the search for potential buyers and is somewhat analogous to the concept of defining the market.

In the preinterview stage the salesperson attempts to obtain certain information about the prospect that will make the interview proceed smoothly. The approach is the initial contact with the prospect and must attract attention and stimulate interest. The presentation and demonstration is the core of the interview. During this stage certain objections to buying are bound to arise. These objections must be overcome if the sale is to be made. The close should take place when the prospect is ready to buy. And the only truly successful close is one that leaves the customer satisfied with the outcome.

QUESTIONS FOR THOUGHT AND REVIEW

1. If all the elements of the promotion mix are designed for persuasive communication, what makes personal selling different from the others? In what respects is it the same?
2. How is the nature of the salesperson changing? What forces in the environment have caused the change?
3. Why is it increasingly important that salespeople have more formal education than was historically necessary?
4. Explain your concept of ethics. Now design a code of ethics for a professional salesperson that would be consistent with your concept.
5. Describe and distinguish among the three kinds of selling jobs: *order-taking, missionary selling,* and *creative selling.* Are they mutually exclusive? What are the objectives of each?
6. Give some specific examples of each of the three kinds of selling jobs.
7. Is there an analogy between *missionary selling* and *corporate advertising?* Explain.
8. Is there such a thing as a "born salesperson"? Can anyone learn to sell? Can you sell?
9. There are certain characteristics associated with all good salespeople. Among these are a positive attitude, a high degree of determination, empathy, and a special kind of ego-drive. Relate each of these characteristics to professional selling. Give examples that show why they are important.
10. Why must a salesperson be a self-starter?
11. Discuss the opportunities and rewards associated with a career in professional selling.
12. What is the purpose of prospecting in connection with the selling process? Explain the notion that it is a two-fold task. Why is it an ongoing process?
13. The systems used in obtaining the names of tentative prospects include personal observation, spotters, centers-of-influence, endless chain, and the party plan. Explain each of these, and give examples of the kinds of selling in which each might be effectively used.
14. Why is a tentative prospect not necessarily a genuine prospect? Should such people be eliminated entirely from the salesperson's list? Why?

15. What are the criteria used for evaluating tentative prospects? Explain the significance of each criterion.
16. What is the purpose of the preinterview effort? Give some examples of the kind of information that might be obtained in this connection and how it might be used.
17. What is the purpose of the *approach?* Discuss the various approach techniques and give examples of each.
18. What is the rationale of the stimulus-response theory of the sales process? Do you think it has any merit? Why?
19. How does the MONEY theory in connection with the sales process differ from other theories?
20. Is planning a sales presentation similar to planning an advertising communication? Explain.
21. If the person with whom the salesperson is dealing is a genuine prospect, could any real objections arise in the interview? Explain.
22. Explain how the salesperson can anticipate objections.
23. When should the salesperson respond to objections? Discuss several ways of handling objections.
24. Describe some of the techniques used for closing the sale, giving examples of each.
25. When should the sale be closed? How does the salesperson know when to close the sale? Is the close the end of the relationship with the prospect? Discuss.

17

PERSONAL SELLING— SALES FORCE MANAGEMENT

The previous chapter described the evolving contemporary salesperson and delineated several aspects of selling. The focus of this chapter is certain problems associated with managing the people involved in performing that function — the sales force.

THE SALES MANAGER

The title *sales manager* correctly implies that the position carries with it responsibilities and obligations beyond those associated with managing the *sales force*. The sales manager is an active participant in the development and implementation of the total marketing program. Such participation requires working with the chief marketing executive as well as with the managers and directors of the promotion function, its subdivisions, and other marketing subfunctions.[1] The degree of participation varies with the level of the position. The advancement track for those who so aspire can be described generally as salesperson, district sales manager, regional sales manager, and field sales manager; and the responsibilities increase with each successive advancement.

The job of sales manager in connection with sales force management is unique, perhaps, among all managerial positions. Unlike managers in many other areas, the sales manager is responsible for people who operate beyond direct supervision. The salespeople's activities are usually difficult to observe directly, and often there is a time lag between undesirable performance and the sales manager's awareness of it. Furthermore, the sales manager may have a conflict of interest. Most sales managers achieve their positions through advancement from the entry level of salesperson. They usually like to sell, and it is difficult for them to make the transition from selling to supervising. Yet as sales managers they must play the supervisory role. It has been suggested that because of this conflict of interest and possible blurring of objectives a policy of management by objectives (MBO) might help. Duties could be more clearly identified, for example, if the sales manager together with the salespeople involved jointly established goals and objectives.[2]

Another complicating factor in managing the sales force is the fact that salespeople often have varying degrees of experience. An interesting analogy has been drawn between the life cycle of a product and the career cycle of a salesperson. The salesperson's career reflects progress through four stages — preparation, development, maturity, and decline — in a manner similar to that of a product through its four stages of introduction, growth, maturity, and decline.[3] Since a sales force may consist of people in each of the stages, the varying needs resulting from the different degrees of experience may complicate supervision. Furthermore, with increasing experience come stronger convictions that one's performance is without fault; if there are some needed improvements, they are difficult to make.

---

[1] Our concern in this book is the sales manager's responsibilities in connection with managing the sales force. Coverage of the sales manager's total range of responsibility may be found in books on sales management such as those listed in the footnotes to this chapter.

[2] J. Taylor Sims, "Industrial Sales Management: A Case for MBO," *Industrial Marketing Management* 6 (1977): 43–46.

[3] Marvin A. Jolson, "The Salesman's Career Cycle," *Journal of Marketing* 38 (July 1974): 39–46.

The productive ability of a salesperson is a function of the time available to make sales calls. Because customer's buying habits are unpredictable and the sales interview is so complex, it is unrealistic for the sales manager to expect salespeople to save valuable time by reducing the time spent with each prospect. Instead, the sales manager must work with the things that are controllable to increase selling time and improve performance.[4]

SALES FORCE MANAGEMENT

The myriad activities associated with managing the sales force seem to fall into seven categories. These include recruiting, selecting, training, compensating, establishing sales territories, motivating, and evaluating.

Recruiting

Just as prospecting should be an ongoing process for the salesperson, recruiting should be a continuous activity for the sales manager. The objective in both cases is to maintain a perpetual list of likely candidates from which selection can be made for their respective purposes. The sales manager who neglects recruiting activities, or whose zeal in this regard is sporadic, will frequently be forced to fill the inevitable openings that arise with walk-ins whose qualifications may be considerably less than hoped for. Good recruiting and selection policies will not only assure the sales manager of qualified people in the sales force, but will also tend to reduce the turnover rate of the sales personnel. Low turnover is desirable because of the enormous expense and waste of employing and developing a salesperson only to have that person leave for what appear to be greener pastures.

But although sales force turnover should be minimized, some turnover is desirable. If a person is not happy in selling, despite favorable qualifications at the time of hiring, it would be better for all concerned if employment were terminated. Productivity is not compatible with job dissatisfaction. Furthermore, a turnover rate that is too low would likely result in a sales force composed only of aging individuals with waning enthusiasm. Thus, a turnover rate should be sufficiently high to maintain a sales force composed of people representing several age groups.[5]

Matching People with Jobs

The recruiting process is costly, and the sales manager should make every effort to find qualified recruits. An essential step in the recruiting process, therefore, is to develop in connection with each job a job description and person profile.[6]

---

[4]Charles E. Bergman, ``All Out for Productivity,'' *Sales and Marketing Management* 118 (14 Mar. 1977): 52–59.

[5]Richard R. Still, Edward W. Cundiff, and Norman A. P. Govoni, *Sales Management: Decisions, Policies, and Cases,* 3rd ed. (Englewood Cliffs, N.J.: Prentice-Hall, 1976), p. 221.

[6]Roy Hill, ``How to Select a Good Salesman,'' *International Management* 31 (Dec. 1976): 30–32.

Job description.   The job description is a detailed written description of the job to be filled. Properly constructed, the job description provides the sales manager with a concrete basis against which potential recruits may be judged. It serves as a set of guidelines to be followed in the search for appropriate sales representatives.

To be completely effective, the job description must represent a total picture of the job. It should identify the position by its title, such as detail person, field sales representative, or product specialist in precise terms so that there can be no question as to the job being filled. This is particularly important in those firms having a number of different kinds of sales positions. Furthermore, there should be a clear indication of how the position fits into the organization of the firm. The lines of authority relevant to the position should be identified as well as the staff personnel with whom the individual filling the position might be associated. In addition, the advancement track and related aspects pertinent to the position should be clearly explained. Finally the total range of duties and responsibilities of the job should be clearly spelled out.[7] The list might include planning, selling activities, clerical duties, and self-management responsibilities.

The job description is the first part of the two-stage foundation necessary in matching people with jobs. Its importance in the performance of that activity cannot be overemphasized, but its value is more far reaching than that. In fact, there may be no other single tool that exceeds the usefulness and significance of the job description in connection with sales force management and operation.[8] A job description given to the newly hired sales representative can be a guideline for his or her actions. It can be used as the basis for developing training programs and compensation plans and can serve as a means of comparing workloads among various members of the sales force. The job description is an indispensable item for the most successful sales managers.

Person profile.   The second half of the foundation for the matching process is the development of a person profile (also referred to as *job specifications, work force specifications,* or *hiring qualifications*). The *person profile* is a complete description of the kind of person best suited for the position delineated in the job description. It not only includes such measurable factors as education, experience, and training but also identifies those personality attributes essential to the successful performance of the job described. It is especially important that the latter be considerations in the recruiting and ultimate selection of sales representatives because such traits cannot be taught easily; they must already have been established.[9]

As easy as it might seem, developing a person profile for each sales position is a difficult task. Different jobs require different qualifications and characteristics. Sales representatives dealing with ultimate consumers, such as those selling Avon products, must usually possess a different set of traits than those selling to whole-

[7]Thomas F. Stroh, *Managing the Sales Function* (New York: McGraw-Hill, 1978), p. 197.

[8]William J. Stanton and Richard H. Buskirk, *Management of the Sales Force,* 5th ed. (Homewood, Ill.: Richard D. Irwin, 1978), p. 101.

[9]Roy Hill, "How to Select," 30–32.

salers and retailers. The sales rep of a drygoods wholesaler is a different kind of person than the engineering salesperson representing an industrial installations manufacturer. Sales positions whose job descriptions require the handling of complaints and making adjustments must be staffed by people with different personalities, perhaps, than those requiring sales calls only. Thus, each job must be considered individually.

Compounding the problem are the facts that different degrees of a particular trait may be necessary in different sales positions and that measurement of many traits is difficult and often impossible. Care must be taken also to avoid including attributes in a person profile that really are not necessary for the related sales position. Failure in this regard can result in artificially high standards that could eliminate consideration of some deserving candidates. Person profiles that are properly conceived in conjunction with carefully designed job descriptions can assure the best match possible of people with positions.

Compliance with the Law

The concern for civil rights, crystallized in 1964 with the passage of the Civil Rights Act and expanded with additional legislation in subsequent years, has had an enormous impact on the recruiting and selecting policies of sales managers. The original act, which provided for the establishment of the Equal Employment Opportunity Commission (EEOC), prohibits discrimination on the basis of race, color, religion, nationality, or sex. Discrimination is further prohibited on the basis of age by the Age Discrimination in Employment Act of 1967, which applies particularly to people in the 40–65 age group. The regulations in both of these acts must be observed by employers of twenty-five or more persons. Companies working with federal contracts and employing fifty or more people must also comply with the regulations of the Office of Federal Contract Compliance (OFCC), which include the use of affirmative action programs.

Proof of compliance is the responsibility of the company, and any firm to which the laws and regulations apply is subject to the scrutiny of federal watchdogs. Sales managers must avoid any "surface" discrimination in their recruiting and selecting practices, such as deliberately excluding from consideration blacks, women, or other minority groups. They must also be careful in using testing procedures for screening purposes. Such devices can be used legally only if the company can empirically show that the test predicts success in job performance.[10]

In light of such legal constraints, therefore, two questions as suggested by Charles Futrell would seem to serve as guidelines for recruiting and selecting efforts: "(1) Are employment practices equally applied and do they have the same effect on all potential employees, regardless of race, sex, religion, or national origin? and (2) Are the employment practices job related?"[11]

Thus, unless the age and sex of the applicant are bona fide occupational qual-

---

[10]See *Guidelines on Employment Selection Procedures* (EEOC, 1 Aug. 1970) and *Proposed Employment Testing and Other Selection Procedures* (OFCC, 15 Apr. 1971).

[11]Charles Futrell, *Sales Management* (Hinsdale, Ill.: Dryden, 1981): 203.

ifications, they must not be considerations. Questions concerning marital status and family composition should only be asked after hiring, and then only for insurance purposes. Physical data (such as information on muscular development) is pertinent only if it can be associated with job requirements. One's criminal record and/or type of military discharge are considered confidential; questions concerning such information should only be used if the job requires pertinent security clearance. In fact, asking for information that would suggest discrimination is to be avoided unless it can be defended in terms of the guidelines mentioned.

Sources of Recruits

Recruits for sales positions may be drawn from a number of sources. Some firms use more than one source; others may rely almost entirely on a single source. Whatever the case, the recruiting effort should be well planned.

Intracompany transfers. Potentially good salespeople may be found already employed by the firm in other departments. Such people may express a preference for selling jobs to whatever they are currently doing, or their demeanor may simply suggest they might be stellar sellers. If they have the potential for sales positions, it would be advantageous to consider them because they would likely already be familiar with the firm's products and company policies.

Recommendations of sales personnel.   The members of the sales force can be a productive source for new recruits. Their sincere recommendations can often be more reliable than those of other people less familiar with the job. They know better than anyone the demands of the job and are therefore in a good position to judge the potential for success of acquaintances. Furthermore, they have the opportunity for many varied contacts through their daily associations with their customers and with clubs and organizations. In considering the recommendations of the sales force, however, the sales manager must remember that friendship rather than ability could be the reason for some recommendations.

Educational institutions.   Educational institutions at all levels are important recruiting sources. Depending upon the job descriptions of the positions for which recruiting is being done, the sales manager may effectively use such sources as high schools, junior colleges, business colleges, night schools, vocational schools, four-year colleges, and universities. Many of these institutions maintain placement services for their graduates, and the sales manager would do well to establish favorable relationships with administrative and faculty personnel.

Employment agencies.   The stigma that may have once been associated with employment agencies no longer exists. Both employers and job-seekers now consider such institutions as a viable means for accomplishing their purposes. In many instances the hiring company pays the agency fee, which makes the use of employment agencies increasingly attractive to people looking for sales positions.

Employment agencies are considered important sources of recruits by many firms; when they are given complete job descriptions, they can do much of the initial screening otherwise done by the recruiting firms. In many firms the management has concluded that even when they pay the fee the cost is no more than that of sending recruiters to college campuses. Both the employer and the job seeker should use care in choosing an agency. The local Better Business Bureau and Chamber of Commerce can be helpful.

Other companies. People with some degree of experience can often be recruited from other companies. Such sources include suppliers of merchandise or services to the recruiting firm, competing companies, and nonrelated firms. The sales representatives of suppliers may be interested in changing jobs; since they are at least somewhat familiar with the recruiting firm, they can be excellent recruits. Sales representatives of competing firms are often interested in improving their positions, which they sometimes feel can be done more advantageously by switching employers. Even companies that are completely unrelated to the recruiting firm may have excellent prospective recruits.

The advantage in "pirating" such people from other companies is that they are not raw recruits; the training required in their indoctrination and assimilation can be less rigorous and therefore less costly than for completely inexperienced people. This is particularly true when the recruits come from competing firms.

On the other hand, the sales manager must be certain that the reason such people identify themselves as possible recruits is not that they were terminated from a previous job because of incompetence. In addition, there is always some danger of retaliation by the firms from which the recruits came.

Advertisements. Advertisements placed in newspapers and trade journals can yield recruits. Although they do not usually produce large numbers of qualified recruits, advertisements often elicit many responses. The lack of qualified applicants makes the later screening and selecting process more difficult and time-consuming than it is when more self-screening sources are used.

The copy used in advertisements for recruiting purposes must be carefully thought out so that enough information is included to attract good prospects but not to turn them off. Whether or not to mention compensation or company name is sometimes a difficult question. Enough detail on qualifications must be included as a screening device, but not so much detail that the ad discourages possible qualified candidates. Conversely, sufficient qualifications should be included to discourage responses from unqualified people.

Walk-ins. Almost every company has some unsolicited applicants for sales positions, and some firms rely heavily on walk-ins as a source of recruits. Such people should be considered as recruits and given the same evaluation as those obtained through the initiative of the company. A strong argument for their serious consideration is that they sought out and obviously have an interest in the company.

Selecting

Selecting is the process of determining the recruits to be hired for the open positions. Properly handled recruiting efforts reduce the task of selection but do not eliminate it, and the selection process is crucial to maximizing the effectiveness of the sales force. The legal considerations associated with recruiting are equally applicable in the selection process; thus care must be taken to prevent any discrimination in its implementation. Furthermore, companies that must include affirmative action programs in their hiring must be doubly alert.

Among the most important tools used in the selection process are the application blank, the personal interview, references, and psychological tests.

Application Blank

The initial tool in the selection process is usually the application blank. One of its major purposes is to serve as a first screening device. The earlier in the process unqualified people can be eliminated, the less costly it is to the firm.

Sometimes called a *personal history statement,* the application blank should elicit only that information related to job performance. Thus any questions that might be considered discriminatory, such as those dealing with age, sex, marital status, religion, nationality, and physical disabilities, should be avoided unless such information is significant to successful job performance. For example, sex might be significant in selling women's clothing or cosmetics if the job requires a personal demonstration of the product. A speech impediment could be a legitimate disqualifying factor in selling, and people of particular nationalities might be desirable candidates for selling certain markets. But unless such characteristics are related to ability to perform, they should not be used as criteria in the selection process; questions designed to get that kind of information could be considered suspect.

The type of information requested on the application blank depends upon the company's specific needs. Most application blanks request, in addition to name and address, educational background and work experience, plus numerous bits of nondiscriminatory information that can provide clues to the applicant's character and potential for success. The amount of formal education can be quite important in some selling positions, and completion of an educational program, such as high school or college, indicates some amount of initiative and perseverance. Furthermore, the course of study may reflect the person's areas of interest.

Information about work experience is always significant, especially if the firm is seeking applicants who are not recent graduates. The kind of employment experienced can indicate interest in the job as well as previous proficiency. A larger than average number of positions held in the time span expressed may show a proclivity to "job-hopping." Although job-hopping may not necessarily be bad, it is grounds for serious investigation. Reasons for leaving previous positions can provide some illumination in this regard.

Personal goals, hobbies, reading habits, civic concerns, and social interests can provide insight into the applicant's motivations and behavior, and stability can be indicated in a statement of assets and liabilities. Of course, references are also usually asked for.

Personal Interview

Regardless of the number of tools used in the selection process, the personal interview is almost universally included. There seems to be no better way to get certain information related to the applicant's appearance, personality, and ability to communicate. A trained interviewer can learn a great deal about such things in a 20- to 30-minute session.

The process usually involves a series of interviews, the first of which serves as an early screening device. The first interview is not ordinarily considered conclusive, except when the applicant is eliminated at that point. An interview session is a somewhat traumatic experience for aspiring job-seekers, and their conduct is often affected by the resulting pressure. Those who appear to be likely candidates are invited for additional interviews with different people, usually at the plant or office and usually at the company's expense. At these follow-up sessions, the applicant's behavior is more nearly normal because some of the tension has been alleviated in the first interview.

In addition to getting the kind of information not provided in the application blank, the interview can also serve to substantiate certain statements made therein. Stated reasons for leaving certain positions, for example, can often be verified through discussions in the interviews. Moreover, interests in various areas mentioned in the application blank can be probed for intensity. The use of good interviewing techniques produces the desired information. Approaches can range from the highly structured interview (guided) to one that is completely free and open (nondirected).

Guided interviews.   Somewhat analogous to a "canned" sales presentation, one completely prepared by someone else and used verbatim by salespeople, the guided interview is based on questions previously prepared by expert interviewers who know what things should be asked and their proper sequence. The technique requires that the applicant's responses be written down by the interviewer as they are given or, in some cases, at the completion of the interview. The results of the interview can be evaluated at a later time by whoever is qualified to do so. In the guided interview not only are the "right" questions asked, but any interviewer can ask them.

Nondirected interviews.   Despite the theoretical advantage of having a "perfect" interview in the guided approach, it is argued by some that the technique is too stilted and that a better picture of the applicant can be obtained if there is complete freedom to talk. The applicant in the nondirected interview is encouraged to speak freely about personal interests, problems, aspirations, and other things that might provide an insight into his or her personality, character, and ability. The technique may generate more spontaneous discussion than the guided interview, but it is time-consuming and usually produces much information irrelevant to the purpose.

Since both guided and nondirected techniques have certain advantages and disadvantages, many companies use a compromise approach in which the interviewer has in mind a kind of framework for the interview but allows the applicant some freedom to volunteer comments. Often, the applicant's spouse is asked to participate in one or more of the interviews since a salesperson's performance can be affected by the attitude of the husband or wife toward the job.

References

It is common practice for firms to ask for references. These can be the names of former employers, teachers and professors, or simply friends and acquaintances. Although their value is questionable because most former employers are reluctant to give unfavorable recommendations, particularly when the applicant has access to the information, and the recommendations of friends will nearly always be positive, they can be an additional factor in the selection process. Most employers can translate vaguely glowing praise into its real unstated meaning.

References can be contacted by mail, telephone, or in person; mail is probably the most common method. Personal interviews with the people named as references is the best method because complete information is likely to be given more freely orally than written in a letter, but it is expensive. When the reference is contacted by mail, the letter is frequently followed up with a telephone call for amplification of certain information contained in the responding letter.

Psychological Tests

Psychological tests of various kinds have been used in the selection process by some firms for many years. However, their significance in the process has been debated. Management in some companies believes that the tests have no value whatsoever, and others argue that they are extremely useful. To reap maximum value from psychological tests they should be designed, administered, and evaluated by experts in the field. Furthermore, psychological tests should not be the only selection tools used. As mentioned earlier, unless the firm using the tests can produce empirical evidence that the results are predictive of success on the job, the tests may be considered discriminatory and in violation of the law. Three of the most important kinds of tests are those dealing with intelligence, aptitude, and personality.

Intelligence tests.   Pardoxically, most sales managers using intelligence tests establish both minimum and maximum scores as cut-off points. Understandably, people with less than a minimum degree of intelligence are unsuited to many types of selling positions. At the same time, some selling jobs are not challenging enough to satisfy people with unusually high intelligence; such people are not likely to perform as well as the less favorably endowed.

The use of intelligence tests presupposes a relationship between intelligence and selling. But beyond some necessarily vague upper and lower limits, it is difficult to equate intelligence with ability to sell. However, as one of several tests used in the selection process and within the legal constraints referred to earlier, intelligence tests can probably be justified.

Aptitude tests.   The purpose in using sales aptitude tests is to measure the applicant's talent for selling. Some of these tests involve verbal role-playing in which the applicant is asked to demonstrate effectiveness in responding to problems posed in fictional selling situations. Others require the applicant to construct a self-profile composed of characteristics related to his or her ability and capacity to sell. Several descriptive statements are given for each of a number of questions, and the applicant chooses the statement that describes him or her best or sometimes the least. And there are other types of aptitude tests.

Sales aptitude tests should be custom-made for the selling situation in accordance with the person profile developed for the position. Even so, it is sometimes difficult to prevent faking answers by test-knowledgeable candidates. The usefulness of aptitude tests is therefore questionable.

Personality tests.   Personality tests are used to determine if the applicant's social amenities are compatible with the demands of selling. The presumption is that the personalities of salespeople are different from those of people not involved in selling. But it is difficult to isolate specific personality traits good salespeople possess and perhaps even more difficult to devise a test that could reveal their presence. Personality tests seem to do little more than identify applicants whose personalities are unusual.

Training

Virtually all firms provide some training for their salespeople. However, the amount and kind of training vary enormously among companies, as do the methods used and the people receiving the training.

The importance of training cannot be overemphasized. Not only does it assure better performance in the strict sense of the word, but it also accomplishes other purposes advantageous to both the company and the employee. A good training program can contribute immensely to alleviating the inevitable problems encountered by the brand new sales rep in becoming oriented to the firm and assimilated into the sales force. Training is a morale builder and a motivation device. A properly trained salesperson is simply happier in the position than one who is operating on a trial-and-error basis.

It is fairly obvious that newly hired sales representatives should undergo some degree of training, particularly if they are hired right out of school and have no experience. But what about people who have been with the firm for several years and newly hired people with some years of selling experience? Training programs should be designed for them too. Everyone needs periodic planned exposure to the myriad changes taking place today. The programs designed for experienced salespeople should be different from those used for freshman reps, and persuading the former of their need to participate is often a problem. But a complete sales training program includes training for all salespeople in the firm.

All training programs should be specifically related to the job and use the appropriate selling language. They should exclude abstractions and theoretical concepts that might be useful to managers but uninteresting and perhaps irrelevant to salespeople.[12] Furthermore, they should include training in the use of creative imagination. It is the creative factor that differentiates the super salesperson from the average type; without creativity a salesperson, in the eyes of the buyer, is pretty much like all other salespeople.[13]

Each company's sales training program is different. Despite the differences in programs, at least two areas must be considered in their planning and implementation — the content of the program and the method of instruction, both of which must be developed in accordance with the objectives and capabilities of the firm and of the job descriptions of the positions to which the training applies.

Program Content

The specific nature of the subject areas included in a program will vary among firms, but most programs include the areas of product knowledge, company knowledge, market knowledge, and selling techniques.

Product knowledge.   Few things are more frustrating to a salesperson than trying to sell an unfamiliar product. Product knowledge is essential to self-confidence and enthusiasm in selling. Not only does a thorough knowledge of the product enable the salesperson to develop a sales presentation that incorporates product benefits appropriate to the buyer's needs, but it also provides answers to objections and criticisms that might arise in the sales interview.

The degree and kind of information necessary depend upon the product line or lines of the firm. A highly technical product usually requires an intensive educational program, but a standardized product sold in a mass market may require only superficial training. Moreover, wholesaler representatives could not possibly be thoroughly trained in the thousands of items that might comprise their lines.

In addition to knowing a good deal about the products of the employer, the sales rep should also have some understanding of competitors' lines. This is important in preventing possible embarrassment when a buyer suggests that a competitor's product has a certain unique feature. The knowledgeable salesperson would be aware of such things and would be in a position to respond effectively.

Company knowledge.   Sales representatives should have a fairly comprehensive knowledge of the companies for which they work. To their customers and prospects they *are* the company; ignorance of the company could create suspicion and lack of respect.

[12]James F. Carey, "Make Salesmen Soar Via Down-to-Earth Sales Training," *Sales and Marketing Management* 117 (13 Sep. 1976): 119.
[13]Tom Alexander, "Creative Training = Creative Selling," *Sales Management* 114 (7 Apr. 1975): 83.

Included in the company knowledge area of the program are credit policies, pricing procedures, service and adjustment practices, delivery methods, and other activities directly related to selling. But the training program should cover more than these directly related aspects. For example, the salesperson should know something of the history of the company, the names of the executive officers, the capitalization structure, and growth plans. The sales rep will not recite all this information in every sales interview; but if a prospect should ask a question concerning such things, a ready correct answer could add much to a favorable impression.

Market knowledge.   It is axiomatic that a knowledge of the market is essential to the successful implementation of any part of a marketing strategy. Personal selling is no exception. The only way a salesperson can perform at maximum efficiency is to have a thorough understanding of customers or prospects. The sales rep should not only know who the customers are but also their reasons for buying and their purchase habits. In fact, most of the concepts discussed in chapter 6 could be the basis for training.

Selling techniques.   The training programs of most firms include some training in selling techniques, which usually involves an adaptation of the stages in the selling process (discussed in chapter 16) to their own particular circumstances.

Thorough instruction in how to sell, together with a knowledge of the product, company, and market should arm the sales representative in the best way possible.

Methods of Instruction

Several instructional methods can be used in the sales training program. The choice of methods depends upon a number of things, including the size of the company, the availability of teaching personnel and financial resources, and management's philosophy on the merits of decentralized versus centralized training. Small companies and those with limited resources will have to use less expensive methods. Companies that have more funds for training may need to decide whether to use a centralized or decentralized format.

Centralized training implies that the entire program is carried on at one location, perhaps at the plant or the main offices. Expert trainers are available, and permanent facilities are usually provided for continuing programs. Decentralized training takes place at the regional or local level and is usually the responsibility of the regional or district managers. In any event, instructional methods can be divided into those requiring group participation and those developed for individual training.

Group participation methods.   Among the most common methods of group instruction is the *lecture*. It is not necessarily the most effective method, but the lecture is economical because it can be used with small and large groups. Its effectiveness can be increased with the use of visual aids. Because *group discussion* requires active participation by the members of the group, it is considered by many people to be superior to the lecture method. Analysis of cases and extemporary discussion of problems are the approaches used. In smaller groups, consisting of perhaps no more than fifteen people, *role playing* is an effective method. In this system various members of the group are given parts to play in a simulated selling situation. One member plays the role of the salesperson, another the prospect, and if other characters are involved, such as the prospect's spouse or employer, members play these roles. Performances are then critically analyzed by the instructor and discussed by the other members of the group.

Individual training methods.   The simplest, least expensive, and probably least effective method of individually training salespeople is simply that of stimulating *independent study* by the trainee. This can be done through pamphlets, brochures, programmed courses of study, and other instructional materials. A major problem is getting the salesperson to use the materials. *On-the-job training* is usually included in sales training programs, regardless of other methods that might be used. The method requires that a senior salesperson first instructs, then observes, and later analyzes the trainee's performance. With a good senior salesperson teacher, the method can be extremely effective because the learning environment is reality and not simulation. A danger is that the trainee may learn some of the bad habits of an inferior senior salesperson. Moreover, some senior salespeople resent having to act in this capacity, even when they are compensated for their efforts.

Compensating

The method by which salespeople are paid is a significant factor in the effectiveness of sales force activity and the profitability of the firm. But because of the ever-changing environment and the constantly evolving nature of the firm itself, a compensation plan can rarely be considered static. A plan once established must be constantly monitored for indications of the need for alterations.

A good compensation plan should provide appropriate rewards for the salesperson's efforts and results, allow for some degree of direction and control by the company, encourage good relationships with customers, and attract competent career-oriented people.[14] Accomplishing all these objectives is possible, but it may be difficult.

Compensation plan development begins with a determination of the appropriate general level of pay. Once the pay range is determined, a plan is devised to accomplish the four objectives listed previously. Such a plan may include some or all of the following elements: a fixed element, a variable element, an expense reimbursement element, and a fringe benefit element.[15]

Fringe benefits have become a necessary part of the total pay package of most firms today. In fact, it is estimated that employee benefits add one-third to payroll costs.[16] Such benefits include health and life insurance, pension plans, stock

---

[14]Stanton and Buskirk, *Management of the Sales Force,* pp. 248–49.

[15]Still et al., *Sales Management,* pp. 332–33.

[16]Fred D. Lindsey, "The Benefit Bonanza," *Nation's Business* 70, no. 12 (December 1982): 70–71.

options, paid vacations, and sick leave. Most companies also provide some means of reimbursing salespeople for their expenses on the road — travel, lodging, food, and limited entertainment expenses incurred in connection with clients or customers. With respect to the fixed and variable elements of a compensation plan three alternatives are available — straight salary, straight commission, and some combination of fixed and variable elements.

Straight Salary

A straight salary plan is predominantly a fixed-element compensation plan. Under this plan the salesperson receives regular payments of a fixed amount regardless of the sales generated or other activities performed. A straight salary provides security of income to the salesperson and maximum control for the company. Beginning salespeople are usually happier with a straight salary because they lack confidence in their ability to sell. Moreover, since their income does not necessarily depend upon their sales volume, they are not inclined to resent requests from their sales managers to spend time on the submission of reports and other nonselling activities. On the other hand, since their income does not depend on it, they may lack the necessary incentive for aggressive selling.

Straight Commission

The straight commission is the antithesis of the straight salary. Its advantages and disadvantages are basically the reverse of those of the straight salary method. Security of income is not guaranteed, and remuneration is entirely dependent upon the volume of sales generated. Because of this, salespeople working under a straight commission plan tend to resist any request of the sales manager that reduces their time available for selling; management's control is thus weakened. But incentive to sell is high under this plan, and proficient salespeople tend to prefer it to the straight salary method.

A question in connection with the straight commission method is whether the commission rate should be fixed, regressive, or progressive. A fixed rate is simply the same percentage figure applied to the sales generated regardless of volume. A regressive rate structure provides for a reduction in the rate as sales volume increases, and a progressive structure allows for an increase in the rate with increasing sales volume. In a progressive structure the commission might be 2 percent on the first $100,000 of sales, 3 percent on the next $100,000 and so on. A progressive rate structure is generally preferred, although there should be a reasonable ceiling on earnings in inflationary times to prevent "windfall" gains.[17]

---

[17]Don Korn, "Paying Off for Profits," *Sales Management* 114 (19 May 1975): 5–8. See also Wesley O. McGee and David T. Norman, "Profit and Growth Through Sales Compensation," *Management Accounting* 58 (Dec. 1976): 32–34.

Fixed and Variable Combination

Because of the opposing advantages and disadvantages of the straight salary and straight commission methods of compensation, most firms attempt a compromise to gain the advantages and offset the disadvantages. Such combination plans assume many forms and involve such basic elements as salary, commission, bonus, and drawing account. A bonus differs from a commission in that it is an amount paid over and above that paid for normal performance. It is not directly correlated with routine job activity as is a commission, but is an additional payment for above-normal services. A drawing account establishes a fund to which the salesperson's commissions are regularly credited and from which withdrawals can be made, including overwithdrawals against future earnings. In some cases, amounts over-drawn need not be paid back by the salesperson.

There are probably as many combination plans as there are firms using them. In any case, the incentive part of the plan should be at least 30 percent of the salary.[18]

Establishing Sales Territories

Sales force deployment must equalize as much as possible both the sales potential and workloads of the sales representatives.[19] Total success is unrealistic, for the sales potential throughout any region varies enormously because of the uneven population dispersion. Customers and prospects may be highly concentrated in the metropolitan areas and miles apart in the sparsely populated sections. Workloads also vary. Required performance of nonselling activities such as missionary work, arranging displays, or making adjustments takes away selling time. In addition, different degrees of sales effort required for various products results in different amounts of time spent on each account. Compounding the problem is the fact that some salespeople do better with some accounts than with others, and it may be necessary to try to match such people with the accounts they are comfortable with.[20]

Good sales management usually requires the establishment of sales territories to define responsibilities for individual members of the sales force.[21] The task is basically a four-fold problem: identifying basic territorial units, estimating the sales potential in each unit, constructing tentative territories out of the units, and making final adjustments.

Identifying Territorial Units

To be useful, sales territories must ultimately be defined geographically. Since the purposes of establishing sales territories include control and supervision of the

---

[18]Korn, "Paying Off," 5–8.

[19]For a model of sales territory analysis using quantitative methods and computer simulation see A. Parasuraman and Ralph Day, "A Management-oriented Model for Allocating Sales Effort," *Journal of Marketing Research* 14 (Feb. 1977): 22–33.

[20]See Leonard M. Lodish, "Assigning Salesmen to Accounts to Maximize Profit," *Journal of Marketing Research* 13 (Nov. 1976): 440–44.

[21]For an in-depth discussion of this topic see Still et al., *Sales Management*, pp. 358–68.

sales force with respect to sales potential and work load, territory delineation must also reflect a consideration of statistical and other relevant data. Once they are defined sales territories must allow for necessary adjustments.

In the light of these prerequisites, therefore, the sales manager must select a basic unit for which the necessary data are available. In addition, since a territory is usually composed of a number of units, the unit must be small enough to be easily added to or deleted from an actual or tentatively defined territory. Possibilities include political subdivisions such as states, counties, cities, precincts, and wards, and other bases including metropolitan and trading areas.

Political subdivisions are convenient because relevant demographic data are easily found in government publications and other sources. Their use is not entirely logical, however, because purchasers' buying habits are not determined by political boundaries. Nevertheless, for purposes of convenience and because it satisfies the prerequisites fairly well, the county is a commonly used basic unit.

Metropolitan areas or trading areas are perhaps more logical units, but they are a bit more difficult to use. Many companies have used the metropolitan area as a unit since the Bureau of the Budget established the principle of a Standard Metropolitan Statistical Area (SMSA). This is an area consisting of a group of adjoining counties or a single county in which there is at least one city or two adjoining cities with a population of at least 50,000, and a total population in the area of 100,000 or more. Because the county is the basic unit in standard metropolitan areas, the data availability advantage is still present. Furthermore, SMSAs more nearly approximate realistic trading areas than do political subdivisions alone. A newer concept reflecting the merging of two or more SMSAs is the Standard Consolidated Statistical Area (SCSA).

Trading areas are the most logical basic unit for sales territory delineation. A trading area is the arena in which groups of people buy and sell. The difficulty in using them is the fact that their configurations may be different for different products, and statistical data are sometimes hard to get.

Estimating the Unit's Sales Potential

Once the basic units have been identified, the sales potential in each unit must be estimated. The approach is identical to that used by marketing managers in determining the sales potential in markets and market segments. It is first necessary to determine who the buyers of the product or service are — college-age sorority women, middle-class 35–50-year-old professional men, or whatever. The unit's total potential is obtained from the number of such people in each unit. This represents the total potential sales of the product in that unit by all sellers of the product. The sales potential of the firm is then computed on the basis of the company's traditional share-of-the-market figures, and adjustments are made as dictated by circumstances.

Constructing Tentative Territories

A sales territory is composed of the number of basic units deemed appropriate for the assigned sales representative. The number and size of territories needed is initially based on the *total* sales potential for the firm and the *total* number of sales-people required. The sales volume an average salesperson can achieve is estimated and then the total market is divided into the number of territories so indicated. This requires combining various numbers of adjoining units, the number depending upon the sales potential determined for each respective unit. The assumption in this step is that since the sales potentials are the same in all territories by design all will be equally achievable by the salespeople responsible.

Making Final Adjustments

Such an assumption is heroic. We have already established that work loads are different, and that the population is unevenly dispersed throughout a single terri-tory and different among territories. Furthermore, salespeople vary in ability, accounts are not all the same, and the physical shape and nature of the terrain are different among territories — even though all the territories tentatively established have the same sales potential.

These factors must be considered before the territorial structure is finalized. Adjustments require the addition and deletion of basic units in certain territories to equalize opportunities and limitations that each salesperson will face. The final structure will no longer be composed of territories with equal sales potential, but will reflect reasonable equality in terms of the total sales environment.

Motivating

Everyone needs a little push now and then to maintain enthusiasm on the job, and the salesperson is no exception. It is the sales manager's responsibility to provide the right kind of push. Motivation is less of a problem if the tasks previously dis-cussed have been effectively accomplished. Proper recruiting and selection pro-cedures should provide the company with competent people interested in selling; a training program that equips the salesperson with the necessary knowledge and skills to sell effectively will minimize discontent; and a compensation plan that is reasonable and administered fairly can be a motivating force. These things, cou-pled with intelligent territorial assignments can go a long way toward sustaining motivation.[22]

But recruiting, training and compensating are usually not enough. The sales manager must often use specific devices to stimulate sales activity. Among those devices available are sales conventions, contests, and public recognition.

Sales Conventions

Sales conventions have long been used in sales force management. They are both costly and time-consuming, but they are effective motivational devices. Not only are salespeople exposed to inspiring talks by experts in the field but they also are

---

[22]See Robert E. Lefton, ''A System to Motivate Salespeople,'' *Professional Trainer* (Del Mar, Calif.: CRM/McGraw-Hill, 1983), pp. 1, 3, 10.

made aware of the fact that everyone has the same kinds of problems. Just talking with fellow sales representatives in the convention environment inspires confidence and enthusiasm.

There are many problems associated with arranging conventions. For example, there is the question of whether to have a single national convention or several regional conventions. National conventions allow for the presentation of inspirational and educational ideas and materials to the entire sales force at one time, but there is a period of time when no one is out selling. Regional conventions are closer to the field of action, but they require more of the top executives' time, and experts may not always be able to attend. Neither type of convention is necessarily better than the other; the choice depends upon the circumstances.

Contests

Contests are fascinating to almost everyone, particularly if there is a worthwhile prize for the winner. When used in sales force management to stimulate sales activity, contests are usually designed with a specific purpose in mind, such as to introduce a new product or to gain new accounts.

Obviously, the contest must be fair, and every salesperson should have an opportunity to participate. Furthermore, the prize should be something salespeople would like, such as vacation trips, merchandise, or cash. Among the factors to consider when designing contests is the fact that the losers are more important than the winner because there are so many more of them. The event must not become counterproductive by discouraging those who fail to win. Also, the contest should be structured so that salespeople cannot "borrow on future sales activity" to win the contest. This borrowing would defeat the contest's purpose.

Public Recognition

People appreciate being recognized for capable work. Good sales managers, therefore, use every opportunity to reward good performance through some kind of public recognition. The names of people who win contests, receive other honors or awards, or simply do an exceptionally good job on a particular activity should be publicized. Bulletin boards and house organs are among the many ways to publicize the names.[23]

Evaluating

Evaluation is important to both the company and the sales representative. It identifies those reps who are not producing so corrective action may be taken or their employment terminated if all attempts by the manager to help them improve have failed. Evaluation is important to the salesperson for purposes of salary raises and promotions.

---

[23]Sally Scanlon, "Let's Hear it for Recognition!" *Sales and Marketing Management* 116 (12 Apr. 1976): 42–46.

A good performance evaluation system should include a positive reward in the form of salary and promotion, a neutral reward carrying a modest salary increase, and a negative reward—dismissal.[24] However, a major problem in the evaluation of salespeople is the difficulty of measuring certain activities. How does one determine the effectiveness of missionary work, for example? Complicating the process, too, is the fact that the responsibilities and working conditions of salespeople vary, and across-the-board comparisons cannot be made among the members of a sales force as with people working on an assembly line or laying bricks. As a result, the evaluation must be approached by considering each salesperson's performance in relation to his or her own peculiar circumstances.

The traditional focus of evaluation systems for salespeople is on the results of behavior. An interesting proposal has been advanced recently, however, that purports to allow management to relate specific behavior to the achievement of desired results. The *Behaviorally Anchored Rating Scale* (BARS) involves the use of a rating scale designed to provide information on how performance can be improved by identifying it with specific kinds of behavior.[25]

Evaluation of any activity requires a benchmark to which actual performance can be related. Thus the first step in the evaluation process is to establish standards of performance for the activities being judged; as previously mentioned, these must be set for each salesperson and cannot be common standards for the entire sales force. Obviously such an approach requires a careful analysis of each sales representative's situation with respect to individual characteristics, territorial assignment, and selling environment.

Once the standards are set, the activity of the salesperson is compared with the standard, and action is taken as indicated by the comparison. Often, the results of the comparison are expressed in ratios or in terms of percent accomplished. The numerical expression makes possible the comparison of performance among salespeople. If sales volume is the activity being evaluated, and Salesperson A's performance is $110,000 with a standard (quota) of $100,000, A would have achieved 110 percent of the quota. Salesperson B, on the other hand, may have had sales of $180,000 with a quota of $200,000, which would only be 90 percent of the quota. Thus despite the lower total sales, the performance of Salesperson A was superior to that of B.

Bases for Evaluation

Most firms use a combination of bases (or ratios) in evaluating their sales representatives. Use of a single base often does not provide a true picture of the salesperson's performance. Among several possibilities are sales to quotas, sales to expense, sales to gross margin, sales to net profit, and orders to calls made.

---

[24]John Moynahan, "With the Wrong Compensation Strategy You Pay Through the Nose," *Sales and Marketing Management,* 118 (14 Mar. 1977): 64–68.

[25]A. Benton Cocanougher and John M. Ivancevich, "'BARS' Performance Rating For Sales Force Personnel," *Journal of Marketing* 42, no. 3 (July 1978): 87–95.

Sales to quotas.   Whether or not any other bases are used, salespeople are almost always evaluated on the basis of the sales they generate with respect to the quotas set for them. The key to fairness and accuracy in the use of the ratio is in setting a quota reasonable to both the sales rep and the firm. Setting a fair quota requires an intelligent assessment of the unique selling conditions associated with each sales rep for whom a quota is to be determined. Interestingly enough, it has been found that sales managers who work with their salespeople in setting the quotas are satisfied that they get honest, helpful information.[26]

Sales to expense.   An analysis of sales volume alone does not show the cost of generating those sales. It is possible to achieve high sales volume, for example, by spending excessive amounts of money on entertainment, travel, and other items that might be particularly persuasive to some customers. One way to encourage sales reps to hold down expenses is to determine their sales expense ratios and evaluate their performances on that basis. Of course, a good sales rep can score high in this regard by not only keeping expenses down but also by increasing sales at the same time. Either or both are desirable from the company's point of view. Only those expenses over which the sales representative has control should be considered. Moreover, a certain amount of expense is necessary, and the sales rep should not be discouraged from incurring those expenses essential to the performance of his or her job.

Sales to gross margin.   Often the items in a company's line of products that are easiest to sell have the lowest margin of profit to the company. It is natural that if the only basis used for evaluation is sales to quotas, the sales reps will push those items. To increase the selling effort devoted to the harder-to-sell, higher profit items, some firms evaluate their sales reps on the basis of the gross profit generated by the sales they make.

Sales to net profit.   To provide some degree of control over both expenses and gross margin, the sales rep can be evaluated on the net profit resulting from the sales he or she makes. This method encourages the salesperson to hold expenses down and at the same time concentrate on selling the higher margin items. Of course, many of the factors entering into the computation of net profit are beyond the control of the sales rep; but to the extent that they are controllable, the sales rep will be encouraged to optimize performance accordingly.

Orders to calls made.   Sometimes called the sales rep's batting average, the order-to-calls-made ratio is computed by dividing the number of orders received by the number of calls made. It provides the sales manager with some indication as to the sales rep's effectiveness with customers. Certainly no sales manager would expect complete success. But if the batting average is too low, or it is higher

---

[26]Thomas R. Wotruba and Michael L. Thurlow, ''Sales Force Participation in Quota Setting and Sales Forecasting,'' *Journal of Marketing* 40 (Apr. 1976): 11–16.

than usual but the orders are smaller than average, the sales manager might conclude that the sales rep is not spending enough time with each customer.

Subjective Evaluation

Subjective evaluation by the sales manager is viewed with suspicion by many sales reps. They feel, sometimes rightly so, that such evaluation tends to reflect unfounded personal judgments based on emotion and individual preferences. Used judiciously as only one of several criteria in the total evaluation process, subjective evaluation can be of advantage not only to the firm but to the sales rep being evaluated. If one of the previously discussed objective ratios indicated inferior performance, for example, there may have been a reason. Perhaps a destructive act of nature occurred in the sales rep's territory during the period for which evaluation is being made. Or perhaps the sales rep had a traumatic personal experience that affected job performance. The sales manager who is aware of such things can temper unfavorable results of the objective criteria.

SUMMARY

The person responsible for managing the sales force is the sales manager. The job is difficult not only because it carries responsibilities above and beyond those directly related to the sales force, but also because the sales representatives comprising any single sales force are not really a homogeneous group.

Among the many problems of managing the sales force are recruiting, selecting, training, compensating, establishing sales territories, motivating, and evaluating. Recruiting is a process of matching people with jobs. The two basic tools in the process are a job description and a person profile; the first is a description of the job and the second is a description of the kind of person best suited for the job. Sources of recruits include intracompany transfers, recommendations of sales personnel, educational institutions, employment agencies, other companies, advertisements, and walk-ins.

The selection process involves determining which recruits should actually be hired as sales representatives. There are several tools used in performing the task. The application blank provides certain initial information, and the interview, or a series of them, furnishes additional insights regarding the applicant's personality and potential success in selling. References are usually checked, and various kinds of psychological tests are sometimes given. Training programs should be established for the entire sales force and should cover such areas as product knowledge, company knowledge, market knowledge, and selling techniques.

Compensation plans should both be fair to the sales rep and provide some degree of direction and control by the company. Three basic plans are available: straight salary, straight commission, and some combination of the two. The advantages of the straight-salary method are, for the most part, the disadvantages of the straight-commission method. In order to get the best of both worlds, most companies have compensation plans that are combinations of the two.

Establishing sales territories involves identifying basic territorial units, estimating the sales potential in each unit, constructing tentative territories out of the basic units, and making final adjustments. Keeping sales representatives motivated is an important part of the sales manager's job. It is accomplished by, among other things, the use of sales conventions, contests, and public recognition.

Evaluation requires a standard with which to compare performance. Standards should be set for each person, not for the sales force as a whole. Usually expressed in ratios, the most common standards are sales to quotas, sales to expense, sales to gross margin, sales to net profit, and orders to calls made. In addition to objective standards, some subjective judgment is often used in the evaluation process.

QUESTIONS FOR THOUGHT AND REVIEW

1. On the basis of your understanding and the inferences you can make, contrast the job of sales manager with that of advertising manager.
2. Why should recruiting be an ongoing process? Why not recruit only when a vacancy arises? Explain why some turnover of the sales force is desirable.
3. Define *job description* and *person profile.* Explain their use in matching people with jobs. Why is a person profile sometimes difficult to construct?
4. Discuss the influence of civil rights legislation on recruiting and selecting practices of companies.
5. What are the advantages of using the recommendations of sales personnel as sources of recruits? What are some cautions to be observed?
6. Why are employment agencies often considered good sources of recruits? What functions do they perform particularly advantageous to companies seeking employees?
7. Discuss the pros and cons of hiring salespeople away from other companies.
8. What information can be obtained from the application blank? Is it against the law to ask for information concerning physical disabilities? Explain.
9. Distinguish between a *guided interview* and a *nondirected interview.* Which do you think is better? Why?
10. Discuss the validity and usefulness of references.
11. Explain the conditions under which psychological tests can be used legally, and discuss their pros and cons.
12. Discuss individually the use of intelligence tests, aptitude tests, and personality tests.
13. Should all salespeople be trained? Explain. What kinds of topics should be included in a sales training program? Why should they be included?
14. Distinguish between *group participation* and *individual training methods.* Mention several of each and discuss their advantages and disadvantages.
15. What should be the goals of a sales force compensation plan? Are they mutually exclusive?
16. Discuss the advantages and disadvantages of *straight salary* and *straight commission,* both from the point of view of the company and of the sales rep. What is the purpose of a combination plan?

17. Discuss the several political subdivisions that might be used as basic units for establishing sales territories. What nonpolitical units can be used? What should be the basic consideration in determining the unit?

18. How is sales potential used in combining units into territories? Why are adjustments nearly always necessary after the tentative territories have been established?

19. Discuss the sales manager's problem in motivating sales reps. What are the various techniques used to motivate salespeople? Discuss their advantages and disadvantages.

20. Explain why evaluation is important to both the company and the sales rep. Why is evaluation of salespeople more difficult than evaluation of other types of employees?

21. Explain the general procedure for evaluating salespeople.

22. Describe and explain the purpose of each of the following ratios used as standards for evaluation: sales to quotas, sales to expense, sales to gross margin, sales to net profit, and orders to calls made.

23. Do you think subjective evaluation of salespeople is justifiable? Why?

18

SALES PROMOTION— STIMULATION OF CHANNEL SUPPORT

The third element in the promotion mix is sales promotion. The term is a bit confusing because all of a company's promotional acitivities are, in a sense, designed to promote sales. But sales promotion has a special meaning. The AMA Committee on Definitions defines *sales promotion* as "those marketing activities other than personal selling, advertising, and publicity, that stimulate consumer purchasing and dealer effectiveness, such as displays, shows and exhibitions, demonstrations, and various nonrecurrent selling efforts not in the ordinary routine."[1] According to this definition any promotional activity that is not advertising or personal selling falls into the category of sales promotion.

In a book that is becoming a classic in the field, sales promotion is defined as "a direct inducement which offers an extra value or incentive for the product to the sales force, distributors, or the ultimate consumer."[2] An even more concise definition of sales promotion is "a short-term incentive to the trade or consumer to induce purchase of the product."[3] Regardless of how it is conceptualized and although it would rarely be used alone, sales promotion is an increasingly important part of a firm's total promotional strategy.[4]

But it must be carefully planned to coordinate with the other components of the promotion mix. To consider sales promotion an afterthought in the promotional strategy of the firm is to weaken its potential effectiveness. Properly conceived and implemented, sales promotion can accomplish many things. For example, it can motivate the company's sales force; generate support from retailers, dealers, wholesalers, distributors, jobbers, and other intermediaries in the channel; stimulate consumer interest in trying a product; and encourage multiple-unit purchases and repeated use.

Sales promotion should never be considered a panacea for the marketing ills of a company, however, as is sometimes mistakenly done. The use of sales promotion cannot solve the problems resulting from poor product performance or inadequate distribution; nor can it ever take the place of advertising and personal selling. It has to be a part of the *total* promotion mix and must be planned in that light.[5]

The orientation for our consideration of sales promotion is the manufacturing firms or firms occupying a comparable position in the channel of distribution. Among manufacturer's sales promotion targets are their sales forces, the intermediaries in the channel, and the consumer. We have covered, directly or by implication, sales promotion relative to the sales force, and we shall consider in chapter 19 those activities aimed at stimulating consumer response. This chapter is concerned with sales promotion aimed at channel intermediaries, and is generally referred to as *trade promotion*.

---

[1] Committee on Definitions, *Marketing Definitions: A Glossary of Marketing Terms* (Chicago: American Marketing Association, 1960), p. 20.

[2] John F. Luick and William Lee Ziegler, *Sales Promotion and Modern Merchandising* (New York: McGraw-Hill, 1968), p. 4.

[3] *The Tools of Promotion* (New York: Association of National Advertisers, 1975), p. 1.

[4] See Roger A. Strang, "Sales Promotion—Fast Growth, Faulty Management," *Harvard Business Review* 54, no. 4 (July-Aug. 1976): 115–24.

[5] See Louis J. Haugh, "Promotion Trends: Defining and Redefining," *Advertising Age* (February 14, 1983): M-44.

THE CHANNEL SUPPORT PROBLEM

A company such as Avon that has an integrated channel is not concerned about getting support from intermediaries in the channel because there are none. But most manufacturers operating in channels that are not completely integrated need some degree of help from such institutions in promoting their products.[6] However, such help is not easy to get. Most middlemen are not concerned about the problems of the manufacturers because they have their own problems. They are not particularly concerned about which products consumers purchase as long as the products are purchased from them. The manufacturer is not really concerned about which store the consumer patronizes as long as the right product is purchased. Thus there is an inherent conflict of promotion goals between the manufacturer and the middlemen, and the manufacturer must resolve the conflict before any help can be expected in promoting the manufacturer's product.

The issue can be reduced to a single proposition: A dealer or distributor cannot be expected to help promote a manufacturer's product unless there is something to be gained. The manufacturer's success in the use of sales promotional devices aimed at stimulating retailer support is entirely dependent upon the retailer's perception of advantage. Obviously the firm's marketing strategy has a bearing on the problem's magnitude. A firm that employs a policy of *exclusive distribution* has a less severe problem than one using *intensive distribution*. Retailers who are given the exclusive rights in their areas to sell the manufacturer's product (exclusive distribution) may see a strong advantage in promoting the manufacturer's brand because under these circumstances that particular brand may be a major patronage motive for a customer clientele. But retailers selling products of a manufacturer who uses intensive distribution procedures are not inclined to devote much effort to any particular manufacturer's brand. They know that their promotional efforts could benefit their competitors as much as it would benefit themselves. In addition, they are probably selling other brands of the same product and do not really care which brand they sell. The manufacturer who distributes intensively must use sales promotion devices that strongly suggest advantages to the retailers in return for their support.

The manufacturer's policies regarding inventory requirements for dealers can also affect their willingness or need to provide promotional support. Some firms have a *loading* policy, for example, whereby they require that dealers purchase excessive quantities of the product in order to handle it at all. The rationale is that forcing the dealers to maintain large inventories will stimulate promotional effort to accelerate sales. The policy is only effective, of course, among dealers whose customers demand that manufacturer's product; even then support is only grudgingly given.

An inventory policy that generates more willing support, perhaps, is a *basic stock policy*. Under this policy the manufacturer simply requires that dealers maintain a minimum stock complete with respect to the nature of the line – sizes, colors, styles, etc. This is not an unreasonable policy, and its purpose is to prevent "outages" of the product at the dealers who handle it.

---

[6]See "Why P & G Wants a Mellower Image," *Business Week* (June 7, 1982): 60–64.

The manufacturer's policy regarding *returned goods* may also affect the dealer's willingness to provide promotional support. Some firms are quite liberal in this regard and allow dealers to return unsold merchandise almost at will. At the other extreme are those manufacturers who accept no returns. Most firms have a returned goods policy somewhere between the two extremes. If there is good reason for returning the goods (perhaps the dealer was oversold, or the style did not sell in a dealer's area), these manufacturers will accept them. Dealers are more likely to stock and promote products of manufacturers that have fair and reasonable policies regarding merchandise returns than of manufacturers who have stricter policies.

SPECIFIC DEVICES AIMED AT INTERMEDIARIES

The sales promotion devices used by manufacturers to stimulate dealer support of their promotional programs may be divided into four general categories: those eliciting quickly concluded response ramifications, those with prolonged response ramifications, trade shows, and cooperative advertising.

Devices for Quickly Concluded Response

Some sales promotion activities require responses whose effects are usually immediate and short-lived. The advantage to dealers in responding favorably to such sales promotion efforts is direct and results in relatively little lingering effect.

Promotion Allowances

Promotion allowances are sometimes offered a dealer for actively promoting the sale of the manufacturer's product for a specific period of time. They generally take the form of a reduction from the invoice price of the merchandise and are particularly useful in the introduction of new products. Dealers are sometimes a bit reluctant to stock a new product if the demand for it has not been established. Yet the manufacturer must see that stocks of the new product are available to the consumer to effectively generate demand. To encourage stocking, the manufacturer convinces the dealer that demand is forthcoming and makes sharing in the promotional effort worthwhile. Accomplishment may be achieved by offering a retailer, say, a dollar per case off the invoice price if the retailer agrees to purchase a certain minimum number of cases and to display the product in a prominent location in the store for a stated period of time.

Caution must be observed in using this and many other sales promotion devices to avoid violating the provisions of the Robinson-Patman Act, which requires that the same proposition be offered to all dealers on a proportionate basis.

Buying Allowances

A buying allowance is somewhat similar to a promotion allowance except that the dealer is not asked to actively promote the product. But its purpose is very much the same — to get the dealer to purchase the product or to buy in larger quantities than usual. Encouragement to do this is provided by a price reduction on each case purchased during a specified period.

The manufacturer hopes that the dealer will voluntarily push the product because of the higher profit margin resulting from the discounted price and the fact that a larger inventory of the product is on hand. A variation in the technique is to offer free goods with the purchase of a specified quantity instead of directly reducing the price per unit on the units purchased. For example, a free case might be given with the purchase of ten cases.

Still another variation is a *buyback allowance,* which may be offered in conjunction with another deal. It provides for a reduction in price on replacement purchases of merchandise whose stock was depleted as a result of successful promotion in the "first" deal. Usually the offer is limited to the quantity of merchandise sold during the other deal.

Devices for Prolonged Response

In other cases, longer-lasting effects of the dealer's favorable response to the sales promotion may be required. The distinction between short-term and prolonged effects is a relative matter because sales promotion activities, by definition, are designed for temporary purposes. Few single devices are intended for continuous use, although they may be repeated periodically, and sales promotion in some form may be used continuously.

Quotas for Dealers

Some manufacturers establish quotas for their dealers. Such a policy works best with dealers who have been granted the exclusive right to sell the manufacturer's brand in a specific area. The manufacturer can insist that the dealer sell a specified quantity of the merchandise to retain the franchise. Thus promotion is encouraged. The policy is effective if the dealer needs the brand and must buy it directly from the manufacturer. But if the merchandise involved is a convenience good available to the consumer at countless retail outlets and to the dealer from numerous sources, the policy cannot be imposed.

Contests for Dealers

The desire to participate in contests seems to be a fairly universal characteristic of people. Under certain circumstances, contests can be effective with wholesalers, retailers, and other distributors who handle the manufacturer's product.

The guidelines are somewhat the same for all contests used by the manufacturer: all eligible people should have a chance to enter and to win, and the losers are more important than the winners. Thus care must be taken to prevent the contest from being counterproductive by "turning off" the losers. Objectives should be set, prizes should be carefully selected, and the contest should be efficiently and fairly conducted.

The general purpose of a contest for dealers is to stimulate activity in pushing the manufacturer's product. In order to generate enthusiasm and to reduce the number of total losers, there should be many prizes. These should range in value from the relatively inexpensive, such as pen and pencil sets, letter openers, and other small but useful items, to such things as vacation trips to Hawaii, new automobiles, and other items of substantial value.

Prizes should be awarded on the basis of percent increase in sales during the life of the contest—not on the total units sold. Because all dealers entering the contest are not the same size, to determine the winners by the total number of units sold would be unfair to the smaller businesses.

Retailers selling convenience goods, however, are not likely to be enthusiastic about contests. Convenience goods are purchased at the most easily accessible locations, and more retailers are involved than is the case with shopping for specialty goods, which require some degree of search by the consumer. Thus, contests are more easily implemented if the manufacturer follows a policy of exclusive or selective distribution than if the policy is intensive distribution. A major problem with the use of contests is that there is always the danger of shifting future sales up to win the contest. As a result, sales may drop to a level below normal for a period of time following the contest.

Contests for Retail Salespeople

Contests for retail salespeople are aimed at increasing the sales of the product in retail stores by stimulating activity among the salespeople themselves. In order to avoid creating any possible ill-will with the retailers, the manufacturer should obtain permission to conduct the contest. The retailer will agree only if there is an apparent advantage in doing so. The advantage might be greater profits because of the increased sales or a better relationship with the manufacturer if that seems desirable.

Ground rules for the contest should be similar to those established for dealer contests. All eligible salespeople should have the opportunity to enter; there should be a number of prizes; and so on.

Spiffs

Another sales promotion device aimed at increasing sales by stimulating the activity of retail salespeople is the use of *spiffs* (also called *push money* or *P.M.'s*).

A spiff is a monetary award paid to a retail salesperson by a manufacturer for selling the manufacturer's line of products. The amount paid is in addition to the regular compensation earned by the salesperson and paid by the retailer. The use of spiffs is not easily adaptable to self-servicing retailing; it is appropriate only where sales depend largely on the effectiveness of the salesperson such as in certain sections of department or specialty stores. The items on which spiffs are paid must usually be fairly high-ticket items. Semiexclusive men's and women's clothing and major appliances are the kinds of products for which spiffs can be effective.

Implementation requires the consent of the retailer. A manufacturer of fashionable men's suits might approach the manager of a men's specialty shop handling the line with the proposition that for each of the manufacturer's brand of suits a salesperson sold, that salesperson would be paid $20 by the manufacturer. There is little doubt that the salespeople would push the line under these circumstances, which of course is what the manufacturer wants. But what is the advantage to the retailer? The retailer might be inclined to allow the spiffs if either that manufacturer's line was the only brand the retailer carried or the profit margin on the line was higher than that on the other lines carried. Otherwise, the retailer would very likely refuse to allow the spiffs.

Training Dealer Salespeople

Stimulating promotional support in the channel can sometimes be accomplished by providing training programs for wholesale and retail salespeople. If such salespeople are trained in selling the manufacturer's brand, they will push that brand in dealing with their customers.

To implement such a program, of course, the manufacturer must obtain the consent of the wholesalers and retailers involved. But the underlying principle mentioned earlier still prevails: These institutions will agree to cooperate only if it is to their advantage. If it is an appliance dealer, for example, and the only line of appliances carried is that of the manufacturer offering the training program, cooperation would certainly be helpful. But suppose the dealer carries more than one line of appliances? Then the manufacturer's training program would be acceptable only if the profit margin were higher on that line than on the other lines carried.

Merchandising the Advertising

Merchandising the advertising literally means selling the manufacturer's advertising program. It means convincing the dealer handling the manufacturer's products and also the manufacturer's sales force that the forthcoming advertising campaign will be highly successful in stimulating demand for the manufacturer's product. The purpose of the technique is to generate enthusiasm by the dealers so they will take an active part in promoting the line. The very least expectation is that they would purchase above-normal quantities of the product to satisfy the anticipated increase in demand.

The success of the method depends upon the manufacturer's ability to convince the dealers of the merits of the planned advertising campaign. It often takes a good deal of selling to accomplish this, and the job usually falls to the manufacturer's sales reps. These people may not be as well qualified to discuss advertising programs as the people in advertising, but they are the logical ones to sell the campaign because of their established contacts and their selling ability in general.

Effective merchandising of the advertising requires a thorough explanation of the total advertising campaign. A complete discussion involves showing the dealer the ads that will appear, the commercials that will be shown, and all the other information about the campaign (except confidential information) that might be persuasive, including a detailed advertising schedule. If the presentation is persuasive enough, the dealer may think that it would be foolish not to participate, and will not only purchase a plentiful supply of the product but will also tie into the national campaign with some advertising in the local media and promotional activities in the store.

Missionary Selling

The primary purpose of missionary selling in stimulating dealer support is to generate and sustain goodwill among present and potential customers. An underlying objective in its use is that it will do its job so well that dealers will be persuaded to actively promote the manufacturer's product.

However, overselling can create resentment. Middlemen are very perceptive and are suspicious of exaggerated attempts to sell anything. But helpful suggestions with respect to the arrangements of merchandise and displays, the effective width and depth of the line, and ideas for local advertising will often be accepted by a retailer to the advantage of the manufacturer.

Trade Shows

One of the most effective, interesting, exciting, and expensive sales promotion devices is the industry trade show.[7] Trade shows provide an opportunity for many competing firms and firms producing complementary products to exhibit their products and lines at the same time to the hundreds or thousands of retailer customers who may attend. The shows range from the two- to five-day regional affairs held annually or less often to the almost perpetual show at the Merchandise Mart in Chicago.

Trade shows provide many and varied opportunities to participating companies. In this excellent selling environment many orders are written for customers and for buyers who may not have been customers previously. Trade shows lend themselves extremely well to giving out sample merchandise to prospective customers; distributing brochures, pamphlets, and other advertising material to obviously interested people; and showing slides, filmstrips, and motion pictures to passers-by of the exhibit booths. In addition to sales that are made at the time, some future sales result from the show.

A trade show is an excellent device for generating good public relations with customers and with competitors and also with the city where it is held because of the business it brings. Representatives of participating companies can gain tremendous insights into the attitudes of people toward their companies and toward competitors just by listening to comments. They can discover what competitors are doing and can share ideas to improve the industry. The entire atmosphere at a trade show is informal; the cocktail parties and other social events are conducive to strengthening relationships with customers.

To be successful, a trade show must be very carefully planned and effectively coordinated. The trade show has been likened to a magazine — the attendees are

---

[7]See *Advertising Age* (23 Apr. 1979). Section 2 is devoted to a discussion of meetings, shows, and conventions.

the readers; the displays, seminars, and programs are the editorial content; and the exhibitors are the advertisers.[8] It takes a tremendous amount of advance planning to arrange for the speakers and participants in the seminars and programs, to line up the exhibitors, and to arrange the exhibition booths into a functional and aesthetic order.

Not only must the total show be carefully planned but each exhibiting firm, too, should thoroughly plan for its participation, beginning with the establishment of objectives whereby the exhibit can be developed.[9] The planners must consider the target audience and precisely what the firm hopes to accomplish with its exhibit.

Cooperative Advertising

The two kinds of *cooperative advertising* are horizontal and vertical. Our concern is primarily with vertical cooperative advertising. However, we will take a brief look at the horizontal kind, which is really classified as advertising, and not sales promotion in the sense that we have defined that term.

Horizontal Cooperative Advertising

Cooperation between two or more firms on the same level of distribution—manufacturers, or wholesalers, or retailers—in an advertising effort is referred to as *horizontal cooperative advertising.* Such an arrangement exists most often among manufacturing firms. The most viable means of implementing such an effort is through the trade association that represents the companies in a particular industry. A good example is the American Dairy Association. This association periodically sponsors an advertising campaign whose purpose is to increase the total consumption of dairy products.

Horizontal cooperative advertising is aimed at increasing the demand for the generic product. Rarely are brand names mentioned, but accomplishment of the objectives is considered beneficial to the entire industry. Participating firms indirectly through the association believe that while their competitors may gain sales as a result of the advertising, they too will benefit and that if all the firms in the industry retain their present shares of the market, they will all gain because the total market will be larger.

Vertical Cooperative Advertising

Because vertical cooperative advertising is particularly related to the stimulation of retailer support of the manufacturer's promotional effort, it is sales promotion as well as advertising. Such advertising is a cooperative arrangement between the manufacturer and the retailer (vertically, "down the channel," and not horizon-

---

[8]B.G. Yovovich, "Trade Show? Think of It as a Magazine," *Advertising Age* (23 Apr. 1979): S-12-13.
[9]See Suzette Cavanaugh, "Setting Objectives and Evaluating the Effectiveness of Trade Show Exhibits," *Journal of Marketing* 40, no. 4 (Oct. 1976): 100-3.

tally, ''across the industry''). It can exist between the manufacturer and any intermediary in the channel, but its primary use is with retailers. The manufacturer and the retailer in the vertical arrangement share the expenses incurred by the retailer, up to a certain point, in advertising the manufacturer's products. Usually the costs are shared on a 50-50 basis, but they can be shared on any basis agreed to by the participating parties.[10]

The technique is not new, but its use seems to be increasing. Among the many companies that have used it recently are General Motors, Champion Spark Plugs, Kodak, Teledyne Water Pik, and Arneson Products (swimming pool cleaner).[11] The National Bowling Council, which represents bowling proprietors and companies, has used the technique in an arrangement particularly suited to the nature of the bowling industry.[12] Other products advertised by firms through cooperative arrangements include paint, clothing, automobiles, appliances, and cosmetics. Cooperative arrangements are more effectively used with established products than with new because retailers are reluctant to participate in advertising a product for which the demand has not yet been developed. Retailers consider generating initial demand to be a problem for the manufacturer alone.

Purposes. The manufacturer's ostensible purpose in using vertical cooperative advertising is to build sales of a profitable product or line. A survey showed that 66 percent of the firms using the technique indicated building sales as their reason; it was also apparent that vertical cooperative advertising is considered as a way to sustain good relationships with their retailer and wholesaler customers.[13] The method serves not only to get retailer support in the specific advertising involved but also establishes an incentive, perhaps, for other kinds of support.

Procedure. The procedure for vertical cooperative advertising is for the retailer to place the advertisement in a local medium; later, the medium bills the retailer for the total cost of the advertisement. The retailer then sends the bill, together with a tear sheet of the ad or other necessary proof that the ad has been run to the manufacturer, and the manufacturer either sends a check to the retailer for a previously agreed upon amount of the bill or credits the retailer's account. The manufacturer usually provides the retailer with prepared ads that can be reproduced, and all the retailer has to do is add the name of the store. This practice assures professionalism in the construction of the ads and consistency among all participating retailers.

Any medium can be used as a vehicle for cooperative advertising. Newspa-

---

[10]For extensive discussion of cooperative advertising, see ''Co-op Advertising: Power in Numbers,'' *Advertising Age* (March 7, 1983): M-9-22; *Advertising Age* (August 17, 1981): Section 2, and *Advertising Age* (September 1, 1980): Section 2.

[11]''The Cry in Co-op: Ready, Set . . . CHARGE,'' *Sales and Marketing Management* 119 (11 July 1977): 30–37.

[12]See Christy Marshall, ''Co-op Ads, New Gear Lead Bowlers Down Alley.'' *Advertising Age* (18 Sept. 1978): 48, 78.

[13]Martin Everett, ''Co-op at the Crossroads,'' *Sales & Marketing Management* 117 (13 Dec. 1976): 41–46.

pers are probably most commonly used, perhaps because they are the predominant medium for retailers. But advertisers are allocating more money to cooperative plans in television advertising.[14]

There are several reasons why the retailer and not the manufacturer should place the advertisements. Involvement is certainly a major reason because one of the purposes of cooperative advertising is to generate support for the manufacturer; this is difficult to accomplish if the retailer is not actively involved. Furthermore, the retailer's knowledge of the local market and the media is important for maximum effectiveness. Even without these reasons, the manufacturer would still prefer to have the retailer place the ads because of the lower rates the retailer can get from the local media. The manufacturer can thus get more advertising for fewer dollars than if the ads were placed at the national rate.

Benefits to the retailer.   The biggest advantage to the retailer is the *reduced cost* of the advertising. On a 50-50 split basis the retailer gets twice as much advertising for the same dollar outlay than if the manufacturer were not picking up half the cost. However, the manufacturer's gain is even greater. Since the rate differential between national and retail advertising as employed by some local media is often quite substantial (sometimes as much as 50 percent), the manufacturer's share of the cost of ads placed by the retailer is half of a much lower figure than if the ads were placed at the national rate. Thus the manufacturer may get considerably more than twice as much advertising for the same dollar outlay under a co-op arrangement with the retailer placing the ads than if there were no co-op arrangement at all.

Other benefits to the retailer include the use of advertising that is professionally done, the increased sales from advertising that probably would not have been run without a co-op arrangement, a feeling of participation in a beneficial activity, and possibly a revival of enthusiasm toward a profitable product. All retailers handling the manufacturer's product should have the same opportunity to realize the benefits on a proportionate basis because of the provisions of the Robinson-Patman Act.

Dealer listings.   A variation of vertical cooperative advertising is national advertising in which the names and addresses of dealers handling the manufacturer's product are listed. There is rarely any financial arrangement between the manufacturer and the dealer, but it can be advantageous to both. Dealer listings help the manufacturer in that people who read the ad know where they can get the product, and the dealer gets some free advertising.

SUMMARY

This chapter is the first of two devoted to a consideration of sales promotion — the third element in the promotion mix. Sales promotion consists of those promotional

---

[14]"Advertisers Using More TV for Co-op Ads," *Editor & Publisher* 110, pt. 3 (6 Aug. 1977): 20.

activities that are not properly classified as advertising or personal selling. It includes temporary devices used for the purpose of stimulating activity by both channel members and consumers; the various techniques designed for the purpose can be divided accordingly. This chapter was concerned with sales promotion activities aimed at channel members.

Some sales promotion devices are designed to provoke an immediate response from the dealer without any necessarily lasting effects. Others produce effects that continue for a period of time. Still others are somewhat special and must be considered separately. Promotion allowances and buying allowances are two devices in the first category.

A dealer's favorable response to some promotional devices produces longer-lasting effects than with promotion buying allowances. Contests, both for dealers themselves and for their salespeople, are among the devices that produce longer-lasting effects. The use of contests is more viable with specialty or shopping goods than with convenience goods. Merchandising the advertising is an attempt to convince the dealer of the demand-stimulating potential of the manufacturer's forthcoming advertising campaign. Missionary selling — the use of goodwill ambassadors — can also serve to generate support in certain ways.

Participating in a trade show can be a highly successful promotional device for a manufacturer. In an environment where many competing firms exhibit their merchandise simultaneously, large numbers of customers and potential buyers are receptive to the presentation of information about the manufacturer's line.

Vertical cooperative advertising is advertising that results from the cooperative efforts of two or more firms on different levels of distribution, such as a manufacturer and a retailer. In the arrangement, the manufacturer provides reimbursement for part of the retailer's cost (usually half) incurred in advertising the manufacturer's product. A variation of cooperative advertising is the practice some manufacturers have of listing in their national advertising the names and addresses of the dealers who handle their products. Referred to as dealer listings, the device does not obligate the dealer financially.

QUESTIONS FOR THOUGHT AND REVIEW

1. Define *sales promotion*. How would you distinguish it from advertising? from personal selling?
2. Why is it necessary for most manufacturers to have dealer support for their promotional programs? Name some companies that you think need such support and some companies that you believe do not need it. Explain your choices.
3. Explain the conflict in promotion objectives between middlemen and manufacturers. Does this conflict exist if the manufacturer's policy is one of exclusive distribution? Explain.
4. Explain the conditions under which a dealer might agree to provide support for a manufacturer's promotion program.
5. Explain and distinguish between *promotion allowances* and *buying allowances*. What is their purpose, and when are they particularly useful?

6. Explain the purpose of contests for dealers, and discuss the guidelines that should be observed in conducting them. What adverse effects may result from their use?

7. If you were a retail salesperson, how would you react to the opportunity of entering a sales contest? Would you see any disadvantages to it as a salesperson? Explain. Would your employer see disadvantages? Explain.

8. What is a *spiff?* Explain the conditions under which a retailer would allow a manufacturer to use spiffs. What difference would the fact that retailer carried more than one brand of the product have on the use of spiffs?

9. What does *merchandising the advertising* mean? How can it be effective in stimulating dealer support?

10. Discuss the part that missionary selling might play in a manufacturer's sales promotion program.

11. Briefly describe a *trade show*. What exactly does it accomplish in stimulating dealer support? How does it generate good public relations?

12. Discuss the planning that must take place for a trade show, both from the point of view of the total show and of the individual exhibitor.

13. Distinguish between horizontal and vertical cooperative advertising. Which is appropriately considered as a sales promotion device and why? What benefits can a specific manufacturer gain from participating in horizontal cooperative advertising?

14. Explain how vertical cooperative advertising works. Why does the retailer and not the manufacturer place the ads?

15. What are the purposes of vertical cooperative advertising from the manufacturer's point of view? What are its benefits to the retailer?

16. What are *dealer listings?*

19

SALES PROMOTION— STIMULATION OF CONSUMER RESPONSE

I. Devices that reach consumers directly
   A. Coupons
   B. Premiums
   C. Contests and sweepstakes
   D. Cash refunds
   E. Sampling
II. Devices that reach consumers through retailer
   A. The package
   B. Point-of-purchase materials
   C. In-store demonstrations
   D. Trading stamps
III. Trends and developments

A completely effective promotion program requires the use of all available promotion tools in a mix appropriate to the circumstances. Since no one knows for sure when the buying decision is made, nor the conditions under which it is made, the only way a manufacturer can be sure of being considered in the weighing of alternatives is to "be there" at all times. Furthermore, the impetus for making the right decision from the manufacturer's point of view must come from all possible directions. Thus advertising, personal selling, sales promotion, and publicity — each in whatever forms seem appropriate — should be implemented into the total program.

National advertising is usually aimed, in some way, at consumer attitudes. That is, the consumer is not expected to rush out to the store to buy the product immediately upon exposure to the ads, but to use the information presented in the advertising in making the buying decision whenever the occasion arises. But when the national advertiser wants a more immediate response than that which might result from advertising alone, sales promotion is used.

Sales promotion directed at middlemen (trade promotion) is important, but a more immediate effect on sales can usually be accomplished by aiming the effort at the consumer — selling *through* the retailer and other channel members and not just *to* them.[1] Both targets are important, but since ultimate success in the sale of consumer goods depends upon the consumer's decision to buy, the more quickly that decision is made, the sooner success is realized.

In the last few years sales promotion has come to dominate the promotion mixes of many firms. It was estimated that in 1983 revenues approached $70 billion.[2] In addition, expenditures for sales promotion in many product categories were 60 percent of the combined advertising and sales promotion budgets — compared with less than 40 percent in the late 1960s.[3]

Sales promotion aimed at the consumer is particularly useful when the manufacturer is introducing a new product. A gentle prod can overcome the consumer's natural hesitancy to try something new. Sales promotion can also be used to encourage consumers to buy more of the product at one time, thus increasing total usage. Despite logic to the contrary, the consumer who has a reserve supply of a product will be inclined to use more of it than if the item in use is the only one on hand. How often have you continued to use a bar of bath soap, for example, when it has become paper-thin because you had no spare bars in the bathroom cabinet? Finally, the manufacturer may simply want to provide the consumer with additional incentive to pick the "right" brand from an often vast array of brands lined up on the supermarket shelves.

It is convenient to divide the various consumer sales promotion devices into two groups: those that reach the consumer directly, and those that reach the consumer through the retailer.

---

[1]See Benson P. Shapiro, "Improve Distribution with Your Promotional Mix," *Harvard Business Review* 55 (Mar.-Apr. 1977): 115-23; Eugene Mahany, "How 'Sell-through' Consumer Promotions Improve Your 'E.Q.'," *Advertising Age* (18 Oct. 1976): 80.

[2]Lee LeFort, "We've Come a Long Way, Baby," *Advertising Age* (August 22, 1983): M-12.

[3]B. G. Yovovich, "Stepping into a New Era," *Advertising Age* (August 27, 1983): M-9, 30-32.

DEVICES THAT REACH CONSUMERS DIRECTLY

Those sales promotion activities involving direct contact with the consumer do not require the retailer as a vehicle of communication, transmission, or delivery. Rather, the consumer is usually made aware of them by such means as advertising in the mass media, using direct mail, and contacting the consumer on a house-to-house basis. After the initial contact has been made and the consumer has been persuaded to respond, the retailer usually becomes involved.

Coupons

Coupons have been tremendously popular in recent years. Estimates are that close to 120 billion coupons were distributed in 1983, or about 1,400 per U. S. household.[4] Seventy four percent of shoppers interviewed in a study of the Newspaper Advertising Bureau said they used coupons in their weekly food shopping.[5] Some retailers are now having "double coupon days" – days on which the retailer allows credit for double the face value of the coupons. In addition, couponing is being used in industries not traditionally associated with the practice. Breweries, for example, are experimenting with it in the 14 states in which couponing for alcoholic beverages is legal. Pabst Brewing Co., Stroh Brewery Co., and Heileman have used it, and Adolph Coors Co. is expected to try it. So far, however, the major brewers, Anheuser-Busch and Miller, have refrained from couponing, but say they are keeping their options open.[6]

However, there is some concern that the practice of couponing is being threatened. Not only are the costs accelerating – it costs more than $550,000 for a single-page four-color insert in 236 Sunday newspapers, for example – but retailers claim that the 7 cents handling charge paid by the manufacturers does not cover their costs.[7] Moreover, the growing popularity of coupons may destroy their effectiveness as a marketing tool.[8]

A coupon is a device used to effect a temporary price reduction. It is a "cents-off shelf price" proposition to stimulate purchase of the product for which it is issued. Coupons are distributed in a number of ways, including daily newspaper advertisements, Sunday supplements (including free-standing inserts on which several different coupons are printed), magazines (as part of the advertisements, or simply bound into the magazine), and direct mail. They may also be distributed in or on the package to be used for future purchases. Couponing almost always involves the retailer after the initial contact because on almost all coupons the consumer is asked to go to the retailer for redemption. There are exceptions to this however. A recent example is a $4.00 coupon offer by Hanes to consumers who ordered a $5.95 pantyhose directly from Hanes; redemption of the coupon and shipment of the merchandise was made by the manufacturer. But this is not the

[4]*Ibid.*

[5]"Consumers" Coupon Clipping Climbs," *Advertising Age* (April 11, 1983): 59.

[6]Robert Reed, "Beer Couponing Foams to the Top," *Advertising Age* (February 21, 1983): 10, 71.

[7]"Retailing May Have Overdosed on Coupons," *Business Week* (June 13, 1983): 147–49.

[8]"Coupons in Danger, P&G Exec Warns," *Advertising Age* (March 28, 1983): 3, 69.

common procedure. Although the retailer is paid about 7 cents per coupon for handling the coupons, most retailers resent having to accept them because they think it interferes with the smooth operation of checkout procedures and is a nuisance. The retailer sends the coupons, sometimes by way of a clearinghouse, to either the manufacturer or to redemption agents such as A. C. Nielson Co., Lees Marketing Service, and others.

Manufacturers consider the use of coupons to be more effective than straight price reductions because, even if they reduce the price of the product to the retailer, they have no assurance that the reduction would be passed on to the consumer. Also a price reduction would imply a permanent change, when what is desired is a temporary stimulus. But beyond that, the psychological effect of a coupon with an expiration date is much stronger than is a gradual realization of a price reduction or even an advertised price reduction.

Table 19–1 shows examples from among the hundreds of companies using coupons in recent promotional programs.

During the course of a year, almost every consumer in the United States is exposed to hundreds of coupon offers. And if a coupon is for a product the consumer wants or needs, it is foolish not to use it. One consumer reported getting

---

TABLE 19–1
Examples of the use of cents-off coupons.

Company	Cents-off retail price	Product
Del Monte	12¢	Any of several Mexican foods
Hi-C	20¢	8- and 12-quart size
Kool-Aid	20¢	3 envelopes or 1 canister
Sure-Jell	15¢	2 packages of Sure-Jell or 1 of Certo
Tender Vittles	15¢	2 boxes of cat food
Hefty	15¢	1 package of garbage bags
Ken-L Ration	40¢	1 bag of Tender Chunks dog food
General Foods	35¢	1 can or jar of Mellow Roast coffee
Arrid	20¢	1 package of roll-on anti-perspirant
A-1 Steak Sauce	12¢	Any size bottle of steak sauce
Borden	20¢	1 package of Lite-line cheese product
No-Pest	20¢	1 No-Pest Strip insecticide
Johnson & Johnson	12¢	Any size package of Band-Aids
General Foods	10¢	1 package of 40% Bran Flakes
Fixodent	20¢	1 package of denture adhesive
Lever Brothers Co.	20¢	Any size bottle of Signal mouthwash
Minute Maid	10¢	1 Minute Maid pure lemon juice
Ralston Purina	13¢	Any box of Chex cereals
Pepperidge Farm, Inc.	25¢	1 frozen cake
Durkee Famous Foods	7¢	1 package of French fried onions
Allerest	25¢	1 package of Allerest allergy medicines
Thomas J. Lipton, Inc.	25¢	Any box of Lipton Flavored tea bags

back from $40 to $90 every week by redeeming coupons.[9] Of course it would be unwise to buy 12 cans of sauerkraut juice just because there was a coupon worth 50 cents on its purchase – unless the buyer happens to like sauerkraut juice! But using coupons on the purchase of staple items can result in sizeable savings over a period of time.

The redemption rate varies, however, by region. According to a Nielson report, for example, 81 percent of the households in the Northeast redeem coupons compared with 68 percent in the Southeast.[10] Furthermore, the design of the coupon often determines the people who redeem it. If product benefits are emphasized, the coupon tends to attract new users. But if the coupon emphasizes the discount aspect, consumers who want discounts will be attracted.[11]

Cross Coupons

A particular kind of couponing is the use of cross coupons, or *cross-ruffs*. Cross-coupon promotions involve several brands of one company or the brands of several different companies. Coupons for use in the purchase of one of the products are made available to consumers with the purchase of another of the products involved. Among the many cross-ruff arrangements in recent years are those of Royal Crown Cola with Hanes L'eggs, Nabisco with Nestlé and Lipton, and Oscar Mayer with Pillsbury.[12]

A recent cross-ruff promotion considered one of the best was a joint effort between Pepsi-Cola and No-Nonsense fashions. Free No-Nonsense pantyhose were offered with multiple proofs of purchase of Pepsi, via order forms on point of purchase displays, and 50-cents-off coupons for the purchase of Pepsi Light and Diet Pepsi were packed in No-Nonsense pantyhose packages.[13]

The Problem of Misredemption

Misredemption is a major problem in the use of coupons. It has been estimated that 20 percent of the coupons submitted for redemption are fraudulent, amounting to as much as $350 million.[14] Some retailers accept coupons without requiring the customer to purchase the products for which they were issued. A few years ago some stores even had coupon-cashing counters staffed by a person who did nothing but add up the coupons presented by a customer and pay the total to the customer in cash. Some store owners and their employees have been guilty of

---

[9]Bob Gatty, "Incentives Move Products – and People," *Nation's Business* 69, no. 9 (September 1981): 66,67.

[10]Louis J. Haugh, "How Coupons Measure Up," *Advertising Age* (June 8, 1981): 58–63.

[11]K. C. Blair, "Coupon Design, Delivery Vehicle, Target Market Affect Conversion Rate: Research," *Marketing News* 15, no. 4 (May 28, 1982): 1,2.

[12]Louis J. Haugh, "Cross-ruffs Gain Ground as Popular Marketer Tool," *Advertising Age* (26 Jan. 1976): 24, 60.

[13]William A. Robinson, "Best Promotions of the Year," *Advertising Age* (June 7, 1982): M-2-24.

[14]Jennifer Alter and Nancy Giges, "Industry Losing $350 Million in Coupon Misredemption," *Advertising Age* (May 30, 1983): 1, 57.

accumulating coupons and cashing them in. And various other misuses of coupons have been discovered.

Constant monitoring has lessened the fraudulent practices, but they are extremely difficult to control. Store inventories are often checked to determine if there is a discrepancy between the number of coupons submitted for payment and the number of units of the product sold. The returned coupons are examined very carefully for authenticity, and the entire couponing program is watched closely. One suggestion for further reducing the misredemption of coupons is to use color in newspaper coupons to discourage running them through copying machines.[15]

Another approach has been to set traps to catch the offenders, although there are questions of ethics in using this tactic. Coupon ads for nonexistent products are placed in newspapers to catch big-scale "fraud operators." But perhaps the most effective curb would be the passage of a proposed bill called the "Coupon Protection Act," which would make coupon fraud a crime.[16]

Premiums

A *premium* is the offer of a merchandise item either free or at a substantially reduced price to stimulate the purchase of the product being promoted. Premiums are not particularly useful in introducing a new product, but they can be quite effective in persuading consumers to switch brands, at least temporarily. The premium does not have to be related to the product, although it is directly associated with the *sale* of the product. But it should be a useful item that consumers would want, but may not want to pay the retail price for.

Some firms use premiums to enhance their brand images by relating the premium to the themes used in their advertising. Referred to as advertising-oriented premiums, they can actually be extensions of product advertising. Philip Morris, for example, in their "Marlboro Country Store" series, offered such things as boots, saddles, denim jackets, bandannas, and hats as premiums. Such items accentuated the Marlboro image of the rugged outdoor individualist created in their advertising.[17]

But a company must be sure to have enough premiums to supply the demand, and this is often hard to anticipate. Gillette, for example, was recently the defendant in a class action suit because it underestimated the response to its offer of an Accent table lighter stand for its Cricket disposable lighters to customers who sent in 50 cents and two proof-of-purchase seals from Cricket lighters. Gillette ran out of the premiums and refunded the money, along with another Cricket lighter to those people who did not get the premium. It was contended in the suit that Gillette had made an explicit "offer to contract," and the suit asks for the payment of $7.95 (the value of the premium) plus an undetermined amount of punitive dam-

---

[15]"How 12 Agencies View Newspapers," *Media Decisions* 11, no. 9 (Sept. 1976):124–40.

[16]Nancy Giges and Jennifer Alter, "Bill Making Coupon Fraud a Crime Being Proposed," *Advertising Age* (June 6, 1983): 2, 68.

[17]Leonard Daykin, "Premiums' Role Builds Brand Image," *Advertising Age* (October 12, 1981): S-13-15.

ages to each of the 180,000 customers who did not get the premium. Gillette erred in not having enough premiums, or in not limiting the response to the offer with an expiration date or the present supply of premiums.[18] The case is presently still pending.

Sometimes premiums are used in conjunction with other sales promotion devices. Star-Kist Foods offered free to customers the choice of a Morris or Sylvester (9-Lives cat food characters) poster with each purchase, together with cents-off coupons on the cat food; and used trade promotion such as case allowances to encourage dealer support.[19] Or two firms with entirely unrelated products or services may cooperate in a promotional effort involving premiums and other sales promotion devices. In an effort to increase the sale of its series 600 cameras, Polaroid teamed up with Delta Airlines with the offer, "Buy a Polaroid 600, Fly Delta Free."[20]

Methods of Distributing Premiums

The two basic ways of getting the premium to the consumer are attached to, or inside, the package of the product itself or otherwise immediately available as the product is purchased; and by mail at the request of the consumer with submitted proof of purchase. Sometimes the distribution issue resolves itself, such as when the premium is too large or bulky to be included with the product. In other cases, however, the company may have an option.

Attached to, or inside, the package, or otherwise immediately available.   Some consumers are more likely to react favorably to a premium offer if the premium is immediately available than when additional effort is required to get it. Furthermore, the cost of distributing the premium on or in the package is much less than the cost for mailing it at the request of the consumer. On the other hand, retailers may resent having to display products with premiums attached, particularly if the attached item makes the product difficult to stack. This retailer resentment is perhaps reason enough to enclose the premium in the normal package without using a plastic "bubble" or otherwise distorting the package whenever possible. Nevertheless, successful promotions have been achieved with the premium attached outside the normal package. An example is Procter & Gamble's Camay bath soap promotion, which was a free razor attached to four bars of Camay, all of which were wrapped in plastic with the razor visible. Other successes in this regard include toothbrushes with toothpastes, razors with shaving creams, and ballpoint pens with numerous products.

One of the oldest continuing successes in the use of premiums enclosed in the package is that of Cracker Jack. There are people today who can tell their grandchildren about the toys and novelties they got with Cracker Jack when they

---

[18]Gary Levin, "The Accent Is on Having Enough Premiums," *Advertising Age* (August 22, 1983): M-18–19.

[19]William A. Robinson, "The Year's Best Promos," *Advertising Age* (August 10, 1981): 40–42.

[20]William A. Robinson, "Best Promotions of the Year," *Advertising Age* (May 9, 1983): M-54-59.

were children. The method has not changed for at least three generations; only the price, size of the box, and the nature of the premiums have changed. The price is higher, the box is smaller, and the toys have no sharp edges (to comply with current legislation). Another old successful premium-in-the-box promotion was that of Quaker Oats Company's "Mother's" brand of oats for oatmeal. For years, a cup and saucer were enclosed in each box. The method was ingenious, too, because there was an additional incentive to continue buying the product to accumulate a matched set of cups and saucers.

Manufacturers of ready-to-eat cereals have put premiums in cereal boxes for many years and continue to do so. Children's books have been included in boxes of Post's Alpha-Bits, and their Honeycombs have been packed with finger writing pens. Cap'n Crunch, a product of Quaker Oats Company, has been sold with a glow-in-the-dark spooky pirate as an in-package premium. Most of the cereals, in fact, whose appeal is directed at children, have premiums connected with their sale.

Certain brands of detergents are among the many other products with which the technique has been successful. Bath towels and drinking glasses have been used for many years as premiums in boxes of some detergents.

Sometimes the premium is immediately available, but is not actually attached to or inside the package. *Near-pack displays,* for example, are frequently used where the premium is on display adjacent to the stock of the associated product. The previously mentioned Star-Kist poster giveaway was handled in this manner. Burger King, in immediately taking advantage of the popularity of the movie *Return of the Jedi,* sold four different drinking glasses with scenes from the film at 49 cents each with the purchase of a Coke.[21]

Sent to consumer by mail.   In contrast to distributing the premiums simultaneously with the purchase of the product, companies sometimes ask the consumer to mail in a request for the premium, usually along with some proof of purchase of the product being promoted. The premium is then sent to them through the mail. Occasionally those premiums are free to the consumer, such as the 16-page cookbook offered by Frito-Lay to promote Doritos or the cooperative offer by Nabisco and Nestlé to send a coupon worth a half-gallon of milk in return for submitting proof of purchase of two packages of Oreo cookies and a can of Nestlé Quik. The by-mail premiums are usually higher in value than premiums distributed with the package, and, in addition to proof of purchase, a specified sum of money is required. In any case, such premiums represent real bargains to consumers who have uses for them.

Free or Self-liquidating

Developers of a premium promotion must decide whether to charge for the premium or to offer it free. Premiums for which there is a charge are called *self-liquidating premiums,* which simply means that the cost of the premium is recovered

---

[21]Scott Hume, "Burger King Drinks to the Jedi," *Advertising Age* (August 22, 1983): M-10-11.

by the company by requiring the payment of a certain amount of money. Consumers do not seem averse to paying for such premiums if they perceive them as real bargains.[22] And they usually are bargains since the company's objective is not to make a profit on the premiums, but to stimulate purchases of the product connected with the offer.

Among the most outstanding successes in the use of self-liquidating premiums was the promotion of Kool cigarettes in 1973, in which over 20,000 sailboats were distributed as premiums, each at a cost to the consumer of only $88 plus ten empty packages as proof of purchase.[23] More recent examples include the Seven-Up Company's premium offer of various items of outdoor gear to consumers who submitted two 7-Up proofs of purchase and the stated reduced price; Kellogg's offer of a Rand McNally Explorer World atlas for $4.99 and two proofs of purchase seals from their Frosted Mini-Wheats; and a T-shirt offered by Scott Paper Company for $2.99 plus 2 proofs of purchase of Soft 'n' Pretty bathroom tissue.

Contests and Sweepstakes

Contests and sweepstakes are similar in that they both imply opportunities to win something. They differ in that contests are games of *skill* and sweepstakes are games of *chance*. To enter a contest it is necessary to create something — a jingle, a name, a product, a recipe — and submit it, together with proof of product purchase, to be judged. But to enter a sweepstake it is only necessary to submit one's name to have a chance to win that is equal to that of anyone else who enters. Many sweepstakes require no proof of product purchase or allow facsimiles of the labels to be submitted.

Contests are less popular than sweepstakes. It may be that people think the possibility of winning is better in sweepstakes than in contests because winning is a matter of pure chance; they hesitate to compete in contests with people who may be particularly capable with respect to the contest task. Relatively few contests have been used recently as promotional devices. A notable exception is the contest sponsored by Campbell's Soup a few years ago that required entrants to submit a soup recipe, along with a proof of purchase, to compete for a first prize of free groceries for five years or cash, plus a number of additional prizes.[24]

Sweepstakes, on the other hand, have experienced a resurgence of popularity in recent years, after having been dormant for a period of time. Perhaps it is because direct-mail marketers have found that sweepstakes can generate about 50 percent more sales than can any other form of sales promotion.[25] Moreover, they can be used effectively in combination with other promotion devices such as cents-off coupons and trade promotions. Their original popularity occurred in the

---

[22]James F. Engel, Martin R. Warshaw, and Thomas C. Kinnear, *Promotional Strategy,* 4th ed. (Homewood, Ill.: Richard D. Irwin, 1979), p. 458.

[23]Robert L. Uebele, "Premiums," *The Tools of Promotion* (New York: Association of National Advertisers, 1975), p. 9.

[24]See Morton B. Elliot, "Campbell's First Contest Becomes Three-way Promo," *Advertising Age* (21 Aug. 1978): 42.

[25]Thomas J. Conlon, "Sweepstakes Rank as Tops," *Advertising Age* (October 6, 1980): S-6, 7.

1960s — a decade in which they were both introduced and abandoned.[26] Countless games of chance cropped up as promotional gimmicks during these years, including numerous types of bingo and TV horse racing. But because of consumer dissatisfaction with sweepstake management and because their legality was considered suspect by certain federal regulatory agencies, their use declined and almost stopped altogether. The sweepstakes' legal problem was that they were suspected of being lotteries, which are, with some exceptions, illegal. A lottery exists if three conditions are present: chance, a prize, and consideration (a price of some kind to enter). The question was whether the requirement that the entrant purchase the product constituted consideration. Although legal opinion seems to indicate that such a requirement is not sufficient to constitute a lottery, companies sponsoring sweepstakes are still cautious. Hence, the practice of requiring no proof of purchase or the submission of facsimile labels is quite common.

Apparently the problems that put a stop to the use of sweepstakes in the late 1960s have been overcome. Games are becoming popular again, both at the national and the retail levels. The existence of numerous sweepstakes sponsored by The Reader's Digest Association and Publishers Clearing House is well known. Recent sweepstakes also include Van Camp's Pork and Beans' "Inflation Fighter Sweepstakes," the Palmolive dishwashing liquid sweepstake of the Colgate-Palmolive Company, American Home Products' Anacin Sweepstakes, and Armour-Dial's "Dial Your Own Environment and Tone Up" sweepstake. Games at the retail level have been popular, too, although it seems that they are more effective for stores with low market penetration than high.[27]

Cash Refunds

The use of cash refunds as a promotional device is really a method by which the manufacturer effects a temporary reduction in price at the retail level. In some ways it is better than reducing the invoice price to the retailer. If the latter were done, there is no guarantee that the retailer would pass the savings on to the consumer (as is also true in connection with coupons). Also, if the retailer does reduce the price, the consumer may perceive it as a permanent reduction, or at the very least resent it when the price goes back to its normal level. And, of course, the psychological effect of a cash refund can be quite strong.

Refunds, called *rebates* on high-ticket items, have been around for many years and have been used by many diverse companies. Perhaps their sustained popularity is due to the fact that they are sure things, whereas sweepstakes and games are long-shot promotions, even though when they do succeed they are extremely effective.[28] The countless examples of cash refunds include a $2.00 refund on a carton of Brown & Williamson Tobacco Corporation's Arctic Lights cigarettes, or 50 cents on 2 packs; the price of 1 quart of oil for proof of purchase

[26]See Fred C. Allvine, Richard D. Teach, and John Connelly, Jr., "The Demise of Promotional Games," *Journal of Advertising Research* 16, no. 5 (Oct. 1976): 79–84.

[27]Ernest Dickinson, "What You Should Know About the New Games Craze," *Progressive Grocer* 55 (Sept. 1976): 91–97.

[28]See Louis J. Haugh, "Refunds: An Old Standby Stands Out," *Advertising Age* (May 3, 1982): M-26–27.

of 5 quarts of Conoco's New Generation All Season motor oil (Continental Oil Company); $1.00 refund from Warner-Lambert for proof of purchase of two products in its line (or $3.00 for four items); a $1.00 refund on the purchase of one Wilson's Western style ham; and a $1.00 refund from Du Pont for each gallon of Lucite paint purchased.

But rebates gained new momentum and increased attention when Chrysler Corporation, appearing to be on the brink of disaster a few years ago, offered a $500 rebate to consumers.[29] The effort was a success, although it also generated a response in kind from other auto makers — a dramatic departure from their traditional image-advertising. When a company offers a rebate, its competitors seem quick to match or exceed it; a firm offering a rebate increases sales mainly by taking them from competitors until the rebate advantage is eliminated.[30]

Sampling

One of the most effective promotional devices for introducing new products is sampling, in which the consumer is given a free trial size of the product being introduced. But the expense of this method is as much as $5 million for a single product in a national campaign.[31] Sampling is effective because consumers are more likely to try a new product if it is free than if they have to buy it. If the product is good, it will sell itself; but the manufacturer had better be certain that the product is equal or superior to existing products because in trying the product the consumer will discover its faults as well as its merits.

The size of the sample is important. If it is too small, it may not provide the consumer with a good test. If it is too large, it may delay the purchase of the product — and purchase is the desired result of sampling! The size of the sample should be smaller than the size of the product on the retailers's shelves, and it is usually packaged in a miniature of the regular product package to generate product recognition.

Distribution of the sample can be achieved in a number of ways. It can be sent through the mail, delivered door-to-door, or enclosed in or included with another product. The method will depend upon the situation, but the goal is to get the largest distribution among potential users for the least cost.

DEVICES THAT REACH CONSUMERS THROUGH RETAILER

Although the successful use of almost all sales promotion devices has an ultimate impact on the retailer, the effectiveness of the devices discussed in the previous section is not initially dependent upon the retailer's involvement. However, other

---

[29]See Lee Hill, "Chrysler," *Advertising Age* (October 12, 1981): S-20.

[30]Betsey Hansell, "When Do Customers Tire of Saving Money?" *Advertising Age* (August 22, 1983): M-16-17.

[31]Otto Kleppner and Normal A. P. Govoni, *Advertising Procedure,* 7th ed. (Englewood Cliffs, N.J.: Prentice-Hall, 1979), p. 281.

very effective devices do involve the retailer in reaching the consumer. Among these are the package, point-of-purchase materials, in-store promotions, and trading stamps.

The Package

The package sitting on the retailer's shelf is often the key element in the consumer's decision to buy or not to buy the product it encloses. Many consumers form their impressions of a product based on their perceptions of the package. But designing a package is not a simple matter. If its use as a promotional device were the only necessary consideration, the task would be difficult enough; but consideration must also be given to the package's other functions and necessary qualities. Furthermore, once a design is established it must be periodically analyzed for possible changes made necessary by technology or by some aspect of the marketing environment.

Purposes and/or Qualities of the Package

As is true in the case of many marketing activities, the multifaceted nature of packaging makes it difficult to maximize the effectiveness of any single purpose or quality associated with the package. Rather, compromises must usually be made to achieve maximum *total* effectiveness of several aspects.

Protection.   The primary purpose of the package is to provide protection to the product it encloses. Sealed containers, vacuum-packed cans, colored bottles, and plastic-coated boxes, for example, keep certain products fresh or prevent leakage or evaporation. Modern packaging is a far cry from the days of the old general store when merchants sold crackers, beans, flour, sugar, coffee, chewing tobacco, and many other items in bulk and when Father took his bucket to the local saloon to be filled with beer to take home.

Convenience.   Convenience to the consumer is an important consideration in modern packaging, although child-proof containers somewhat negate the convenience of some packages. The consumer wants a package that is easy to open, handy to use, and suitable for storing. "To open, pull tab" or some similar statement appears on many packages. Unfortunately, in too many cases the tab fails to work and frustration rather than convenience prevails. Using the product should require as little effort as possible. Aerosol containers (whose use is now discouraged because of possible atmospheric damage) were designed for easy use. Finally, the consumer wants a package that can be stored conveniently in the home.

However, the package must not only be designed for convenience to the consumer but must also be convenient for the retailer to stock and display. Odd-shaped packages or packages that do not stack easily on the retailers' shelves should be avoided. Perhaps one of the most appropriately packaged products ever was Log Cabin syrup in a can that was a replica of a log cabin; its chimney was the pouring spout. But because of the chimney, the cans were extremely difficult to stack in store displays. The use of the can was discontinued years ago in favor of bottles, perhaps in part for that reason.

Appearance.   The package should be functional and have a pleasing appearance. It should be appropriate for the product and aesthetically appealing so the consumer will be attracted by the impression created by the package.

Promotion.   Finally, and the most important aspect of packaging from our point of view, is its use as a sales promotion device. The other package characteristics add to the product's saleability, but promotion is a special part of the package.

In recent years the package has become an increasingly important sales promotion tool. The growth in significance of the package is due, in part at least, to the proliferation of mass-merchandising outlets. Self-service shopping makes it mandatory that marketers devote considerable attention to the package.[32] It is a member of the manufacturer's sales force sitting on the shelf; it can say nothing or it can say a lot.

The importance of package design becomes even more significant when one realizes that consumers tend to perceive the package and the product as one entity. They do not distinguish clearly between the product and its package.[33] Thus the design must not only attract attention — stand out from competitors' packages — but must also be compatible with the product.

The actual designing of the package is the task of specialists in the creative field. However, those involved in the promotion function usually provide input during package design. Three elements of the package label relevant to promotion are identification, product information, and use of promotional techniques. The brand and/or company name, as well as that of the product itself, should be clearly indicated. If the firm's national advertising is to be totally effective, the consumer must be able to immediately identify the product on the retailers' shelves. This is especially true if several competing brands are displayed together.

Information about the product must also be incorporated into the package design. In addition to that which is required by law, certain other information may be helpful. Alternative uses of the product, and methods of prolonging its life or otherwise getting greater enjoyment from it might be beneficial to the consumer and could help in selling the product.

In addition, some firms are including *instant coupons,* cents-off coupons affixed to the package that can be used immediately upon purchase of the product, and on-package sweepstakes or games. Examples of the latter are rub-off game cards placed in a specific number of packages with many chances to win. These have been popular with fast-food outlets.[34]

Finally, specific promotional techniques should be used in the package design.

---

[32]See Anna Sobczynski, ''Avenues of Design — Old and New,'' *Advertising Age* (August 9, 1982): M-5-7.

[33]See Walter Stern, ''Design Research: Beauty or Beast,'' *Advertising Age* (March 9, 1981): 43–44.

[34]Ed Meyer, ''It's in the Package,'' *Advertising Age* (May 17, 1982): M-27.

Color (red for hot, blue for cool, etc.) should be carefully selected. Limericks, slogans, special product benefits, and other reflections of effective promotion appeals can be worked into the design. Even the sizes and the number of sizes available to the consumer can be factors in promoting the sale of the product. An effective promotional feature of some packages is their usefulness for other purposes after the product has been consumed. For years, cheese spreads have been packaged in glasses that can be used later for breakfast juices. Pharmaceutical items sometimes come in old-fashioned apothecary bottles that can later serve as decorations. The decanters used in packaging alcholic beverages at Christmas time are attractive reusable containers. A few years ago, even the sacks in which cattle and other stock feed were sold were of material that could be converted into homemade dresses!

Changing the Package

A package design can never be considered permanent. Periodic design audits are essential, and they should be complete analyses covering everything from the original objective of the design to consumer acceptance of the package.[35]

A package design can last for years, but it is sometimes necessary to alter the design to be consistent with changing objectives, to maintain a contemporary image, or for some other reason. Classic examples of package changes over a period of many years include Morton's salt, Kellogg's corn flakes, Quaker Oats, and Coca-Cola.

A package change may be implemented gradually or suddenly, and the method selected usually reflects the reason for the change. A gradual change may take several years to complete, and each part of the change is made in such a subtle way that the consumer may not even be aware of the difference. If the reason for changing the design is simply to keep up-to-date, the gradual change is recommended.[36] Satisfied customers do not like to see their "old friends" change. Moreover, a radical change in the package design may make it difficult for the consumer to find the product on the retailer's shelf.

On the other hand, if the reason for changing the package is not simply to keep up-to-date but is rather to reflect a major change in objectives or strategy, a sudden change may be desirable. If a company wants to completely change the image consumers have of the product (such as the case of Marlboro cigarettes when its feminine image was changed to masculine), it is usually desirable to erase the old image quickly and make a sudden, radical change in package design.

Point-of-Purchase Materials

Of the several sales promotion devices that reach the consumer through the retailer, perhaps none is as important as point-of-purchase materials (POP). Formerly called point-of-sale, but changed to reflect the consumer orientation

---

[35]Roy Parcels, "Ten Steps to Profitable Packages," *Advertising Age* 48, pt. 3 (5 Sept. 1977): 31–34.

[36]See Walter P. Marguilies, "Don't Shock Buyers—Subtle Package Updates are Best," *Advertising Age* (19 Feb. 1979): 53–54.

espoused by firms today, its volume exceeded 5.88 billion dollars in 1981.[37] POP is said to have the lowest cost-per-thousand of all media.[38]

POP advertising consists of those promotion materials to which the consumer is exposed at the point of purchase (the retail store). It includes merchandise racks and displays of various kinds; signs and posters such as counter cards, or banners and streamers hung on walls or on wires suspended from the ceiling; window arrangements; and any other promotional device in connection with the product at the point of purchase. Some firms even use compact projectors placed at the counter or some other convenient location to project promotional films continually.[39]

A point-of-purchase device first introduced in 1971 and now enjoying a revival is the shopping cart medium. Eight- by ten-inch laminated cards, or *mini-billboards* are inserted into plastic holders attached to the fronts of the carts. The medium is operated by companies such as Actmedia, Ad-Va-Carts, and Grocery Impressions, Inc., who sign up supermarkets and pay them a flat fee for the use of the carts. They then sell space to advertisers in four-week *flights,* up to 13 per year. The average cost-per-thousand (CPM) is between 70 and 75 cents; clients have included General Foods, Bristol-Myers Co., Quaker Oats Co., Kellogg Co., and Procter & Gamble.[40]

Companies spend a great deal of time and money to produce effective POP materials, although a survey of dairy products by the American Dairy Association showed that the height of materials and their location were more important than the materials themselves.[41] POP does more to trigger sales, perhaps, than any other single promotional device. One study showed that it is superior to a price special in producing increased product sales, although a synergism exists when the two are combined.[42]

Major Purposes

POP materials are especially effective in accomplishing two purposes: to serve as reminders, and to stimulate unplanned purchases. Consumers become rather fickle in the contemporary purchasing environment; when faced with countless choices in the supermarket they tend to forget any brand loyalty they had before entering the store. Point-of-purchase materials may restore brand loyalty by reminding consumers of the information they were exposed to in the mass media. Of course, a completely effective promotion program requires that the consumer be kept aware of the manufacturer's brand and its appeal at all times to insure consideration of the brand in connection with the purchase decision.

---

[37]As reported in an untitled, undated pamphlet of the Point-of-Purchase Advertising Institute.

[38]Howard Stumpf, "Point of Purchase has 'Lowest' CPM: Study," *Advertising Age* (25 Oct. 1976): 80.

[39]"AV Stops Them in the Aisles," *Sales and Marketing Management* 119 (12 Dec. 1977): 51–53.

[40]See Bernie Whalen, "Need for Competitive Edge at Retail Creates Boom in Shopping Cart Ads," *Marketing News* 15, no. 10 (November 13, 1981): 1, 5, and Anna Sobczynski, "Inside the Store, the Selling Never Stops," *Advertising Age* (March 15, 1982): M-30–33.

[41]"How to turn P-0-P into Sales Dollars" *Progressive Grocer* 56, pt. 1 (June 1977): 83–89.

[42]Arch G. Woodside and Gerald L. Waddle, "Sales Effects of In-Store Advertising," *Journal of Advertising Research* 15, no. 3 (June 1975): 29–33.

The number of impulse purchases and the kind that occur when shoppers do their meal planning in the store are greatly increased by POP materials. How many times have you walked down a supermarket aisle and picked up a jar of olives just because a particularly enticing sign urged you to buy it?

Major Problem

Reaching the consumer with point-of-purchase materials requires the cooperation of the retailer. The problem of getting retailer cooperation is somewhat the same as with trade promotion activities, except that the devices used in trade promotion are aimed *at the retailer* and POP is aimed at the *consumer* through the retailer.

In addition to the natural resistance to the manufacturer's pleas for promotional help, there is another very good reason for the retailer's defensive attitude toward allowing the placement of POP materials in the store. Imagine the clutter if the POP materials of all the hundreds of manufacturers producing the thousands of items sold in a supermarket were displayed in a single store!

Thus much of the material received by the retailer is simply thrown away without ever being used; or it if is used, it is often discarded too quickly. Although supermarkets seem to be using more materials than they formerly did, they are being very selective.[43] Perhaps the traditional methods of getting the POP materials to the retailer need revision. Indiscriminately enclosing counter cards, shelf stickers, and other items in the cases of merchandise shipped to the retailer may simply invite their immediate disposal, and materials left by sales reps without explanation or sent by mail can very easily end up in the trash. The solution may lie in merchandising the POP materials. Using this approach and presenting superior materials might decrease the waste. If in addition to these measures, the manufacturer's representative discusses with the retailer the kinds of materials the retailer wants or would use, there might be less resistance to the manufacturer's request.

In-Store Demonstrations

Another sales promotion device aimed at the consumer through the retailer is the in-store demonstration. It is less frequently used than some of the other devices, but it can be quite effective for some products under the right conditions.

A professional "demonstrator" employed by the manufacturer, with the permission of the retailer, sets up a booth or an area in the store and demonstrates the product to consumer passers-by. The method is successfully used in connection with several different product categories. Cheese spreads or crackers are sometimes demonstrated in supermarkets. The demonstrator offers each consumer in the area a sample of the product to be tasted or eaten on the spot. In this case, the sales promotion is a combination of in-store demonstration and sampling. Another product category with which the method is used is cosmetics. The proper selection and use of cosmetic items are demonstrated, often by using cooperative customers as models.

---

[43]"Supermarket Panel Cites Growing Interest in P.O.P." *Advertising Age* (30 Aug. 1976): 2, 50.

The demonstration method is also used with some hard goods items, such as vegetable choppers and blender-type appliances. In some cases, cookware is demonstrated, and in one demonstration eggs were actually fried in a pan coated with a substance that prevented sticking.

The retailer will agree to such in-store demonstrations if it appears that they will increase the sale of the product in the store or generate store traffic. Otherwise, the natural resistance to such things usually prevails.

Trading Stamps

Trading stamps are not a part of the manufacturer's promotion program, but are initiated by the retailer or the stamp company. Trading stamps seem to have peaks and valleys of popularity. A few years ago they were used extensively by many retailers including some of the large chains, but their popularity now seems to be low. Their purpose is to serve as a patronage motive for buying at the store giving the stamps. The customer is given stamps at the rate of ten for each dollar's worth of merchandise purchased; when a sufficient number of stamps has been accumulated, they can be exchanged for desired premiums displayed either in a catalog or in a stamp redemption store. The retailer buys the stamps from stamp companies, the oldest of which is Sperry & Hutchinson (S&H), at a cost of between 2 and 3 percent of sales.

The justification for using stamps, however, has been vigorously debated over the years. From the retailer's point of view, it is argued that when not many different "brands" of stamps are available at the various stores in an area, their use can build a kind of pseudo-loyalty to the few stores giving them. But when many different stamps are given in an area, no single store benefits greatly. From the consumer's point of view, there is a question as to whether stamps are actually free or whether prices are higher in stores giving stamps than in stores not giving them. Stamp-givers deny that they raise their prices to pay for the stamps.[44]

TRENDS AND DEVELOPMENTS

Current trends and developments in sales promotion include an increase in group promos, or co-op promotions. Such promotions involve two or more companies in a single promotion; while they are sometimes difficult to organize and implement, they can be quite effective. Furthermore, they can reduce costs enormously. To be completely effective, there should be one large brand as a principle focus, with smaller compatible brands tying in.[45] In addition, retailer cooperation with respect to proper displays is essential for maximum success.

Many firms are using *overlays* in their sales promotion programs. This involves using two or three devices at the same time, such as cents-off coupons

---

[44]See Ed Zotti, "They Take a Licking but Keep on Sticking," *Advertising Age* (March 15, 1982): M-40-41.

[45]Louis J. Haugh, "How Group Promos Work," *Advertising Age* (April 27, 1981): 56.

combined with a self-liquidating premium, or a refund combined with a sweep-stake. The combined impact seems to increase consumer attention and involvement. The use of "800 number" promotions is also increasing, and allows consumers to call the toll-free number for free coupons or entry blanks for sweepstakes.[46]

Manufacturers are making use of self-liquidating premium offers to gain in-store displays. These are often referred to as *dealer loaders* because they tend to encourage dealers to stock more than average quantities of the merchandise. Any way that the manufacturer can use a tie-in with the trade (middlemen) adds to the effectiveness of the promotion. Associating the promotion with some event — national (such as the World Series) or regional (such as state fairs) — may be successful if it is carefully planned. Coupon books and "everybody wins" sweepstakes are also becoming popular. Not to be overlooked, either, is the universal marketing tenet of market segmentation. A promotional effort can be quite effective when it is targeted at a specific segment.[47]

SUMMARY

As a tool of promotion, sales promotion is used both to generate support for the manufacturer's activities and to directly stimulate consumer response after national advertising has presented product information. The latter has been the subject of this chapter. Sales promotion devices are conveniently divided into those that reach the consumer directly, and those that reach the consumer through the retailer.

Promotion devices that reach the consumer primarily by means other than through the retailer, such as national advertising, direct mail, and door-to-door delivery, include coupons, premiums, contests and sweepstakes, cash refunds, and sampling. Coupons are used to effect a temporary price reduction. A variation of traditional couponing is the use of cross coupons, which involve several different products in a manufacturer's line or several different brands of products. A premium is an item of merchandise given to the consumer or sold at a substantially reduced price (self-liquidating) as an incentive to purchase a product. Premiums may be attached to the product in some way, or they may be mailed to the consumer upon the submission of proof of purchase. Contests and sweepstakes both involve an opportunity to win something. They differ in that contest winners are determined on the basis of the skill with which the entrants perform some activity, and sweepstakes winners are determined by pure chance. Cash refunds are sums returned to the consumer by the manufacturer upon the submission of proof of product purchase and actually represent temporary price reductions. Sampling is providing the consumer with a free trial size of the product; it is effective if the product is equal or superior to existing products.

---

[46]See William A. Robinson, "Promotions Spruce Up," *Advertising Age* (October 12, 1981): S-4, and Russ Bowman, "Advice of Redeeming Value," *Advertising Age* (May 4, 1981): S-8-9.

[47]See *ibid.* See also Ed Myer, "Promotion: 29 Things to Remember About It," *Advertising Age* (December 21, 1981): 35.

Some sales promotion devices require the cooperation and/or utilization of the retailer in reaching the consumer. The package itself is a sales promotion device as it sits on the retailer's shelf. Point-of-purchase advertising consists of promotion materials displayed in the retail store. Their purpose is to serve as reminder advertising and to stimulate unplanned purchases. In-store demonstrations sponsored by manufacturers are effective in promoting the sale of some products. The use of trading stamps – a promotional device of the retailer – is sometimes effective in building store loyalty.

Among the trends and developments in sales promotion are an increase in co-op promotions, the use of overlays, toll-free telephone numbers, dealer loaders, coupon books, and sweepstakes where "everybody wins" or where there is a large number of prizes.

QUESTIONS FOR THOUGHT AND REVIEW

1. Explain how sales promotion activities in general supplement a manufacturer's national advertising campaign.
2. What specifically are the objectives of sales promotion activities directed at the consumer? Give some examples of activities you have observed.
3. Why are coupons used for temporary price reduction? Why do manufacturers prefer to use coupons for that purpose rather than simply lower the invoice price of the merchandise?
4. What are *cross coupons?* Can you give some examples?
5. Discuss the problem of coupon misredemption. Can you suggest methods other than those mentioned in the book that can be used to minimize the problem?
6. What is a *premium?* How is a premium different from a coupon? Discuss the pros and cons of attaching the premium to the package versus sending it to the consumer by mail.
7. What is a *self-liquidating premium?* When should it be used instead of a free premium?
8. Compare and contrast *sweepstakes* and *contests.* Why are sweepstakes more popular than contests? Under what conditions would a sweepstakes be considered a lottery? Discuss.
9. Attack and defend the use of cash refunds as a promotional device.
10. When sampling is used as a promotional device, why is it important that the product be as good as or better than existing products? Do you use samples when you receive them?
11. Discuss the various functions of the package. Why is it necessary to consider convenience to the retailer as well as to the consumer in package design?
12. What should be included in the package design with respect to its function as a promotion device?
13. Name some conditions that might suggest the need for a package change. Can you think of examples of package changes?
14. Discuss the question of whether a package change should be gradual or sudden.

15. What are *point-of-purchase (POP)* materials? Why is it important to the manufacturer to try to get retailers to use them?

16. What are the major purposes of POP materials? What is the major problem in connection with their use? How can the problem be overcome?

17. Describe some in-store demonstrations you have been exposed to. Do you think the in-store demonstration is effective as a promotional device? Explain.

18. Discuss the pros and cons of trading stamps.

19. Name some current trends and developments in sales promotion, and explain why in your opinion they are occurring.

20

PUBLICITY AND PUBLIC RELATIONS

Unlike the other elements of the promotion mix (advertising, personal selling, and sales promotion) publicity is not under the direct control of the organization sponsoring it. Whether or not any particular item of publicity is used depends entirely upon decisions made by representatives of the media in which its appearance is proposed. Nevertheless, a carefully planned publicity program can be an extremely valuable component of an organization's promotional effort.

Publicity is a part of public relations and is one of the tools used in creating favorable relationships with various groups inside and outside the organization. When it is used as an element of the promotion mix it is, in a sense, "borrowed" from public relations for that specific purpose.

CONCEPT DISTINCTIONS

The concepts of public relations and publicity are sometimes erroneously considered to be synonymous. Therefore, let us distinguish between the two and indicate their places in the promotion scheme of things.

Public Relations

Public relations is really an umbrella term because it refers to the totality of an organization's behavior with respect to the society in which it operates.[1] It is at the same time a condition, a philosophy, and a function. It is a condition in that it refers to existing relationships between the organization and the social environment; such relationships are reflected in the notions "reputation" and "image." It is a philosophy because effective management requires a clearly defined perspective regarding the most appropriate kind of relationship the organization should have with its publics. And it is a function when management designs and implements programs and activities for the purpose of creating or maintaining the desired relationships.

Thus public relations affects and is affected by promotion, but it is much broader than that. Virtually all the functions of an organization should be performed in the name of public relations if maximum effectiveness is to be achieved. The same can be said for other activities not specifically identified as *functions*. An effective public relations program reflects positive action in many aspects of the organization's behavior and concern for public relations in its total behavior.

Publicity

Publicity is primarily one of the tools of public relations, but it is used in the promotion mix when circumstances warrant.

Any newsworthy item about an organization appearing in a mass medium at no cost to the organization is publicity. The items might deal with products or ser-

---

[1]For definitions of public relations, see Scott M. Cutlip and Allen H. Center, *Effective Public Relations*, 5th ed. (Englewood Cliffs, N.J.: Prentice-Hall, 1978), ch. 1, and C. Thomas Wilck, "Toward a Definition of Public Relations," *Public Relations Journal* 33 (Dec. 1977): 26–27.

vices; the people in the organization; ideas, activities, and events identified with the organization; or any other information of potential interest to the public. The fact that the sponsor does not pay for the space or time in which the item appears differentiates publicity from advertising. Publicity's primary use as a part of the promotion mix is in connection with publicizing products and product-related ideas; it has been suggested that publicity is not used enough.[2]

PUBLIC RELATIONS IN CONTEMPORARY SOCIETY

Every organization has public relations if it has been in existence for any length of time. An organization has to have some relationship with its publics; the relations may be good or bad. A public's perspective of an organization's relationship with it is reflected in the organization's reputation or image.

The reputation of business in recent years, rightly or wrongly, has become considerably tarnished. Almost no segment of business has escaped the attack of activists identified with some social cause such as environmentalism, consumerism, civil rights, welfare, medical care, employee safety, and women's liberation. The very institution of business is denigrated on the grounds that it is so involved in the pursuit of its self-interests that it is blind to the needs of society. Certain industries have been particular targets. The energy "industry" for example — oil, gas, coal, and nuclear — is especially vulnerable to attack, as is the lumber industry.

Not only are entire industries criticized, but specific firms in their respective industries are singled out for attack at manufacturer, wholesaler, and retailer levels. Some of the criticism is justified and some is not. In any event, adverse public announcements about a firm or its products can affect consumer attitudes toward the product.[3]

Negative publicity, with its adverse effect on a company's image, is much more prevalent in the media than is the positive kind. This is understandable, of course, when one recognizes the traditional and perhaps desirable position the press has always taken with respect to the behavior of any institution whose activities can affect large segments of society. Members of the press see it as their duty to expose the practices of any organization that can be detrimental to any group of people. As a result, many marketers have had to deal with blots of varying magnitudes on their images and reputations. Unfortunately, such exposés can be damaging even if there is no proof of ill effects on the consumer, or if there are ill effects but the firm involved is itself innocent.

Manufacturers of artificial sweeteners such as cyclamates and saccharin have been affected by the considerable publicity in recent years regarding their possible connection with cancer. Companies in the asbestos industry have also been attacked. Procter and Gamble voluntarily withdrew its Rely tampons from the mar-

---

[2]See Donald G. Softness, "What Product PR Can Do for You in Today's Advertising World," *Advertising Age* (2 Aug. 1976): 19–20.

[3]See Terrell G. Williams, "Adverse Product Publicity and Consumer Attitudes," *University of Michigan Business Review* 29, no. 5 (Sept. 1977): 1–8.

ket after the publicized charges that it was the cause of toxic shock syndrome. Johnson & Johnson was an innocent victim in the highly publicized Tylenol (McNeil Consumer Products Company) episode involving the deaths of several people who purchased packages of the product in which poison had been injected by persons totally unrelated to the company. Nevertheless, the company had to overcome the public's resulting resistance to using Tylenol.

Equally disastrous or perhaps more so are the unfounded rumors that find their way into various facets of the press. "Wearing Jockey Shorts makes men sterile," "The Coors Brewery supports gun control," and "R. J. Reynolds Tobacco owns marijuana fields in Mexico" are three examples of many that have been started and of more that will undoubtedly arise. Sometimes, of course, a rumor is so absurd that it will simply die out in time. Usually, however, the affected companies must try to kill such rumors before they do irreparable harm. A firm may tackle the rumor head-on—publicly recognizing it but presenting counterarguments; or it may rebut the rumor without really repeating it.[4]

Negative publicity can also result from product recalls whether they are voluntary or not. The very fact that a company calls a product in for adjustment, for whatever reason, tends to cast suspicion of inferiority or slipshod work on the part of the company and its products. Because of this, it is to the firm's advantage to cooperate with the media in publicizing the recall so its side of the issue will be presented.[5]

Thus a growing number of corporate executives are expanding their public relations programs to counteract possible damage to the reputations of their companies from adverse publicity. In fact, they are increasingly taking the position that their best approach is to identify possible areas of vulnerability in advance, to correct them if necessary, and to forestall adverse criticism by means of carefully planned public relations programs.[6]

The Public Relations Department

Most major nonprofit and business organizations now view public relations as a function—that is, requiring some sort of positive action to achieve the desired relationships with appropriate publics. Even the government has public relations people, properly called government communicators but perhaps better known as "flacks," whose job is to publicize such government concerns as product recalls, helmets for motorcyclists, and drunk drivers.[7]

Thus public relations has finally "arrived." Historically considered a nonessential function, or even the practice of cover-up or deception, it has now achieved

---

[4]Jim Montgomery, "Rumor-Plagued Firms Use Various Strategies to Keep Damage Low," *The Wall Street Journal* (February 6, 1979): 1.

[5]See R. Seymour Smith, "How to Plan for Crisis Communications," *Public Relations Journal* 35, no. 3 (March 1979): 17–18.

[6]For an in-depth discussion see "The Corporate Image: PR to the Rescue," *Business Week* (22 Jan. 1979): 47–61.

[7]"Washington PR Staffs Dream Up Ways to Get Agencies' Stories Out," *The Wall Street Journal* (May 23, 1979): 1.

a status comparable to production or marketing.[8] The essence of this view has been expressed publicly by representatives of such firms as Crown Zellerbach, Ford Motor Company, Chase Manhattan Bank, and others.[9] The result is that most major firms have set up a public relations department whose prime responsibility is listening to the firm's various publics and responding appropriately.

An Organization's Publics

Any organization has many publics. The *general public* is everyone whom the organization affects in any way. The size of the general public varies with different organizations. The oil industry's general public consists of almost everyone in society because the actions and the behavior of the firms composing the oil industry affect almost everyone. The same is true with labor unions and numerous other organizations with national significance and impact, as well as the Federal government. On the other hand, hundreds of businesses and other organizations have general publics much smaller than the whole of society because the effects of their actions are restricted to smaller groups of people.

Certain parts of a PR program can be addressed to the public as a whole, but any general public is composed of people with so many different backgrounds and interests that opinions, beliefs, and attitudes with respect to an organization are not the same among all the people whom its actions affect. The range of an organization's reputation in its general public often runs the gamut from shabby to sterling. And if an organization is to build and maintain favorable relationships with everyone whom it affects, it must subdivide its general public into smaller publics and create public relations programs designed specifically for each group.

The situation is analogous to developing marketing (and promotion) strategy in that the general public must be segmented into groups delineated by factors such as age, sex, income, and education; and strategies are developed to reach each segment. Thus, the pair of terms *general public* and *smaller publics* is analogous to the pair of terms *total market* and *market segments*.

The number and kinds of publics an organization has depends on its nature and the circumstances associated with its operation, but certain publics are common to all corporate firms. These can be conveniently divided into those directly related to the firm and its operation and those whose relationship is somewhat indirect.

Directly Related Publics

Among the publics directly related to the operation of the firm are stockholders, ultimate consumers, middlemen, employees, and suppliers. At first glance it may seem odd that a firm must maintain good relations with its owners (the stockhold-

---

[8]See B. G. Yovovich, ''Skills Needed, Status Growing,'' *Advertising Age* (January 5, 1981): S-1–4.

[9]See ''How Business Faces a Hostile Climate,'' *Business Week* (September 16, 1972): 70–72, and Joseph Nolan, ''Protect Your Public Image with Performance,'' *Harvard Business Review* 53, no. 2 (March–April 1975): 135–42.

ers). But since many corporate firms are owned by hundreds of investors who play no part in the management of the firm but whose invested capital is necessary for the firm's survival, it is essential to perpetuate their approval. Ultimate consumers must think favorably of the firm and its products or, given a choice, they may transfer their loyalties to competitors. The attitudes of retailers, wholesalers, and other middlemen toward the firm are significant to the success of firms requiring their services. Employees, of course *are* the company to many outsiders, and they reflect their own perceptions of the company to those with whom they come in contact. And suppliers can often help or hurt the firms to which they sell.

Indirectly Related Publics

In addition to the various publics directly related to the firm, there are certain other publics that are indirectly affected by the operation of the firm, or that have a special interest in the firm for some reason or other. These publics, too, must be the targets of public relations effort if the entire program is to be successful. Such publics may include the people in government at all levels, environmentalists, civil rights proponents, women's liberation advocates, the people concerned with the whole area of health, education, and welfare, and others. It is these publics that are especially vocal in their criticisms of business and firms; they are prime targets for concentrated public relations effort.

Instruments of Public Relations

If an organization allows relationships with its publics to develop naturally, public relations is not a function for that firm because *function* implies positive action of some sort. Management that deliberately chooses not to take any positive action may be expressing a public relations *philosophy*. But where management plans and implements programs for the purpose of creating or perpetuating favorable relationships with its publics, or building a reputation or image, *public relations* means condition, philosophy and function. As a function, public relations requires the use of certain tools in the same sense that promotion as a function does.

The foundations for an effective public relations program are a clean house and societal concern. No amount of public relations effort can repudiate the manipulation or exploitation of consumers. Nor can it camouflage social unconcern, although it is not to be inferred that every business organization should necessarily participate actively in the promotion of social "causes." Every organization should be aware of the impact of its activities on society and should govern its behavior to serve society most effectively in the purposes for which it exists. At the same time, it should prevent any deleterious effects on society that might result from its actions.

On the other hand, a firm may choose to become actively involved in social causes.[10] And if such is the case, the payoff is not only self-satisfaction but also a

---

[10]See William A. Robinson, "Promotion Through Good Deeds," *Advertising Age* (23 Oct. 1978): 72, 74.

building block in the creation of good public relations. Participation in social causes and other facets of civic improvement comes under the general heading of *public affairs,* and as such it is an instrument of public relations.

But just being a good business citizen is not enough for a company these days. People must *know* that such is the case, and letting them know is the purpose of a public relations program. Public opinion with respect to the organization and its behavior must be changed, or strengthened as the case may be, by informing people of the angelic nature of the organization and its activities through the use of certain tools, or instruments, identified with the function. The purpose is to create an accurate picture of the company; if the public portrayal of an organization is merely a facade to conceal undesirable behavior, the public relations program is doomed to failure from the start.

Thus the instruments of public relations are designed to inform and "educate" the people composing the various publics of an organization. The number of such instruments is limited, perhaps, only by the imagination of public relations practitioners. But certain devices are of particular importance. Lobbying, for example, is used to generate favorable opinion toward an organization and its causes among legislators considering bills which, if passed, would have an effect on the organization. Lobbying activities are not restricted to business firms; environmentalists, consumerists, labor unions, and others are extensive users of the lobbying device.

Corporate advertising is another device often identified with public relations, although it is equally appropriate to consider it a tool of promotion.

Perhaps the most important instrument of public relations is publicity. The very nature of public relations, in fact, is interwined with publicity. Whatever good that an organization is or does should be publicized for maximum success in building or maintaining the desired image or reputation.

Opportunities abound; none should be overlooked. In making donations to charitable organizations, for example, it has been suggested that the cause of public relations can be served more effectively if rather than sending a check, management requests that a representative of the receiving organization come to the firm to pick it up.[11] In doing this, greater visibility is possible since the representative can then be exposed to various aspects of the presenting firm and perhaps be inclined to spread the good word voluntarily. Many things a firm does can be successfully exploited for public relations purposes if management is only alert to them. Good public relations programs reflect attention to every opportunity to gain favorable publicity for the organization.

PUBLICITY AS A PART OF THE PROMOTION MIX

A strong public relations program is essential to a firm's survival in today's critical and questioning society. An unsavory reputation virtually precludes success in any

---

[11]See Richard R. Conarroe, "How to Turn Up Acres of Publicity in Your Own Back Yard," *Sales and Marketing Management* 117 (9 Aug. 1976): 66, 71–72.

activity of a firm. But *market-oriented* public relations, particularly as it is reflected in publicity, has a more specific purpose than does the public relations program in general.[12] It is strictly a marketing tool identified with promotion, and is used to complement the other elements of the promotion mix.[13] In fact, when publicity is coordinated with advertising, personal selling, and sales promotion, a synergistic effect is bound to result.

Typically, however, publicity's role in the promotion mix is smaller than that of the other three components, due largely to the fact that it is more difficult to plan and implement than the other three. But in recent years it has begun to play a larger part in the promotion mixes of some companies.[14] Bacardi Puerto Rican rum, for example, gives much credit for an increase in sales to a publicity campaign developed for it by the firm Compton Public Relations, involving the creation and publicizing of recipes calling for rum. The firm of Manning, Selvage & Lee launched a very successful publicity campaign for Johnson Wax on how to face up to and eliminate cockroaches.[15]

Beech-Nut, Inc., a major baby food producer, used publicity as the main component in its promotion mix for introducing its baby foods with no salt and little or no sugar. The baby food industry had been pressured for several years by nutritionists, physicians, consumer activitists, and others to remove the salt and sugar from baby foods. Beech-Nut listened — and acted. The campaign included the use of a number of techniques, such as providing samples of the product to editors of appropriate publications, arranging interviews with media personnel, issuing original and creative press releases, and using numerous other devices to attract press coverage. An underlying theme of the campaign was that the firm would "make baby food for baby's taste, not mother's mature tastes."[16]

Responsibility for the Publicity Function

Since publicity is a kind of hybrid among the elements of the promotion mix (being identified with both public relations and promotion), responsibilities are not standardized. Even the names by which it is identified in the promotion function confuse the issue. Sometimes it is referred to as "market-oriented public relations" and other times as "product publicity." Thus in some companies the responsibility lies in the public relations department while in other companies it is the responsibility of promotion in the marketing department. Many companies rely heavily on outside public relations agencies, somewhat analogous to advertising agencies in connection with the advertising function.

Compounding the issue even further is the fact that some advertising agen-

---

[12]Publicity is also effectively used by trade associations. See Ronald N. Levy, "The Role of Publicity in Association Public Relations," *Public Relations Journal* 33 (Mar. 1977): 14–17.

[13]See John Peters, "Good PR Strategy Can Reinforce All Efforts in Communications," *Industrial Marketing* 61, pt. 1 (Feb. 1976): 50–51, 54–55.

[14]Theodore J. Gage, "PR Ripens Role in Marketing," *Advertising Age* (January 5, 1981): S-10-11.

[15]*Ibid.*

[16]Jeanne Gumm, "Public Relations is Primary Element in Beech-Nut Food's Marketing Program," *Advertising Age* (February 6, 1978): 3.

cies have established public relations departments, or have merged with public relations firms. The latter has given rise to questions about possible conflicts of interest with respect to clients. When mergers occur, the public relations "partner" may have clients who are direct competitors of clients of the advertising agency "partner." The 1980 merger of J. Walter Thompson, the second largest advertising agency in the United States, with Hill & Knowlton, the largest public relations firm, is such an example. Among the Thompson accounts were Goodyear, Chevron, Lever Brothers, Ford, and Hyatt. Hill & Knowlton accounts included Goodrich, Texaco, Procter & Gamble, Mazda, and Marriott.[17]

Regardless of who is responsible for handling publicity, however, when used as a tool of promotion, publicity's function is the same as that of the other elements of the promotion mix — persuasive communication related to products, services, and ideas. Immediate objectives associated with its use might include announcements of new products, information about new features of existing products, new production techniques, and new uses for existing products. Its use may be aimed at simply informing consumers of such things, or it might be designed to change attitudes. In any event, favorable opinion of the product is the desired result.

Characteristics of Publicity

A major characteristic of publicity that differentiates it from the other elements of the promotion mix is that it always involves a third party (editor, a program director, or someone else outside the sponsoring organization) who determines whether to use the item, as well as when and how. Such mandatory third person involvement puts the use of publicity items at the discretion of an outsider and beyond the control of the promotion manager. Thus it is sometimes difficult to make concrete plans regarding its use in the total promotion program. On the other hand, the fact that an outsider is involved makes the message more credible then when it appears in an advertisement. People exposed to the message tend to perceive the medium through which it is transmitted as the source of the message rather than the sponsoring organization which, they feel, would be presenting a biased viewpoint. They know who the source is in advertising.

Publicity is free. Or so it seems. There is no charge for the space or time, but costs associated with generating the activities or events to be publicized may be extensive, and it can be expensive to prepare and merchandise publicity releases. Furthermore, it is philosophically wrong to consider publicity free because this implies that it is not worth anything. Such an opinion does not encourage acceptance of the item by an editor.[18]

People tend to read publicity items more than advertisements because publicity items are perceived as news. Thus publicity may not only reach people with a greater impact than advertising does but also reach people who do not read

---

[17]Jeffrey H. Birnbaum, "Merger of Thompson, Hill & Knowlton Could Produce Conflict over Clients," *Wall Street Journal* (June 4, 1980): 10.

[18]See Martin Isherwood, "Editorial Publicity: How To Reach Your Audience Anywhere," *Industrial Marketing* 63 (Oct. 1978): 76–82.

advertisements at all. Moreover, the credibility of the medium may favorably affect the reader's perception of the message.

There is no opportunity for repeat exposures to a publicity message. Editors only consider publicity items if they believe them to be newsworthy; once run, they are no longer news. Of course, an item may occasionally come to the attention of the editors of several different media at the same time, and if more than one editor uses it, some people may see the message more than once. But rarely, if ever, would the same item appear twice in the same medium.

Forms of Publicity

Among the most common forms of publicity as a promotion tool are news releases, feature articles, pictorial releases, tapes and films, background editorial material, speeches, and news conferences.

News Releases

The most widely used form of publicity is the news release. It consists of from 200 to 300 words describing a newsworthy event concerning the subject for which publicity is sought. It should be typewritten and should always include the name and telephone number of the person to call for further information. An editor considering using the release will often have questions that must be answered by a representative of the sponsoring firm. If appropriate, glossy photos should be included with the news release sent to print media.

Feature Articles

Feature articles are longer than news releases, usually consisting of from 1,000 to 3,000 words. They differ from news releases, also, in that they are not necessarily "news" as such but often deal with stories about the company and its products, or management philosophies, or some other topic of interest to people whom the medium reaches and who might respond to such promotion. Moreover, unlike news releases that might be sent to any of several media, feature articles are usually tailored to fit a specific medium.

Pictorial Releases

Pictorial releases are pictures or illustrations submitted to media. They may or may not accompany a news release or a feature article and, as with all publicity items, the decision to use them or not is the editor's. Thus the admonition is to make them relevant, interesting, and newsworthy.

Tapes and Films

Taped or filmed information about a company or its products is sometimes sent to radio and TV stations. These devices are somewhat analogous to news releases and feature articles in that they can be as short as a 5-minute film clip to be presented as a news release or they may constitute a 30- or 60-minute ''program'' corresponding to a feature article.

Background Editorial Materials

Sometimes background material for use by editors in composing the items on the editorial page can be submitted and accepted. The editorials themselves are usually written by the media staff, but if information submitted by a company can provide ideas for editors, some degree of publicity for the company can result.

Speeches

Speeches by organization executives are increasingly popular as publicity devices. They are used more, perhaps, in connection with the total public relations program than as a publicity device in promotion, but under certain conditions they can also aid in the promotion function. Unique features of a product, for example, or unusual aspects of the production process that may be newsworthy to certain publics may be appropriate topics for speeches at various kinds of meetings. It has been suggested that executives should not only accept opportunities for such public appearances but actively seek them out.[19]

News Conferences

News conferences are used more rarely, perhaps, than any of the other devices. They involve inviting a number of representatives of the press to a meeting at which executives of the organization discuss the publicity item. They are particularly appropriate when understanding can only be complete through discussion and question and answer exchanges. They are probably inappropriate when a news release would suffice or when it is inadvisable to stimulate rivalry among various media with respect to the item.

Implementation of Publicity in Promotion

Publicity is a particularly useful element of the promotion mix in connection with the introduction of new products. But it must be coordinated properly with the other elements. This means that it must be planned in such a way as to appear *before* exposing people to the other elements. In fact, unless publicity is used first, it is unlikely that it can be used at all. Editors will agree to run publicity items if the items are newsworthy, and they are not newsworthy if the public is already aware of them! Properly used publicity can condition consumers to be more receptive to appeals made in the subsequent promotional effort.

Using publicity is not the hit or miss venture it might appear to be, but

---

[19]Carl R. Terzian, ''Going to Communicate? Try Speaking!'' *Public Relations Journal* 32 (May 1976): 16–19.

requires careful planning. Publishing lead time, for example, necessitates advance planning to time the appearance of the items appropriately vis-à-vis the use of the other elements. Furthermore, publicity items must be merchandised to editors, much as advertising is to middlemen and other people relevant to its effectiveness.[20]

All publicity items should be expertly written. Editors have the prerogative of rewriting the items, deleting certain things or not using the item at all, but they are more inclined to be receptive to well-written items. News releases, and all publicity material, should be real news and should be presented from the user's or reader's point of view of the sponsoring firm.[21] This is consistent with our earlier discussions of perception and communication theory. Moreover, the most important points should appear first in the release or article because often readers do not read the entire thing and an editor may simply cut out the last part.

It is usually unwise to send a release to a number of different editors hoping that one or more will run the item. Rather, it is better to select appropriate media on the basis of their editorial philosophy, content, and circulation and to tailor the items for those specific media.[22] Better acceptance can be obtained, too, if the sponsoring firm deals directly with the editorial specialists in the appropriate fields rather than with someone whose interests and responsibilities are more general.

Evaluation of the Publicity Effort

The standard procedure for achieving maximum effectiveness in evaluating any activity is to follow a sequence of four steps

1. Establish objectives
2. Measure performance
3. Compare performance with objectives to determine the degree of accomplishment
4. Take corrective action

Unfortunately, because of the nature of publicity and the lack of control a promotion strategist has over it, accurate evaluation is almost impossible. To be sure, objectives can be established (in communication terms) as was indicated in our discussion of promotion objectives earlier in the text. Thus if the objective were to inform a certain number of people in a defined market within three months about a forthcoming new product, one could survey the market at the end of the period; if the statistical techniques were soundly conceived, the resulting figures could be compared with the objective and whatever corrective action was necessary could be taken.

But because of the ever-present uncertainty associated with the use of pub-

---

[20]See Gerald S. Schwartz, ''Planning Product Publicity Pays Off,'' *Nation's Business* 66, no. 9 (Sept. 1978): 35.

[21]See Paul Hugh Zahn, ''European PR Uses New Approach in Bid For Editors' Attention,'' *Industrial Marketing* 63, pt. 2 (July 1978): 60, 64.

[22]See ''Why New Product Releases Don't Get Published,'' *Public Relations Journal* 36, no. 1 (January 1980): 43.

licity, it is not likely that many firms use that approach. The approach most firms take is to count the number of exposures — news releases, feature articles, etc. — that appeared in the media during a given period of time. The items are clipped and kept, along with such information as the date of publication and the length and placement of coverage (press clipping services can be retained to do this). The same "count" is made with respect to the minutes of air time on TV and radio devoted to the company's publicity items. These space and time amounts are then used in computing comparable advertising costs, and some idea of the value of the publicity is obtained.

SUMMARY

Publicity differs from the other elements of the promotion mix in that it is not under the direct control of the organization sponsoring it. Its use always requires the concurrence of someone outside the organization, such as an editor or program director. Publicity is primarily a tool of public relations, but it has a specific use in an organization's promotion effort.

Public relations is a multiple concept. It refers to the relationships an organization has with its publics, a philosophy of management in the sense that management determines the kind of relationships it wants, and a function when positive steps are taken to create desired relationships. Publicity, as one of the tools of public relations, is any newsworthy item about an organization that appears in a mass medium at no cost to the organization to which it relates. Negative publicity about a company, including unfounded rumors, frequently appears in the media and must be dealt with by the company. Many firms now have public relations departments to handle these problems and to implement positive policy.

A public relations program must be built on ethical behavior and concern for society; but worthy behavior and commendable actions are not enough. The public must be informed of them, and that is the task of a public relations program. Of particular importance in this regard are lobbying, corporate advertising, and publicity.

It is the publicity part of a public relations program that is especially significant to promotion, and, when used in this sense, it is part of the promotion mix. Publicity is especially important to the introduction of new products and is free as far as space and time costs are concerned. But there is no opportunity for repeat exposures because an item is only news the first time it is run.

Publicity as a promotion tool can take several forms, the most important of which are news releases, feature articles, speeches, and news conferences. News releases are short statements about a product or service; feature articles are longer pieces that are more story or philosophy oriented. Speeches given to interested organizations can be an effective publicity device, as can news conferences. But news conferences should probably replace news releases only when the editors might need a chance to discuss the topic with company representatives to understand the information. Other publicity devices include pictorial releases, tapes and films, and background editorial materials.

Planning is the key element in implementing publicity in promotion. People must be exposed to publicity items before they are exposed to the other elements of the promotion mix. Because of this and also because of required publishing lead time, advance planning is essential. Furthermore, great care should be taken in writing publicity items and in choosing the media in which they appear.

Evaluation of the publicity effort usually is accomplished by counting the number of times a publicity item appears in a given period of time, noting the amount of space or time devoted to the item, and then determining the advertising costs for comparable space and time. Some idea of the value of the publicity is thus obtained.

QUESTIONS FOR THOUGHT AND REVIEW

1. Discuss the notion that all of a company's activities are in the nature of a promotional effort. Is it logical to isolate certain functions? Explain.
2. Define *public relations*. Why might it be considered an "umbrella" term? How does promotion fit into the concept of public relations?
3. What is publicity? Give some examples of publicity items.
4. Explain the statement that all firms have public relations whether they want them or not. How do they develop naturally?
5. Why are firms strengthening their public relations programs? Discuss.
6. Define a *public*. How is it that organizations have several publics? Why is it necessary to develop public relations programs for each one?
7. Explain the analogy of market/market segments to general public/smaller publics.
8. Distinguish between publics directly related to a firm and its operation and those indirectly related. Give some examples of each.
9. Explain the multiple concept of public relations.
10. What is the foundation for an effective public relations program? Can an effective program be developed without it? Discuss.
11. What are the major instruments of public relations? Give some examples of the use of each.
12. Discuss the advantages and disadvantages associated with the fact that publicity involves an outsider to the sponsoring organization. Why is publicity more believable than advertising?
13. Is publicity free? Explain. Why is there no opportunity for repeat exposure?
14. Who is responsible for the publicity function? Explain and discuss.
15. Distinguish between *news releases* and *feature articles* as forms of publicity. Explain the circumstances under which each would be used. Are speeches effective as publicity devices? Why?
16. What is a *news conference?* When can it be appropriately used?
17. Why must publicity appear before advertising or other elements of the promotion mix? How does it help the other elements?
18. Discuss the significance of planning in the use of publicity.

19. If editors are likely to rewrite publicity releases, why is it necessary to use care in writing them? Why put the important points at the beginning of the message?
20. Discuss the importance of carefully selecting the media to send publicity items to, and describe some of the characteristics to use as criteria for the selection.
21. How is the performance of publicity as a promotion tool evaluated? What are the problems?

PART SIX

EPILOGUE

In chapter 21 we shall take a look at what the promotion environment might be in the future and how promotion may have to adjust.

Change in the promotion environment has always been both inevitable and evolutionary. However, it seems that in recent years the process has accelerated. The promotion manager, most certainly, must not only be aware of the changes but must anticipate them.

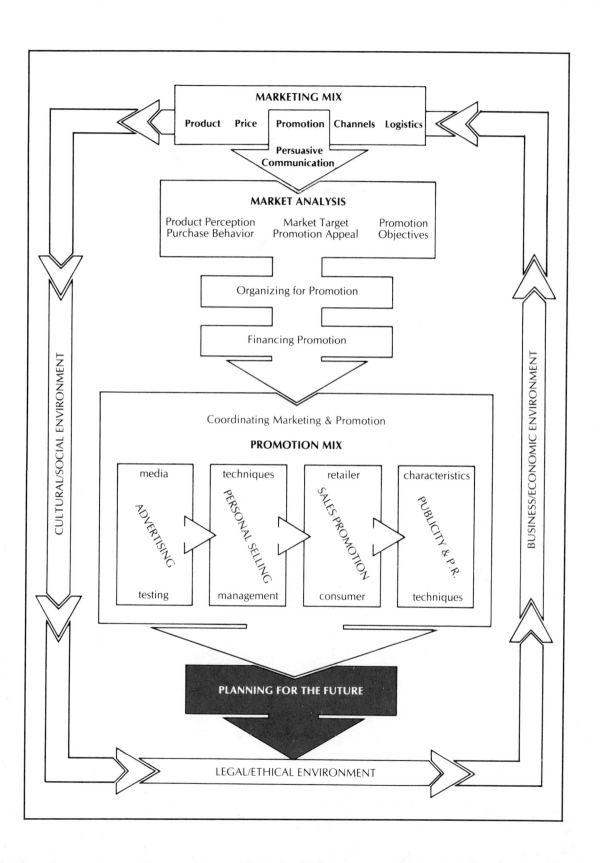

21

PROMOTION IN THE FUTURE

To presume that certain conditions will prevail in the years to come is really nothing more than pure conjecture. Nevertheless, since decisions made in the present determine, in part, an organization's ability to cope with the future, it is necessary to anticipate the direction and magnitude of change. In all matters of speculation, visions differ among the prophets, and the future of promotion is no exception. If you happen to disagree with the inferences presented in the following discussion, draw your own; you could be right!

It seems appropriate to develop our prophecy within the now-familiar framework of relating promotional strategy to the environment in which it operates. Therefore, we shall begin by reexamining certain environmental factors in the light of what they *might* be in the future. Then, with the future environment in mind, we shall focus on the elements of the promotion mix.

THE PROMOTION ENVIRONMENT OF THE FUTURE

A three-way classification of the factors composing the environment for promotion was established as a framework for our earlier discussion. We shall use the same classification for the present discussion (cultural/social, business/economic, and legal/ethical) and select certain factors from each that appear to be particularly significant to environmental conditions in the future. *We shall project these factors to some future date and speculate on their nature.*

Cultural/Social Factors

Among the many characteristics of our culture that have changed, four seem to be especially worth noting: culture homogenization, influencers of behavior, attitudes and values, and life-styles.

Culture Homogenization

Cultural traits that have historically distinguished subcultures within the United States have greatly diminished in number and influence. In some cases they are virtually nonexistent. As each new generation has arrived on the scene, there has been an increased commonality among representative groups of people earlier identified with various subcultures. Traditional tastes and values formerly associated with specific subcultures have been diluted through the declining influence of traditional transmitters of such things and the increasing impact of other influencers. Family life-styles; tastes in foods; fashion acceptance in clothing, furniture, housing, and recreational activities are fairly universal throughout society.

Influencers of Behavior

As individuals in a society, we are at the same time more individualistic and more conforming than ever before. We are a highly educated, perceptive people inclined to chart our own courses. But the courses we chart bear striking resemblances to those of everyone else.

Our individualistic/conforming behavior stems, in part, from the declining influence of the family and the church. Our exposure to model behavior comes from other associations. Peer groups at every stage in the life cycle influence our behavior. As preschool-age children spending a big part of each day in nursery schools or day-care centers because both our parents are pursuing careers, we tend to emulate the behavior of others of our kind. The same tendency prevails throughout our school lives.

Success in our jobs depends a good deal on our behaving in a manner acceptable to those with whom we work. We tend to avoid nonconforming behavior for fear of ostracism; yet we are expected to be our own men and women. We wear the same kinds of clothes, eat the same kinds of food, live in the same kinds of houses, attend the same cocktail parties, hold the same political views, and generally reflect the behavior of our peers — all with a bit of an individual touch. Even when we retire, we join senior citizen organizations of some kind whose unwritten prescribed behavior becomes a pattern for our own.

The common behavior among peers, however, has not resulted from peer pressure alone but also from the influence of the mass media. Advertising, through that vehicle, has played its part, but other stimuli presented through the mass media have been equally influential. Articles, stories, pictures, books, movies, speeches, and television talk shows, for example, have for years depicted a normative behavior that has been accepted by people in their respective peer groups. The forces influencing our behavior, in short, have gone beyond the traditional ones of family and church.

Attitudes and Values

Our attitudes and values are considerably different from what they were a few years ago. It would be impossible to discuss all the changes that have taken place in this respect, but a few are especially significant to promotion.

A major change is our attitude toward ecology in all its ramifications. Just a few years ago, most of us were apathetic in this regard. We took our environment for granted, blithely assuming that ours was the land of plenty capable of supporting an unlimited population. We were unconcerned about pollution. If we gave any thought to it at all, we somehow assumed that our paradisaic environment was self-perpetuating, or that its immenseness precluded its destruction.

But we have now come to the frightening realization that we must be concerned. And we are. We know now that, unless the rate of population growth is somehow stemmed, food supplies may be insufficient for survival. Furthermore, we are now convinced that a polluted environment is not self-cleansing, but must be attacked through the positive efforts of everyone. Our concern is reflected in most of the things we do and the thoughts we think, but our attitude is not a comfortable one. We would like to have a spotlessly clean environment; but we came to the conclusion, after several years of agonizing, that to supplant the exhausted supplies of oil and natural gas we have to resort to the use of coal and nuclear energy. There is still the actuality and the threat of pollution from each of these, but we are aware of the problems and have taken steps to minimize the ill effects. The important point is that the polar extremists in our society have reconciled their viewpoints, and the attitude that has emerged is now positive and constructive with respect to this and other problems of ecology.

General attitudes relative to certain other issues divisive in the past have become reasonably unified in our society. Problems of discrimination, for example are less severe than they have been. Doors formerly closed to women and minority groups are now virtually wide open. But the significance of such attitudes is not that the doors are open but that they are open *de jure* and not *de gratia*. The result is that legal impetus is no longer necessary, and entry is gained because of qualifications and not because of sex or race.

Our attitudes toward moral values have stabilized somewhat. The seeming rush toward conditions of amorality has apparently subsided and our attitude toward such things has crystallized at a point about halfway between humanism and Puritanism. It is a comfortable attitude, and probably right for our society. It encompasses a sufficient degree of freedom of thought and action to satisfy most people and still provides sanctions against behavior contrary to reasonable religious standards.

A negative attitude toward business still exists, unfortunately, among large segments of our society. Business is aware of and is no longer complacent about this. But despite efforts to overcome it through publicity and corporate advertising, business remains the scapegoat for many of the ills of society, real or imagined. Although some progress has been made toward convincing people that business is not the ogre it is alleged to be, it appears that some people still believe business is not assuming the responsibilities it should.

Life-styles

Life-styles are freer and less regimented than ever before. Prescribed routines in family living are minimized, and family members tend to pursue their own individual interests. The roles of husband and wife are not severely defined; either or both (usually both) serve as breadwinner. Chores associated with the home — shopping, cooking, doing the laundry, and maintaining the yard — are viewed simply as tasks to be done by whoever has the time to do them when the need arises. Often they are performed jointly. Responsibilities with respect to the children are shared between husband and wife and with outsiders such as baby-sitters and nursery schools.

Eating out is increasingly common. The combination of less time available for preparing meals at home, the growing number of fast-food restaurants, and the rising price of groceries has made frequent dining out both necessary and possible. Families now have a considerable amount of leisure time, but sometimes have a problem filling it productively because of economic conditions and lack of available recreational facilities. Life-styles in general are casual and informal.

Business/Economic Factors

The business and economic environment reflects the increasing need for a global perspective. The economies of the world are truly interdependent now, and the days of provincialism are over. Not only are our decisions necessarily influenced by the quagmire of international debt and unstable world currencies but also by the strongly entrenched foreign competition. This larger perspective presents a real challenge to marketing and promotion managers. The problems are not insurmountable, but their solutions require considerable creativity.

Population

Although world population continues to expand, the population in the United States has stabilized. The typical family has no more than two children, and the number of immigrants has been severely reduced. The nearly zero growth rate in population is the result of prevailing attitudes and life-styles in the United States and the fact that there is less incentive for foreigners to emigrate than has been the case historically. Although there are exceptions, the disparity between conditions in their own countries and those in the United States has been greatly reduced, particularly in the Western-oriented countries.

The average age of the population is higher than it has ever been. This is due to the facts that people are living longer and fewer children are born. The population is less mobile than it has been in the past, partly because of economic conditions and partly because of attitudes; people now tend to resist the demands of employers for location adjustments.

Economic Conditions

Two of the conditions that plagued us for so many years are still with us — inflation and energy and other product shortages. Although we are solving the energy problem through greater use of coal, the continuing development of nuclear power, and making the use of other energy sources more feasible, we are still not completely self-sufficient. Shortages in other product categories develop periodically because of the lack of energy supply as well as for other reasons, and inflation seems to be a permanent way of life.

But there is reason to be optimistic. The high technology age is now well established, and continued innovation will lead to further growth and productivity. Not only will there be a personal computer in every household, but most homes will have the facilities for viewing video cassettes or discs, in addition to large TV screens and two-way video information systems. Furthermore, they will be able to pick up satellite transmissions.

Legal/Ethical Factors

Consumerism keeps business alert to the changing demands in the market place. The radical arm of consumerism, "consumerist groups," has almost disappeared. Business is increasingly responsive to the legitimate demands of consumers. Management is cognizant of the need for ethical behavior, not only for the self-gratification it engenders but also to prevent the passage of more restrictive legislation to add to the plethora of existing laws.

Management has not been entirely successful in this regard, however, because legislators continue to legislate. And they probably always will until people are convinced that business is really the layer of the economic golden egg.

THE PROMOTION MIX OF THE FUTURE

With the changes in the promotion environment over the years, there have been corresponding changes in marketing strategy and the promotion mix. There are fewer new product offerings, which is due not only to the periodic shortages of materials but also to consumer resistance. People tend to use products longer, and many have become convinced that it is an economic waste to discard still useful products. This does not mean that marketing innovation is dead. On the contrary, it means that creative marketing is more essential than ever. Markets must be carefully defined, and the concept of demand management seriously considered.

Professionalism in marketing and promotion is mandatory. The typical consumer is a highly intelligent person with a formal education that goes considerably beyond high school. That kind of consumer is very discriminating with respect to both products and promotional appeals. Any kind of promotional effort that lacks professionalism and some degree of sophistication is doomed to failure from the start.

Advertising

Advertising is still an important element of the promotion mix. But the media mix has changed somewhat. Television provides the advertiser with many more options and problems than it once did. Cable TV, satellite transmissions, video discs, and the large number of "superstations" offer many opportunities for reaching markets that in previous years were out of reach. Magazines are increasingly attractive to advertisers. Not only are there more of them than ever before, but more special fields are covered. Local magazines, too, are quite common now for those advertisers wishing to reach local markets. Coupled with this is the fact that people are reading more than they did in the early days of television. Newspapers are using electronic delivery systems and have become more customized, thereby offering unique opportunities to the advertiser.

Outdoor advertising has declined in use because people are traveling less. It is still an important medium for some products, but its popularity peaked several years ago. Advertising specialties, on the other hand, have assumed a more important role in advertising. Newspapers and radio are still significant media for local advertisers, and radio is now used by national advertisers much more than it had been for a number of years. Advertising in all media is much more creative than it was a few years ago.

Personal Selling

Overall, the relative importance of personal selling in the promotion mix has declined. The concept of self-service merchandising used by retailers in almost every field has been extended upward in the channel. Wholesalers and retailers in many fields now send in their orders for merchandise by returning to their suppliers preprinted order books on which they indicate their requirements. In addition, they attend trade shows frequently to examine new merchandise and to get fresh ideas. Thus the need for salespeople in institutions at all levels has been reduced.

Coupled with the foregoing changes is an increasing prevalence of direct marketing — the system by which the entire marketing process is initiated and consummated by mail or other remote contact. Large consumer mail-order houses utilizing extensive seasonal general catalogs together with catalogs of merchandise in special fields furnish the most obvious example of the system. But other firms are using the system, too. Many such firms do not use catalogs, but initiate the process by means of advertisements in magazines, newspapers, and Sunday supplements. The consumer deals directly with the seller by mail.

Personal selling is still strong in some industries, however, and it probably always will be. Products that require extensive explanation to induce purchase cannot be promoted effectively without the personal touch. The salespeople involved are very professional in performing their jobs. As with respect to advertising, the appeals they use and the methods they employ must be designed to match intelligent and sophisticated markets.

Sales Promotion

Sales promotion is the most important element of the promotion mix. Manufacturers have found that both trade promotion devices (those aimed at wholesalers and retailers) and sales promotion devices (aimed at consumers) are more effective than any other promotional tool. This is due, primarily, to the nature of the current environment. Consumers, and therefore wholesalers and retailers, are increasingly conservative and discriminating in their buying because of environmental conditions. Thus they are more likely to be persuaded to buy if they can see immediate advantages in doing so. Sales promotion devices provide such a stimulus.

Publicity

Publicity is now recognized as an extremely valuable component of the promotion mix. The stature of publicity in a firm's total behavior, in fact, may exceed that of any other function when considered holistically. It is a vital part of a firm's public relations program, and a public relations program is vital to a firm's survival. Thus publicity is a key element in all aspects of an organization's operating strategy.

Business learned its lesson several years ago: favorable public opinion toward it and its products does not just happen; it must be cultivated. Business no longer remains silent when it has something good to say about its policies, actions, or products. The art and science of capitalizing on newsworthy events associated with business in general, as well as with individual firms, is now in full bloom.

CONCLUDING COMMENTS

Promotion is a legitimate tool of business in every sense of the word. It is a necessary function of any organization that wishes to survive and perpetuate itself. Some people think that in promoting itself and its products business is engaging in nonessential activity and that there is something morally wrong with this idea. People with that opinion should look at the behavior of any organization. Churches, schools, fraternities, sororities, social clubs, civic groups, charitable organizations, labor unions, farm groups, and every other kind of organization promote their causes to their publics. If the promotion is unsuccessful, that organization does not survive.

The cause of business is to produce and sell products and services to satisfy human wants and needs. Unless the products and services are sold, the cause is merely fictional, for goods piled up in warehouses do not satisfy human wants. The fact that business is rewarded with profits for successfully promoting its cause does not make the cause or the effort unjust. There are unethical methods of promoting any cause, and probably every organization has been guilty of using unethical methods at one time or another. Business is no exception. But contemporary promotional activity in the business arena is certainly as ethical as in any other. It has to be; it is so conspicuous.

QUESTION FOR THOUGHT AND REVIEW

Write your own prediction of what the promotion environment and the promotion mix will be in the future. Explain why you made the prediction you did.

AUTHOR INDEX

SUBJECT INDEX